My Lunches With With Henry Jaglom

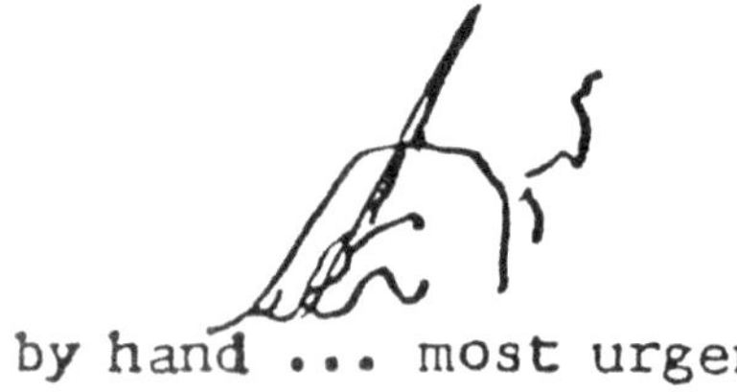

by hand ... most urgent

THE ENEMY OF ART IS THE ABSENSE OF LIMITATIONS

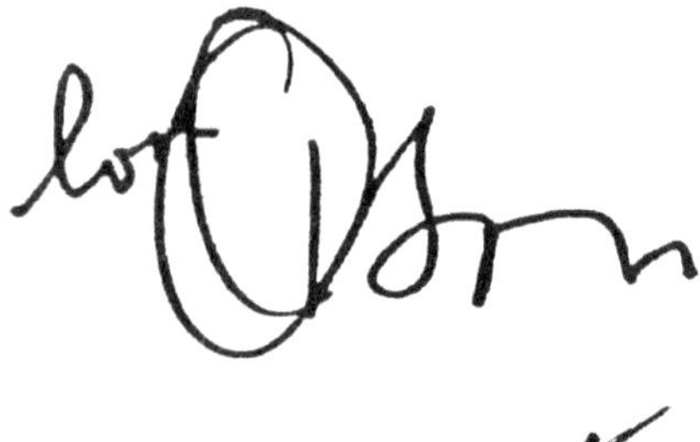

My Lunches With Henry Jaglom

A Biographical Dialogue Starring Orson, Gadge, Marlon, Judy, Liza, Ingrid, Marilyn, and the Others

Daniel Kremer

Sticking Place Books
New York

ISBN 978-8-89976-050-1

I must dedicate this book to Henry.
There's just no other way to do it,
and no one else who deserves it more, in this case.
I wouldn't be where I am today without you, Henneleh.
You were a crucial player in my own life story.
Love and miss you, my dear friend.
Here it is, your book, at long last.

And to my recently departed old film professor
Allen Barber (1947–2025) of Temple University,
who was always either amused or bemused by my
Henry stories around the time I was first telling them.

And as always, I couldn't have done any of this
without my husband Evan. So, once again,
I dedicate another book to him, with love.

The filmmakers of tomorrow will express themselves
in the first person and relate what has happened to them.
The films of tomorrow will be an act of love.

François Truffaut

Contents

Foreword by Candice Bergen

Henry was my weirdest friend. He was also one of the smartest. Many, many years ago, I recall often going to a now non-existent restaurant called Ma Maison in Los Angeles. Henry was always there, proudly lunching with Orson Welles. He could hold his own with Orson, as he could hold his own with anyone. He would simply take charge of whatever conversation he wandered into and some people found this presumptuous, which it was. Which he was.

He came from a wealthy, indeed very wealthy, family. He said, when his father was a boy in Russia, he rode a white pony. I'm not sure if the family helped in financing—or single-handedly financed—his films, which were as singular and weird as he was. They had a home movie-quality to them: intensely personal, nervy, open, honest, sometimes interesting, sometimes boring. I can't imagine they earned a dollar, but he sort of seemed like he knew what he was doing. He was fearless and ambitious, compulsively creative… and deeply eccentric.

If you were with him outside, he would position himself precisely. He was completely in shadow with only his feet and ankles in the sun. Which brings me to his shoes, which were daringly feminine, worn with lightweight, silky socks. His shoes were thin-soled and thin leather, almost like ballet slippers but with laces. And then, those thin and drapey socks. I used to partly judge men on their footwear and Henry's shattered the chart. He was off the scale.

He was generous with his time and friendship. He spent hours with me going over my first book, always encouraging, drilling me that I could do it, and that I could be as honest as he felt I should be. We often sat at a table towards the front

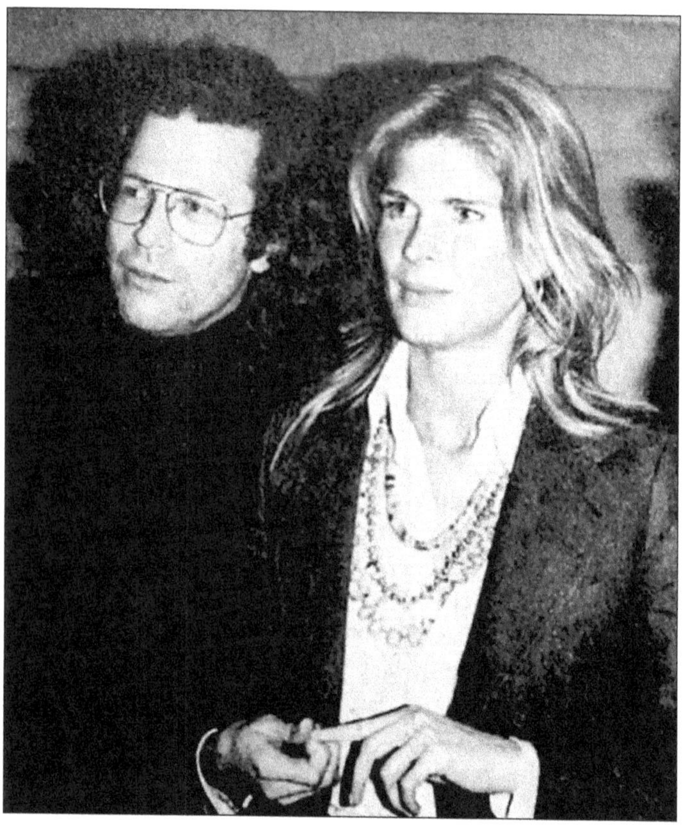

Candice Bergen with Henry Jaglom, circa 1976.

of the Russian Tea Room on West 57th Street, going over it chapter by chapter. He kept pushing me to be open about my life, and I ultimately was, even though I'd barely lived it yet.

I could trust him to keep a secret, even though I didn't yet have many. Oh, and he always wore a hat. Always. I never asked him why. I assumed it was to cover a bald spot. I didn't want to prod or delve. It became a kind of trademark of his.

The last time I saw him was at the bar mitzvah of his son at his house in Santa Monica. It was a large, rambling old Spanish house. He may have moved out of it after he'd separated from Victoria, his second wife. Henry wasn't religious but gave the bar mitzvah anyway… I'm not sure why. Maybe to cover the bases? To honor his son? He was very proud to be Jewish, I'll say that much. Quirky wouldn't begin to describe him but "Great Friend" would. The space he occupied is far less creative and colorful today. No one has stepped in. I can't imagine anyone will. He was the definition of "one-of-a-kind."

Candice Bergen is the winner of five Primetime Emmy Awards and two Golden Globe Awards for her work as the title character on Murphy Brown *(1988–1998). She was nominated for the Academy Award for Best Supporting Actress in* Starting Over *(1979).*

Introduction

I have little frame of reference for someone like Henry Jaglom. As I told my husband multiple times recently, Henry was sui generis. I never met anyone like him, and I never will again, no matter how long I last on this earth. Even when he was exasperating, as he could sometimes be, I loved Henry and I had some of the best lunches of my life with him, as this book bears out.

When he died on September 22, 2025 (and he would have wanted me to say "die" rather than "pass on," which he hated), it felt like losing a family member. I took into consideration how, by that point, I had known Henry for most of my life and looked to him as a close friend—almost like a favorite uncle, in some sense. I also wouldn't have my funky little film career without him. One of his ex-wives called me in the days that followed, telling me, "You know, Henry didn't have very many male friends. You could have counted them on a single hand, just barely. You weren't only one of them, but you might have been the closest. He spoke of you all the time." Though that was nice to hear (or confirm), our relationship wasn't always "sunshine and rainbows," as it were. Henry had a reputation, you might say, for being irascible sometimes. I certainly saw that side turned on me now and then. In a piece for *Interview* magazine, Peter Bogdanovich related that "Jack Nicholson best summed up what it's like to be susceptible to Henry: one way or another he will have his way with you." In his final years, though, he had mellowed considerably. By the time I moved down to Los Angeles from San Francisco in 2023, it didn't take long before we took our—you might say, "storied"—friendship to the next level. He was there for me as a favorite lunch date at a time I needed it most. But that's later on.

I first met him back in 2003, as a teenager. At that point, one could only secure a copy of his first film, *A Safe Place* (1971), on a specialty VHS that his company sold on the sly, as it had never been properly released on home video. It was a Columbia/Sony property, and they were evidently not eager to renew the extensive music licensing on an experimental feature that flopped so resoundingly back in its day. I had a keen interest in the New Hollywood—and still do—but how could any film from the legendary BBS Productions, starring Tuesday Weld, Jack Nicholson, Orson Welles, and Gwen Welles, have managed to remain so obscure and MIA? I got my answer when I first ran the tape copy I ordered from Rainbow Releasing, Henry's company. The critics were not kidding about the radically avant-garde nature of the editing and its ostensibly inscrutable narrative. I watched it a second time immediately following the first viewing. Soon enough, I'd grown obsessed with *A Safe Place*—it felt like I somehow connected with it, especially with its soundtrack of Thirties and Forties standards (including old French cabaret stuff by Charles Trenet and Edith Piaf) and its New York Jewish feminist Borges-by-way-of-Salinger sense of itself. (Read that last part again slowly to savor the diversity in its palate of influences, both deliberate and accidental.)

The film spoke to the "old soul" that all the adults in my life long told me that I uncannily possessed. I had also scored a VHS copy of Dennis Hopper's *The Last Movie* (1971) around that time—Jaglom had a bit part in that one, and its similar, radical approach to montage likewise tantalized me. It was an exposure to, and an education in, an alternative American cinema. I drove my college roommate, an obnoxious comic book dork, to certifiable madness by re-playing both films incessantly. (Truth be told, I was also kind of getting off on his aggravation, as I disliked him intensely, not merely because of his limited and even restrictive taste, but mainly for other vexing domestic reasons.)

I decided to write a letter to Henry, recounting how much I loved the film, expressing the largely ineffable to him: all the things I saw in its jagged but sinuous cuts, my intensely personal interpretations of its poetic codes and coups. Of course, I also told him a bit about myself. I was an aspiring filmmaker at that point, and had serious designs on making the type of envelope-pushing, formally gutsy personal films for which he was known. I not only got a response, but I got a big package in the mail containing the entire Henry Jaglom catalogue, some on DVD and others on VHS (keep in mind, this was still the early aughts and not everything was out on disc by that point). In short order, I came to treasure and outright relish how all his films had a homemade, handmade quality. Miloš Forman once said, "Henry has elevated home movies into an art form." I was granted access to Henry's private email address, and we started a little correspondence. I had all kinds of questions, mostly about how he managed to carve out such a niche for himself. This was the first meaningful contact I had had with anyone in the film industry at large. Sometimes the emails could be curt, and maybe a little tartly worded, depending on the day, but we remained in constant touch.

In 2006, I completed my first narrative short film, *Charles at the Threshold*, about two intellectual 18-year-old kids who elope, believing it a very "adult" thing to do, only to soon realize marriage is trickier than they've been led to believe from literature and second-hand observation. It felt in some ways like my pass at a French New Wave outing, à la Éric Rohmer (the title itself was a wink to Rohmer-type titles). I had also started shooting my first feature, *Sophisticated Acquaintance* (2007), around then as well. In some sense, I was running before I learned to walk, but I committed myself to making personal films honestly, rather than aping the flashy, trendy movies that most titillated my classmates. I was emulating Henry, in my way, trying to find my own voice while simultaneously immersing myself in his. Also, without legally securing the music rights, I had scored *Charles at the Threshold* with the Charles Trenet music that I loved from *A Safe Place*.

I shared the finished short with Henry, and it turned out that he was launching a film festival in Iowa with his star—and then-girlfriend—Tanna Frederick, an Iowa native. Lo and behold, they wanted me to bring my short to screen! I enthusiastically booked my flight and made the arrangements, borrowing money from my aunt. Henry and Tanna were to attend as well, to kick off the first festival in style, but they were also bringing distinguished friends of theirs, including Karen Black and her husband Stephen Eckelberry (still a friend to this day), David Proval (of *Mean Streets* and *The Sopranos*, ditto still a friend), and a whole entourage of others. This was a golden opportunity, my first real festival, and I was not going to miss out. I grew a truly terrible moustache, thinking I would maybe look more grown-up. Instead, it appeared as if I'd glued on a ridiculous Groucho beaglepuss and then lost the remover. Suffice to say, I was green, real green.

At the end of the three or four days, an after-party at a local watering hole following the awards banquet proved formative. I was signaled over to the VIP table with Henry, Tanna, Karen, David, and the others. I can only assume I looked lonely and awkward hovering around the bar all by my lonesome, not wanting to disturb the celebrity guests like some nudnik or pisher. In other words, I didn't want to be a "What-About-Bob" nagging at them. But the moment that they collectively beckoned me over to them, my heart skipped a beat. Keep in mind, I was barely legal for the beers I was so cloddishly sipping, so this was like a dream. Soon, it became evident to them that I was "Mr. Encyclopedia" when it came to films and film history. The day before, I had freaked out some local Iowan festival workers by letter-perfectly reciting some of the more intricate Meredith Willson lyrics from *The Music Man*, a show based on their hometown. When Henry remembered playing the "*12 Angry Men* Game" during his days at the Actors Studio (i.e. merely naming the dozen actors in the film), I not only did so but I named them in order of juror number, going around the table in my head. I even got the obscure ones, like John Fiedler, Eddie Binns, and George Voskovec. "Who is this kid?!" I remember David Proval bellowing in amazement. Before

I knew it, I was being invited out to L.A. and given private phone numbers. I was "in"! While being ushered around in a van with the other L.A. guests—including one woman, writer-actress Wendel Meldrum (the "low talker" on *Seinfeld*, among other things), who later became a very close friend and confidante—I cultivated other meaningful relationships that, to this day, I've kept.

This was a crucial turning point in my life. Before I knew it, I was living with Karen Black and her husband Stephen, as their houseguest. A movie-savvy college chum was interning in L.A. at the time. He drove by to pick me up so we could enjoy a few beers, but I encouraged him to come inside. Upon meeting Karen, who was lying on the floor with a big pillow watching television, he found himself speechless. Here was an actress he'd loved so much from *Five Easy Pieces* and other movies, in her home, lounging, completely unwound, talking to *him* of all people. When we got out to the car, his first words were, "Seriously, what the fuck, dude?!" This and beyond is the world that Henry opened and revealed to me.

I returned to Iowa the following year with a short, very personal documentary, on the subject of my stutter, which was far more severe growing up. I won one of the festival's awards. That year, special Hollywood guests at the fest included director Randal Kleiser (*Grease*) and the great André Gregory, there with his wife Cindy Kleine, who was showing a documentary. I got to have daily private "breakfasts with André," at the Mason City bed and breakfast where the festival had us staying. I would come down to the dining table each morning and catch him reading Ford Madox Ford's *Parade's End* before we started in on conversation. Our principal topics were theater, the art of directing, and the George W. Bush administration. I remember him explaining how he figured out his character in *The Mosquito Coast* (something external, a Nixon-esque hairstyle, informed the internal).

I may have come off as slightly arrogant at my film school around that time, because it felt like my classmates knew little about the exalted folks with whom I was hobnobbing. Honestly, it was hard not to feel special or privileged in my way. Think "Well, *I* had private breakfasts with André from *My Dinner With André* just days ago!" It was a lot for me though. I do believe some of my film professors were duly perplexed, enchanted, and entertained by stories of my recent exploits. One professor, for her vested interest in my friendship with Jaglom, got a full Rainbow package of Henry movies on video herself! When I had a rough cut of my thesis project, which turned out to be my second feature-length film, I got a full page of notes from Henry, who was especially intrigued by its Jewish touches.

My relationship with Henry waxed and waned through the years that followed. There were a few squabbles (to be expected in the course of any Jaglomian relationship). By the time I moved from New York to San Francisco, though, we were speaking on a wavelength of respect and admiration that was now reciprocated. Around then, I was finishing my first book, the official biography of director Sidney J. Furie (*The Ipcress File, Lady Sings the Blues*). I'd visit L.A. more and more as my friendship with Sidney progressed, and no trip was complete without a stop down at Henry's lunch table in Santa Monica. I likely would have never met Sidney without Henry in my life. I had gotten to Sid through a chain of people I met through Henry at those Iowa festivals—specifically from Wendel Meldrum, to Saul Rubinek, to another intermediary, finally to Sid, who wouldn't have talked to me at all without the references that such a solid chain could provide. I felt gratitude to Henry, as that Furie book was the first thing to really establish me.

I remember Henry working on his play *Train to Zakopané*, and him asking me about certain Yiddishisms he used in the dialogue. Like a couple of Chatty Cathys, we would sit for hours plumbing a wide range of topics. Our mutual love of old music would often inspire spontaneous rounds of table singing. I would share my new films with him—he would tell me, "You keep getting better and better. They're weird but they're very you, and that's the best thing about them." He got to witness me carve out a comfortable film career for myself, as a director and as a historian, and I think he took some pride in seeing me grow. It was in 2017 that Henry asked me if I'd be interested in writing my follow-up book on him. "All roads seem to point to this happening with you," he wrote me that summer. He claimed that others had approached him, but he wanted me to do the honors, I think because he knew by then I was familiar with even the most obscure names that were likely to be brought up in the course of the taping sessions. He could save time by not needlessly explaining things, and maybe have some fun for himself by doing it with me. He knew I was a rapt appreciator of obscura. I of course jumped at the opportunity.

I knew how storied Henry's life had been. Even for those who disliked his films, the tales and the way they were told would win the day, I was sure. Any book would be a coup. So we started taping. Many of those recordings formed the basis for this text—along with any number of later lunches. By the time I was ready to pitch the project to publishers via my literary agent Georges Borchardt, the publishing industry had taken a serious downturn as a result of the Covid pandemic. Henry was disappointed, of course, but never held it against me. Some time later, I retooled the approach, intending to eventually use only a portion of these Jaglom recordings in a first-of-its-kind book about the three fiercely independent American improvisational cinema mavericks: Rob Nilsson, Jon Jost, and Henry. Having been close with all three, I also know of their involvements with the leftist movements and personalities of their day, and how these associations factored into especially their early film works. I may still pursue that book, one day. It took listening back to my recordings of Henry after his death to re-realize that he deserves his own volume. It felt in many ways like I was attending to unfinished business in putting the finish on it, at long last.

I'd call him on the phone during the lockdown and we'd have our compulsory epic schmoozes at a fairly steady clip. At one point, I got him to lecture to a film class I taught on Zoom. Those students still remember that night. When I decamped from San Francisco to Los Angeles in October 2023 to move in with Evan, the man who would become my husband the

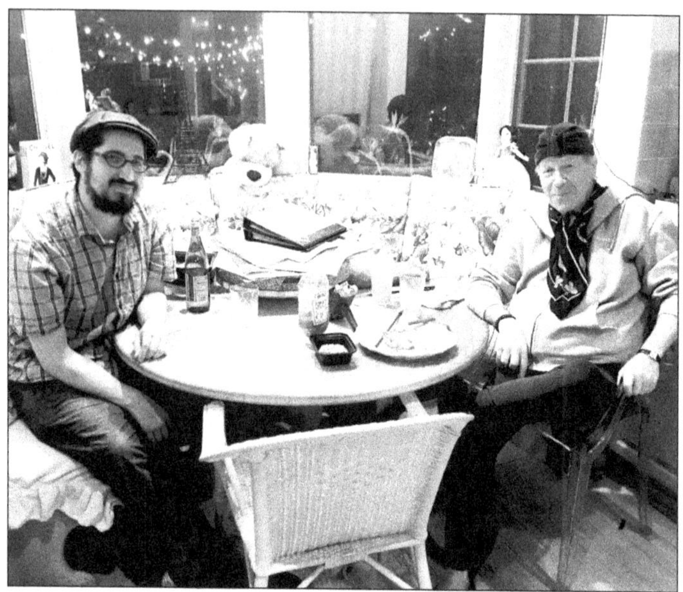

Henry and I seated in his kitchen nook, in 2017,
during the first round of taping. Photo by Ron Vignone.

following year, lunches with Henry became a cornerstone of
my existence as a fresh Angeleno. If I told Evan I was going
down to Santa Monica for lunch with Henry, he always knew
to expect me late, because the lunches would sprawl out into
consummately unpredictable six-hour talkathons. Movies,
music, life, love, the news, family, Jewish stuff, and on and on.
His magnum opus is actually a book of Jewish history (tentatively titled *The Third Stone on the Second Row*) that he spent
decades writing and revising, constantly debating whether or
not to finally put the cap on it. He would ask my input on the
project, as he knew I was something of an observant Jew, or
at least had Jewish orthodoxy in my background. Everything
was on the table, literally and figuratively—and when I say
"literally," he always traveled in his final years with a gigantic
binder, and piles of newspapers and clippings, which he would
scatter among the plates and utensils. Red-pen doodles and
notes were scrawled across every item.

I also took people down to meet him and lunch with him. Probably the number one thing on my mother's list of "things to do in L.A." was to meet and spend time with Henry. That lunch was a "hoot and a half," as they say. She kept digging candy out of her purse (mainly Necco wafers and Blow pops) and handing them over to him. When she commented on Henry's (indeed) shapely "sexy legs" (which were usually clad in skin-tight leggings), he actually squealed in delight, and marveled that "This is your mother?!" Once, I brought along my

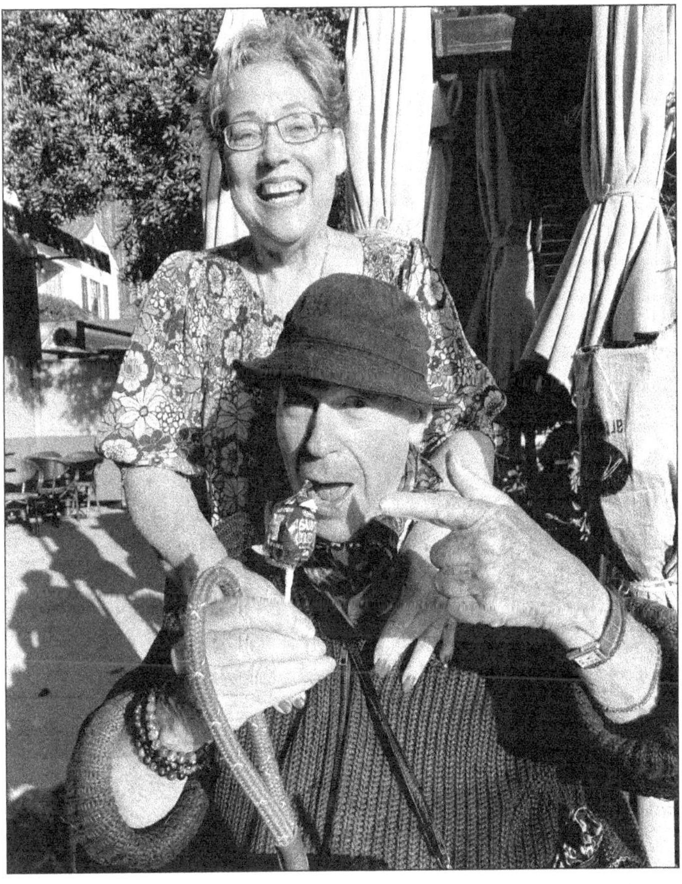

My mother met Henry at a memorable and even zany lunch in 2024, after years of hearing stories about him.

chanteuse friend, Tara DeMoulin, and that 3:00pm lunch appointment mushroomed into a confab that ended only when the restaurant closed for the night.

Countless late nights were spent in his kitchen booth. When my political statistician husband went off on the campaign trail in May 2024, Henry invited me down to show him a film I'd been telling him about: Irving Rapper's *Forever Female* (1953). "With that title, how could I not want to see it?" he quipped. We had a blast watching Ginger Rogers and Bill Holden together in a frothy comedy about an aging Broadway actress struggling to stay in the game, plus I got to listen to him rhapsodize the mostly forgotten Pat Crowley, an actress Paramount once groomed for superstardom, who quickly fizzled after an initial blush of success. When he would call me with computer questions—he was the absolute *worst* with technology—somewhere in the course of our chatter after the tutorial, I would mention how I missed Evan. He would be the one to offer, "You want to come down here for lunch?" He knew I was vulnerable and lonely without Evan around. I took him up on many such invitations, and he would suggest bringing "another old movie I might enjoy—something like *Forever Female*." I'll never forget how outright giddy he was watching Claude Rains very theatrically order dinner at a swanky restaurant in *Deception* (1946).

We'd often arrive in his kitchen singing duets of "Our Love Is Here to Stay" or "I Like Myself"—originally performed by Gene Kelly in the famous roller-skating dance sequence in *It's Always Fair Weather* (1955)—in a way that acknowledged our affection for the music of an earlier time. Beyond that, I think we felt an affinity for each other because we were both avowed sentimentalists, with hearts perennially pulled toward the poetry of a vanished past. The thing that is rarely mentioned in most public considerations of Henry is that his heart was huge—he did many things for people that they'll never forget. He could also be vexing and impossible—but also incredibly funny. I mean, *really* funny. He did, at one point, try to forge a career as a stand-up comic, after all. I'll be forever grateful that he kept me company through a difficult year, and would watch whatever new film or essay documentary I was working on. "You sound so butch when you narrate," he once told me, smirking. "You sound professorial, not like the weirdo I know."

To consider the times and places to which we traveled in our chats is a dizzying exercise. The last time I saw him, on August 7, 2025, I filmed him discussing his romance with Natalie Wood and his encounters with Gene Kelly, for my documentary on Irving Rapper. It's likely the last bit of film shot of him. I of course didn't know this would be our last visit. In many respects, I still can't believe he's gone. I've thought so many times, "I can't wait to tell Henry about this," only to get unbearably sad and forlorn when I realize I can't. I would have told him all the things people said about him at his memorial service, and he would have loved hearing every word of it.

He was such a part of my life for so many years, even when we were at odds during certain times. I'll miss him taking a note on a yellow pad or newspaper with his hand-written, instantly identifiable "Jaglom font" or "Jagscript" as I called it. I'll miss him drilling me, not out of rage but of genuine interest, and the impetuous need to get to the bottom of something I'd said or referenced. I'll miss his impertinent tech questions (the concept of having multiple open internet "windows" constituted one such frustrating tutorial). I'll miss singing old, obscure Forties tunes with him. When I listened back to us singing "Someone Nice Like You" from *Stop the World! I Want to Get Off*, I got misty, wanting my friend back with me in the usual booth. I'll miss his stories (and boy, did he have many, from an extraordinary and very eventful life, as you will read in the pages that follow). There's simply so much I'll miss about him.

I think most of all, he loved that I knew of old things: songs and movies and authors and obscure history. During a certain period, he'd send me news clippings about something along those lines, and in the margin would be his handwriting: "Dan, you would have loved it back then!" Even with later short-term memory lapses, he was still so present during a conversation, albeit with some noticeable repeats.

My last sight of him was in the doorway of his building, as I was leaving for the night with all my equipment. We spoke of my then-recent wedding, and he concluded the evening on a longtime conversational refrain, asking, "When are you going to lose that beard?" He always hated my beard. "You'd look so good without that thing. Why can't you just shave it off? Don't you even want to try it?"—always with an incorrigible, charming grin, essentially tipping you off that he never really meant anything by it. I started singing the title song from the musical *Hair*, which at first puzzled him because it wasn't familiar. When I told him what the song was, he chuckled and said, "Well, think about it. Can't blame me for trying!" He asked me to procure full copies of the movies from which I'd shown him only clips that night, then he retreated upstairs with his faithful pooch Cagney. A fitting coda, in its way. Weeks later, I got word from his daughter that Henry had suffered a serious stroke, but that he was expected to recover. I'd be able to visit him at some point in the hopefully near future. About a week and a half after that, he was gone.

I poured myself a small glass of scotch and retreated to my office, where I put on Charles Trenet's "La mer" (his favorite song, featured in not all but I'd say the majority of his films). I sat there listening to it in his honor, toasting him alone, not without some tears. I'd wash the dishes from dinner and ask our Alexa to play "Our Love Is Here to Stay" by Gene Kelly. Listening to our mutual favorite music was my way of mourning. His was one of the toughest losses for me. I remember a couple years back, Henry and I got to talking about religion and the afterlife. Henry was a proud Jew, but a staunch atheist, with not a lot of patience for religion, to say the least. As the years progressed, in discussion of my own Jewish observance as a theist, he grew morbidly curious rather than miffed (as he used to get with me, back when). Henry huffed that the afterlife conversation was silly. He would often quote a Russian proverb: "Blessed be the believers. Life is infinitely sweeter for them." Sure, Jews don't really talk much at all of an afterlife, but I don't think I know a soul who doesn't have some vision in their head of what a heaven would look like, at least for themselves. I prodded him to play along, and finally, one little part of him relented: "I'd want to see Orson again, and I'd want to see my parents again, and so many others like Richie Pryor or Karen Black or Bert Schneider. I'd just want to see people, not 'do' anything. But why I even talk like this? It's silly! It's childish!"

That aside, I really hope he's at a corner booth with Orson catching up on the years as if no time had passed, and singing old tunes with Karen, and trading barbs with Richie, striking new movie deals with Bert Schneider, and embracing his folks. A guy can hope—that's what we've got, the hope. My heaven is also people rather than things. How could Henry's not be about people when his films were *entirely* about people? In listening back to these tapes, I laughed when I'd refer to someone as "no longer with us," and without missing a beat, he'd retort, "It's called 'dead,' Dan." I was beyond astonished at how bracingly honest he was in relating the stories he told me. There was more gold herein than I had remembered by the time I started listening back, imagining him once doing the same with his Orson tapes. I was evermore grateful that I'd made the recordings and kept them safe.

I figured this would make a perfect sequel to Henry's *My Lunches With Orson*, so I essentially copied that book's editor, Peter Biskind's basic format and started curating the meatiest bits. Henry kept very odd hours—his Circadian rhythm was dissonantly off-tempo, openly in rebellion against nature, pseudo-jetlagged in perpetuity—so some of these "lunches" were actually free-association kitchen nook rap sessions that lasted into the wee hours of the morning. He would buy burgers earlier in the day for the two of us, then heat them up in the microwave. These were the "lunches," as it were.

So long, my dear friend. I'll never forget you. I know, I know… yes, he was 87, it was only a matter of time. But it doesn't blunt his absence. When I called to break the news to my mother, she paused and said, "He just seemed to have so much life left in him." Indeed, all this happened quite fast. He was part of my artistic family, not to mention that as an artist, he always preached, "Make your own movies your own way.

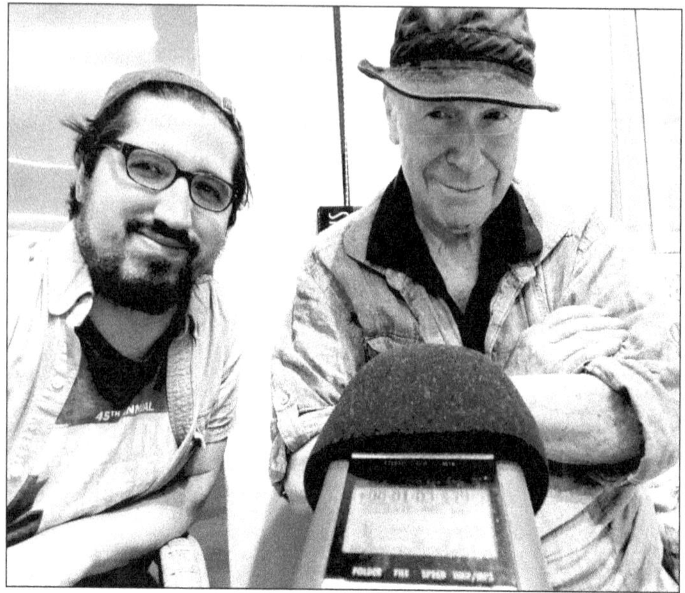

Henry and I recording audio commentary tracks for
upcoming video releases of his films in the summer 2024.

Don't let anyone tell you 'No'." That's been my method,
motto, and mantra, ever since we sparked our friendship all
those years ago.

I do intend this book as a biography—an untraditional bio
for a very untraditional filmmaker, as loose and freeform as
one of his entirely improvised movies. I present to you Henry
in his own voice, the best way to experience him, in transcripts
of our conversations that are as precise as possible. I wish he
could have been around to see it get published. I almost hear
him castigate me, "Why did you wait so long? I would have
loved seeing this come to fruition in my lifetime!" But… better
late than never, Henneleh (the Yiddish diminutive I often called
him). Herein are the experiences, the people, the works of art,
the loves gained and loves lost, the longings both hidden and
unhidden, that—to invoke a phrase from his oft-used anthem
"La mer" by Charles Trenet—"cradled his heart for life."

1.
"Don't be a dumb kid"

In which Henry discusses a life-saving afternoon with Judy Garland, the dramatic engagement party of an Oscar-winning chanteuse, a piece of advice from Paul Newman, and a bumbling chance lunch with Ingrid Bergman.

Henry Jaglom: Is that going to be good enough?

Daniel Kremer: Yeah, it'll be fine.

HJ: It's funny. This is a modern version of the old-fashioned little thing. We had a Nagra in the old days. What's this thing here?

DK: Yeah, this is a handle. And these are mics.

HJ: Mics! For Orson, I didn't have something this fancy.

DK: So, as I was getting set up, you were talking about dating Georgia Brown.

HJ: You know who that was?

DK: Yeah, she starred in *Oliver!* on Broadway.

HJ: That's right, good for you! And she had great albums—Gershwin and all these others. And she was a friend of Judy Garland, so I went to all these parties. This was early Sixties. I was going to open for Noel Harrison; he had a singing act and he was opening at the Blue Angel, and I was going to do a stand-up comedy opening for him. I was writing material. I was just a young kid, a young guy in my early twenties. And I started getting sick, and I started feeling really miserable, and everybody said, "What's wrong with you?" I said, "I don't know." And Georgia Brown and my other friends, which [included] Noel Harrison, who was Rex Harrison's son.

DK: He was in [your movie] *Déjà Vu* later.

HJ: That's right, yeah. And he was a very good friend, but they all treated me like I was a hypochondriac, because the doctor came—they had sent for a doctor. The doctor looked me over and prescribed some pills. And the way they do it in England is, they just laid out the pills and I said, "What is it?" He said, "These are the pills you should take at night and in the morning." I said, "But what are they?" He said, "Well, you just take them." You know, being an American and a Jew, you don't just take stuff, you know. And I finally got out of him, "These are sleeping pills and these are nerve pills." So I said, "So what does that mean? There's nothing wrong with me physically?" "No, it's just your nerves. You need good sleep, and you need to relax." And I didn't believe him, because I knew something was wrong, so I got mad. I threw him out. Georgia got mad at me because I wasn't taking the pills I was supposed to take. We had a big party the next day, at Dirk Bogarde's house.

DK: Oh wow!

HJ: And it was in Sussex, outside of London. And we went to this party and it was a very small luncheon of about twelve people… and sitting next to me was the woman I loved more in this world of show business than anybody else. That was Judy Garland. And I'm sitting next to Judy Garland, and I mean, it's Judy Garland! So I'm talking to her about this and that, and everybody else gets up at the end of the meal to play croquet, which is going on outside. What I remember is Leslie Howard's sister was an agent. She was one of them. Leslie Howard was my mother's favorite actor.

DK: Sure, *Of Human Bondage*, he starred with Bette Davis.

HJ: Well, known mostly for, you know, the big one. The biggest one of all. The biggest movie of all time.

DK: *Gone With the Wind*, of course.

HJ: Yeah, and also many other very good things. He was *The Scarlet Pimpernel* and he had been a spy in World War II. I don't know if you know about him. His plane was shot down; they think it was because there was a faux Churchill on his plane. Churchill had six doubles flying around. He was on his way to Lisbon doing a spy thing. The reason big stars could be spies—I don't know if you know this—was because they would go to neutral countries. They were invited to embassy parties and everything, and everybody just thought of them as stars. So, Cary Grant, Leslie Howard and… who else? Really big stars. Noël Coward. They were all stars for the British intelligence, and they hung out socially at these parties, which included German officers, and they found out what they could and acted like they were loosely talking about things. And then they reported back to MI5. Leslie Howard was on one of those missions, to Portugal. Neutral capitals, because in the neutral capitals, they could meet Nazis from the German embassies. It's fascinating. If you don't know about that, it's fantastic. And the big one, the big three: Noël Coward, Cary Grant, nobody knows about him practically… and Leslie Howard. That was his life. He was really great at that. And they shot down his plane, and nobody knows if it was shot down because he was on it, or shot down because one of the faux Churchills, one of the lookalikes, was on it. He died in that crash.

DK: Noël Coward wrote those early David Lean pictures, like *In Which We Serve*.

HJ: And he wrote "London Rose," you know. And, anyway, there were a group of unexpected people, because you think of him as a prima donna. You think of Cary Grant out in Malibu not being involved. And they're spies, right? And the biggest one was Leslie Howard, which I liked as a Jew, since he was a Jew from South Africa, of Lithuanian background So, anyway, how do we get off on that?

DK: The party at Dirk Bogarde's house.

HJ: Oh, right, so Georgia's my date. But she's treating me badly, she's treating me like I'm a hypochondriac. "Oh, Henry. That's okay. You'll feel better," because the doctor said there's nothing wrong with me and gave me these pills, which I wouldn't take, which were just placebos essentially. And everybody left the table to go out and play croquet, except me. I felt lousy, and there was one other person sitting next to me who didn't feel good. It was Judy Garland. And imagine me at 24 with Judy Garland. She had been the hero of my life. I went to concerts for Judy Garland at the Palace in New York.

DK: She would have just done that film *I Could Go On Singing*, with Dirk Bogarde.

HJ: Which is one of the greatest performances, I think, in movie history. Her performance is so underrated. Nobody talks about that. I once told Bette Midler that she should remake that movie. She'd never heard of it. Nobody has heard of that, right? It was great, who directed it?

DK: Ronald Neame.

HJ: Ronald Neame? I didn't know that. I knew him earlier through… I forget. I know I met him. Portland Mason was my friend. You know who Portland Mason was? The daughter of James Mason. So I got very friendly with James Mason. James Mason told me the best story, I'll tell you just quickly. He's in Ireland. It's the Sixties. He's a little past his main fame, right?

DK: Right.

HJ: Still looking great, though. I can't do an Irish accent, but it's important that whoever tells you the story should have an Irish accent. I can't do it. But the story is he goes into a pub in Ireland, and a guy keeps looking at him and looking at him and looking at him. This guy finally comes over, and he says with the Irish accent I can't do, "Would you happen to be James Mason in later life?" And he says, "Yes, I suppose I am." He was the most elegant man I ever met. "James Mason in later life!" It's a good story.

DK: It's like Malcolm McDowell talking about how he went to a commemorative showing of *A Clockwork Orange*. I just heard this recently. Some guy approaches him and is like, "You're in the movie, right?" And he's flustered and just kind of squints at the guy and goes, "Yeah." The guy says, "Which one are you?" And he goes, "Well, you know, I'm the guy." And he says back at him, "The old guy?"

HJ: That's how it goes, right? But yeah, James Mason in later life. I told him he should write a biography called *James Mason in Later Life*. That's a great title. Yeah. So, anyway, I'm left alone. Georgia's gone outside. Everybody's gone, including

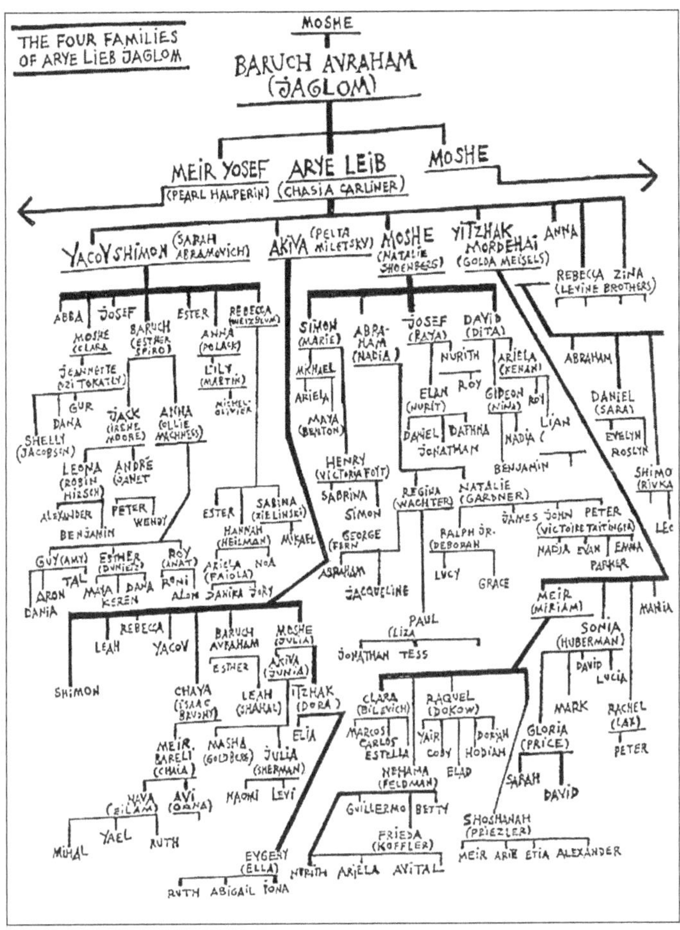

The Jaglom family tree, charted by Henry
(in his classic "Jagfont").

Noel Harrison and his then wife. And Dirk Bogarde, who
was very pleasant, but I didn't get to know him all. They all
went outside to watch the croquet players, or play croquet.
I start aching and moaning, and Judy Garland says, "What's
wrong?" I ended up spending the whole afternoon crying on
Judy Garland's shoulder because she was the only one who had
sympathy. She had enough of her own mishegas, you know.
And she was the only one who treated me like I was really

sick! She told me I had to go see another doctor, because it doesn't matter what this one doctor says. She asked me how much sleep I was getting? And she said, "Here, take these." She had some kind of very gentle tablets which helped you sweat it out, or I don't remember. But she spent the whole afternoon with me! Judy Garland, who was my idol, you know! So that's the only good thing that came out of it.

I told my aunt about my illness and she said to come to her house—she lived in Hampstead. And she said, "Go to the bathroom." I said, "I don't have to." She said, go to the bathroom and try to force a bowel movement, and she said, "Don't flush it!" When she looked, the shit was white. That's a bad sign. I had hepatitis. She said, "You're not leaving here. You go right upstairs and go to bed. You'll be in bed for at least five, six, seven weeks." I was all upset and told her, "But I was going to open at the Blue Angel. I'm going to do comedy opening for Noel Harrison. It's been announced." She said, "You're not opening for anyone. You're opening the toilet!" And she sent the doctor who confirmed it, and my mother flew in from wherever she was. And I was in bed for many weeks in London, upstairs before there was a television upstairs. They only had one TV downstairs in the house in those days.

DK: So what did you do with yourself?

HJ: My cousin Gideon Jaglom and his best friend Michael Chaplin…

DK: Charlie's son?

HJ: Yeah, they sat on the floor of my room to keep me company and smoked grass. I read a lot of books, a lot of film criticism. That's how I got acquainted with my favorite film critic. Who would that be?

DK: I'm going to guess James Agee.

HJ: Jesus, that's right! Good for you!

DK: Really, I'm right? Yeah, that was just a guess.

HJ: Well, I'm impressed by the guess. That's where I came across James Agee, and that's how I fell in love with film criticism. Just, oh my God, what he could do! But it's funny you knew that!

DK: I just… it was just a total guess.

HJ: Yeah, out of all of them! Good guess. I also read his amazing *Letters to Father Flye*. That was a major education. His film reviews have never been equaled, as far as I'm concerned. You didn't even have to have seen the movies he was writing about, the writing was so amazing and compelling, like Shaw's music criticism. But anyway, the point is, Judy actually listened to me. She's the only one, other than my aunt. I never forgot that. She told me all about her MGM childhood and Louis B. Mayer and the pills they gave her—the uppers and then the sleeping pills, and all those now famous stories.

So I guess, after about six weeks, I was well enough to gingerly walk, because you're supposed to keep the liver flat. You're not supposed to move it. It heals itself, if you don't do anything wrong. Georgia came out to Hampstead once, for dinner to visit me before we broke up. This is when I could finally go downstairs, carefully. My aunt, who was quite a snob—though very kind toward me—was very impressed that Georgia Brown came for dinner, because she was a star on the British stage and a big singer. She was my older girlfriend... the older woman.

DK: Where would you have gotten hepatitis?

HJ: I'm convinced it was a dirty needle at a clinic in Israel. I was there just before all this. I turned yellow, you know.

DK: You were jaundiced.

HJ: Yeah. So, very gingerly, I would go downstairs, because downstairs, they had a TV that showed one movie at night, on the BBC. So that was 1964. Yeah, one movie per day. With 5,000 movies every night nowadays, they take it for granted. It was such a great thing, though. I'd go from James Agee to whatever movie they happen to have showing, which just naturally seemed to be the best movie of all time, you know? Because that was your one movie that day, right? Sorry, I went way off there. That's the danger with me. You have to direct.

DK: No, it's an interesting way to begin the whole taping, with the story of Judy Garland.

HJ: I swear, she... in a way, she saved my life because she treated me seriously enough that I thought, maybe I've got something serious. I don't know that I would have gone to my aunt before. Somehow, Judy Garland made me know. It's funny, because this is *Judy Garland*!!! She helped me not accept people telling you you're making it up. She said, "They used to say that to me all the time. 'Here, take this pill, dear. You're just imagining it. You're just nervous. Take this pill to go to sleep." And that's what the British doctors were doing to me, right? And they weren't accepting that something critically was wrong. Yeah, that's a weird way to start, but okay.

DK: That's the good thing about free association.

HJ: "The Judy Garland Show" was the greatest thing in its time for me. I stayed home and you know, at that age, you don't stay home on a Saturday night. I was 22 or whatever, and my mother said, "What's the matter, are you feeling alright?" And I'd just tell her, "Judy's on." And I just watched this brilliance. Everything she did was just magnificent to me.

DK: I've seen clips of the show, including duets with Liza and, I think, Streisand.

HJ: Of course, of course! You know, I have journals going back forty, fifty years. I wrote them every day. You know, my thing to people: The most helpful thing I ever do to anybody is, when certain people are in certain conditions of needing certain things, I always think the thing they need to do is keep journals. And that saved my life too. And I say to them, you know, your obligation is to make a commitment that, every night before you go to bed, to write the day, the date, the time, and at least one word. And it can be "Fuck" or "I don't want to write this bullshit." It doesn't matter. And then the next day, in a contiguous place after, not on another page unless you've filled up that page, you write the day, the date, the time, the city you're in, and one word minimum. And you keep doing that for one month, and I promise you, you will be keeping a journal for life. And it'll help you through so, so many difficult times and loneliness and fear and everything. But as a book, it becomes your friend. I've been keeping a journal since 1961. Since I got out of college, I've been keeping a journal. So I have all the stuff that I'm telling you. That's why it's all so vivid, because I read it over and it's in my voice at that time, you know?

And after getting well, I got to know her better, Judy I mean. There was a club in Beverly Hills, and she was there with Mia Farrow a lot, and other people. I wrote in my journal, I remember, "I think Mia and Judy are both going to be dead within a year. They're going to kill themselves." As I said, "These are the saddest two people I've ever known," at that point. They seemed doomed. The interest here is that Mia grew out of it. Judy, of course, didn't.

And, of course, I've got this sick ego thing. I've always had this. I hardly knew Judy, really. I had that one meeting, then in Beverly Hills, then at the Improv in New York, she and Liza used to come. I became friends with Liza Minnelli completely separately. And at the Improv, you met Richie Pryor there and we worked together there, doing stand-up together. And like I said, Liza would come with her mother, and they'd sing and it was great nights, after hours. I remember once in particular, when my friend Dudley Moore played the piano and Judy sang. Having all this going on, with all these people, never failed to amaze me, though I acted very blasé and cool about it all. Fantastic stuff.

But I didn't really *know* Judy. I mean, I never had her phone number. And yet, when she died, I had this… this is part of my illness: I thought I could have saved her. I never even spoke to her separately from being in a public place. But my image of myself, yeah, it was, "If I'd only called her, I could have figured out what the problem was and…" And I have the sickness a little bit. Is this the kind of stuff you want to hear? I don't know.

DK: No, no, it's great! Everything is great!

HJ: Because I don't know any other way to do it. You ask me anything and it triggers stuff, but you got to then stop me.

DK: No, no, really, it's great.

HJ: Because I can go on. I don't know how it applies, but I'm happy to give it. I just don't want to censor anything.

DK: You know, it's life. It's all part of your life. It's a vivid memory.

HJ: Oh, big! Huge, huge. I'll tell you another thing that just occurred to me. I went to Liza's engagement party.

DK: For which husband?

HJ: First. She was just a girl. What's his name? The singer from Australia, Peter Allen. So I'm at the engagement party. It's at Il Mio, which is one of the earliest discotheques in New York, in a fancy hotel on the east side. It was run by Timmy Everett. I went in the bathroom to pee, and I didn't know him but I knew her very well. I was gonna meet him, but had not yet met him. And then this guy came on to me in the bathroom. Usually, I go into a stall because I'm kind of private. But I was at a urinal, and this guy starts very clearly coming on to me. And I said, "No, no, I'm not interested, thank you." And then I look at him and I say, "Oh, you're... you're Peter Allen." I zipped up, I remember that [*laughing*], and he said, "You don't really have to zip up"—some line like that. "Yeah, I do, thank you though. I'm a friend of Liza's, and I..." It was awkward because he had definitely come on, and that was their engagement party! Now, you know, I'm faced with a dilemma. She's my friend, not a good friend, but a friend. Somebody I know well enough, and she's getting married, and she's a young girl... to this guy who I now know is gay.

DK: Yeah.

HJ: Is there an obligation here to say something to her? So I go out—I'm going to sound like I'm doing a lot of name-dropping, but this is just the way life then was. I go out and I happen to have been sitting with Paul Newman and Joanne Woodward. Joanne was at another table talking to some people. So I'm sitting with Paul Newman. I think I got some pictures of us there. And he's drinking a bit. And I said, "Oh, shit, I don't really know what to do." And, he said, "Why?" I said, "I really like Liza. She's a kid. I just found out that the guy she's going with is gay." He said, "How did you find out?" I told him and he said, "Jesus Christ! At her engagement party!" I said, "Yeah, so that means he's not only gay, he's also a bit of an asshole, and drunk obviously. And I'm scared for her. Doesn't she know?"

And that's when Paul Newman told me her father was gay. I was like, "Vincente Minnelli?!" He explained, "Yeah." He told me her father was kicked out of a movie theater where they were from, because of a gay scandal. He said, "So I wouldn't say anything." I said, "Well, does she know?" He said, "Who knows? Obviously it's okay. Don't be a dumb kid." I looked like a kid to him, you know. He said, "Just keep it to yourself." And I felt really like I was doing something wrong. I felt she should know that. And, of course, in her own way, she knew whatever she needed to know and found out. It wasn't my business, and that's what he was telling me. It was a good piece of advice, but at the time I was shocked by the blasé way. Aren't you obliged to let somebody know something that they should be aware of? But he brought up the fact I had not known at that point that Minnelli was gay, or her father's story, or any of that. And I got friendly for a while with Peter Allen, and they were a nice couple for a while. And, of course, then they broke up and she married, you know, four more people, three of whom were gay. And her mother had gay boyfriends, with the only exception being what's his name, who produced *A Star Is Born*.

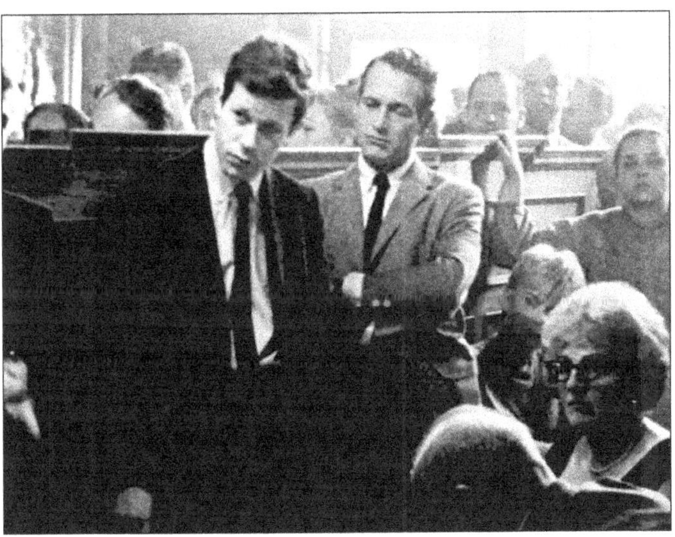

Henry with Paul Newman at a meeting
of the Free Southern Theatre, circa 1965.

DK: Luft.

HJ: Luft, who left her, took all her money. Unfortunately, he was her one Jew. In later years. Liza used to tell me, "I'm Jewish," and I said, "Why are you Jewish?" And she said, "My stepfather."

DK: And then, of course, George Cukor, who directed Judy in *A Star is Born*, was one of the first in that era to be "out," or at least as "out" as one could be.

HJ: Oh sure, they had those parties. My God, people he told me about those. Natalie Wood told me, a lot of people told me about those parties. I never met Cukor. The last movie he did was with Candice.

DK: *Rich and Famous*, with Jackie Bisset.

HJ: Yeah, Candice, did you ever read her book?

DK: Yeah, yeah…

HJ: *Knock Wood*?

DK: I know she thanks you in the opening of it.

HJ: It's great, I think brilliant. It's only dedicated to me because I encouraged her to write it.

DK: Right.

HJ: She's just extraordinary. She really captured the Sixties.

DK: I was very happy to see her again recently in the new Noah Baumbach film. I was surprised, and I was like, "Oh my God, look at Candy Bergen there." Sid Furie and I were having breakfast yesterday, and we were talking about that film, and neither of us could believe when she came up on the screen. "We haven't seen her in a while!"

HJ: You know, she's one of my closest friends. Lifelong friends.

DK: I've gotten that sense, yeah.

HJ: But, you know, I got her together with Bert Schneider, which was probably the worst thing I ever did, but they both they both needed somebody. And they had five years of… if you ever read *Knock Wood*, it's really a good biography of the Sixties. It really captures the Sixties like very little else. She's a terrific writer, I think. Yeah, I'm skipping all over the place.

DK: However it comes out…

HJ: I feel that too. But, I mean, I don't want to interfere with you asking questions.

DK: The charm of this is that, as it comes out, it's going to be more truthful, I think, and you're going to remember more if you're in that zone.

HJ: I'm going to remember more in the zone. That's true, but "truthful" you don't have to worry about because I'm almost insanely requiring that of myself, because there's so much bullshit going on, even in my head, too. Like, for instance, I can't be sure what that doctor said in England, except that he whispered something. Judy implied—because I told her about all that—was that he whispered something like "Neurotic American, just give him these pills to calm him down." And Georgia treated me… I mean, that was the end of our relationship. She was a wild person, she was ten years older, and I was getting in the way of her social schedule, and she wanted to go to this and that. And Judy was her hero, and I don't blame her for that. In New York, we had quite a passionate, strange time, because she was the older woman in my life, and it was… cool. And then in London, I could not be, you know, passionate. I couldn't even basically walk. I'm trying to remember another name. He was starring in London—there was this one guy who took me seriously, a gay guy. Blonde hair, American. But he was in *West Side Story*.

DK: George Chakiris?

HJ: No, George is out here. He is gay, though. When I first met George—don't let me forget the other thing—because this other guy, David Holiday was his name! You wouldn't know it, but he did a lot of musical theater during the period, and he was in the company of *West Side Story*. And I had met him and liked him, and we had gone out for a lot of dinners. And when I got sick like that, I called him up and I told him, "They're telling me I'm a hypochondriac. I don't know what to do, and Georgia is treating me like shit," and he said, "Come over here." He took me in two nights or three nights into his flat, got a bed made up for me, soft drinks. And he had to go out because he was going out to a party that Noël Coward was giving. He says, "Too bad you're not well enough." Now I know how really sick I was, because Noël Coward always meant a great deal to me. I could hardly walk. But he was the first person who took me seriously, and Judy was the second.

DK: So, circa 1964, Coward would have been doing Otto Preminger's *Bunny Lake is Missing*, which came out in 1965.

HJ: I just kept thinking, "Fuck, I'm missing Noël Coward's party!" I was not as much a Noël Coward fan then as I am now. I became a fan because of Andrea Marcovicci, because she sang all his songs. But anyway, all this brought my budding comedy career to a screeching halt.

DK: What kind of comedy were you doing? What was your style, if you can define it?

HJ: I was doing political satire. I was a little bit of… what was his name? You know, the guy who did the political stuff — always had a newspaper.

DK: Oh, Mort Sahl!

HJ: Mort Sahl! Very good! He turned out to be an asshole. I was kicked out of his show later on, for questioning him. Yeah, it'll all come to me. So, anyway, I don't know. I'm rambling.

DK: I was supposed to go to Poland a couple weeks ago to screen my new film at the Joseph Conrad Festival. I was down with the worst flu. I couldn't go, so my partner in crime had to go.

HJ: It's terrible to miss those things.

DK: [Krzysztof] Zanussi was there, the Polish filmmaker, and he loved the film. But I missed that. I'm kicking myself, but there was no way I could fly. I mean, even if I have a little head cold on a plane, I can't breathe, I can't get a full breath.

HJ: I remember one time I tried doing that. The flight attendant had to give me oxygen, in the back.

DK: Yeah, I can't breathe when I'm sick on the plane.

HJ: You know, the thing I missed most was, I made *Sitting Ducks*, and it opened at this new cinema in London, right on the park, which was a state-owned arts center. I don't remember the name. It's still there, right off the park. *Sitting Ducks* was the opening event, for God only knows what reason. And Ingrid Bergman was the hostess of the evening, opening it, and it's my film. I wasn't sick or anything, I was in L.A. working on another film by that point. There's no good story here. I just didn't fly to London. I was lazy, you know, and I thought for years, "I didn't fly to London for Ingrid Bergman opening my film!" That crazy little film *Sitting Ducks* ran for months and months and months there. Every review was great.

DK: I wonder what Ingrid thought of it.

HJ: Years before that, I was editing *Easy Rider*. I'm with that group in Hollywood at Columbia and it's pouring rain. You don't mind if I just free-associate, right?

DK: Henry, please! Not at all!

HJ: I go to lunch… I always went to lunch at the executive dining room, where I was allowed to go to lunch, because for some reason, Bert Schneider, who was the producer of my first movie and producer of *Easy Rider*… I'd just become known there and accepted. They were very strict about who could go; it was a small room and you had to cross a little outdoor ramp to get to the dining room, the executive dining room at Columbia. And there's only one table, it's facing the door. So they let me sit there and I'm sitting by myself. I've got my Israeli army hat, which is like an Australian big thing. I was just back from the Six-Day War at that point.

So there's a seat next to me—a two-person table. And a woman comes in over that ramp, and I've got still my army hat on, and I took off this big, British Bobby coat that I was wearing. I look up, because the voice says to me, "Excuse me, but there's no other seats. Do you mind if I sit with you?" And I look up, it's Ingrid Bergman! I said, "No, sure, what the hell?" I didn't know what to do. So she sits down next to me. We're at this little table for two. She orders something from the waiter and she's trying to make conversation. I've been reading a book; I put down the book, but I don't know what to say because it's Ingrid fucking Bergman! I'm blown away.

She introduces herself. I said, "I know who you are," and she said, "And your name is?" I said, "Henry Jaglom." She said, "Jaglom, Jaglom, interesting name. What is that?" And I swear to God, I spent the next—it seems like hour, but at least twenty minutes—going into this unnecessary, boring history

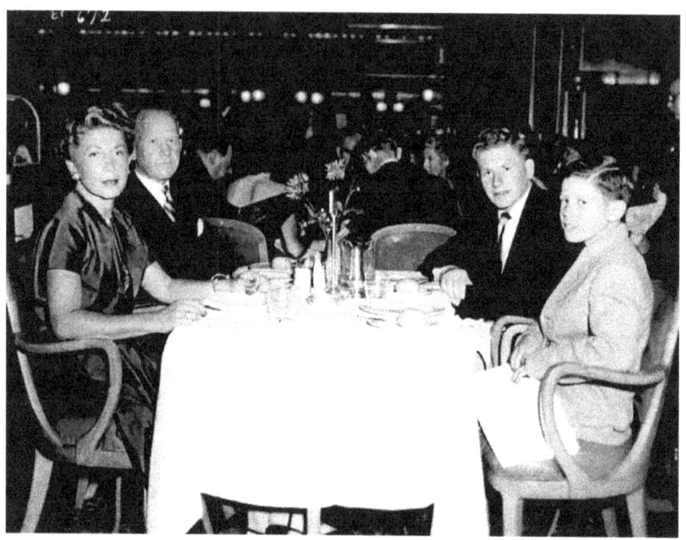

Henry seemed primed early on in life for an unceasing parade of star-studded chance encounters and run-ins with important people. Here, circa 1950, he is pictured with his parents and his older brother Michael on the R.M.S. Queen Elizabeth.

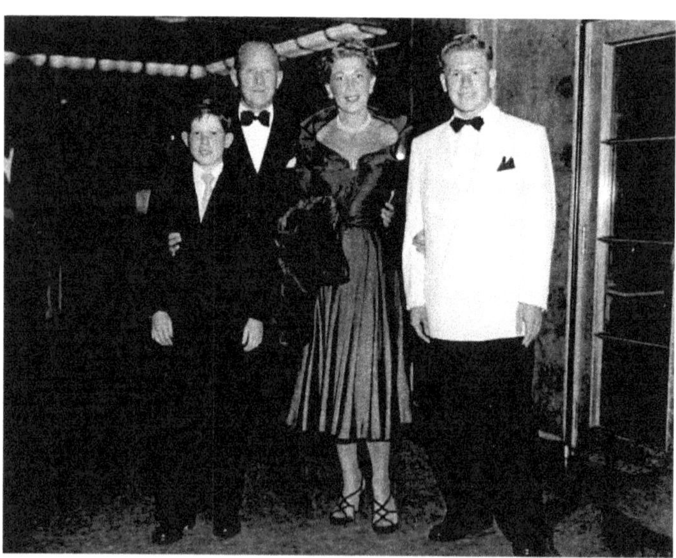

about how the name was taken in Russia, but it's a Jewish name from the Bible. It's Hebrew, Yahalom, but in Russian there's no "ha," and this part becomes a "jah" and this other part becomes a "gah." And I'm saying all this, going on and on. It's Ingrid Bergman, so I want to make believe I'm Bogart, and it's raining out and all that. And she's very polite, looking at me, smiling, and I'm fucking madly in love, but her eyes are clearly glazing over. Instead of doing Bogart, I'm telling a story about how my great, great, great, great great great… wait a minute, no, my great great great great great great great great grandfather…

DK: [*laughing hysterically*] And the little man in your head is saying, "Shut the…

HJ: …the fuck up!!!" Right? And I'm instructing her in the history of Russia, names, the Bible, language, how a J becomes a "ha" and how a "ya" is this and a that. And that's how I became Henry Jaglom! It seems to me that that's all the conversation was. Then it felt like she then said, "Well, it's been very nice to meet you."

[*HJ and DK both laugh.*]

HJ: And somehow it felt, "Oh, wow, she's eaten her whole meal!" [*more laughs*]

HJ: The waiters have come, served it, she's eaten it, gotten some coffee. And I'm there babbling on the entire time.

DK: If it were Katharine Hepburn, I think her line would have been (in Hepburn imitation) "Well, good for you!"

HJ: But she was very polite. "Very nice meeting you." And I didn't say one fucking word about, "Holy shit, you're Ingrid Bergman! I'm in love with you! I feel like Bogart here, except I'm acting like a schmuck, and I can't stop my mouth. I can't stop it! I don't know what to do! I can't talk!" Years later, I've made *Sitting Ducks*, with Ingrid Bergman hosting the whole opening of the arts center and therefore introducing my film. Thank God, maybe she wouldn't remember the schmuck who she had lunch with all those years ago, but I didn't go, and I missed the chance to really meet the real Ingrid Bergman.

[Author's note: In a 2012 oral history, writer-director Frank Pierson recalls this space at Columbia as, indeed, somewhat cramped. He remembers going there often while working on The Looking Glass War, *"and you'd see Henry Jaglom sitting in the corner reading his Jewish newspaper." He also remembers once sitting at a table with Jack Nicholson and Bert Schneider as Marlon Brando sat three feet away. "I was giving a blow-by-blow play-by-play of Brando eating his lunch, because Bob Rafelson didn't have a clear view of what was going on."]*

2.
"Kazan, you're a shit"

In which Henry discusses his brief (and abruptly ended) friend-ship with Jerry Lewis, his fraught relationship with Elia Kazan, his biggest childhood crush, his earliest girlfriends (including Brenda Vaccaro and Tuesday Weld), his romance with Natalie Wood, and an intervention into the Sinatra-Farrow marriage (which ties in with a friend of the author).

HJ: It's 1963, maybe 1964. I was obsessed with Jerry Lewis, and he had a new deal at Paramount to direct and write, and had huge offices. And Steve Blauner was a partner of Bert Schneider and Bob Rafelson.

DK: Blauner was the S in BBS [Productions]: Burt, Burt, and Steve.

HJ: That's right. That's where I made *A Safe Place*, and edited *Easy Rider*, and where I got started. Bert had been my coun-selor at summer camp, Camp Kohut. Bob had gotten me my shots on *The Flying Nun* and *Gidget*, where I guest-starred.

DK: For Screen Gems.

HJ: Right. Somehow it comes up in conversation that I've had this childhood thing about Jerry Lewis. Blauner says, "Do you want to meet him?" I said, "Yeah." "Well, he's starting a movie over at Paramount." So I said, "I'd love to meet him."

So he takes me over—and I'm a kid, you know, in my early twenties—and he takes me over and he's sitting across a big desk... Jerry, I mean. And I sit down. He said, "Sit down, kid, sit down. I'll be right with you." He gets off the phone and then he pushes a button on the table, an intercom, and he says,

"Who's the funniest man in the world?" and six programmed voices come back shouting "Jerry Lewis!" He says, "That's right, and don't forget it!" and he looks at me and laughs.

I still smoked in those days, you know, and I've got a jacket on, which… I still wore jackets and there was a whole inside thing for cigarettes. So he says, "Don't be nervous, kid. What are you nervous about? It's just you and me meeting, two people meeting each other." And I said, "Well, you know, I don't know what," and I'm looking for my cigarettes because I'm nervous. He said, "Oh, you want a cigarette? Here!" And he opens the thing with his face on it, a cartoon of his face and takes out a cigarette. He reaches over and says, "I just want you to know, there's no reason to be nervous, because we're just two people. You happen to not have done anything. I happen to be world famous. If you're nervous, you're dead." All the while he's talking, he keeps pulling back the cigarette, and I keep on reaching for it. It looks like he's just about to give it to me, and just as I reach for it, he keeps pulling back and says, "Please just understand that." And I'm starting to laugh and he keeps going. He says, "Sincerely! We are the same!" And then he breaks the cigarette, and I fell down on the floor screaming with laughter. "You like that, kid?" and I'm on the floor. And then he pushes the intercom again: "Who's the funniest man in the world?" This time, these women's voices come back: "You are!" And we became incredible friends.

DK: That's hilarious.

HJ: So now, for a month or two—maybe two and a half months—he's got me on the set of his new movie. And every time I come in, I'm fascinated. I can't get on sets of big Hollywood movies, you know. So I come in and he's setting up a shot and all these men are around him… big Hollywood crew. In that Jerry voice, really loud: "Henry! Henry's here! Henry got to kiss me. I can't do anything. No more work till Henry kisses me." I said, "It's okay, Jerry," "Henry! I don't do nothing until Henry kisses me on the cheek! He gives me a kiss, I can work. I can't work otherwise. Because without a Henry kiss, it's impossible." These men are glaring at me. They want to work and they're now being stopped by a kid. I'm walking over there self-consciously, trying not to look like an asshole, and I go all the way across a huge soundstage, he's over at the other side, and I kiss him on the cheek. He says, "Now I can work. Henry's here. Henry kissed me, so I can work now." And these guys learn to hate me. And this would happen day after day. Whenever I came on: "Henry's here! Stop! Cut! I need a kiss!" So he was using me to get them fucking crazy. But he was also himself, whatever that was. And this went on for, I want to say, months.

Maybe it was weeks, maybe it was only ten days. It felt like forever. I had a great time and he showed me the camera and how he invented this thing for playback. You know he invented that, which was absolute genius. I'd never heard of it before because it hadn't existed before. And at that point, I want to be a director, and I'm making my own judgments because he's not making exactly the movies I wanted to make. I would have rather been with Fellini. And he said, "Do you want to come see the rushes?" And I said, "Oh, sure. Thank you"—he hadn't invited me ever. He says, "We'll go see the rushes and we'll get a bite to eat." I said, great. No idea where his family was all during this period, or anything.

His house was always empty. He took me out to the house. I took a shit in his bathroom, and I found out that he had it on camera. He had two cameras in the bathroom. He had cameras everywhere in his house. I found out later that I was on there, from some girl who he was having an affair with, who saw me taking a poop. Who was that? She was an actress who never had much of a career. I don't remember.

Anyway, so I go into the screening room. He's running his dailies, and, he says, "What do you think?" And I said, "Well, you know, can I make a suggestion?" He said, "Sure." So I gave a suggestion, because this would maybe be a little better. I'm a young wannabe director. So I say, "You know, you can't cut that this way. So you'd have to cut to that. But if you do this, it'll work." And he looks at me and says, "Oh, you know better than me," cold as ice. I said, "No, I don't know better than you. I don't know anything. I'm a kid. But you ask my opinion, and I do know that…" I still think in my head that he's going to be impressed, because it was a smart comment, whatever it was. It would have been helpful to him for when he went back in to do his coverage. "You know more than I do. What do you need to hang out here for? Goodbye." And that was the end of our friendship. That was the end of it!

DK: I've met directors like that. I want to say, I'm friendly with one in particular. He'll have rough cut screenings and he'll only ever want to hear praise.

HJ: Thirty years later, I get a message from a girl I knew from Vegas. "Jerry said to tell you he likes your films." Forty years later… I had it framed in my office, a sweet little note from him, and he sends me a collection of his films. I was his best friend for three weeks, and then I made an opinion that suggested that something could be improved of what he did. And not only was he disappointed, but I was a piece of shit.

DK: [Joseph] Losey was like that too. Same type.

HJ: Oh, don't tell me Losey was like that! Don't tell me this!

DK: I love Losey, but from basically all accounts, he didn't accept notes gracefully.

HJ: I love his work. Oh, how could Losey have been like that? That's disappointing.

DK: I have a few books about him, because he's one of my favorites. There's also a Japanese documentary that touches on this a bit. He could be rude, or "right cross" as the British would say. He was not a nice man.

HJ: Because of the blacklist, I'm so sympathetic to him…

DK: He's probably a top five filmmaker for me.

HJ: …and the guts of what he did, just going over there and continuing his career and, you know, making some great films. He's such a hero of mine. You know what happened when I met Kazan? Do you know about Kazan and me?

DK: No, not you and him. I, of course, know about what he did.

HJ: But you don't know about me and him. Okay. I got a thing to send you, which you'll enjoy. It's an exchange of letters between us. I had read his book. Should I tell this? I'm not sure, because you looked at that.

DK: No, no, no, I'm just making sure the recorder is still running.

HJ: Oh, I did that all the fucking time. Whenever I was doing things, I was always checking, making sure. I did that with Orson all of time. Yeah, I know I didn't mention you said. He'd say, "What are you looking at?" And I'd say, "I'm just making sure we're still running." I would want to know if it's run out or something.

DK: If it's run out for me, I have my laptop here, I offload, it takes a few seconds, no biggie. But I just do these little checks.

HJ: [*putting on a gangster voice*] 'Cause I'm givin' you gold, kid.

DK: [*laughs*]

HJ: Where was I?

DK: Kazan.

HJ: Okay, so… during the Fifties, the best movies were made by Kazan. Hollywood was full of shit, did a lot of junk, and Kazan was incredible. How about *A Face in the Crowd* for what's going on right now?

DK: Yeah, it's perfect for now.

HJ: Jesus Christ.

DK: You know, I met with a fellow biographer yesterday for breakfast.

HJ: What's his name?

DK: Nat Segaloff. He wrote the Arthur Penn book. He did a book on Friedkin as well, and lots of others. He's a friend, and I was telling him about *our* mutual friend Paul Sylbert.

HJ: Oh, Paul!

DK: I was telling him something that Paul told me about when he worked on *A Face in the Crowd*. Him and his brother Dick.

HJ: Oh wow, they worked on that? Really?

DK: Yeah, they did.

HJ: Boy, the visuals of that were incredible. That apartment…

DK: Yeah, you'll be very interested in this. This has never been reported publicly, but Paul told me this over dinner years ago, that he and Dick unveiled this scale model of that apartment, and they're very proud of it. They're showing it off to Gadge, to Kazan, and pointing out all the particulars, and the amenities for camera placement, the wild walls, the sleekness of everything. Basically, they're priming him for how beautiful that set is going to look. And they finish their presentation, and Gadge looks like he's thinking hard about something. Everyone's looking at each other, wondering what's going on, why Gadge isn't reacting to this beautiful thing. Finally, he asks them, "Where's he fuck her?" meaning, where does the Andy Griffith character fuck… it was Lee Remick, I think—or one of the other girls that he takes to bed. Of course, Paul and Dick are taken aback by the question, and one of them takes the little pointer and says, "Well, probably in here, Gadge." He noodles it for a moment, just says, "Okay," then walks away, and everyone there is just look bewildered at the whole exchange. That was it. Paul told me that at dinner.

HJ: That's strange.

DK: Paul and Dick worked with Hitchcock too, but I get the sense they found Hitch a little less inscrutable, at least in situations like that. They worked on *The Wrong Man* with him. Paul said that Hitch told him, "There's only one way to shoot a piano," because I guess they had the piano not too visible, against something else. Hitch said an upright piano had to be shot from the side.

HJ: Huh. I never actually saw Gadge shoot, but I saw him direct theater when I was with Lee at the Studio. Anyway, it's insane to me that that actor, Andy Griffith, after doing that work, was happy to do this stupid TV sitcom…

DK: Mayberry.

HJ: And the next one was the lawyer.

DK: Matlock.

HJ: And I mean, he gave up this brilliant career, for money, an easy life. But boy oh boy, he was magnificent. And boy, is that character resonant now in some ways.

DK: Yeah, it sure is.

HJ: And yeah, so I read Kazan's book [*Elia Kazan: A Life*, published in 1988], and what can I tell you? It's a great book. It's brilliant. It's the best book I've ever read about both movies and plays. And we've seen each other—at least I've seen him, because he's Kazan. I don't know if he noticed me as a kid at the Actors Studio from time to time. We were at Strasberg's house, at the same parties, you know. But I didn't know him at all, and I wrote him a letter. Dear Kazan… or no, not dear, because I was even unwilling to put "Dear Kazan." Basically, I wrote him—and you'll see the exact writing—"You know, it's an article of faith in my life that you are a shit. Now, I've just read your book, and it's the most brilliant book about Hollywood movies and theater that I've ever read. I cannot reconcile these two facts. How is it that a shit like you could have written a book like that?" That's the basic. You'll see the exact letter.

DK: Wow, yeah. Guts!

HJ: "Signed, Henry Jaglom." I never expected to hear from him. "Dear Henry Jaglom, What a fascinating letter! I've gotten thousands of letters," he feels the need to tell me, "but yours was the most intriguing," or something like that. "So please,"—now he's the director—"Please be specific. 1. In what way am I a shit? 2. In what way is that the best book you've ever read?" I'm paraphrasing, but it's pretty close. You'll see the exact thing. And I wrote him back about himself and what he what he did in his life. And yet I can't reconcile… you can imagine. He writes me back. "See, life's more complicated than you think." "Very interesting letter." "Love to meet you sometime." I'm on my way to Toronto for the film festival with a film, and I go to meet him in New York. He's like a little bantam cock. He's, like, short. He puts his hand out like that, walks upstairs—his wife is working upstairs. We go up to his little private area and we have a couple of hours. I was in heaven. It's Kazan! Not the shit, but Kazan, the filmmaker, and he's talking to me and I'm having a wonderful time. And I think, "Shit, I'm not supposed to like this man. I don't know what I'm supposed to do here." And anyway, we left and we wrote a series of letters to each other, back and forth, all of which I have in a collection.

Then he says, "I'd like to see some of your work," and I sent them some of my films, and he basically says, "You're good with actors, but your films aren't about anything. They should be about life and death, films of struggle, a boxing match, a war, or something where somebody has got something at stake. Not "he loves her, she leaves him, who gives a shit?" Basically like that. And I write him back, "Well, you're really going to hate my next movie because I'm making a movie called *Eating*. It's about, like, 36 women and their issues with food, which to you might be silly, but to them can be a life or death issue. And I know you might not understand this, but I'm going to send it to you anyway," or something like that. And he writes back, "You're right, I don't give a shit about these women. Who cares?" Then he said, "But then, it's just me and I'm an artist. You're an artist. We're artists so we don't have to…"—you know, something like that.

You can see again the exact writing, and I get crazy. When this all began, I told Orson at lunch. And Orson hates this man ever since what happened. He won't talk to him. He said, "I'll tell you a story." And he tells me a story, then I tell Kazan, "Orson Welles told me a story." I don't say that it was about him, I play coy. "And it made me think of you." And the story that Orson told me is about the actor who starred in *The Blue Angel*, who got the first Academy Award.

DK: Emil Jannings.

HJ: Good for you! Yeah, Emil Jannings, who got the first Academy Award for Best Actor. And then he went back to Germany. When Hitler came to power, most of the decent people—no, *all* the decent people—left. Marlene Dietrich, all of that. But he stayed and worked under the Nazis and became the head of the Nazi film industry. And then when the war ended, and Germany got the shit kicked out of it, he stood on his doorstep in this little town, and when the Allied American troops came marching in, he stood on his doorstep holding his Oscar on high, shouting "Artiste! Artiste!" And I said to him, "I know you think as an artist you're exempt from all human consideration, but we're not," you know, something along those lines. I was with Andrea Marcovicci, and she begged me not to send it. He had already had a heart attack. I explained to her, "But we'd been honest with each other" and I didn't hear from him for years.

Then I met Victoria [Foyt], we got married, we had a baby, my darling Sabrina. I sent a postcard out to a lot of people, a picture of me, Victoria and baby Sabrina. And for that I got back from Kazan, "Good looking kid. Congratulations." I always had a hat you know. So he said, "Listen, get rid of that hat. You need $1.79, I'll get you a new hat"—it was actually kind of sweet. And we continued a gentle correspondence, but nothing ultimately. So that's the Kazan story.

DK: Amazing. You had more guts than I. I would have just melted in such a presence.

HJ: But "Who cares about those women?" He was so fucking contemptuous. And a "real movie" was about what he deemed important. And yet, I go back to the Fifties and he was the only one making real, good films. Everybody was making these stupid kind of… well, I mean, not everybody, obviously.

DK: Fluffy.

HJ: Yeah. The good stuff in the Forties was gone, you know, and the good stuff in the Sixties and Seventies hadn't begun yet. He was making one great film after another. But his book is brilliant, because it's so true. The people I know are perfectly described: Strasberg, Harold Clurman… that's how I know it's true. Perfectly captured.

DK: You know, Paul Sylbert wrote a novel that's unpublished. I have the manuscript to it. He gave it to me to read, and he never got it back because he died before I could hand it back over to him. It's called *Nothing Happens*. It's about his memories of being at the Actors Studio. And there's a whole character based on you.

HJ: What?!

DK: Your character name is Marty Jelnick in the book.

HJ: Oh yeah, you said something in an email like about this. But he hardly knew me! Well, I mean, he knew me for a short time. What is my character? Tell the truth.

DK: Your character holds a lot of parties, and basically always carries around a little movie camera all the time, and films everybody.

HJ: Both those things are true. I actually have pictures of Paul at some early parties, somewhere.

DK: I'd love to see those.

HJ: How do you know for sure it's based on me?

DK: He told me. When I was in college at Temple University, where he taught, he knew that I knew you. I was his TA. And years into our friendship, including after I graduated, he gave me the manuscript and said, "You'll probably appreciate this now that you know Henry well enough." So he gave it to me, and I never got it published. I still have it. He never asked for it back. He was very erudite, fluent in Greek and Portuguese, could quote philosophers and new a kind of art-speak, but there was a kind of caprice about him too.

HJ: Caprice?

DK: As in capricious.

HJ: Oh! Wasn't that a terrible Doris Day movie? But late Doris Day.

DK: Yeah, with, I think, uh, Rod Taylor.

HJ: I always liked Rod Taylor.

DK: Richard Harris, I think, was in it too.

HJ: Richard Harris and Doris Day?!

DK: Yeah. Strange. [*Author's note: Frank Tashlin's* Caprice *does not feature Rod Taylor, but it does star Doris Day and Richard Harris. I made a factual mistake here.*]

HJ: That was not her best period.

DK: She did *With Six You Get Eggroll* around that time, which I think was her last film.

HJ: Boy, she meant so much to me in childhood! I mean, I was in love with her. When I married [first wife] Patrice, I took her to my high school reunion. Three different kids — no longer kids, but kids from my school — came up to me at three different times and said, "Well, you did it." And I said, "Did what?" They said, "Well, you said you were going to marry Doris Day and you found her." Yeah, Doris Day, I was madly in love. The first person I was ever really in love with, was Doris Day in the movies. But not that later Doris Day, the early Doris Day. You know, "Once I had a secret love." *That* Doris Day.

DK: From *Calamity Jane.*

HJ: The only girl I ever cut photos out of magazines and had them up on my wall was Doris Day.

DK: Sal Mineo was my first movie crush.

HJ: From which movie? Not *Rebel*.

DK: Of course *Rebel*!

HJ: Not the older, sexy Sal Mineo?

DK: No, the young and beautiful and insecure Sal Mineo in that movie. Plato in *Rebel Without a Cause*.

HJ: Plato was such a kid, though.

DK: Well, so was I!

HJ: Oh, I see. I would think later he became sexier. Do you think you saw *Exodus* first?

DK: Probably.

HJ: Because that makes much more sense.

DK: [*laughs*]

HJ: No, because he was sexy in *Exodus*.

DK: Sexodus!

HJ: [*laughs*] I knew him, you know. I knew him very well. I dated with him when he was still playing straight. I have photos of us somewhere. I went to the Actors Studio and put on the second act of my play, *A Safe Place*. And I was in a dinner jacket because I was going that night to the world premiere of one of the Jesus Christ movies.

DK: *The Greatest Story Ever Told*?—because Sal was in that one.

HJ: My date was Tuesday. And his date was that little girl…

DK: Jill Haworth?

HJ: [*flabbergasted*] How the hell do you know that?

DK: Because they were in *Exodus* together, and they famously were an item for a bit.

HJ: She was a good friend of mine. Sweet girl. And we double-dated and went to the movie, but I had my dinner jacket on earlier because I was going to the premiere. So yeah, I have the tie open, but I'm wearing a tuxedo as Clurman is commenting on the on the second act of the play, and I sat there at the Actors Studio smoking in that dinner jacket, then went out to the opening with Sal and Jill and Tuesday. We all drove around.

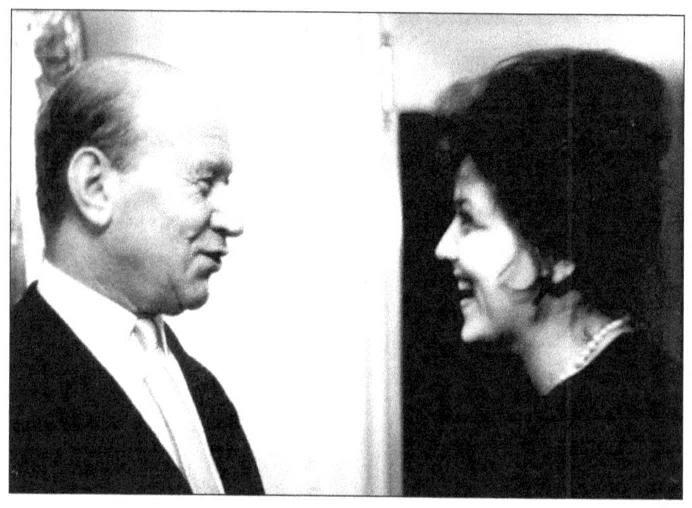

Brenda Vaccaro with Simon Jaglom, Henry's father,
at a party on the Upper West Side in 1962.

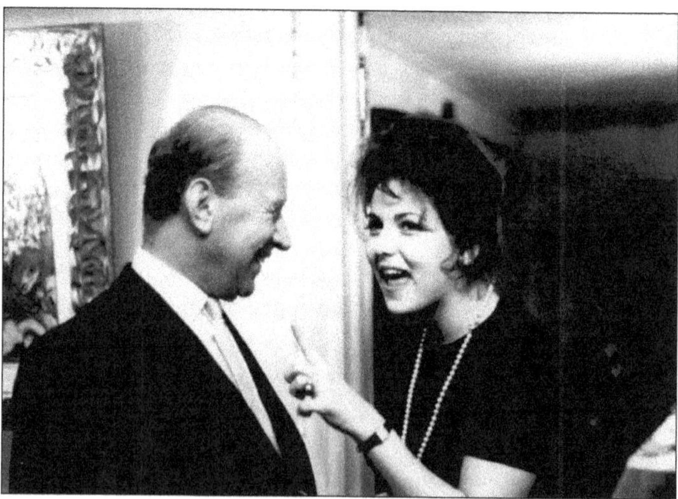

DK: I mean, as a teenager, I'm watching *Rebel*, I found Plato gorgeous and the whole movie, he is just throwing himself at James Dean, and Dean is after—and I know you dated Natalie Wood, but it was different for me as a little gay boy—he is after Natalie. But I couldn't fathom having a Plato in the wings who was in love with me, but going after a girl. I was envious of Dean in a way, because Sal was infatuated with him.

HJ: I liked that kid, but we lost touch around the time he started getting into more dangerous stuff, like rough trade.

DK: Well, he did *Fortune and Men's Eyes* for the stage.

HJ: You know, he went out, got beaten up a few times. He let it be known when he gave up the pretense of being straight. Elliot Mintz was incredibly close with Sal.

DK: You mentioned Tuesday, but Brenda Vaccaro was your first girlfriend, right?

HJ: Yes… no, what am I saying? My first girlfriend was in college, a girl named Sheila, who I still see to this day. She comes to my movies and plays and all the things. She moved out here. We were in college for three years together; she was a year older than me. We met on line auditioning for *Death of a Salesman*, and we both got cast. We started boyfriend girlfriend, this was in the Fifties. We never slept together. Ten years. We broke up because she wanted to get married. "Ten years," I told her. "I'll get married in ten years. I've got a career to get first." Brenda Vaccaro was my first where sleeping together was included. It was in New York, and she was packing chocolates, wrapping them for this Hungarian in this candy store. That's all I remember: she wrapped chocolates. That was after college. Then I was with Karen [Black], and we were together for a year.

DK: Natalie Wood is in there somewhere too.

HJ: Oh yes, of course, Natalie! It's funny, I'm remembering another double date. I was with Natalie, and Warren Beatty was with this girl from the Bolshoi ballet, I think. She hardly spoke a word of English. Natalie translated for us all night long.

DK: Her Russian was that good?

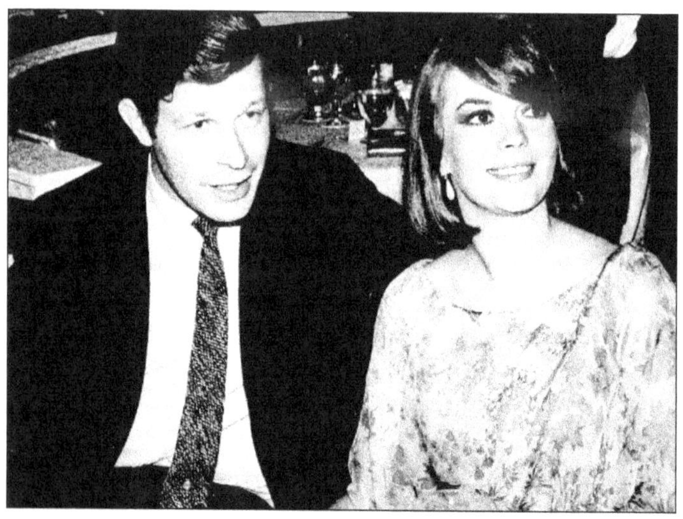

Henry and Natalie Wood were seen together at
multiple parties and events throughout 1965 and 1966.

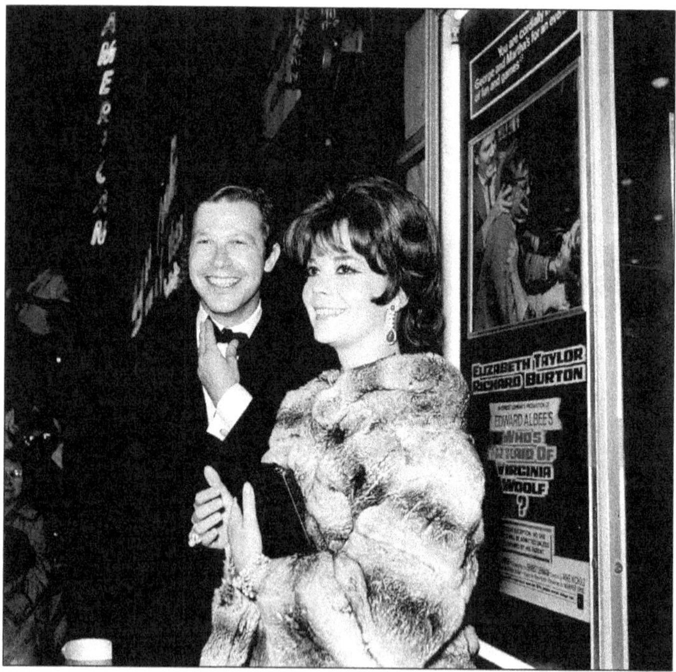

HJ: Oh yeah. She grew up in a very Russian household. Her parents were Russian immigrants.

DK: How did you meet Natalie?

HJ: I met her at The Daisy, which was a club everybody went to. I don't remember much except that she said, "Would you take me home?" It sounds like I'm omitting something, but I don't remember anything more than that. And I said, "Sure." We had flirted and talked for about an hour or two. Warren Beatty was there, and she had broken up with him about six months before, or something.

DK: Yeah.

HJ: So when we got in her door, she said, "Warren hadn't spoken to me in months. Watch this," and she points to the phone with a slow gesture like this [*demonstrates pointing in a kind of slow-motion move*]. And it's amazing, the phone actually rings and she tells me, "Get on the extension. You know how to do it quietly?" I told her yes, and I go in the bedroom, I pick it up, and it's Warren. It wasn't an especially memorable conversation, but we… started our affair that night. I did not succeed on the one thing I wanted to do, which would have saved her life, I think. She had a lifelong fear of water, of swimming, and she ended up drowning, as you probably know. She got out of that place where they were having an argument — Wagner and Walken. It's just speculation, but, she wouldn't otherwise, she wasn't drunk. She wouldn't have gotten onto any boat to go back to shore because, you know, she knew what she hated. She was terrified. I tried to teach her to swim. I would hold on to her in the pool, and she'd help hold me with one hand and the edge of the pool with the other. She just was terrified of being in the water. You just made me think, by the way, something I'm proud of: I was responsible for the pairing of Sydney Pollack and Redford. *This Property Is Condemned* was a movie…

DK: That was 1966.

HJ: That's when I was with Natalie, when we were dating.

DK: Yeah, I saw that newsreel of the two of you at the *Who's Afraid of Virginia Woolf?* premiere. That was also 1966.

HJ: That was quite a party! Still Old Hollywood going on then. I'll have to tell you about that some other time. But Natalie, she was at the height of her fame. She was the number one star in Hollywood. She could command whatever she wanted, she certainly could decide who her directors were, and which writers. She was interested in Redford and Redford wanted Sydney Pollack to direct, and she didn't want Sydney Pollack because… I don't know what he directed before.

DK: He had only done one other movie. *The Slender Thread.* That was his first.

HJ: Yeah, you're handy to have around with all the titles and the years. What year was that one?

DK: 1965.

HJ: Yeah, that sounds about right. But I knew him—I knew Pollack. I was a friend of his from the Actors Studio. I started selling, and I'm really good at that. I was just in the key position at the right time. Pollack always said that his whole career he owed to me. And Redford, in a way too, because he took Redford with him on this journey, starting with *This Property is Condemned*, doing a bunch of movies together. They both became huge. You know, I remember we were drawing each other. I sent you those drawings, right?

DK: Yeah, I have them.

HJ: And I had… what's his name was there of a French actor, gorgeous French actor, Alain Delon. He was drawing us while we were drawing each other. I also have a drawing of him that I did at the time.

DK: I only saw the one that Natalie did of you.

HJ: Not very good. Mine of her is hanging out in the hallway out there, I think. We can prove that very easily if either one of us has the energy to get up.

DK: I trust you.

HJ: But… I'm trying to stay on topic here, but I forget was I saying. Sydney was a friend, a compatriot of mine at the Actors Studio and I was a kid. I just felt he was going to be great, and I really sold him to her, and that changed his whole life and his whole career. Natalie always told people about that too, because you know I could sell. Another thing with Natalie was,

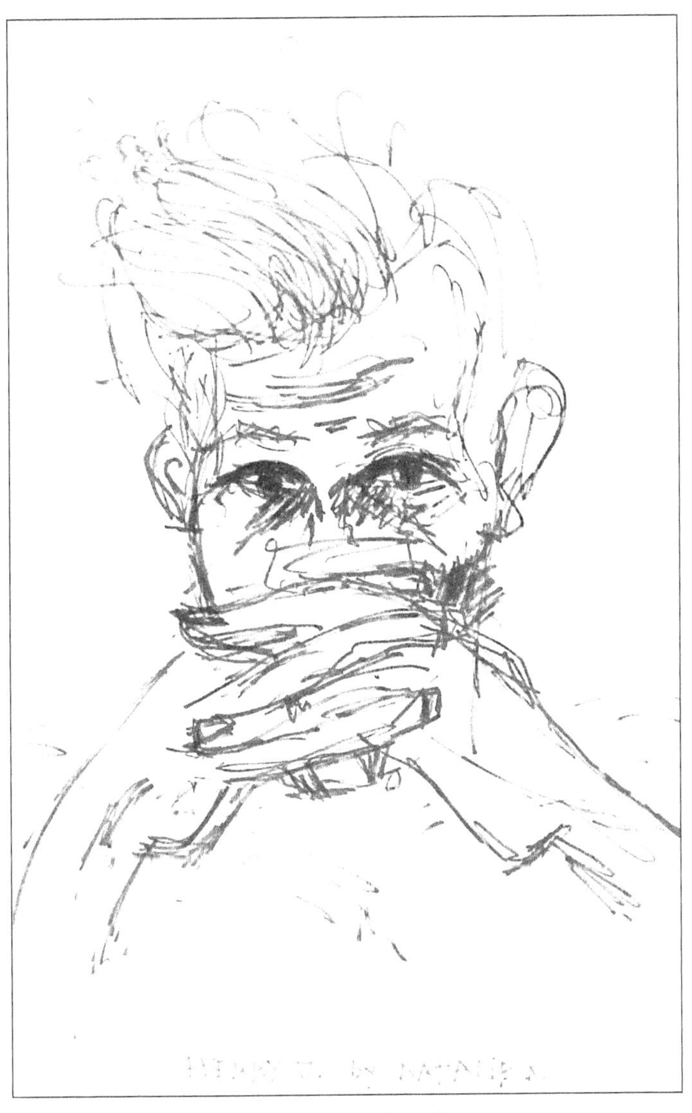

Natalie Wood's drawing of Henry.

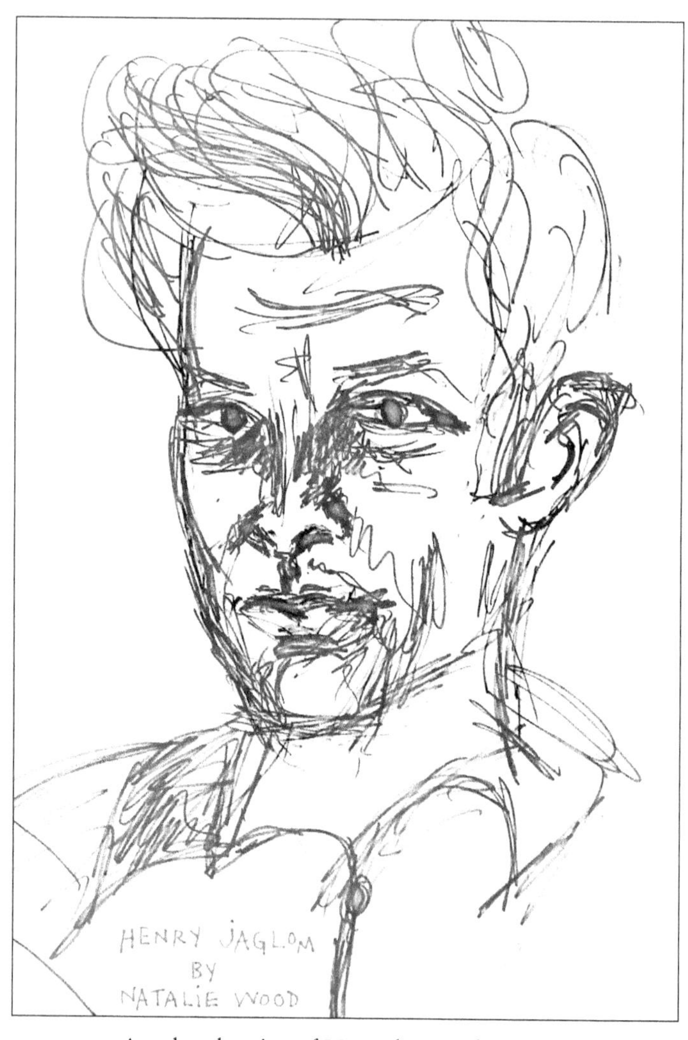

Another drawing of Henry by Natalie Wood.

I remember Sinatra came over to Natalie's house, to visit. I answered the door and… he was in no mood, let's put it that way. We had a very, you'd say monosyllabic conversation, and he leaves in a huff. Not the way I wanted it to go, because I always worshipped Sinatra. It gets back to me somehow that Sinatra has told someone, such-and-such a person, that "Natalie's living with some drug addict."

DK: What?!

HJ: Something like "puny" or "half-pint" drug addict.

DK: You never touched drugs though.

HJ: No, of course not. Just a puff now and then. You know who it was? It was Rosalind Russell! She called Natalie at Sinatra's behest, saying "You know about this guy? He's a drug dealer from New York!"

DK: That's funny.

HJ: He just didn't like coming to see Natalie, she's not home, and getting me. I mean, I can only guess. I told him, "Natalie will be right out. Would you like a drink?" "I know where the bar is!!!" He was like an adolescent. Another time, she went out with Frank, and I was just going to hang around at her place for the night, writing. She told me, "When I get back, I'm going to lean on the doorbell." I said, "This is like high school." She said, "Yeah, that's the only way to deal with Frank, because he wants to sleep with me and I don't want to sleep with him. You come, answer the door, and be very friendly." And that's exactly what happened. They went out, came back, he was kissing her at the doorstep, she's leaning on the bell, I come and pull open the door, and he looks at me, "Oh, hi, did you have a nice time?" Something like that. He looked at me with straight up daggers, like he hated my guts. He had this furious look in his eyes. "Good night," real cold, and storms off.

DK: You were just waiting at home, at her place? You didn't want to go out with her?

HJ: Well, I stirred up a lot of shit in those days. We'd gone to Dean Martin's house. All these guys are playing pool. There was a big, beautiful billiards room. I started running my mouth about Vietnam, and how it was gauche to have a party like this when terrible things were happening in Vietnam. Deano didn't want to hear it, everyone else just kind of rolled their eyes. My thing was, I was outraged. And Natalie and I had a big fight, and that's around the time I just started staying home, staying away from these big celebrity parties she was going to all the time.

DK: You were guilty and agitated.

HJ: Agitated, but also the agitator. There's another story… I don't know if I can tell you this one.

DK: Uh-oh.

HJ: I guess it's no big deal. Sinatra is dead. Well, what's-her-face, she's not dead. Woody's ex, you know… Jesus, what's wrong with me these days? I'm getting terrible with names.

DK: Mia.

HJ: Yeah, Mia. I did something amazing out of the arrogance of my youth. I was with Joan Collins and her husband.

DK: Anthony Newley.

HJ: Tony Newley and Joan Collins. Jewish couple, they both were Jews. We used to talk about Jewish stuff together. They gave a dinner party. I was there with Natalie, and Mia was there with Mike Nichols. As I remember, there was only the six of us, but I think there might have been another couple, so maybe eight people. It was a very small dinner party. I had gotten very friendly with Newley in London when he was doing *Stop the World! I Want to Get Off*, which I still love beyond belief. You never saw it.

DK: I saw the movie.

HJ: Yeah, the movie, but this is before you were born. On stage, oh my God. Wait, there's a movie? How is it as a movie?

DK: Yeah, I think it's fine.

HJ: Fine? That's all? It's magnificent on stage. It's one of the tour-de-force performances, along with Burton and *Camelot*. Earth shattering. Brilliant, brilliant fucking thing. I also became friendly with, what's-his-name who wrote with Newley.

DK: Leslie Bricusse.

HJ: Good for you! Jewish also, by the way. And his wife. Brief aside, I took Andrea Marcovicci up to their house. Oh, this is great. I'm invited to go to have lunch, in the heights

SHEILA O.
BRENDA V.
KAREN B.
GEORGIA B.
TUESDAY W.
NATALIE W.
SANDRA S.
BARBARA F.
PATRICE T.
NELLY A.
ANDREA M.
VICTORIA
TANNA F.

At lunch one day, I asked Henry to clear up confusion by listing his girlfriends and wives in chronological order. This is the result.

above Cannes. It's a drive and Leslie Bricusse and his wife Evie—you know that song from *Stop the World!* [*singing*]: "Why can't someone nice like you, Evie? Why did someone like you, Evie, fall in love with someone like me? If I think of all the guys you could have loved, who should have loved, who would have loved you. You're so much more than me, Evie. Believe you me, Evie. You know it's true. [*DK joins the chorus.*] And if I could live twice, I'd make life paradise, for someone really nice like you." That gives me goosebumps. Newley was such a great performer. When you saw him on stage, you can't imagine. His other big one was, um…

DK: Uhhh, he liked long titles. *The Roar of the Grease Paint, the Smell of the Crowd.*

HJ: Yeah, that one. Yeah, he was magic on the fucking stage. It didn't translate to film. So Andrea and I are driving up for lunch, with Bricusse and his wife. They've got another couple coming for dinner. A car pulls up, a limousine with a dog in the back. We can't see a person yet. Door opens, dog hops out, and it's Elizabeth Taylor. All I remember was she and Andrea spoke about jewelry during the entire lunch. That's all I remember—diamonds and things. Anyway, getting back to where we were. See what happens, with the association, I get lost.

DK: You were starting to talk about Mia and Mike Nichols a little bit back.

HJ: Oh yeah, dinner party at Tony and Joan's. I'm with Natalie. Mia runs off to the bathroom at one point, and she doesn't come back. I guess I was her age, more than anybody else there. I kind of figured she was smoking dope, so I said I'll go and get her. They all were talking, so nobody minded, including Mike. I went in there and she's crying… and smoking dope. I start smoking some grass with her, and she's crying. The grass is an important part of the story, because I am a bit of a megalomaniac, but when I got high, you cannot imagine what a megalomaniac is. And this is a big part of the story, because I can't even believe now when I tell the story. I've kind of always asked myself, "What made you think you could do this?" and I'm sure it was just being high. I said, "Why are you

crying?" She said, "Mike wants me to go to Rome with him."
Do you know about Mike Nichols's hair?

DK: His hair?

HJ: Yeah.

DK: Can't say I do.

HJ: Mike Nichols woke up at 13 or 14. All his hair was in his bed. He had this disease or whatever.

DK: Alopecia?

HJ: Whatever it is, every every hair on the body—gone. Everybody knew this in Hollywood, right? But he wore very good eyebrows and lashes and toupee. Everybody talked to everybody, so everybody knew it here. Anyway, not the point. She knew it, and she said, "He's going to want to sleep with me. And I don't want to sleep with him in any way. He's got no hair. What, does he take it off at night?" She's very high. And I said, "Well, what do you want? Just tell me what you want. I can take care of it." Something insane like that. She said, "What do you mean you can take care of it?" I said, "What is it that you're crying about?" "I don't want to sleep with him." "Then don't sleep with him!" "But I want to show Frank!" I was ignorant. I said, "Frank?" It was Sinatra, of course. I'd heard, of course, like everybody, that he had just walked out on her and said he wasn't gonna marry her because she was too young and wasn't going to see her anymore. "I'm still in love with Frank. And he won't even see me, or talk to me. And now Mike really wants to sleep with me, and I don't want to go to Rome with him because he's going to want to sleep with me."

And I said, "You want me to take care of this?" Here's how arrogant and unbelievably confident, or whatever you call it… nuts or something, but especially when a little high. She said, "What do you mean?" I said, "Tell me if this is right. You don't want to sleep with Mike Nichols. You want to marry Frank. Frank's not talking to you and refuses to talk to you. Mike wants you to go to Rome." She said yes. I said, "Okay, you got to Rome with him, but tell him you want a separate room, because you've got to get used to the idea." She said, "Well, what good is that going to do on the second night?" I said, "There's not going to be a second night." "What are you

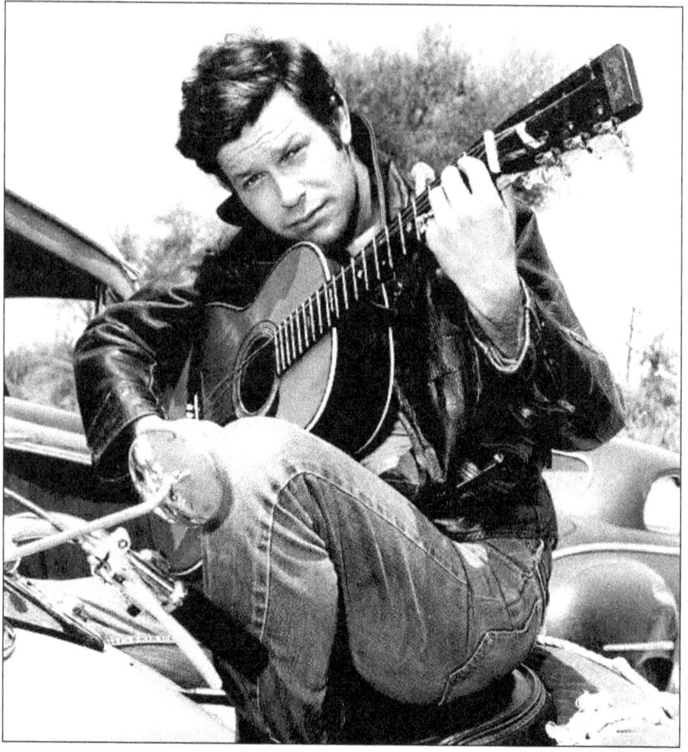

A publicity shot from Henry's guest-star spot on *Gidget.*

talking about?" I said, "You just trust me." "I don't know, I don't know." She was stoned, we came out of the bathroom. I wasn't stoned, but I was a bit high. I can't remember the rest of the evening, to be honest with you. I just remember Tony Newley singing some songs, which was so exciting for me.

We went home, and what I remember was, I didn't go in the house with Natalie. I said, "I got work to do. I'm writing a screenplay." She said, "Come in and write it." "No, I can't, you know. I'll see you tomorrow." So I go home and I had this phone book, which I had taken from Tuesday. That's a whole other story, which I don't want you to tell you about now, but someday I'll tell you. She tried to throw it out of the window in a fit of hysteria. She was mad at me and she threw the whole thing out. I went down, I got it, never gave it back to her. But I had this phone book. Anyway, I made phone calls that night, and it wasn't as easy as now, you understand. I made a tremendous amount of phone calls. I spent the whole night awake.

Mia flies to Rome with Mike Nichols. She later told me she was completely depressed, she remembers being stoned and my telling her to go, she doesn't remember why, she doesn't know why she's even doing it, but she trusted me. That was what she said. I don't know why she trusted me, but I was on the phone. I called everybody I knew who knew Sinatra, and I knew a lot of people. Plus, I told Natalie, who knew Sinatra—Frank was trying to date her again—all kinds of things. She got to Rome. Her separate suite was filled with roses, and a big sign, and a telegram: "Come back immediately. Do not stay another night. We're getting married. Frank." That's the story. I let everybody in this town know that she was going with Mike Nichols. I knew enough to know that Sinatra was an incredibly jealous human being. I met him when I was with Natalie. I knew enough to know that Frank might not want her, but he didn't want anybody else to have her. Mike Nichols was a big, famous director, and it was obvious that the word got back from probably ten people... or fifty people, I don't know. I spent the night calling everybody in Tuesday's phone book, sometimes under assumed names. You understand? It was a fucking amazing scheme. You don't seem too impressed.

DK: No, I'm very impressed. I'm smiling!

HJ: That's a smile? That's very small, but okay. I just couldn't believe it worked. That one telegram from him was followed by, like, six more telegrams. "Don't stay there another night." He found out that she had a separate room. I knew he would do something. I knew enough about him, his insecurities. Much later, I learned from Mike that she slept on both plane trips, to Rome, and then all the way back home. But it's like the greatest stunt I've ever pulled in my life.

DK: You know, there's a Sidney Furie tie-in here. He was about to direct Frank in *The Naked Runner* in 1966. They're way into pre-production when Frank went missing without a trace. They had to put the project on hold. No one knew what happened to him. He resurfaced, newly married to Mia, who would hang around on that set.

HJ: So are you going to tell him this story?

DK: I'll see him for breakfast tomorrow. I'm sure he'll be fascinated.

HJ: Sinatra was absolutely not going to marry her! So it's my fault his production was shut down. Give him my belated apologies.

[Consult the appendix for the complete correspondence between Jaglom and Kazan.]

3.
"I don't think I'll hang myself today"

In which Henry discusses coming into possession of a haunted Marilyn Monroe heirloom, his time at the Actors Studio in those mythic days, and irritating Lee Strasberg twice.

HJ: I'm sorry, names again. Names are the first thing to go. Who wrote *Picnic*?

DK: William Inge.

HJ: Inge wrote a play. It was his last play. In the play, three murderers are on death row in three cells, and you see all three cells. Don't try to figure it out, because it never was done anywhere else except that the Actors Studio West, starring me in the middle, Joe Don Baker…

DK: [*amazed*] Joe Don Baker?

HJ: Is that his name or…

DK: Yeah, just not a name I was expecting.

HJ: Baker on one side and this other great character actor on the other. It's easy to find, I guess, in my journals. Three of us on stage divided by cells. My big speech, what I can remember is, I guess it's to the priest or someone who comes visiting us… the warden, I don't know. "Death? My enemy? Father, life's my enemy, not death!" Something like that. Also, I'm gay and I asked Harold Clurman, "What do I do with that information?" He said, "Well, can you play gay?" Jack Garfein was directing, Clurman was my teacher. Do you know who Bill Archibald was?

DK: Rings a bell.

HJ: He wrote a play about ghosts and Broadway, became quite famous. Bill Archibald had befriended me in New York, brought me into the Actors Studio, in the Playwrights Unit, because I refused to go for the audition as an actor. I'd won an award, $50, for a play I'd written in college, called *Room 322*, so I decided I was best equipped to make it into the Playwrights Unit. I had fancied myself more a playwright as an undergraduate.

The Studio was tough. What actors went through as actors, as people, to get rejected ten times, and that wasn't going to be my way. I knew Strasberg really well, and I knew I'm wasn't going to put up with that bullshit. But I always think of Bill and Roscoe Lee Brown as the first gay guys I really knew well who were gay. Roscoe was flamboyant. He tried to seduce me at one point. When I begged off by telling him I was straight, he said, "But you'll be much better with women once you've been with a man."

DK: Ha! And you cast him later, in *Last Summer in the Hamptons*.

HJ: I didn't take him up on it, but we remained friends. Bill Archibald was this intellectual and a very nice man. He took me under his wing. I'd already been studying with Strasberg as an actor.

DK: Without the infamous audition.

HJ: Right, without the infamous audition. I'm not going to lie. But the way to sneak into the Studio was to become a member of the Playwrights Unit, which I was made automatically and for life. And so I'm a Studio person, and that allowed me to go to all the acting classes, watch them and so on, and do our scenes at the acting class.

Archibald had a boyfriend or husband. For thirty and forty years, they were monogamous, and he was playing piano at a club on the East Side that I used to go to because… Janice Mars. [*pause*]

DK: Janice Mars?

HJ: Oh my God! She was a singer at a club on the East Side. And Beau Bergersen, or Baldwin Bergersen, the husband or boyfriend of Bill Archibald, played piano there. I would go to acting classes at Eli Rill. You know who that is?

DK: I've heard you talk about him.

HJ: He taught me the Method. My first classes, where I was sneaking in from college every Thursday, staying overnight because I couldn't come home—my parents thought I was in college. I couldn't come home till Friday night. So I always stayed with Seymour Cassel and Rupert Crosse; they had a place owned by Katharine Hepburn's brother in Hell's Kitchen, on 45th way over. We were buddies and I'd sleep on the floor. After Eli's class, we went to hear Janice Mars sing at The Back Room, and then I had to find a place to sleep. Mostly where I slept was on the floor at Jim Downey Steakhouse, where we all hung out. You know about Downey's?

DK: Vaguely.

HJ: Oh my God! Downey's was the only decent place you could go without a tie, period, in New York. Those people who could afford it went to Sardi's. All the unemployed actors and even the new Broadway actors, like who came from London and everything, they hung out at Jim Downey's, with all the pictures of on the wall of all the other actors. The goal was to have your picture up there. And I had done summer stock. The Improvisation [comedy club] had just opened, and I painted the original sign of Improvisation in return for free meals for six months.

DK: You met Cassavetes around this time too, correct?

HJ: Yeah, Seymour [Cassel] introduced us. Seymour I knew through the larger network of actors, including people like Rupert Crosse. You know who Rupert Crosse is, right?

DK: Yeah, he's in *Shadows*, of course. And I know him from *The Reivers*, among other things.

HJ: Very good! Yeah, he was very close with McQueen. He would have been a huge movie star if he hadn't died of cancer. And *Shadows* changed my life, of course. Seymour took me to see it at a midnight show at the Paris Theatre. It proved to me that cinema—especially American cinema—could be personal. We remained friends for a long, long time after that… until he died. Anyway, I got carried away. That always happens with you. You have that effect on me. Anyway…

DK: Janice Mars?

HJ: Yes, Janice Mars… Brando made a record of her for private use and spread it around. Marilyn Monroe's masseur, whose name I've forgotten, Ralph something. Big guy, gay. He later played cards with me one night in Hollywood when I was visiting Bobby Walker's house—that's Robert Walker, Jr. the son of Jennifer Jones and Robert Walker. Maureen Stapleton was in that game as well, and that little scared, bald guy with the glasses in *12 Angry Men*.

DK: John… Fiedler?

HJ: Boy, you're good! I love how you keep up with me!

DK: That's how we got to be closer, Henry. We were at a bar in Iowa for the film festival, and I named the twelve angry men in order of juror number.

HJ: Yeah, I remember I wanted to get to know you better. You came up with the name of the foreign guy, um…

DK: George Voskovec.

HJ: That's right. That was a game we used to play in college. We used to be proud that we could name all twelve angry men. Anyway, Ralph… Roberts! I just remembered his name. I think he had a little thing for me. Masseur to Marilyn Monroe. I talked to him about Janice Mars and how much I loved Janice, somehow it came up. I was lamenting that she has kind of disappeared off the scene and I missed hearing her sing. He said, "You know I have an album of hers. Brando made the album. He put her in all his movies and loves her work. It's a private album." I said, "God, that's fantastic." And I went on and on. The next night, or whenever we played the next card game, he brought the album to me. This copy of the album would have been Marilyn Monroe's. She had died, I think, the year before. I never told you my Marilyn story?

DK: Nope.

HJ: Fuck! This isn't possible. I'm going to be going on forever.

DK: [*laughs*]

HJ: It's such a good story. It's the best story in the world, really the best. Don't let me forget to tell you. It takes two minutes. So I play the album when I get back to New York, and there's a song, "Oh, I don't think I'll hang myself today." I mean, her famous songs were "Bye Bye Blackbird" and she's phenomenal doing that. But this "Oh, I don't think I'll hang myself today," the part of the album at that part was scratched to oblivion. Marilyn had, I guess, played it and replayed it to death, and maybe she scratched it all up herself in some fit of rage. But you see this thing that belonged to her, and you see how scratched this record album was at that part, and you start imagining all the pain she must have felt.

DK: Wow, do you still have the album?

HJ: I must have it somewhere. I keep everything. But Jim Downey's Steakhouse—did I tell you I offered to marry Mel Brooks there, when I met him?

DK: [*chuckling*] No.

HJ: I walked in one day a couple of years after all this. There was Mel Brooks there. I fell to my knees, and he was there with his wife and with other people… I fell to my knees and said, "Will you marry me?" And without missing a beat, he said, "You're too short." And I screamed in laughter. I reminded him of that many years later. He said, "You gave me a straight line, kid. I couldn't not take it." It was a great moment in my life. I remember we were on a flight together. I was in business class, and he was in first class with his wife.

DK: Anne Bancroft.

HJ: Yes, Anne Bancroft. She was sitting there reading a script, I think. But he wasn't doing anything. I walked over, got into a conversation with him. I was leaning on the arm-rest, and Bancroft kept shooting me dirty looks. A deep scowl. He told me he was adapting *The Producers* into a Broadway show and was having trouble casting the part that Zero Mostel plays in the movie. I didn't think that *The Producers* would make a good stage show, and boy was I wrong! But I said, "I know just the guy!" I had just seen Jon Robby Baitz's play *Mizlansky*… what was it called?

DK: I don't know.

HJ: It was a play by Robby Baitz. [*Author's note: The Jon Robin Baitz play is* Mizlansky/Zilinsky, *or Schmucks,* staged in 1998.] Anyway, whatever it is… I said, "The guy in that would be superb. It was Nathan Lane." Mel balked because he wasn't Jewish. I, of course, said, "Who gives a shit?" I sat there and really sold him on Nathan Lane, and these terrible looks from Anne Bancroft keep getting worse. She was not pleased. These were, like, hateful looks I was getting. Months later, I read that Mel Brooks has cast Nathan Lane, and the rest is history. [*Author's note:* The Producers *premiered on Broadway in April 2001.*]

DK: You playing a vital role in performing arts history. That's hilarious.

HJ: Completely true.

DK: So you were going to tell a Marilyn story.

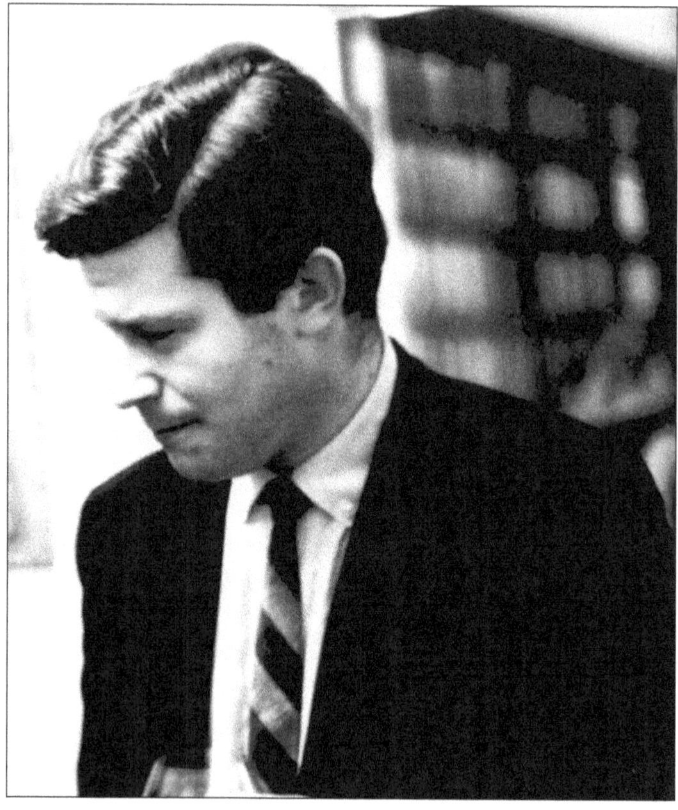

Henry around the time he was studying at the Studio.

HJ: Yes, the Marilyn story! I'm new to the Actors Studio, my first year. We're still at Carnegie Hall, before we headed to the other place. All I wanted was to be famous. I didn't give a shit about the work or anything. Paul Newman was there, Ben Gazzara was there. These people were my heroes. I'd acted in college and directed, and I was more interested already in directing. But I still wanted to be a famous actor.

Now, I'm on a stage, and we're doing a sense memory. I'm up there with six other actors in chairs. We're working on something very simple, like, I think it was orange juice in the glass, imagining the feeling of the glass, the cold, the taste, the smell, all the sensory work. And to me, it's bullshit. I'm thinking, "Okay, goddamn it, nobody's going to ever pay attention to me. There's five other people here and I'm all the way at the end. What can I do to get attention?" All the wrong things, but now I'm telling you the truth. "Oh my God, that's Paul Newman here, if he sees me and likes me, he'll maybe cast me in the next movie," you know. And I see Kazan and I'm like, "Oh, that's, that director Kazan! Holy shit!" And I'm completely obsessed with, frankly, bullshit. And out of the corner of my eye, I see a light in the back of the class. A door opens and in comes a figure, a woman, with a white scarf around her hair. "It's fucking Marilyn Monroe! Marilyn Monroe!!!" This is maybe two years before she died." Nobody makes a move, nobody says anything. She comes in, she sits in the seventh seat, exactly on the opposite end of me at the other end of the stage, with five people between us.

I remember it clearly, "Fuck, now really nobody is going to pay attention to me, everybody's going to be looking at her." The idea of my doing this with Marilyn Monroe being there made me giggle. And I thought, "Well, I'm supposed to go with whatever comes along," and I started kind of laughing. I thought that this'll be interesting because that's going to look like I'm really into something they don't know, they're not privy to. Like. As I started really laughing, I hear, on the other end, Marilyn Monroe sniffling. Suddenly, holy shit, I'm doing a scene with Marilyn Monroe! The more I laugh, the more she cries. Whatever it's doing, I think, this is working.

I'm thinking, "I'm a star. I'm sorry. I've made it. It's me and Marilyn Monroe. We're doing a scene. Who's going to watch the five people in between us? Are you kidding? We're doing this scene, this is brilliant!" And I just let myself go laughing hysterically, and she's sobbing now.

I'm a cruel motherfucker, I'm not thinking about anything but myself, you understand. It goes on for, I don't want to exaggerate, got to be ten minutes. It might have felt like an hour, but it's probably more like ten, eleven, I don't know. But a long time! The lights come up, I hear her pulling herself together. I'm sitting right content because I know the world has been watching the two of us. I know Paul Newman's probably going to cast me. Kirk Douglas happened to be there. And Lee starts with Marilyn. "It's very good, darling. I saw how full that was. I saw the depth of your expression. You really overcame the last problem with that, and it's very specific, very truthful. It was very, very good work." She thanked him, meekly because she was still coming down from it all. And he goes to the next person, "Johnny, that was terrific," etc. Next person, Phyllis, "Good work." And he's being awfully nice, which was not his m.o.

Then he stops one short of me and says "Class dismissed!" He doesn't say anything to me, not a word. He left me hanging. Everybody gets up and start stretching. Other people are coming to congratulate the others. I'm like a schmuck sitting at the end by myself, not knowing what to do. Do I get up? Where do I go? He got it—he saw that I was full of shit and he wasn't going to give me anything. It was a great, great fucking lesson. Then, the worst part of it is that, wherever we have coffee afterward, at Horn & Hardart or whatever it was, Marilyn comes to me with that white scarf. I'm sitting alone, like I'm an outcast and she asks very tentatively, nervously, "Do you have a scene partner?" And I said, "I'm sorry." I was scared, I didn't know what to do. Right? Like a schmuck, instead of getting to do a real scene with Marilyn. I was so devastated by how Lee handled it. Can I tell you one more quick Lee story?

DK: Yeah, just keep on going.

HJ: These are all the stories about what an asshole I am. I call these "my two asshole stories." My other one was in class. Now we'd moved to where we had classes, where it is now. It was a nice, much nicer place—this Greek church. I still thought that acting was bullshit, and I don't remember what exactly I did, but I faked my way through something and I thought it was just damn great. After it, Lee said to me, "Now that's good work, Henry. That's very truthful." I told you, I faked it, and he is just going on and on, that he saw finally what I had reached. Like the asshole that I am, I couldn't resist. So I said, "Really? Good? Well, I didn't do any of the work you're saying. There was nothing internal, it was completely external. It was bullshit."

A hush went over the class. You kind of never forgot that sound of silence… and no movement. And Lee said, "Henry, well, you know more than I do. Obviously, you don't need me, so you can leave the class." I said, "What? What?!" "You have no need for the actors. You know better. You did it, and you're convinced that you got it right and I made a mistake. I saw good work when it was only superficial and false, right?" "Well, no, I didn't say that." "Yes, you did. That's precisely what you said. So since we don't need you here, would you please leave the class?" That was one of the hardest things. And I babbled on, and quietly, he just said, "Leave the class, Henry." Forty or fifty people looking on.

It took me four months to get back in, because I was barred from there. I would come back during the breaks and hang around, and the secretary came up to me and said, "I'm sorry, you can't come in again. He won't let you in." I was like a pariah—persona non grata, not too much grata at all. They didn't know what to do with me. I was twenty-two, you know, and this was about six months after the Marilyn thing, which must have been still in his mind, I don't know. He had congratulated me on good work, and I had made him look like he didn't know what he was doing. The arrogance is unfathomable now. I don't think anybody in the history of the Studio has ever done anything like that with him. But I kept coming back.

Months went by, he came out during a lunch and I was standing there looking like in the corner or something. He came over, and he said, "Why aren't you inside, Henry?" I took that to mean I was allowed to go back in. Months on from that, I'm doing an exercise, singing "The Star-Spangled Banner" one syllable at a time, drawing everything out. Lee gets up from his seat. I don't know if I'm real, if I'm faking, I don't know what the fuck's going on. And, you know, I've never been able to cry in acting in front of people. That was my biggest thing. I could fake every kind of behavior except crying. "Aaaaaand. Ooooooour. Flaaaaaag." And he sticks his his knuckle in my back. I started getting emotional. "Waaaaaas. Stiiiiiill. Theeeeere." And now I'm crying. I don't think I ever had cried since childhood. I don't even know why, but I'm shaking and I'm crying. Since then, I know how to find the emotion. He keeps digging in, finding the spots where tension is. He later explained to me, I don't know, I thought it was all bullshit, but clearly it wasn't.

DK: Right.

HJ: The only three words he said when he sat down was, "Very good, Henry." It was like God had spoken. Everybody who criticizes Strasberg—and there have been so many of them over the years—that's what I remember. From then on, boy, I went to listen to him, I took notes on everything and paid attention, even when he bored everybody and people were sleeping, because there was always something important that he gave. For those few years, I went every single class, twice a week.

DK: Yeah, I know you're a firm disciple. It's interesting there was an arc there.

HJ: I didn't really finish telling you about the Jack Garfein thing, with the Inge prison play.

DK: Did you ever see his movie *Something Wild*?

HJ: With Carroll Baker, right?

DK: Yeah, Garfein did that one and *The Strange One*.

HJ: I knew Carroll, of course, too. So Garfein is directing the play with me as the gay prisoner. He's taken me up to, what's the penitentiary—San Quentin. He wants me to sit in the

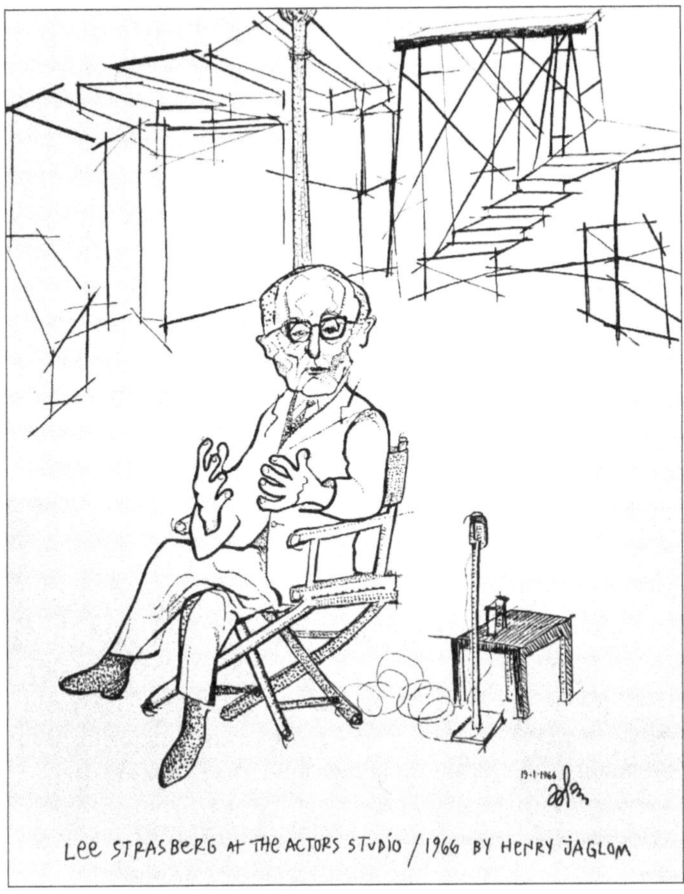

Henry's 1966 drawing of Lee Strasberg,
during his days at the Actor's Studio.

the electric chair there, to get into the part. I was freaked out, I said, "I'm not doing this." He wanted me to meet some of the guys on death row. I could have said, "What, are you crazy?" He had been through a lot, you know. He was in concentration camps. I was conscious of that, and I didn't do with him what I would have done with anybody else. I just simply said, "Jack, I can't do that." And I was all fucked up, obviously, about death and everything. I mean, everything terrible had happened to him… but I couldn't do that. But we went to San

Francisco together, I walked around with them—the warden took us around.

So Jack wants me to really ham it up, and play gay as effeminate, like a caricature. I got these two actors on each side, very famous character actors. Joe Don Baker and I forgot the other's name—bald guy, very talented guy. During the rehearsals, Jack keeps saying "More! More! Henry, I said more!" What is more gay? I said, "Jack, what does that mean?" He said, "He's a big queen. Much more effeminate." Effeminate effeminate effeminate. So I was flying on that stage, doing everything I could, and he said "More! More!" That was the main direction he gave me. "Great, great, more!" We do this thing for the Actors Studio and for Strasberg. Strasberg says to Joe Don Baker, "What wonderful work!"

And then he says to me, "What were you doing, Henry? That's like a caricature." I said, "I know, I know." And Jack jumps in and opens his mouth. Instead of saying, "I told him to do that," he said, "I warned him, Lee. I did warn him! I said take it down." Inside, I was like, "What the fuck? He's selling me out." But I can't say so out loud because of his history. I can't say he's a liar or "You motherfucker!" which I normally would have, because he'd been in Auschwitz, for fuck's sake! What right did I have to say anything? So I took it, which is not like me, as you can imagine. Only two people came to my defense—she became a very famous actress. Names again, they're the first to go. But they roundly attacked me. Once they heard Lee saying so, everybody jumped in. In the audience was the playwright. What's his name…

DK: William Inge.

HJ: And that was his last play, I think. [*Author's note: The Inge play to which Henry refers is* The Last Pad. *It was performed for paying audiences in New York in December 1970, with Tim Lewis, Warren Pincus, and Jack Kiernan in the three principal roles. When the play was workshopped at the Studio is unclear.*]

4.
**"The trouble with you is, you're a weak,
sentimental humanitarian"**

*In which Henry discusses some of his aborted projects, his
sporadic relationship with Gene Kelly, a disagreement with Jane
Fonda and Donald Sutherland involving Barbra Streisand and
politics, the occasion when Henry's mother met an incognito
Abbie Hoffman, and the greatness of Bert Schneider.*

HJ: Did I tell you that Anaïs Nin gave me the movie rights
to all her books for one dollar, so that nobody else would do
them. She was scared. I was interested in her *Cities of the Interior* at one point. Paramount offered her $100,000 for *Spy in
the House of Love*. And I said, "Do it, you need money!" She
said, "I would be up all night worrying about what they're
going to do with it. You, at least if you *do* do it, I'd trust you."
I said, "I don't know if I ever would be able to. I'm not an
adapter." She said, "At least if you do it, it'll be the sensitivity
that shines." You know, she love my movie *A Safe Place*. Have
you read her book *In Favor of the Sensitive Man*?
DK: Yeah, I know she wrote the essay on you and *A Safe Place*
in that book.

*[Reader reference: After the disastrous original theat-
rical run of* A Safe Place, *Henry continued screening
it for small, select audiences in feeble attempts to find
an audience. Writer Anaïs Nin was invited to such an
event by someone at the National Organization of
Women. She fell in love with the film and started her
own crusade for it, procuring a 16mm print, carrying it*

under her arm to feminist collectives, women's groups, and women's colleges. She cut Henry's credit off and presented it to receptive new audiences as if a woman had directed it. Nin referred to Henry as "the magician of cinema" and was heard to have stated, "Now there's a second 'genius Henry' in my life," in reference to her famed relationship with Henry Miller. Henry stated, "She gave me my first audience!" These efforts inspired an essay included in Nin's collection In Favor of the Sensitive Man, and Other Essays, *not to mention a vital friendship between Nin and Jaglom that lasted until her death. Nin did indeed sell Jaglom all the film rights to all her books for one dollar. The deal was extensively covered in the press at the time. Around this time, Henry met Patrice Townsend, who would become his first wife, when she applied for an assistant job at his production company. The daughter of a Hollywood genre director, she found Henry "arrogant and impossible" during the job interview, and walked out in rage. As she was exiting, she saw a poster for* A Safe Place, *a film she deeply loved, hanging up in the office; she realized that Henry had both written and directed it. It so happens that she had first seen the film at one of Nin's special screenings. That was the beginning of their relationship. This is merely to prove the film's power with certain female audiences, and that Nin's efforts to give it new life after its initial failure were substantial.*]

HJ: Anaïs loved *Tracks*. You know, I was up for, uh, whatchamacallit, Sylvia Plath…

DK: *The Bell Jar*?

HJ: Yeah, I was up for *The Bell Jar* too.

DK: Really?

HJ: I had the rights for a brief period.

DK: Larry Peerce wound up doing it.

HJ: Yeah. Terribly.

DK: I agree, it's pretty awful. You knew the lead actress in that film, Marilyn Hassett.

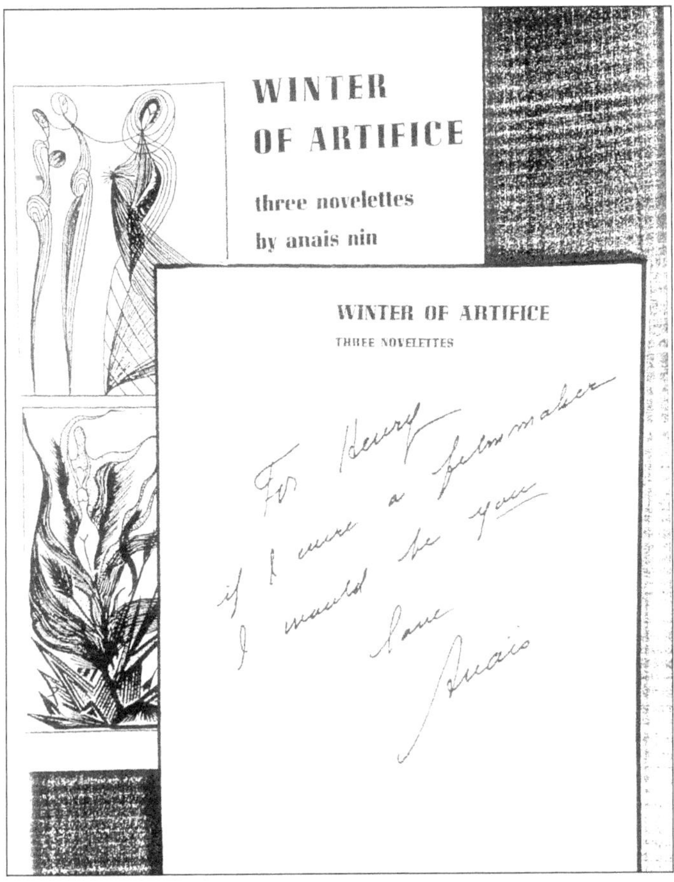

A personal note from Anais Nin to Henry.
"If I were a filmmaker, I would be you. Love, Anais."

HJ: Very well. Very, very well. Wow, I haven't thought about her in a while. We had a little romance.

DK: Pre Larry Peerce? Because you know he wound up marrying her.

HJ: Definitely pre Larry. Before I became involved, somebody owned *Bell Jar* and it went through all these directors and then it came to me. I remember signing something. Oh, do you know who else owned it at one point? The guy who died in the plane crash, married to Elizabeth Taylor.

DK: Mike Todd?

HJ: Michael Todd!

DK: That's a weird thing for *him* to have owned.

HJ: He owned it. Somewhere along the line, it came into my hands. Funny. Boy, this is great, having all this resurrected!—because I forget so many of the ones that never happened. You know, what you don't remember—Orson said this to me, and I realized I was about to say this as myself: What you don't remember are the movies that didn't happen… unless there's one big one that you feel you should have seen through and it lives as a kind of regret.

DK: Or as Maximilian Schell says in [your movie] *Festival in Cannes*, "It's enough to dream them. You don't necessarily have to make them. It's enough that they're up here [in your mind]."

HJ: That was a line I gave him. He never felt that himself. I remember him arguing with me about that particular line. And I said, "You know who I'm quoting here?" And he said, "Of course I know you're quoting Orson." I said, "And you're playing Orson. You've even gained the weight for it." He wasn't amused. He was the sweetest man, though. I really liked him so much. But with *The Bell Jar*, I started looking for someone to play the part—as best as I remember, and you know everyone's memory is a little fucked up—but I couldn't find the right actress. You know you have access to all the journals I kept, that probably has all this stuff in it. But you probably don't want to see everything, because there's just so much.

DK: Honestly, as a biographer, it's… as we say in Jewish, *it's a m'chaya*.

HJ: Oh, my father used to use that word. How do you spell that?

DK: Oh, um… it's a transliteration of the Hebrew word, so it would be M apostrophe C-H-A-Y-A.

HJ: That sounds right. [*he writes it out*] I haven't heard that word since my father died. All these projects we're talking about, that I never made. You get me thinking, did I ever tell you the Gene Kelly story?

DK: Nope.

HJ: It wasn't you? I was telling someone recently sitting in that very spot.

DK: No, I haven't heard your Gene Kelly story.

HJ: Mike Medavoy was my agent after *A Safe Place*. I couldn't get arrested in Hollywood. No one wanted to do business with me. Danny Melnick had just done *That's Entertainment!* at MGM, which was a tribute to the studio's musicals. I had this idea about a guy who comes to the Cannes Film Festival, who was a big star and now he's a businessman. He's way past his stardom. "Gene Kelly in later life," to use the James Mason thing. He meets this girl, and Candice Bergen was going to play the girl, and he starts feeling like his old self again. And they're treating him like his old self at the festival. I go and I meet Gene Kelly, and… it's Gene fucking Kelly! Years back, I had come to talk after a class that was watching a rough cut of *A Safe Place*. Columbia arranged it for film students, and the host was Gene Kelly. Afterwards, he comes up to me and says, "You really know how to pick music!" I had no rights yet to any of the music in this rough cut, so I laughed. He told me he liked the film. He saw himself more as a director by this point.

DK: He just got off directing *The Cheyenne Social Club*.

HJ: He directed that?

DK: Sure did.

HJ: Anyway, we got on very well. He said he thought the movie was very poetic and it touched him. I was surprised that Gene Kelly would like this kind of work. So, years later, I've got this project. We wind up meeting at his house, and I started talking him into doing this movie with me. It was to be shot at the 1973 or 74 Cannes Film Festival, when they were showing *That's Entertainment!*, and Danny Melnick, who was heading MGM, was going to give me a million dollars budget to make it. The film was to end with him taking off his hat and seeing himself without his hair, looking in the mirror, and then calling his daughter. Fred Astaire and God knows who else was going to be there in Cannes, because they were showing *That's Entertainment!*, so I was trying to arrange cameo appearances and such.

We're at his house, and he's telling me, "Judy Garland sat right next to where you're sitting, and she sang over there at that piano," and all this. And it's amazing… he's showing me his old dances a bit. Anyway, to make a long story short—which, unlike my father, I never seem to do—two or three weeks before we're supposed to go, he calls me up and says, "I can't do it." And I'm panicked. "Why?!" He said, "That last scene when I take the hat and the toupee off, I can't do that. And you're going to work with improvisation a lot, and available or natural light, without the studio lighting I'm used to, and makeup," and everything else. I must have told him I didn't want all that. I told Orson later that I wanted the real Orson on *Someone to Love*, his last movie. He showed up with all these fake noses and disguises, and I put my foot down. These guys needed the protection. But it was really the last scene that scared Gene Kelly.

Melnick got crazy at me. I said, "He told me he's going to spend every day worrying about how's going to look, and it was going to worry him long after, and it's Gene Kelly! I can't do that to him!" Melnick said, "You can talk anyone into anything, Henry." "Yeah, but he'll be unhappy! If he's unhappy and anxious, he's not going to give me what I need." It got to the point where Melnick was like, "Make him do it!" He really loved the idea that much. I explained how much Gene Kelly meant to me my whole life. I didn't want to be cruel to him in any way. He was a hero to me.

Thirty years later, I was at the 50th anniversary of the *Hollywood Reporter* at DGA. I'm with Candice, and she says, "Oh look, there's Anouk Aimée!" She knows her and I ask her to introduce me. I open my mouth and I say, "Oh, I've been looking all over for you." That was a lie, I hadn't been looking all over for her. She says, "Really, why?" I say, "I have a movie I want you to do." Candice is looking at me funny. I say, "I can't tell you now. May I come to your hotel room." She says she's seen two of my movies, *Eating* and something else, she likes them very much and is interested in talking. She asks if I

9 feb 76
PARIS

Dear Gene Kelly —
Hello — It is a month since I saw you,
And since then I've been extremely busy:
interviews + promotion for the opening of my
1st film here (It opened 3 days ago to, I am
happy + somewhat amazed to be able to say,
fantastic reviews, everywhere, all the papers +
the weeklies, they really love it over here);
Preparation for the late-spring opening +
distribution of my 2nd film (All now arranged,
made much easier, you will understand, by
the carryings-on over the first film); And —
mainly — sorting everything out to be able
to accomodate your needs (as told to me quite
clearly by your Agent, who I've been in
regular touch with, as I hope you know);
my needs. And the needs of the money-
people — (Caméra One — The Schlumberger
people I mentioned to you.) As they are
Also the European distributors of my 1st 2 films,
And as the required % of gross asked by your
Agent was quite different from my original
deal with them, it took a little doing,
giving up some of my participation (happily,
that really is secondary to me) And —
though they won't admit it, I'm convinced
they were wanting to see the response to their
1st venture with me. Having been practically
compensated by me And greatly pleased by
the films success, they agreed to exactly what
I presented As your unbending terms I felt like an Agent.

and enjoyed the game, and much relieved i wired your agent a general statement of confirmation—that all was done + would be ready to go for the week in May as we discussed + then the 4 or 4½ weeks I need of you + Candice in June or whenever it suited us all, + that I would return in 10 days + see him then.

And i went to London for a 4-day rest.

On my return, I received a very confusing phone call from your agent, asking who the distributors were as you needed to know that up front to protect your percentage. I said that I understood that we understood that I was avoiding pre-shooting distribution deals for reasons of freedom + much else, and he said yes, well, and would I call him when I got back.

I proceeded, within 24 hours, to catch the worst flu of my life, something particularly virulent raging through Paris at the moment called R × 21 Victoria or somesuch.

4 days later, still fevered but able to at least cross the room, and promised full recovery within 4 more days, I write you this letter.

Why? I know, understand and truly appreciate your not wanting to discuss the business part of it all, I dearly hope to achieve that for myself someday. But since my communication with you has seemed

so streaight, so open — since your initial
reluctance was so cleare And you've subsequent
willingness to hear me And then be agreeable
was so without bullshit — I would hate to
blow this, for either of us to not do this
film, for reasons of non-communication,
or 3rd party confusion. It happened to me
one before with an agent — my own —
And Donald Sutherland has just berated me
for not using him in my last film as I
promised + wanted to (I used Dennis Hopper) +
for not checking with him, eather than accepting
an agent's indirectness + other motivativeness.
    <u>So</u> : I want to check with you, to tell
you everything that's transpired, to be able
to call <u>you</u> (even before I call you're agent)
when I come back next week, and find out
If there is some problem other than the
only one I knew about, And happily, after
much fighting, was able to solve. I know
that for you doing a film like "Festival"
with me can only be an adventure, creative-
ly, And economocally, a gamble. I, of course,
think it would be an absolutely breath-
taking, touching, warm, moving film And
I would hate for us to have missed the
chance to make it. The pressure of time

1

is of course, off-putting, but I felt so very relieved at having overcome all the business details, and was preparing, with gusto, to plunge into pre-production on my return here in 3 weeks.

So please forgive the somewhat feverish pitch of this hand-written letter, I honestly, simply felt that the only way to deal with it all is directly in this fashion, and so I am doing so.

Obviously, it is redundant to add that if there are any problems I don't know about, I would do everything in my power to satisfy whatever they are —

I don't want this movie to not have happened, is my entire point, and hope you will give me the six (at the most) weeks of your life, from which to create it.

I hope you're well and happy —

Best — HENRY (JAYlorr)

can bring copies of my other films. "Send them in the morning, then we'll meet in the afternoon." I pitch to her another version of the same Gene Kelly movie story, except for a great female star coming to Cannes, and that's how *Festival in Cannes* was born. She was great. Did you know she was Jewish and during the war, as a small child, she and her mother traveled with false papers?

DK: I did not.

HJ: She loved to talk about all that. But yeah, Danny Melnick never forgave me. "I can't believe how soft you are," he told me. Years later, Victoria [Henry's second wife] and I are leaving a restaurant, when she was pregnant with Sabrina. And who should be entering but Gene Kelly, who by this point is quite old. He was very pleasant, and I tell him that we're expecting, which he can plainly see, because Victoria was very much showing. He crouched down and into Sabrina's womb, he sings, "It's very clear, our love is here to stay."

DK: Wow, that gets me emotional, kind of.

HJ: My heart just swelled. It was unforgettable. I tell Sabrina sometimes that Gene Kelly serenaded her in the womb. I met Leslie Caron around that same time. *A Safe Place* was at a festival in this place in France called Avoriaz. It was gorgeous, in the Alps near Switzerland. The festival called itself the Festival du Film Fantastique. Why I was in that festival, I don't know. I guess it was about breaking conventional logic. Leslie Caron was on the jury. I remember meeting her by a fireplace. On the jury along with her was… the great Yugoslav. Was it the great Yugoslav?

DK: I have no idea. I don't know anyone who would qualify as "the Great Yugoslav."

HJ: Well, he was definitely eastern European. Major name, famous in the theater, and I was so excited that he loved my film so much. You don't know who I'm talking about?

DK: The Great Yugoslav? I don't have a fucking clue.

HJ: He's celebrated! Okay, maybe it's not Yugoslav.

DK: Polish?

HJ: No, could have been Czech. Wait, he wrote *Rhinoceros*.

DK: Oh, Ionesco!

HJ: Ionesco! Yes! Eugène Ionesco. Madame Ionesco let me know he had voted for me and not *The Texas Chainsaw Murder*.

DK: *Massacre.*

HJ: What?

DK: *Texas Chainsaw Massacre.*

HJ: Whatever. That film won, and I lost by one vote. But Leslie Caron and Ionesco both voted for me. I dined out on that for months. But imagine those two films competing in the same category! The Festival du film fantastique, this was, after all! But getting Ionesco meant something to me, and still does. Jean Seberg and her husband or boyfriend, something Berry…

DK: Romain Gary?

HJ: No, that was earlier. This was someone related to John Berry, the blacklisted director. Seberg and her husband Berry both claimed they loved *A Safe Place*, which was quite a hit in Paris. I was just crazy about Leslie Caron, though, because of *American in Paris*. When I met her, she was having a thing with Warren, which really got me pissed off. I wanted her to have a part in the Gene Kelly movie, but we never got that far for me to ask.

Speaking of big casting switch-ups, did I ever tell you about Donald Sutherland and *Tracks*?

DK: Nope.

HJ: So Donald Sutherland is going to do *Tracks*. I'm writing it with him in mind, and he's excited as hell. We're meeting at the Saturday nights with Jane Fonda — meetings of The Entertainment Industry for Peace and Justice, or EPIJ, which we're on the board of. We're sending troops out to do FTA, Fuck the Army shows and all of that.

DK: Which became a documentary, *FTA*.

HJ: Yes, which I actually never saw. So we're trying to get this person and that person, mostly unknown people, but good, solid entertainers too, because we want to draw troops away from the army bases and stop support for the troops' attention to these Bob Hope shows and the war people. And do it with an anti-war message, in between this entertainment. But we don't have real names like Bob Hope does. I'm able to get

Streisand. I may or may not tell you personal stuff about Streisand, but I knew her from my earliest days in New York, when I was at the Studio and going to the clubs and all that. The point is, I can get Streisand. That changes the whole nature of the show. We're going to be able to get all those people away from a huge army base to hear the messages in our anti-war program. It was near a big, huge base. This is 1970-71, still during the war obviously. Everybody is so psyched that I can get Streisand, because the level of entertainment has just gone up 7000%. We didn't have any stars, right?

So, I go to a meeting and I said, "Are we all prepared for the Streisand thing?" "Well, there's one problem." I said, "No there isn't, I just spoke to her. I'm the contact." They said, "Well, she doesn't want to stay overnight." I said, "So? What's the problem? She wants to fly back. She's not asking for money. She's even going to pay everything." And I'll never forget this: "Well, she has to be educated." I said, "I beg your pardon? She has to be educated? What do you mean she has to be educated?" "Well, she's just doing it because she's liberal and she's sympathetic against the war." I said, "That's right." Jane said, "She doesn't really understand the basic reasons that America is in the war." And they start giving me all this Marxist bullshit. Jane was very into that at that point in time. Her and Sutherland. And I said, "You know about me getting Makavejev out of jail, in Yugoslavia?" [*Author's note: This is all Henry says in the recordings, but upon Dušan Makavejev's death on January 25, 2019, Henry emailed me, "Dan. Makavejev just died! Did I ever tell you my extraordinary story about chess with Tito to get Makavejev out of Yugoslav jail?" To my shame, I never followed up.*]

HJ: I remember Jane saying to me, "Your problem, Henry, is that you're a weak, sentimental humanitarian." I said, "Are those dirty words? Humanitarian? Is that a bad sentiment?" All these comrades, or whatever they were, got down on me, and they said, "Streisand has to come at least for two days to be educated." I said, "What are you, fucking crazy? We're talking about Barbra Streisand! She's not going to come and be instructed. She doesn't want to be instructed. She knows the war is wrong. She wants to help the effort against the war. She's willing to come in and entertain the troops, and go home in her private jet. She doesn't need any of your Marxist horseshit." They wanted her to stay there for indoctrination, from this Marxist fucking Leninist who they had designated to do this. It's why I left that organization finally. I remember they also said, "We can't exploit her." And I said, "She wants to be exploited. She said, 'Use me.'" "Well, she's got to know why and she's got to be educated." I said, "You can all go fuck yourselves. You're crazy. She doesn't want education. She knows she's against the war. That's enough. She's willing to put herself on the line, come and entertain troops against, you know, Bob Hope and the whole establishment and endanger her career."

Yeah, at that point, you know, I had had enough. They got mad at me because I called it bullshit, all this Marxist Leninist stuff. I remember that whole thing. They wanted Barbra to sign something, too, with all this loaded language. Then they wanted everybody to stand in a circle and go "Ohm," very culty, so that they could re-center—that was their word—after that big argument. That's right when I left. Donald and Jane were a little extreme at that point. I had originally tried to get Jack [Nicholson] involved, but his attitude was that nothing like that would make much difference. Jane, for her part, since became many other things, including Christian, for a while now.

DK: Godard went through his Mao period, quite infamously.

HJ: Oh, Godard was one of the biggest assholes. I met him at Cannes at one point. I loved many of his movies in the Sixties, but he was a dreadful human being, based on my experience. Horrible Jew hater too, one of the worst. But I was so passionately left wing. Paul Robeson was my hero. I would defend the Rosenbergs. But the Fonda-Sutherland stuff was too much for me.

DK: So, you had mentioned Mike Medavoy.

HJ: That's separate from this story. Like I said, he was my agent, and he was Donald Sutherland's agent. Sutherland is beginning to climb in popularity and he is excited because we're together in this group, the Entertainment Industry for Peace and Justice.

He's very politically "with" *Tracks* and Medavoy says to me at one point, "Listen, Donald's very fond of you, and he feels obliged to you because you made an agreement. But since then, his price has gone way up," and so and so, "and you were offering, I think, $25,000. I've got a situation where he can make $600,000." The real thing is that Medavoy could make $60,000 instead of $2,500, with his 10%, right? He said, "He won't ask. He's too nice. He won't ask you to release him from the obligation." I said, "Look, if that's going to interfere with his career and he's got that kind of a shot, I completely understand." He said, "Oh, I appreciate that a lot." A year goes by, I shoot the movie. Another year goes by, I edit the movie. Now I'm in the Redd Foxx Building, and Donald comes to see the screening of the movie, now starring Dennis Hopper, then comes into my office. He's emotional, got real tears in his eyes. He says, "It's really exciting, I'm incredibly moved," and then he says to me, "By the way, I hope you don't mind my asking, but why am I not in this movie?" And I said, "Well, you know, I didn't want to force you to do it. It's no money compared to what you were make you're making now. Mike told me that you wanted out. He said, "Mike told you *I* wanted out? He told me that *you* wanted out! And that you didn't know how to say it to me, that you wanted Dennis Hopper."

So he had lied to both of us. Of course, he was doing what was right for Donald's career. What good was he going to be in this little art film about Vietnam? So Donald was very emotional at that moment, because he really wanted to do it, and he was passionate politically. We had gone through all these things together. Yeah, they all went a bit nuts. Some people went more nuts than others. But to my dying day, I'll never forget Jane saying "You know your trouble, Henry, is you're a weak, sentimental humanitarian." Yeah, I didn't want Streisand to be "educated," sorry. It's in my journal. Completely shocked me! Her father was a liberal, my mother being a liberal, even my father, though he betrayed me by voting for Nixon.

DK: Oh God, he did? Really?

HJ: And I didn't talk to him for years, you know. I wrote him a letter. I can't believe I wrote that to my father. I didn't talk to him for… at least a year. Candice wanted me to read it to a Jewish audience outside of Canter's on the street. There were like three thousand people at an antiwar thing in that heart of the Jewish section there.

DK: In Fairfax.

HJ: Fairfax. And I read this letter. Oh God, I was crying. I couldn't believe she got me to do that. But she had been so affected by it, and I was basically telling my father he was like a "good German," you know. The good Germans who just didn't really believe in Nazism, but didn't say anything. I made that analogy, which is horrifying to me now. My mother used to always say, "Don't worry, I'm cancelling out his vote."

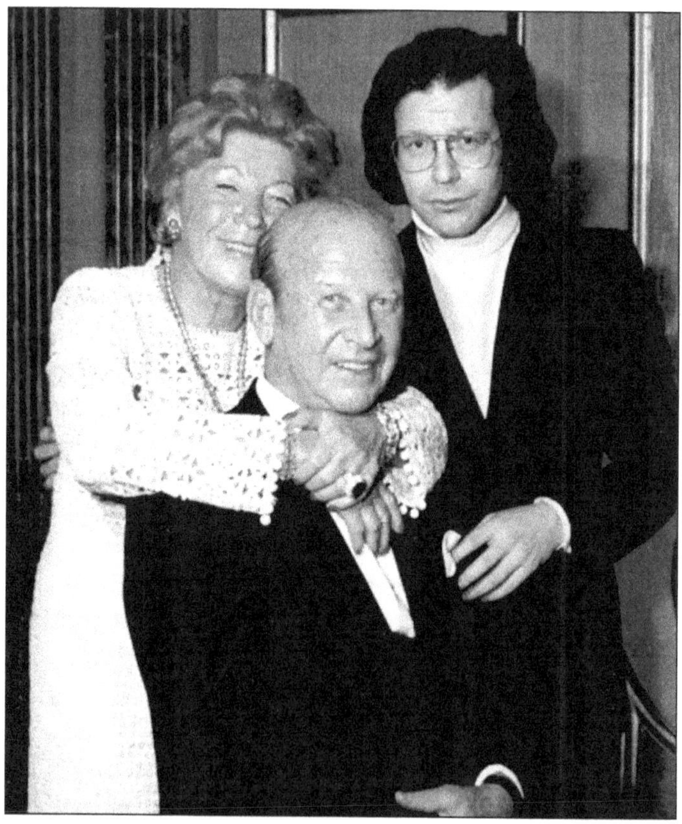

Henry with his parents, sometime in the early 1970s.

DK: Holy shit! My mother says the same thing. My own mother and father are so similar in this regard. They've been married for years, but you look at these people and you kind of ask how they've stayed together for so long because they're so different, politically and otherwise. Especially politically. She also says, "I'm canceling out his vote."

HJ: My mother was trying to make peace between us at that point and she told me, "Don't worry, I'm canceling out his vote."

DK: Mine says the same fucking thing! That's incredible.

HJ: That's funny.

DK: She also says, "We always cancel each other out."

HJ: Wow. I do know one thing for certain, my father would not have gone for Trump. I know that for sure. Did I ever tell you about when my mother met Abbie Hoffman?

DK: I can't say you did, I think I would have remembered. [*laughing*]

HJ: It was at the first screening of *Can She Bake a Cherry Pie?*, for critics before it opened. He shows up incognito. He was underground then. He came to two or three of my screenings—he was also at *Sitting Ducks*. We knew each other through Bert Schneider and we were good friends, actually. We spent a lot of time on the phone when he was in hiding.

DK: Man, that's really wild. Crazy! Wow. [*Author's note: Henry might be only slightly mistaken here. Hoffman lived as a fugitive from the law between the years of 1974 and 1980. It's more likely that Hoffman attended a screening of either* Tracks *or* Sitting Ducks. *Henry did however, at one point, share Hoffman-related mementos with me, from his vast collection of personal memorabilia. Bert Schneider, the son of Columbia Pictures president Abe Schneider, was one of the co-founders of BBS Productions, the vaunted company behind many of the New Hollywood's most important films.*]

HJ: You don't know that whole section of my life. Huey Newton was going to go to jail, and... I couldn't talk about any of this for the longest time, obviously. Bert arranged for Huey to be smuggled out of the country by our friend Artie Ross, on a boat to Cuba. Artie Ross died in a weird way.

A lot of people, including my brother, were really into inhaling nitrous oxide to get high.

DK: Laughing gas.

HJ: It was a big thing. Bert Schneider had a lot of parties at his house, and people were inhaling this stuff, along with grass and coke. And fucking, that's another story. There were these big plastic things for the swimming pool.

DK: Floaties.

HJ: I guess. And they would fill them up with nitrous oxide, and my brother would be sucking the stuff out of this plastic shark in the pool and getting completely high. I was scared to death, telling him to stop it, because he always overdid everything. But Artie Ross, the guy who smuggled Huey Newton to Cuba, got so into nitrous oxide—and he was a writer— I just got a chill. I get a knock on the door one day from Judy Schneider, and she says, "Artie Ross is dead." And how did he die? He was writing, and he strapped the nitrous oxide thing on his face, fell asleep and suffocated to death. [*Author's note: Director Paul Williams recalls Henry and Artie Ross not being particularly friendly. In Williams's estimation, Henry was jealous of Ross's closeness with Bert Schneider, and seemingly attempted to exclude Ross from their core group of friends. Williams remembers an instance of being called upon to defend Ross in front of others, by aggressively confronting Henry about his behavior.*]

DK: Just looking this up. [Ross] died in 1974.

HJ: '74!

DK: [*reading*] "By such a misadventure, the recreational use of nitrous oxide diminished."

HJ: It doesn't say how old he was?

DK: No.

HJ: I didn't realize his death had such repercussions about the use of nitrous oxide.

DK: The person who found him walked into his home after rounds of knocking to no end, and heard a hissing sound. That was the gas. Jesus! At the time of his death, he was planning a trip to Havana to visit Huey Newton, it says. Oh, it says here he was 30.

HJ: 30?

DK: 30.

HJ: 30?!

DK: Yep.

HJ: Fuck!

DK: It says 1975 in this one. The other one said 1974.

HJ: Wow! That gives me chills! The internet is something else, isn't it? But Bert was financing a lot of Huey and Abbie Hoffman's stuff. I remember Abbie told my mother at that screening, "Any mother of Henry's is a mother of mine." Later, she asked, "Who was that?" And I said, "You're not supposed to know who that is, because he's in hiding." He had a different name, a different nose. "Yeah, but he came to your party," she said. She was confused. I said, "Yeah, but he was disguised." "Who is it?" she demanded to know. "Whatever, I don't think you'll know the name. Abbie Hoffman." "My God," she said, "That was Abbie Hoffman?" She knew, and I didn't think she would know.

Yeah, Bert and I and others, we used to have dinners with Huey Newton and his mom. He was this great looking, extraordinarily articulate, brilliant, fucked-up guy. And they did so many drugs together, Bert and he. That's another story about the Black Panthers. You know another think about that *Cherry Pie* screening, my mother was in the audience. She's sitting in the theater in the back, and in the movie, I have my brother [the lead actor Michael Emil] looking at home movies of us. And suddenly, I'm there as a baby, and she hasn't seen me as a baby at that point for forty-something years. She goes "Henry!"—shouts it out loud, in front of all these critics, who laughed. Nobody mentioned it, but they all laughed and they understood. And she was so embarrassed afterwards, she said, "What did I do?" I said, "It was okay." She said, "I was just so shocked." It was just like this, it was: "Chennryh!" with this German accent.

DK: That's a cute story.

HJ: That *is* a cute, cute, cute story. And I have stills of her at that screening of *Can She Bake a Cherry Pie?* Somewhere in the background is Abbie in disguise. I can talk about this now, because everyone's dead. You know, the man who I loved the most, out of anyone outside of my father and brother, the man I loved the most was Bert Schneider. The *most*! He didn't speak to me in the last twenty-five years of his life because he wanted me to denounce Israel and stand in solidarity with the Chinese Cultural Revolution, which to me was senseless murder. Bert was very pro-Mao and a cheerleader for Red China. We got into a number of major fights, all political. He just went completely crazy in his later years, just out of it. He got paranoid and conspiratorial, almost schizo. But he remains the man I was closest to out of any man. Him and Orson.

I told you the story of how we saved *Hearts and Minds*, didn't I?

DK: Yes, but let's get it on the record.

HJ: I couldn't get money for another movie after *A Safe Place*. Along comes Zack Norman, or Howard Zucker, which was his real name, to my rescue. There was this tax shelter system going at the time, for funding movies. Zack was this eccentric who was in real estate, and he had been involved in a few movies, including as an actor.

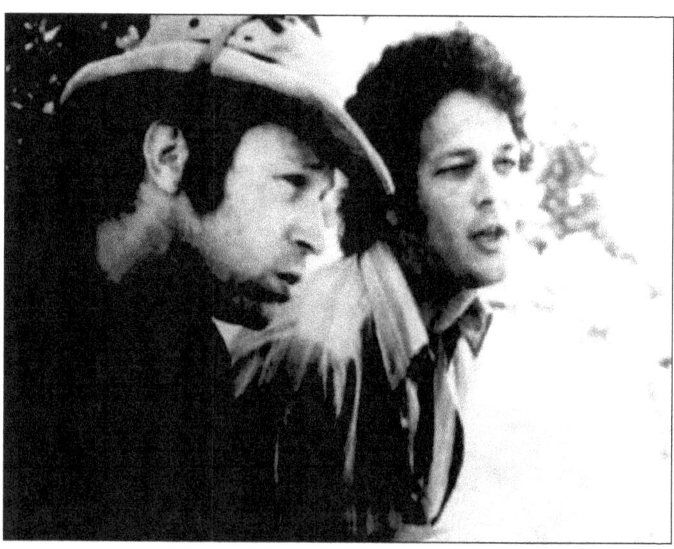

Henry with Bert Schneider, on the set of *A Safe Place* (1971).

DK: Yeah, I saw him in *Been Down So Long It Looks Like Up to Me*, and I was amazed. That's the youngest I ever saw Zack look.

HJ: I think I went to an early screening of that. Was that… what's his name…

DK: Barry Primus?

HJ: Yeah.

DK: You later distributed Barry's only movie as director. *Mistress*—I like that movie a lot.

HJ: *Been Down So Long*, I wound up thrown in a pool at the after-party for that film, but that's another story. [*Author's note: Years later, I met and spent time with Barry Primus. He remembered Henry winding up in a swimming pool after offending somebody at the* Been Down So Long… *premiere party, but he didn't remember the precise details.*] So Zack went out and raised a million dollars from lawyers, dentists, doctors, professional people looking for tax shelters. It was a very corrupt system, but Zack knew all the ins and outs. Michael, my brother, never trusted Zack with business and money, so he became the bean counter once we were actually off and running on *Tracks*, but that was much later. The point is, Zack knew how to game it, and he was good at raising the funds.

So we raise a million for *Tracks*. I start casting and working on the script. There was a big, long script for *Tracks*, that I wrote. Rafelson and I had done this train trip cross-country—that's also another story. So anyway… things are looking good, we're gearing up. Bert Schneider around this time was having all these problems with *Hearts and Minds*, which he produced. Columbia was the studio that was supposed to put it out, but [Walt] Rostow and General Westmoreland were threatening to sue, so Columbia was terrified. The banks wouldn't support them, and they refused to release the film.

[*Reference: Walt Rostow, a major architect of U.S. Vietnam policy as advisor to Presidents Kennedy and Johnson, did sue to prevent the release of* Hearts and Minds, *on the grounds that it "defamed his character" and "invaded his privacy." Following a preliminary injunction, during which time Schneider and the film's director Peter Davis adamantly refused to cut out the offending sections, a Los Angeles district judge dismissed all charges in December 1974, effectively clearing the film's path to distribution. Columbia Pictures, despite everything, were still intending to sit on the film. Henry and Zack Norman, a.k.a. Howard Zuker, formed The Rainbow Company to buy back the film, obtaining a letter of agreement from Warner Bros. to distribute it. This whole affair, and Henry's involvement, was widely covered in the press at the time. Every memo that circulated credited Jaglom and Zuker as the film's "presenters." Henry told the press at the time, "We feel comfortably within our legal rights, and Warners has been very brave and totally supportive."]*

HJ: Bert explained that he needed to find about a million dollars. Columbia would let the film go if we paid them a million—they were just demanding the money back that they'd spent on it. I got Zack to agree to use the money we had raised for *Tracks* in order to buy back *Hearts and Minds* from Columbia. We had arranged a deal with Warner Bros. to distribute. Zack was reluctant, but he did it.

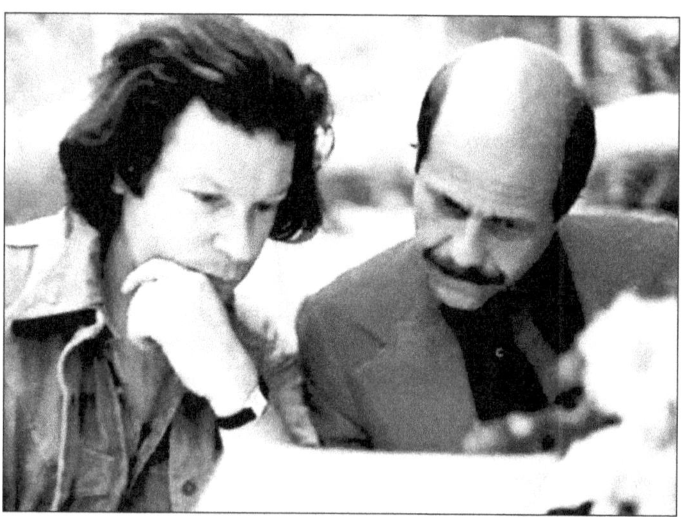

Henry with Zack Norman, a.k.a. Howard Zuker,
making a deal at the Cannes Film Festival in the late Seventies.

DK: And the rest is history, because *Hearts and Minds* famously won the Oscar.

HJ: Did you see Bert Schneider's speech?

DK: Of course, it's famous as one of the most controversial Oscar speeches of all time.

> *[Reference: Upon winning his Oscar for* Hearts and Minds, *Bert Schneider ascended the stage at the Dorothy Chandler Pavilion. He started off by seemingly endorsing what he referred to as the "liberation of South Vietnam" before reading a telegram containing "greetings of friendship to all American people" from the Viet Cong delegation to the Paris Peace Accords. The telegram also thanked the American anti-war movement. The speech set off a major firestorm of controversy, including a famously tense backstage altercation between Bob Hope, Frank Sinatra, and Schneider, which nearly escalated to a brawl. The network switchboard immediately jammed with complaint calls from viewers about "communist propaganda." Shirley MacLaine, to keep the peace, read a disclaimer engineered by Hope, which Sinatra promised to read himself if she didn't. The Oscar hullabaloo did the film a great favor at the box office in the weeks that followed.]*

HJ: It was quite something, but Bert had absolutely no fear.

DK: The FBI had a big file on Bert, from what I understand.

HJ: Bert was a true radical. He lived it. I think the fight on *Hearts and Minds* really wore him down, and his dream kind of ended with that. He was the glue that held it all together. Without him behind everything, we all went our separate ways. *[Author's note: A May 4, 1975* New York Times *article by Stephen Farber claims that after the initial run of BBS films, "gradually Schneider became less interested in films and more concerned about politics." Farber quotes Schneider: "Once I was out of the corporate structure and on my own, my life became more political. I got involved with the Daniel Ellsberg trial, and that was a major turning point. I had been involved* *in the peace movement for a long time, but that pushed me over the edge." This, he said, pushed him to make* Hearts and Minds.]

DK: So did Zack have to raise the money for *Tracks* again?

HJ: He was able to raise another half-a-mil, so we shot it for half-a-million. Everyone had to take a pay cut. We got Dennis, who was willing to do it for what we offered. I put Zack together with Michael, and they're in the movie. Michael was there to help with money, because like I said, he didn't trust Zack. So they became actors too. That was the birth of them as a team.

DK: Dream team.

HJ: Dream team, yeah.

DK: You were close with Jack too, right? Nicholson?

HJ: I was close with Jack, yeah, but Bert, Orson, and I were on another level.

DK: How did you two meet?

HJ: I was invited—I don't know by who—to the screening of one of those two Monte Hellman movies. [*Reference: Monte Hellman actually directed two feature film duos in the Sixties: the Philippines-shot adventures* Flight to Fury *(1964) and* Back Door to Hell *(1964), and the American Westerns* The Shooting *(1966) and* Ride in the Whirlwind *(1966), all of which starred Jack Nicholson—and two of which were written by him.*] I told the two women behind me to shut up and one of them was Carole Eastman, who wrote the movie, and the other was Helena Kallianotes.'[*Author's note: Henry may have slightly misremembered this. In other interviews, he accounts having been introduced to Jack possibly at the restaurant Old World by Rupert Crosse, then being invited by Jack to those Hellman pictures. In any event, in both versions of the story, the Hellman screening was a bonding experience.*]

HJ: They all became my group, you know? That was our clique. And Jack, of course, was there. Jack and I always used to go to Barney's Beanery, this Hollywood kind of saloon. He got me the audition on that silly Haight-Ashbury movie...

DK: *Psych-Out?*

HJ: Yeah, Richard Rush directed. Jack knew him really well, they were close, so he could do all the convincing. I got the audition and I beat out John Strasberg. Lee's son.

DK: I, of course, know Lee and Susan, but I can't say I know John's work.

HJ: He didn't have much of a career, in movies anyway. But originally, it looked like John Strasberg was going to play that role, and I wound up getting it.

DK: You've got some pretty memorable moments in that film, especially the bad acid trip.

HJ: It's fun to watch now, in that faux Sixties way, but it's so silly. But as I was saying, Jack and I had this drive to be directors. We used to wait for each new Kubrick film, that was our big thing. But we also went to a small theater on Sunset, right behind the bookstore, where they showed 16mm prints of different kinds of eccentric, unique movies. My brother used to take me to Amos Vogel's place in New York...

DK: Cinema 16.

HJ: That's right! Jesus, you're good! Jack and I were in our early twenties, and it was an education. We saw Olmi there for the first time.

DK: Ermanno Olmi.

HJ: Right. And we saw the less famous guys like that. We used to play bridge.

DK: Bridge? Like, the card game?

HJ: We used to take bridge lessons at Bert Schneider's house. Bert, his wife Judy, me, and Jack. Bridge lessons, can you imagine how bourgeois that is?

DK: I was gonna say, yeah, I was thinking, it's a game I imagine older women playing, like mahjong.

HJ: Mahjong is very Jewish nouveau riche. My parents played bridge till their last days and that was their favorite thing to do. It's an intelligent game. But our bridge lessons, this was before the change in the culture, let's call it. Before the long hair, before smoking dope. It was there when I first got to California. Judy and Bert were the golden couple in Hollywood, when I first met them. I remember, around the time of the Watergate hearings, I accidentally hit a police car and broke

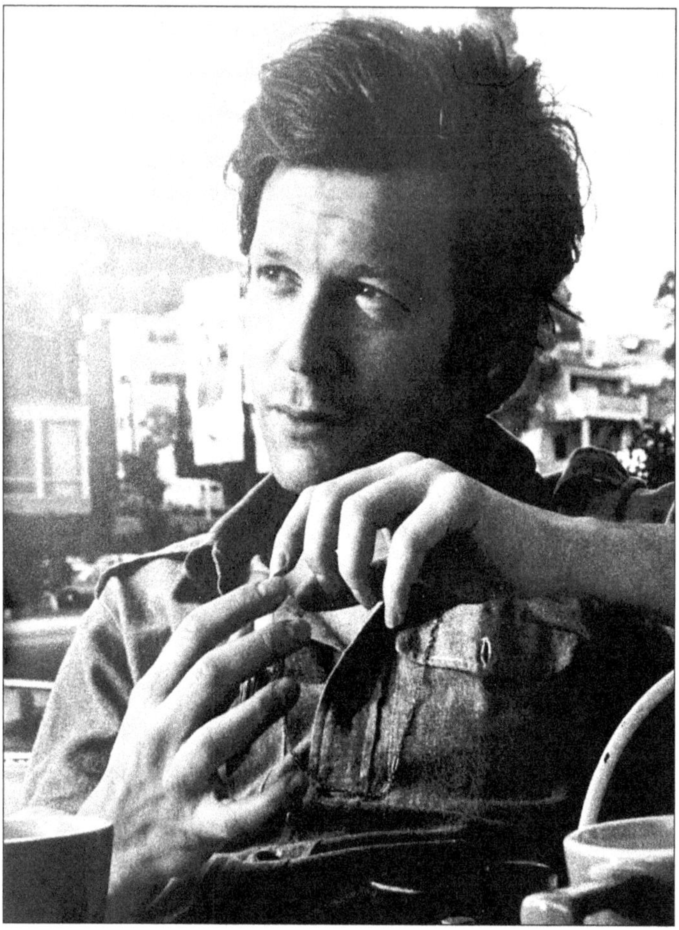

Young Henry, in his first Hollywood years, around the tim
he guest-starred on *Gidget* and *The Flying Nun*.

my leg. I was laid up at Bert and Judy's house and stayed
there for a while with them and their two kids. They were like
family to me.

Then he started cheating, she threw him out, he did so many
drugs, and he self-destructed in a terrible way. Bert I knew
in camp, and he was the very opposite of my goofy brother.
He was the all-American boy, blonde, baseball-playing golden
boy, and my brother was this weird kid with the German

accent climbing trees and playing chess. Though I will say, my brother and Bert were, early on, the most politically engaged people I knew. When everyone was voting for Dewey or Truman, my brother and Bert were voting for Henry Wallace, the progressive third-party candidate. So Bert was always on the more radical side of things, even back in—what would that have been?—1948, I guess.

But bridge lessons, can you imagine? Me, Jack, Bert, and Judy. This would have been around 1965 or 1966. Jack and I… we were both going to be directors. He never expected to be a star. He had given up acting, he was working at Disney or MGM as some kind of delivery boy, and somehow he got in touch with Bert and they did *Head* with Bob Rafelson. That was the first BBS film. I remember reading Jack [Nicholson]'s script for *Head*.

DK: I love Rafelson talking about how, if they'd made another Monkees movie, they would have put on the poster, "From the people who gave you *Head*."

HJ: I went into rehearsals and watched the Monkees all the time. I watched those kids. I knew Davy Jones, because I'd gone out with Georgia Brown. He'd been on Broadway as the Artful Dodger, with Georgia as Nancy.

DK: That's good casting. I can imagine that.

HJ: The thing is, he was short enough. And that's when I first knew him, when we were in New York. But you got me sad with all the Bert stuff and the Artie Ross stuff. Bert, you know… that's the stuff of the great Hollywood story: the rise and fall of Bert Schneider. It's got all the stuff of classic Greek tragedy. He was the hero of this town! You can't even imagine. He was the golden boy to such an extent for so long, the icon of the New Hollywood. Everything he touched was turning to gold. And then he just sort of did himself in, with all the bad stuff that the Sixties brought. I never saw such a decline.

I told you what he said when he saw my cut of *A Safe Place*? He said, crying, "This is going to lose every penny, but I'm not going to ask you to touch a frame of it, because it made me cry." And he never tried to make me change it. He went for his emotions in a way that no one did. It's the most un-Hollywood behavior. This was the same guy who turned this endless Dennis Hopper thing [*Easy Rider*], which had gone on for hours of rides. You can't imagine how many more songs, and rides on the bikes. Everyone in the room was high for the screenings. They'd say, "Great, great!" and fall asleep for stretches, then wake up. Dennis wanted to release it as a four-hour movie, and some big French director had told him, "Don't let them touch it! It's perfect as is."

One day, Bert says to me, "You're a great editor!" I said, "I am?" He said, "Yeah, that Israel movie you did, that was edited very well." What he didn't know is, during the Six-Day War, when I was making this five-hour movie with my little 8mm camera, I was cutting in camera—literally running up to a tank and getting close-ups right after I'd done a wide shot. What little actual editing I did, I was using Scotch tape to join the different ends together—the different reels. It was extremely primitive, but it impressed Bert, and he brought me on to help edit down *Easy Rider*. Bert got all of us in there, with Rafelson and Jack and myself, and we brought it down to its current length. I did the commune and campfire stuff. Peter [Fonda] did some stuff on it too.

DK: I think Dennis, to his dying day, swore that no one touched a frame of *Easy Rider*. He did the work all himself. [*Author's note: Depending on when you asked Hopper, he would invariably say he did the edit mostly himself, or that he had some minor help in doing so. Others involved refuted that account. In Paul Joyce's 1988 documentary* Out of the Blue and Into the Black, *Hopper says, "With all the things that everybody wants to talk about, the editing of* Easy Rider, *Dennis Hopper [referring to himself in third person] spent a whole year editing* Easy Rider. *And all the riding scenes were edited by Dennis Hopper. No one ever touched the cemetery. The only thing is that some scenes were lifted out of the film. The one scene that four people worked on was the restaurant sequence."*]

HJ: Of course he'd say that. Why wouldn't he?

DK: Success has many fathers, and failure is an orphan.

HJ: Jack's got his own Dennis stories. But the final cut of *Easy Rider*—Dennis went with it, but it had everything to do with

Rafelson and Jack and me. And Bert and Bob rewarded Jack and me for our efforts. I got *A Safe Place* and Jack got *Drive, He Said*. Have I told you about the time we were ousted from Figaro's, Jack Nicholson and I?

DK: Nope.

HJ: That's why he used me. You've seen *Drive, He Said*?

DK: Yes.

HJ: I mean, do you remember I play this professor and I'm jumping all over…

DK: Yes, I know the scene. [*imitating*] "My university is full of shit!"

HJ: That's right. I had that awful beard. I got a telegram on the set of Dennis's *Last Movie*, Jack telling me to "grow my Scrooge McDucks." I had these shaggy sideburns that they pasted on in *Psych-Out*—it was kind of our joke. And I went down to the Columbia barbershop with him when he had to get his haircut for *Easy Rider*. He was definitely not happy about having to lose his hair for the part. Anyway, we were at

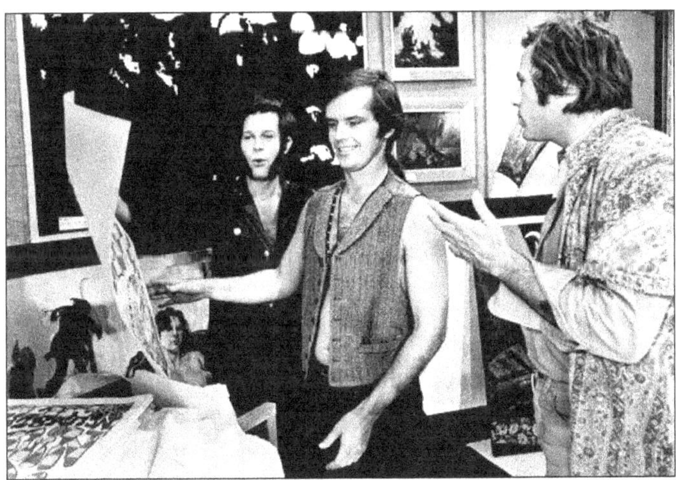

Henry appeared with Jack Nicholson in Richard Rush's counter-culture carnival *Psych-Out* (1968). Henry's LSD freakout scene has become a classic of psychedelic cinema.

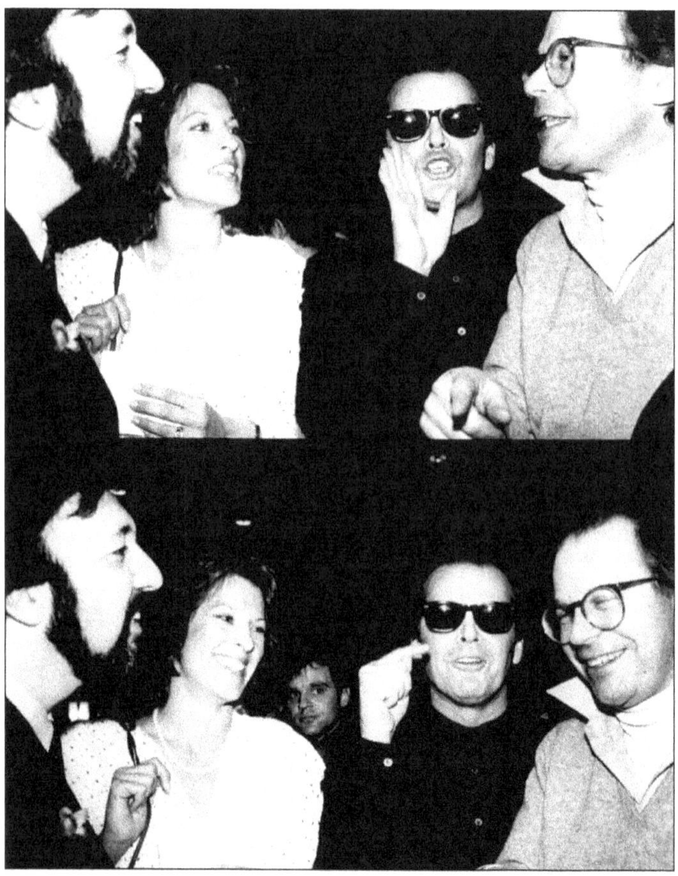

Henry's relationship with Jack Nicholson spanned nearly
six decades. Here, the two of them are together at a party with
James L. Brooks and Holly Brooks in the early Eighties.

Figaro's and I saw the owner, whoever that was then, peeing
in the coffee in the back. I told Jack, "The guy unzipped his
fucking pants and pissed into the coffee! I saw it!" We were
with one other person and Jack said, "Don't make a scene."
I said, "No, of course I'm gonna make a fucking scene. Are
you crazy?" And I started screaming and ranting and raving.
The police came and it was a whole big mess. Jack used that.

We were also in a Chinese Japanese restaurant on Sunset
once. It was Jack, myself, and whichever woman I was dating

at the time. And the Chinese started doing something, I don't remember, and then they tried to add something to the check that wasn't right. I said, "I'm not paying that!" So they called the police. They locked the doors of the restaurant and Jack said, "Great, now I'm trapped in a fucking Chinese restaurant because you won't pay. Just pay the bill!" I said, "No, we can't do that. It's the principle of the thing!" Jack claims he used stuff about me. Did you read that in any of the books? I think it's in at least a couple.

DK: I don't think so, but I haven't really read books about Jack.

HJ: You know about why he did *A Safe Place*?

DK: *Why* he did it? You mean how you paid him by getting him a color television he wanted?

HJ: Yeah, we were friends, and we were going to do each other's first movie. We had promised each other, but by the time I got to do *A Safe Place*, he said, "You can't afford me now, but I tell you what: there's this particular television I want." It was this big, huge thing with the red, blue, and green lights, and it would project, or whatever. I think he wanted to watch the ballgames in a super-sized way. He said, "If you can get me that, I think I can do it." And that's how we paid him. He shot it in a day. Pretty great.

DK: Nice to have friends! [*Author's note: This is Jack Nicholson's recollection of his time on set: "I came to New York, I still don't know what the part is. And they're getting ready to shoot the part, there's nothing written down and I still don't know what the part is. I went back to my hotel thinking, 'What the hell?' And Henry says, 'Here's what the part is. I got Tuesday over here. And after you, she's gonna commit suicide in the bathtub. That's the part! Fill that in!' I improvised the whole part all in one day!"*]

HJ: That movie *As Good As It Gets*, he claims he used me.

DK: He "used" you? You mean as like, he based the character on you? You're not OCD though.

HJ: Not OCD at all, so I don't know what part of me he thinks he used. But he told interviewers that a couple of times. Interesting. But Tanna agrees with that. She likes to tease me.

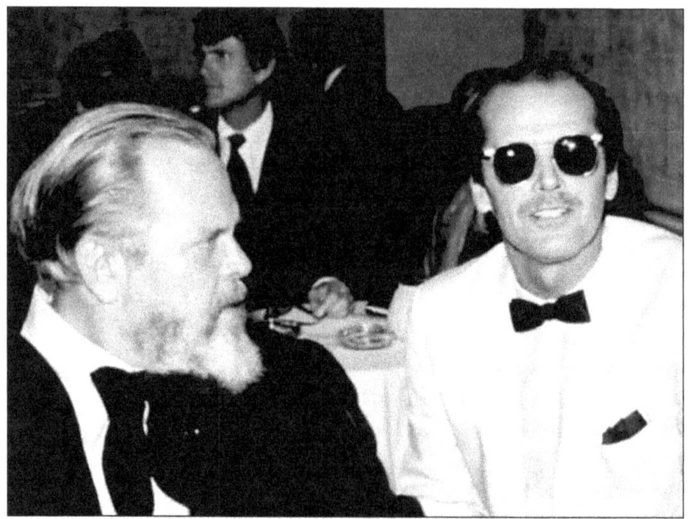

Two of Henry's closest friends, Orson and Jack, mingle at
AFI's Tribute to Orson in 1975. They never shared a scene in
Henry's *A Safe Place* (1971).

I always told him, "All you have to do is smile. Just smile."
Jack's teeth did a lot of work. When *Batman* came out and he
played the Joker, I told him, "See? What did I tell you? All you
had to do was smile!"

[Author's note: Bruce Dern claims in his own memoir,
Things I've Said But Probably Shouldn't Have, *that
Henry graduated in his class at University of Pennsylvania. When he crossed paths with Henry again
years later, after they had both entered the movie
business, he recalls that "he was hanging around Jack
Nicholson all the time." Once, Dern asked him why
he was "making movies for one million dollars" when
he had "a gazillion." Henry replied simply, "I don't
ask my family for any money." Dern's final verdict on
Jaglom was equal measure praise and condemnation:
"Henry's got gifts. He just can't shut up. That's his
problem."]*

5.
"Orson said, 'We're going to drive him fucking crazy' — and he actually said 'fucking'"

In which Henry doubts that Orson Welles's The Other Side of the Wind *is ever going to come out (the film was released the year after the recording), he remembers his relationship with the troubled Christopher Jones, explains his longtime tension with Paul Mazursky, recounts Dennis Hopper trying to strangle him in a restaurant, and relates the story of a cross-country train trip with Bob Rafelson.*

HJ: I just hope if you're right [that *The Other Side of the Wind* is going to be released), but I don't believe you're right. I just don't believe it's coming. I don't see how it *can* come out, but they did spend $1 million and Oja got some money. I'm scared of what it's going to be, and I'm also scared they're going to cut me down. That's my own ego part. But I'm more scared for Orson. How are they going to do it? Peter [Bogdanovich] can't be Orson. I love Peter, but he can't be Orson. He was making a really difficult movie, as you might have seen from some of those clips. I mean, very nonlinear… very, you know, experimental for him. I don't know.

DK: Yeah, I have about an hour of material. It's pretty radical.

HJ: The stuff that they let out, yeah. How do you put that together?

DK: I mean, I think there's only been about thirty to forty minutes that's been made public. One is the entrance to the party, with Susan Strasberg.

HJ: Oh, I've never seen that.

DK: You never saw that? She's the Pauline Kael character.

HJ: I know that, yeah. She was a good friend of mine. Very good friend of mine. You know, she was married to Chris Jones. You know who he is?

DK: Yeah, I've heard I've heard you talk about him. *Ryan's Daughter.*

HJ: Yeah.

DK: Which I think is a pretty good film.

HJ: You know what they did to him? Despite everything, they overdubbed him. It killed him.

DK: I saw *Ryan's Daughter* in a big 70mm print and it's just gorgeous.

HJ: Gorgeous, yeah, but is it coherent?

DK: I think it's completely coherent.

HJ: Mitchum's good in it, isn't he?

DK: He's fantastic. He plays the cuckold in that.

HJ: Oh, I know the film very well. If you don't know the film well, if you don't know anything about it, would you know what Christopher was dubbed?

DK: I mean, I saw the film when I was very young. I saw it when I was 11 or 12. I've seen it many times since then, but sometimes, initial childhood perceptions are burned into your brain. I didn't know as a kid that he was that dubbed. No clue. I don't think it's bad per se, but you know…

HJ: Good, good, good. I want it to work, because it killed him. It ended his career. He was on the rise, and they were they were married… you know, Susie. And the director puts his arm around him and says, "You're the worst actor I've ever known." Yeah, David Lean, everybody says he's the greatest one, and I have such a hostile feeling to him because of this story. Christopher came back haunted, hiding behind cars, whispering to me at the Old World, switching coffee cups for fear that I was going to poison him, then getting arrested for being naked on the Strip, following me and Andrea back to that hotel, then urinating on us from the balcony. Complete crazy shit.

DK: Wow.

HJ: And then one winter showing up outside where we always went to eat, Dan Tana's, and he's naked and shivering. And then another time, he's with some woman, a girl he introduces as his wife, and a baby, and they're out in the cold, what seems like homeless, and he doesn't want to come inside when I welcome him, and I give him some money. He's the other kind of tragic story, with Bert Schneider being the first kind. I used to go with him to movies and 42nd Street. Gay men loved him, loved him, loved him. And they loved me, but they really loved him, and Larry Dove, this guy who appears in *A Safe Place*.

DK: He's the one who has the monologue about the dead cat, right?

HJ: That's right. He's credited as something else in the movie though. Dov Lawrence, I think. Something like that. He and Chris Jones used to bed girls together, in the same bed.

DK: They'd orgy together.

HJ: Orgy? Odd way to look at it.

DK: That's what it kind of sounds like.

HJ: Those were the times, though.

DK: That they were.

HJ: I was not at all inclined to fuck in the same bed with another man, especially if they were hairy.

DK: Yes, you've told me of your aversion.

HJ: Chris flirted with everybody. He had a big affair with Shelley Winters…

DK: Really?

HJ: …which was just unfathomable to me. They did that silly movie together with Richie. [*Wild in the Streets* (1968)] I remember Chris saying to me—because he was very mad at something that Lee said to him in class—he said, "I'm going to fuck that old Jew's daughter and make her marry me," and that's exactly what he did. I'm not saying he didn't love her, but he did it to piss Strasberg off. He was like a vagrant James Dean. A gorgeous hustler, came from an orphanage, hustled on 42nd Street, as he told me— I don't think Lee knew this. He used to joke that he wanted to do the same thing as James Dean: get famous, and then die in like a plane crash and disappear, but actually just go off to an island somewhere and paint. He was very self-destructive.

And he was basically straight, but he liked to use his sexuality for power—and he had that power over gay guys completely. He just would make them crumble. An extraordinary character in every way. They put him in an institution at one point, in North Carolina.

DK: I often paired him together with Jordan Christopher. You remember him? Similar kind of career.

HJ: Yeah, I knew him a bit too. I remember at one point he grew a beard, and I told him to get rid of it.

DK: Don't you do that with everyone though? Including me?

HJ: Beards! Beards were big back then.

DK: He must have heeded your advice, because I never saw Jordan Christopher with a beard. Or Chris Jones for that matter.

HJ: I grew a beard for Jack on *Drive, He Said*. Fucking hated it, but I had fun in that part. I miss acting sometimes. You know, Paul Mazursky… I was going to work with him once, as an actor. I originally had the lead role in *Alex in Wonderland*. I had the part for sure, and it was announced in the press. Biafra was falling around that time. I was constantly listening to news reports on the radio about Biafra. I was feeling really shitty about myself that I wanted this part. This terrible thing was happening, and I was so superficial, and I was mad at myself. Mazursky started doing all this stuff with me, like, "Come sit in my chair. You're playing me. You need to feel what being a director is like." He started calling me in the middle of the night, saying, "I know you're just aching your guts out about playing this part." I said, "No, I'm not. I'm aching my guts out about Biafra. I wanted the part and I got the part, so now, I don't know what you want from me." He said, "Ah nothing, never mind. You go back to sleep." And it kept going on. He had me sit behind his desk, showing me all the aspects of his life and kept saying, "You're playing me! You're playing me!"

Then he started testing me, saying, "I need you to want this part more than anything in the world." I said, "I do. I want a starring role in a movie. I'm not proud of it. I want more decent things about world peace," yada yada, "but yeah, I want this. What do you want from me?" He said, "Well,

I want you to need it enough, so you give up going to Peru on Dennis Hopper's movie." I said, "That's bullshit. It's seven months apart." He said, "I just need to know." I said, "Fine, I won't go to Peru. It's a bit part." Then he came up a week or two later, and said, "I don't want you to go to Oregon to do Nicholson's movie." I said, "What has that got to do with this? They don't interfere." It was getting neurotic. When it got to the point where he was saying, "I need you to tell Bert Schneider that you can't make your movie"—that was *A Safe Place*—"for at least two years." I hung up the phone on him. And that was the end of it. I went to Peru, I went to Oregon, and those worked out.

Another thing Mazursky didn't like was, he was testing me against all these other actresses. Jackie Hellman, Monte's ex-wife, was great, and we were great together. But he didn't like it. Paul liked Ellen Burstyn, who's a terrific actress, but for some reason, she wasn't really connecting with me. We weren't connecting in that way, and I kept telling him that. But he wanted her, and he wound up using her. And he'd say, "I don't know if you're committed enough to this part." "Well, you said I'm great in the part," but he kept raising the stakes and driving me crazy. The last straw was him saying "no *Safe Place*," and I actually said "Go fuck yourself," and hung up.

[Author's note: Paul Mazursky's memoir Show Me the Magic *offers a different take of what went on. "Henry had auditioned for the leading role of* Alex in Wonderland, *and when we decided not to use him, he accused us of bowing to studio pressure. This wasn't true, of course, but we could never convince Henry. We weren't exactly enemies, but we certainly weren't friends." He goes on in the book to account how Orson Welles directed them together in a shared scene of his* The Other Side of the Wind, *only a glimpse of which is featured in the final 2018 Netflix cut. In a 2008 oral history of Mazursky, he admits that he was definitely "not on good terms" with Henry then. Though he conceded, likely out of courtesy and*

diplomacy, that they were "on better terms now," he required a pause in the recording to tell the interviewer something obviously not complimentary off the record. In my onetime encounter with Mazursky, at the mention of Jaglom's name, he went cold. I think it's safe to assert the two were not terribly fond of each other, but a kind of mutual respect existed between them.]

HJ: I did go to Peru for Dennis, which I wish I hadn't done for other reasons, because I got really sick. But for Paul, it was so personal for him. He was so into being Fellini that he needed someone to pretend to be so much like him. I don't know what Donald Sutherland contributed, but he did have a much bigger name. The interesting part of the story is years later, when Orson knowing all this—because I'd told him— has us do that scene in *Other Side of the Wind.* I said, "What are we gonna do?" He said, "Oh, we're gonna drive him fucking crazy." He actually said "fucking," I remember that. "We're going to drive him fucking crazy!" I was worried that Paul was going to think *I* was doing this, that *I* was behind it, and just using Orson as a way to get back at him. Orson told me, "I'm going to keep feeding him alcohol," and he did. Paul was so enamored of the fact that this was Orson Welles, so much so that he would have done anything. I was already very close to Orson, so we could hatch the scheme and play this trick together. [*Author's note: Their onscreen argument was far nastier and more ad hominem than any of the extant footage suggests. Henry called Mazursky's then only movie* Bob & Carol & Ted & Alice *"bullshit" while Mazursky basically called Henry the equivalent of a talentless nepo-baby, in so many words. Neither party held back.*]

HJ: That movie [*The Other Side of the Wind*] is never going to come into being.

DK: They're editing it right now.

HJ: Bullshit.

DK: Netflix struck the deal. It's official. They have a specific official release date.

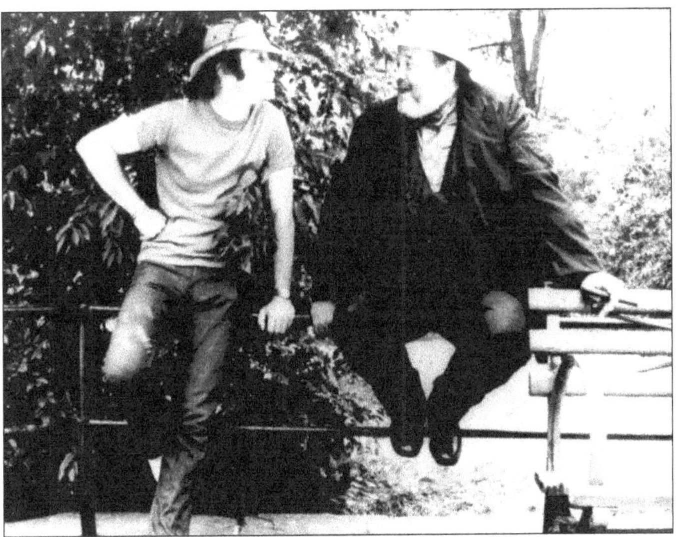

Henry and Orson on the set of *A Safe Place* (1971).

HJ: I know all about that. Listen to me: it's never gonna happen. It's not going to be Orson's film, anyway. Who's supposed to edit it but Orson, who's gone? [*Author's note: When the film was eventually released, I did have a conversation with Henry. His reaction was a big mix of emotions, including ambivalence and disappointment with various aspects, but he was impressed with the production team's efforts and was happy and relieved that it got some type of release. He was especially happy to hear that I admired the final result. He was crestfallen, however, that the final edit used precious little—indeed, only a flash—of his scene with Mazursky.*]

HJ: I went off to Peru not long after the thing with Mazursky. I got down there for *Last Movie* and I couldn't take the altitude. It was way high in the Andes and I could hardly breathe. Everyone else is throwing down vodka and all kinds of drinks. I'm afraid to drink anything because of germs. I'm a total sissy. I had to leave in the middle of shooting, before my big scene. I'm basically not in the movie at all. There was this obnoxious doctor, who was the on-set doctor. He was Synanon and he wouldn't give me aspirin, he wouldn't give me Bufferin, yet everyone else was taking enormous quantities of illicit substances. [*Author's note: Synanon is a dangerous and now long defunct religious movement originally established as a drug rehabilitation program, which explicitly rejected prevailing medical treatments for addiction.*] Everyone seemed like they were twice my size. That's what it felt like. All these big guys! I broke a window out of rage and left, flew back from Peru to Miami, and all I wanted was a bed and a television… a color television, that was the thing. *A Safe Place* was shot in the summer of 1970, later on that year. Dennis was out of his mind on *Last Movie*… absolutely out of his mind. [*Author's note: Henry's diary of the time accounts the location conditions: "No toilets on location! Toilet's [sic] below filthy, overflowing, disease-ridden, and unusable. No washing facilities. Water is brown and polluted. No soap. Sinks unusable. Feces, urine, and vomit mixed with mud everywhere." One account in a Hopper bio suggests that Henry had drafted a letter he was ready to send to the Screen Actors Guild about the untenable conditions. Hopper dared him to send it. I never personally asked Henry about this detail.*]

HJ: Did I ever tell you when Dennis attacked me in a restaurant?

DK: Like, physically?

HJ: Yeah, physically. We were at the Old World on the Strip. Dennis was with a woman, I don't remember who. They were both zonked out. I had originally cast Cayle Chernin in the role in *Tracks* that Taryn Power wound up playing, because Dennis started working with Cayle for the movie, and he'd gotten her so hopped-up and out of it that I couldn't talk to her. Dennis just broke her, and he got into this sadomasochistic thing with her, where she'd show up with fresh bruises. Mentally, she was just gone. She's still in the movie, but in a smaller part. So he's with this girl when he comes to meet me. At one point, I complimented whoever it was on a piece of jewelry she was wearing, just in my very girly way, and he says, "What'd you say?" Dennis was paranoid, but he offered her to me like a piece of meat, and I say, "No, thank you." Before I know it, he's jumping across the table trying to strangle me, then he's holding a ketchup bottle over my head trying to hit me on the head with it.

DK: Jesus!

HJ: He had a very frightening violent side. So, we're on the floor of the restaurant tussling, they call the cops, it was a big mess.

DK: This is after *Tracks*, or before?

HJ: Before.

DK: Jesus, and you still worked with him?

HJ: Well, we could afford Dennis. He was a great actor, and he did great work. On some level, you just had to accept the fact that he was going to do something crazy, because what you got out of him was worth it.

DK: Feels like taking your life into your own hands.

HJ: Oh, it would have never gone that far.

DK: He was really persona non grata at that point in his career. There was *Last Movie*...

HJ: Which was a disaster.

DK: Right, and then there was *Kid Blue*, and he did a film by Silvio Narizzano in Spain, which shows him shooting up right on camera.

HJ: What was that one?

DK: It's known under various titles. People in America would know it as *Bloodbath*, if they'd know it at all, but the real title was *The Sky is Falling*.

HJ: And what year was that?

DK: Scattered release, but the initial showings were 1975.

HJ: So just before me, probably.

DK: And probably around the time he tried to choke you at the restaurant.

HJ: You know, the ending of *Tracks*, did I ever tell you that story?

DK: Not sure.

HJ: I either did or I didn't.

DK: Well, I mean, I know the ending that's in the movie isn't what was originally written.

HJ: I had written pages of this big speech, which is the finale of the movie. He tears it up and improvises this amazing take,

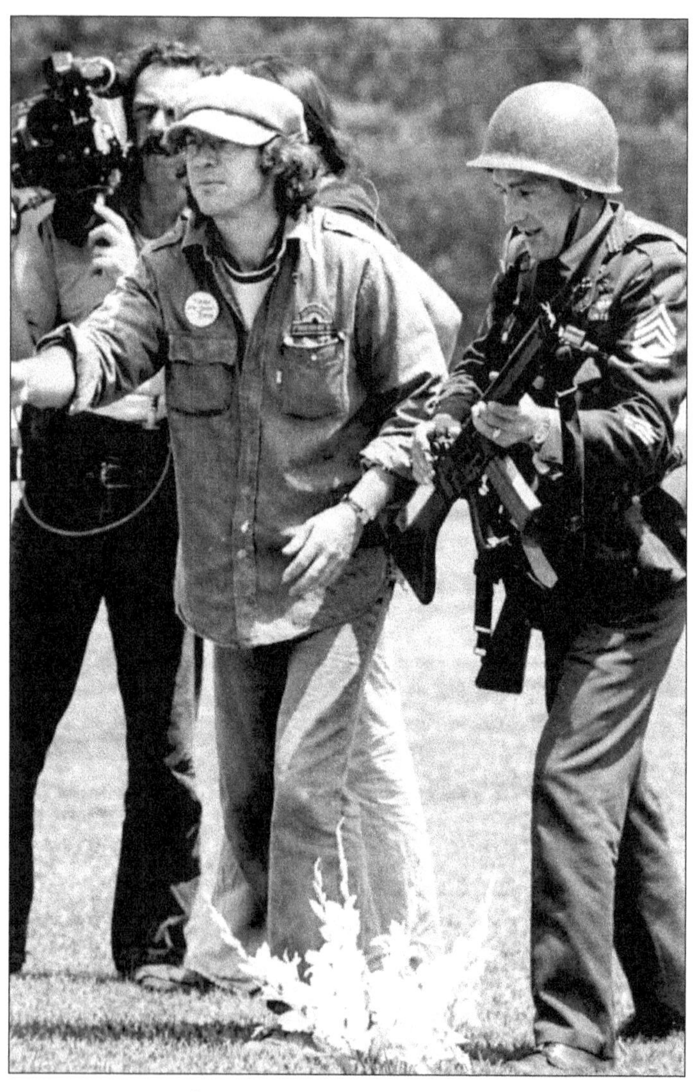

Henry directs Dennis Hopper in *Tracks* (1976).

the one that's in the final movie, with the "You wanna go to 'Nam?! You wanna go to Nam?!" I yell "Cut!" and tell him how great he was…

DK: Didn't he say something like, "You're not my friend"?

HJ: No, he said, "You don't love me," and just walks off. We can't get another take because he just walks off. I don't know how anyone handled him during that time. I handled him by never working with him in the afternoon, because by that point he was angry and intoxicated and wanted to fight about everything. But in the morning, he was great and very easy. It was just… very tricky. I had four or five great hours per day. But I knew him so well that I knew I could deal with him. At that point, I didn't think he had much time left. I thought he'd be dead within a couple years. The funny thing is that, years later when he cleaned up, he became a big Republican.

DK: Talk about "we blew it"! I just can't believe he tried to strangle you.

HJ: At Old World, yeah. I was there all the time. I'd go there with Jack [Nicholson]. That's where that story—I told you this—my brother is back from Israel and I didn't know. I'm having lunch with Jack and there's my brother Michael walking down the street, and I didn't know he was back. I run over to him, and I said, "Michael, hi!" "Hi, I need to get these glasses fixed," which he's holding in his hands and going on and on about. I interrupt him and go, "Michael, it's Henry, your brother! I haven't seen you in a long time. How are you?" And he goes, "I'm fine, but you see these glasses…"

DK: Yeah, you told me that.

HJ: That was one of my haunts. I get back to the table and Jack says, "That's your brother?! He's a goldmine! He's a natural comedian! You need to put him in your next movie!" And I put him in a whole string, as you know. *Tracks*, *Sitting Ducks*, *Cherry Pie*—he was in everything during that time.

DK: He was great. A lot of fun to watch.

HJ: Old World, Dan Tana's, Ma Maison where I would go with Orson. Wolfgang Puck was there, then he got his own place, Spago. I went there a lot too.

DK: How did the people at Old World react when you came back? That must have been quite a sight for them to behold, someone trying to choke someone else in their establishment.

HJ: I have no idea, but I did go back, a lot. Did I tell you the story of where *Tracks* came from? When I went on the train trip with Bob Rafelson?

DK: You've told bits and pieces about this, but it would be nice to get the whole story. You know, Rafelson tells his own version of this same story in Nelly's documentary. [*Author's note: I was referring to an Eighties video documentary about Henry, directed by Nelly Alard, who starred in* Eating *and* Venice/Venice. *She later went on to become an acclaimed novelist.*]

HJ: I want to watch that again. Can you show where I can find it?

DK: We can go up to your computer before I leave, and I'll get it for you.

HJ: Thank you. I'm bad with that stuff. So I met Bob though Bert Schneider. I had quit acting after Mike Nichols had cast Dusty Hoffman in *The Graduate*, instead of me. I really thought I was going to get the part for a time. Mike seemed excited by the idea. That was the last straw. That really triggered me to become a director, because I was so upset over that. Then, around that time, Bob told me he was going to do a movie, and we knew it was going to be about a soldier coming back from Vietnam accompanying the body of a friend of his, who said he was a war hero. And through that process, it would reveal our feeling about the horror of the Vietnam War. It wasn't my idea originally. I wasn't going to write it with him… I can't remember exactly.

All I know was, he and I got on a train in New York to come to California. By the time we got to California days later, he was so fed up with me. I had been such a pain in the ass, as far as he was concerned, that he decided—for that reason, but also because he wasn't interested any more in doing this movie about a Vietnam veteran—to move on to something else. I took over and rewrote the script. And I decided that this would be my next movie after *A Safe Place*.

The only thing that remained from it was the one scene that I wrote but he revised and later claimed for himself, which was actually my scene—the lunch scene from *Five Easy Pieces*, with the "You want me to hold the chicken?" bit. We had a big falling out over that scene, because I think we genuinely both believed that we had created that, and that scene is now famous, of course. I thought he had forgotten the origin of all that. Doesn't that sound like something I would do?

DK: Actually, I have to admit, yes. There is something very "Henry" about that interaction.

HJ: [*chuckling*] I like that, "very Henry." Bob was also my neighbor, when I lived behind the Chateau Marmont. So it was logical to use him when I shot *Always*. He played one of the neighbors, who comes over for the barbeque. He played a perfect little part.

[Rafelson's account, as recorded in Nelly Alard's documentary On the Tracks of a Filmmaker: *"I had known Henry for a few years. He was a friend of my business partner. When he'd come to Los Angeles, I had tried to get him some help as an actor. I always had a desire, since I was a young boy, to make a movie on a train. It had been some time since I had traveled cross the country on a train. I needed somebody who would be helpful to me in thinking about the story and doing some research on the story. So I called Jaglom, and said, 'Would you arrange for a train trip. Get the tickets, but I don't want to know where I'm going.' We encountered a number of strange people. And Henry's idea, of course—and this was 1967 or '68— before Henry was a movie director. This was before, I think, Henry aspired to be a director. One of the things that Henry was doing at the time was making home movies. No matter where he went, or who he confronted—and we were to confront some very serious adversaries—Henry always had the camera up against his eye. For example, at one point, there were about thirty or forty young teenage students who were celebrating their graduation. They were in a very good*

mood and wanted drinks, but they were too young to buy a drink on board this train. They asked Henry if he would get them drinks. He went and he started ordering these drinks, a big order. The bartender asked for his identification. Henry said, 'My identification? Why do you ask for my identification?' The guy said, 'Without identification, I won't serve you a drink.' Henry began to scream at this man, as if he were an SS officer from Nazi Germany who was demanding papers. It appealed to Henry's sense of drama. The old Black man was irritated by the way Henry was speaking to him. It became more and more escalated, until it became a major confrontation, with the Black man holding the knife for lemon slicing and holding it up to Henry and threatening to kill him if Henry didn't walk away. You have to understand that one of the reasons the Black man was irritated was not simply the argument, and not the absence of identification, but during the whole thing, as Henry was talking, he was also filming him. Eventually, I decided not to make this movie and I gave it to Henry. The movie became Tracks. *When I say I gave it, I wrote the script partly with Henry, and kept the one scene, the lunch scene from* Five Easy Pieces, *and the rest was all his."]*

HJ: Women loved Bob. He had a dynamic personality. They went crazy for him. He was a major attraction for almost every woman I knew. Extraordinary stories that I know involving him with women. He was also very funny. A little bit angry, a little bitter. I always got the sense that he felt he didn't fulfill what he wanted to fulfill. He felt that his dream got thwarted somehow. Complicated guy, and sweet, despite himself.

DK: Were you around during his *Mountains of the Moon* period? That was Rafelson's pet project, his dream or passion project.

HJ: I don't remember much about that, but what year was that?

DK: Like 1990.

HJ: I know he was passionate about that film, obsessed with it, and I maybe had one conversation with him. I do remember Bert Schneider telling me, "Be careful when you get obsessed with something. Bob is totally obsessed with this *Mountains of the Moon.*"

DK: I don't have much of a sense of when you arrived in Los Angeles. Was there a lot of hopping back and forth for a certain time?

HJ: I came out three times in the summers of the early Sixties. Then I came out for good in 1965. Tuesday picked me up at the airport and took me to her house down in Malibu. It was Karen Black's birthday, July 1. That first Fourth of July, we went up the road to Jane Fonda's house. She was married to Vadim then. This was a famous party—written about endlessly. For me, it was mind-boggling, because all the old stars were there. Her dad was there—Henry. Jimmy Stewart was there. Some of the New Hollywood too—Jack and Dennis and Bert and Warren, all my friends. Bobby Walker, Jr. whose house we'd always gather at. All the people who would become my friends. I almost died there. I almost killed Rafelson, and Saul Rifkin... Ron Rifkin, but his real name is Saul.

DK: Oh wow. I know Ron appeared later in *Last Summer in the Hamptons.*

HJ: Tuesday drove a red Porsche convertible, which was a stick shift, and I had just basically learned how to drive in New York. I always had a Mustang out here. I didn't know anything about a shift, but I told her I did. So we were at this party—huge, amazing party. The Beach Boys were there, and they were the entertainment. [*Author's note: Research indicates that the band was actually The Byrds.*] Can you imagine? They were the hired help! Everyone smoked a little grass then. I and Ron Rifkin, who was Saul Rifkin, and Bob Rafelson. I was never a big pot-head. We all went out in Tuesday's car. I drove and we went somewhere to smoke some dope. We're heading back and I make this U-turn on Pacific Coast Highway, and this being a shift car, it froze on me. I didn't know what to do, because I never drove a shift. Right in the middle of the highway division as I was making a U-turn, it froze. Behind me,

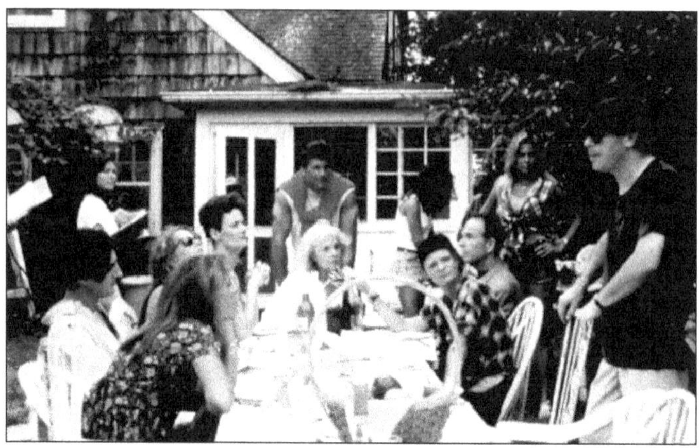

Henry reunited with two old friends, Ron Rifkin and
Roscoe Lee Browne, by casting them in his
Last Summer in the Hamptons (1995)

in the backseat, are these two guys. Rafelson is saying, "Shit!
Fuck! Shit! Fuck! Fuck, Henry! Shit!" Rifkin is going "Shema
Yisroel, Adonai Eloheinu, Adonai Echad." [*The Shema,
the last thing a Jew is supposed to say before the moment of
death.*] It was quite the contrast. I'm hearing "shit" and
"fuck" and then this Jewish prayer. I put my hand out as if I'm
Superman or something. I just knew nothing bad was going
to happen. I see this woman heading toward me in her car,
terrified. I felt the heat of her car on my hand. She screeches
to a halt. According to Rifkin—Rafelson's eyes were closed
shut, but Rifkin saw—I all of a sudden seemed to know
what to do, I shifted the thing and got us back on the road,
back to the party. They were so shaken that that's all they
talked about for the rest of the night. It was scary, though.
I almost killed Bob and Ron that day.

My highs, whenever I got high, were normally very good
though. Did I tell you about the high that Richie Pryor had,
when he tried to jump out the window?

DK: No.

HJ: I don't know if I have the strength to go into that right
now.

6.

**"Are you a Jew who's prepared
to kill your parents?"**

*In which Henry remembers his close friendship with Richard
Pryor, discusses Pryor's fascination with his parents' famous art
collection, relates a story involving his father and André Gregory's father, and relates the story of his first time being a girl.*

HJ: Bud Friedman at the Improvisation never liked anyone
cursing, or saying "Fuck" or "Shit" during their sets. Richie
[Pryor] started doing it, and… did I ever tell you this thing he
did when we were competing to make each other laugh?
DK: No.
HJ: So, the thing was, we had to make each other laugh. In
My Lunches With Orson, Jack Lemmon was sitting at our
table once so, and I remember telling him and Orson. Richie
goes right for the props. There was a tray with condiments on
it, and he takes the ketchup and puts it on his head. I'm not
laughing. The job was to make the other person laugh. It was
a game, a competition.
DK: Right.
HJ: He throws the ketchup on his face, and I'm not laughing.
Then the mustard, I'm still not laughing. And then the mayon-
naise. All this stuff is dribbling on his ears. It's not doing
anything to me. Then takes a whole dish, dumps it on his
head—like seven different colors of horrible shit, all while
I'm not laughing. And he picks up a napkin that is covered
in crap. He does this delicate Chaplin-esque thing with the
napkin, daintily wiping the corners of his mouth clean. I fell
down on the ground screaming with laughter. That's when I

knew I had no future as a comic. Richie Pryor was that much of a genius that I realized I couldn't hold a candle to him. I've never laughed as hard. I'd been holding in any willingness to laugh. The dam broke. I don't know if you can get how brilliant that is.

DK: No, I think you did a pretty good demonstration of the move.

HJ: But it was much funnier. My stomach hurt. And he won the game! I got pissed off at Richie because he would hang out with Amiri Baraka.

DK: A.K.A. LeRoi Jones.

HJ: One time, I sat down with them, and they would tell me that I wasn't allowed to participate in the conversation unless I was willing to kill my parents. I said, "Well, my parents are Jews from Europe, so I've got you just copped." He didn't like that, he got really pissed off. Richie had acted in *A Safe Place* when it was at the Actors Studio.

DK: He did? I never knew that.

HJ: Yeah. And one night we were sitting around, and they were really getting into their Black Power thing. I said something innocuous, and Baraka said, "Listen, I have no interest in hearing what you have to say. You're so fucking white. What are your credentials?" And it eventually led up to me saying, "I'm a Jew." And he said, "Are you a Jew who's prepared to kill your parents?" I said, "I beg your fucking pardon?!" Richie didn't come to my defense, and he didn't want to get into a fight with this guy who was now becoming his hero. Richie told me later that I was the first person who'd ever talked to him like that. I said, "Well, he told me I should kill my fucking parents!" Richie hadn't been interested in politics at all, then all of a sudden he's hanging around this asshole, and I was really fucking depressed. You know, we were trying to pitch a show, a sitcom, a Black guy and a white guy. Detectives. Then that other show came along, with Bill Cosby, um…

DK: "I Spy"

HJ: Yeah, we couldn't do it because "I Spy" beat us. Later on, I was going to do a *Sitting Ducks* sequel, with Richie and

Dustin Hoffman. They were actually scheduled to do it, if you can believe it.

DK: You know, you're like a counterculture Forrest Gump, in a way.

HJ: [*laughing*] Counterculture Forrest Gump? Thanks a lot!

DK: No, just that you've met all these people. They've just breezed into your life. It's quite something!

HJ: That's how it was in those days. Richie was doing some drugs back even then, and I was never as much into that. And he'd say, "Why are you always straight?" I'd say, "Straight? In what sense of the word are we talking?" And he'd say, "Not sexually, you asshole!" I was never stoned. And I'd explain, "I like it here, just like this," and he'd say, "Yeah, I saw your parents' apartment, I don't blame you!" Then I realized, yeah, growing up in his mother or grandmother's whorehouse in the Midwest, it made sense. I never thought much about class differences, and where we each came from. I was trying to hide being a rich kid, and was very intent that people not know that. Louis Malle and I would discuss that. He came from wealth too, and it was always important for us that others know we weren't dilettantes or just in it for the money. I think the way we made films put any doubt to rest.

DK: Yeah, you're definitely not driven by storming the box office.

HJ: But early on, I did hide that a lot... that part of me.

DK: You were embarrassed?

HJ: I just didn't want people looking at me different for something I couldn't help or change about myself.

DK: Yeah, you can't help who or what your parents are.

HJ: You know, Richie had been over to my parents' apartment on the West Side, and we'd stay there, especially when they were away during summers. He used to bring people up to see my parents' famous art collection. They had great collections of impressionist and expressionist paintings, all by major artists: Renoir, Degas, Chagall, and so on. He said, "Would you mind if I do The Tour?" He'd call it "The Tour." He took a few people up, on a few different occasions. I'd get a call, "Do you mind if I bring someone up for The Tour?" Richie got fascinated, not surprisingly, by the life of Van Gogh during all this. He would stare at our Van Gogh—we had just one—for such a long time. And it wasn't a psychologically settled one. You could tell things were brewing—it wasn't a famous painting of his, I don't think. He had never thought about painters having different, what we call periods. He had very little frame of reference, but he got interested in art thanks to my parents' collection. You know, they opened up a wing of the Tel Aviv Art Museum, the Simon and Marie Jaglom Wing, with that art collection.

DK: Yeah, I've been to it.

HJ: You were?

DK: Oh yeah, I've walked through it, so I probably saw some of the same paintings Richie did.

HJ: Yes, his eyes were on that very collection. Do you remember which Van Gogh it was?

DK: No, I don't.

HJ: I don't remember right now either. Polly Platt pissed me off when she told some journalist that my parents had hung a priceless painting, a Van Gogh or Picasso or Gaugin, in a bathroom over the toilet. That was never true. I was outraged by that.

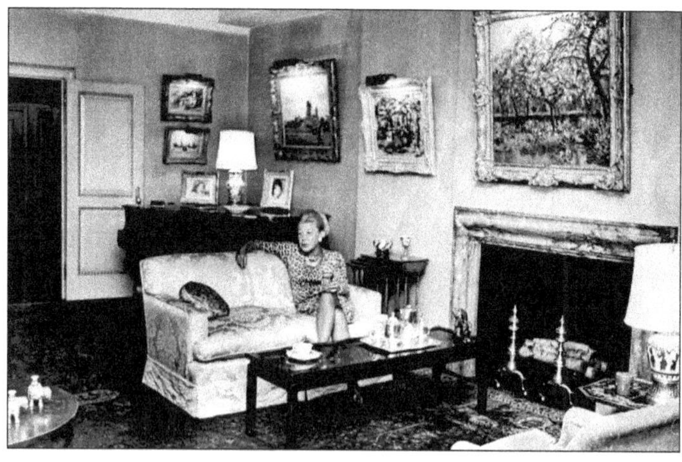

Marie Jaglom, Henry's mother, pictured with the family art collection in the *New York Post* on April 1, 1968.

[Reference: The multi-talented Polly Platt was a producer, screenwriter, and production designer, married to Peter Bogdanovich from 1962 until 1971. In 2020, critic and author Karina Longworth dedicated a podcast series to her, focusing on her considerable contributions to American movies. Polly discusses the "toilet painting" in a 1990 Jaglom profile piece in Movieline, *called "The King of Spago" by James Kaplan. She mentions a Picasso hanging in a bathroom, and is quoted as saying, "I have never seen so many paintings on a wall. It was like a woman wearing too much jewelry."]*

DK: So, she made it up?

HJ: I think it was just a good line to make us look ridiculous. I liked Polly, but that upset me.

DK: You must like *Lust for Life*, right?

HJ: Great movie. Great, great movie. I remember talking with Stanley Donen about Vincente Minnelli. Stanley was a great friend, and I loved *Two for the Road* and, of course, all those great musicals he did. Stanley especially loved Minnelli though; he thought he was beyond just an entertainer. He had a peevish side too. Once in a restaurant, Stanley got mad at me and got up and left.

DK: I've been there.

HJ: What are you talking about? You've never left one of our lunches.

DK: You've exasperated me enough where I've sometimes been on the edge.

HJ: Really?

DK: I mean, it doesn't matter really. I get too much out of these sessions to ever leave like that. You know you can be a pill sometimes though, right?

HJ: A pill?! I mean, I don't mean to be, unless I get the sense that someone's not being honest or something, but I haven't had that problem with you, at least recently.

DK: In any event, Henry, those who love you wouldn't have it any other way.

HJ: Donen could be insecure, though. Deeply insecure.

DK: He's still with us. I know he's in his late 90s and he's dating Elaine May.

HJ: Dating? Does one date at 98?

DK: And does one go steady with Elaine May?

HJ: She was a trip! Boy, talk about neurotic!… but brilliant.

DK: Yeah, she's one of the seats of Jewish-American humor and sensibility. All part of a picture.

HJ: Did I ever tell you the story of André Gregory's father?

DK: You know, Cindy Kleine [André's wife] made that documentary about André and his relationship with his father?

HJ: This is an interesting story. André's father and my father were partners, and they had real estate together. They had different businesses together. The great story toward the end of my [Jewish history] book… They're collecting money for Israel. I think it's the Six-Day War. Might have been 1973, but I think it was the Six-Day War. They've got all these very wealthy European Jews. My father was the head of the European division of the United Jewish Appeal, which meant European born Americans. They had a distinct… all these accents was fascinating: Russian, German, Polish, French, everything. And he was head of this division. So during the Six-Day War, during the critical period, he was raising money and he had all these very powerful men, businessmen, in our apartment. One of them was André's father, his partner. George in English, and Grisha was what they called him. His real name wasn't Gregory. I don't remember what the Russian was, or whatever, but it became Gregory when he came to America.

DK: I think it was something like Josephowitz.

HJ: That's plausible. André was sent to some Episcopalian prep school and I told you, I think… he didn't know he was Jewish till he was 21. So, you have to know that that's a key part of this story. They're all sitting around, including his friends, several of them good friends, but other just wealthy men who were born in Europe. Sol Hurok was most interesting to me because of show business. Do you know who he was?

DK: No.

HJ: He was an impresario who brought the Russian ballet to America, all of that. So, he asked each person how much he's

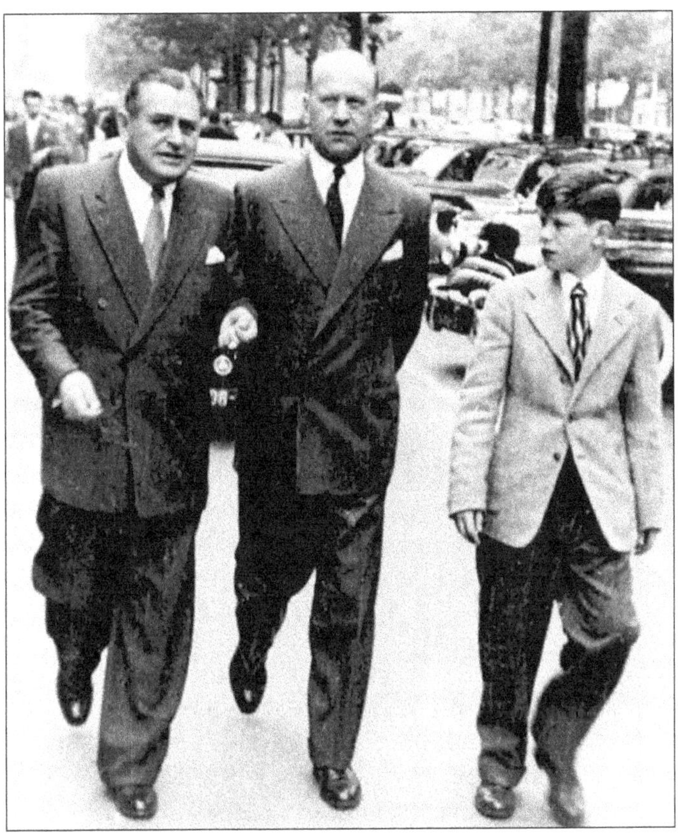

Henry walking the Champs Elysees with
his father and uncle.

going to contribute, and they do it publicly, which I found embarrassing. But they were wealthy men, and they said an amount. He asked one man, and the one man says, "I don't know, let's say $20,000." And he says, "Thank you very much." And then he asks Mr. Gregory… Grisha, his first name. "Grisha, what about you?" And whatever he says, it's like $30,000. That's $10,000 more than the person before. My father said, "No, I don't accept that, Grisha. Forget it. Next. Maximilian!" Grisha says, "What? What do you mean, you don't accept it? You just accepted less from so-and-so right before me, and now I'm saying more than him." My father said, "Okay, Grisha, not important," and he keeps going on, and André's father gets infuriated. He says, "What are you talking about? How can you treat me this way? What do you know? I'm not even Jewish!" He had become Episcopalian.

My father looks at him, puts down the pad and pencil and says, "Listen, Grisha, I'll tell you a story. In Russia, there was a priest, and he went around and dealt with the Russian Orthodox people. But every once in a while, a Jew would come to be converted. So this Jew he said, 'Father, I want to be a Christian.' And the priest said, "Good." He puts holy water on him and said, 'You're no longer Moshe. You're now Ivan.' And so he says, 'But, you know, there are many rules to being a Christian. You have to come to church on Sunday. You have to eat fish on Friday,' and on and on. He says, 'Yes, I know. I'll be a good Christian and a good Russian Orthodox,' da da da, 'I'm no longer a Jew. I thank you, Father. So the priest makes his rounds the next Friday, and he looks through the window at the formerly Moshe and now Ivan's house, and he sees that he and his family are sitting around a big chicken. He comes and he says, 'What is this? You said you understood that this Friday you eat fish. You don't eat chicken.' Ivan tells the priest, 'But Father, this is a fish.' And the priest says, 'What kind of fool you take me for, you dirty Jew? I know chicken when I see it! It's got legs, it's got wings. How can you call this a fish?' Ivan says, 'Father, if you can put a few drops of water on my head and turn me from Moshe into Ivan, I could pour a few drops of water on top of this chicken and make it a fish.'"

And my father says, "I know you think you're a fish now, Grisha, but to me, you'll always be a chicken." And then, to his credit, André's father blushed or whatever—got embarrassed—but then increased his amount. You know, it was an aggressive thing for sure for him to say that in front of all these other people, and to make fun of the idea of being a convert.

By the time I was nineteen or twenty, and started showing an interest in show business, my father was basically like, you know, "Just like Mr. Gregory, he's got the same problem with his son." I was luckier because he came first in that social set. Somebody went off into show business, somebody's son, so my father already had the unfortunate experience of knowing that Grisha Gregory's son also was in show business. So it wasn't completely as shocking, I guess, or something. André always said it was better for me, because I didn't have to break the mold, because the idea was outrageous to them. "You're going to be what?" "I'm going to be an actor. I'm not to try to direct." "What? Plays? Movies? Well, come to the office. You sit in the office, and three months of the year, you can go out and be a crazy artist."

DK: Your father knew Yiddish, right?

HJ: He knew a number of languages. I've had to get over my prejudice. You know who got me over my prejudice, who is not even a Jew?

DK: Prejudice toward the Yiddish language? You told me Andrea Marcovicci.

HJ: Because she did *Ghetto*, it's a musical written by a very interesting Israeli. She did it down here at the Mark Taper Forum. It all takes place in one of the ghettos, I forgot which one, during World War II. And she sang songs in Yiddish. She had to learn to do that, and the beauty of the language she was overwhelmed by. I grew up in a culture with Israeli cousins who all were told to be contemptuous of Yiddish as the language of the ghetto. It's a dead language, and this linked to Nazi killing, you know. It's for the galoot.

DK: In Yiddish, we say *galus*. It means exile.

HJ: Right, and everybody outside of Israel are the galoot. So kids were taught not to talk to their grandparents, I don't know if you know that. That is, if they spoke Yiddish.

DK: No.

HJ: An overreaction, obviously, so I always had this attitude prevalent among this generation of Israelis, thinking it's a bad ghetto language that corrupts Hebrew. I hated the grotesque mispronouncing of the Hebrew words, as I saw it. Then Andrea did this play, and learned all these songs, and they were beautiful. I didn't understand a word of them because I can't understand Yiddish, but they were gorgeous and moving. I could hear the beauty of the language, is my point.

DK: I worked in Borough Park for a time when I lived in New York, and I worked at a video production company, believe it or not, run by Satmar Chassidim.

HJ: Are Satmars allowed to do that?

DK: Well, here's the thing: we were recording plays in Yiddish with all-male casts.

HJ: Oh my God, there are no women allowed?

DK: When I was doing these behind-the-scenes videos, I remember putting in a shot that I thought it was a pretty handsome looking shot. I thought it looked great. My boss with the curly *payis* [sidelocks] comes in and he's like, "Oh, you have to cut that out." "Why?" "There's a woman in the foreground." I was like, "What?!" I was affiliated with Lubavitch, and the Lubavitch weren't like that. But I had to learn at least rudimentary Yiddish, enough to listen and understand fluently.

HJ: Yeah, they're nuts. So you can understand it?

DK: [*says a full sentence in Yiddish*]

HJ: I understand a bit of that because of German. I don't know a word of Yiddish, but I can understand exactly that. Interesting. So many of the words are German-based.

DK: Then when I did an acting part for Rob Nilsson, I had to sing a Yiddish swing tune by the Barry Sisters.

HJ: "Bei Mir Bist du Schön"?

DK: No, it was a swing version of "Yidl Mitn Fiddle." [*sings a bit*]

HJ: It was real prejudice I had though. Andrea was a big help.

DK: You used to get really miffed at me. You used to rage and then correct me on my Yiddishized pronunciation of certain words, far more than you do now. You used to jump on me.

HJ: I remember that, yeah. There was Ladino too. In my [Jewish history] book, I talk about after the Nazis devastated Greece, that was the end of Ladino. Five hundred thousand Jews of Spanish origin, Sephardic Jews, were killed.

DK: I have still heard it spoken. I know someone who does.

HJ: Yeah, there are a few people, obviously, who do, but there was a huge language in this. Wiped out.

DK: Getting back to your father, what did he think about your interest in the feminine world and lady's clothes and all that?

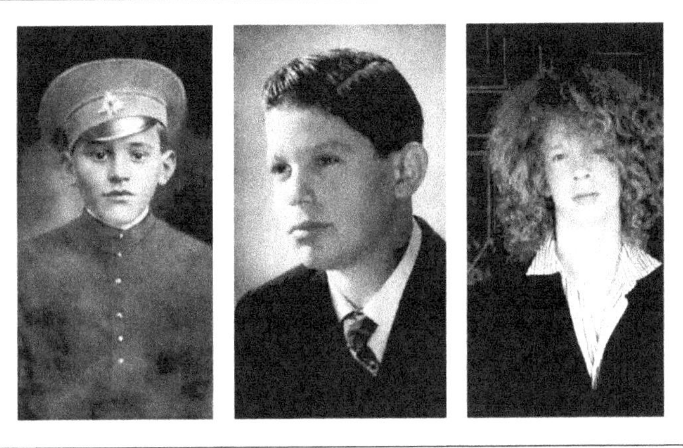

Three generations of Jaglom family bar mitzvah photos.
From left to right: Henry's father Simon/Sioma, Henry,
and Henry's son Simon.

HJ: He had no idea about any of that. That was part of the fun of it. It was like, with my mother and I, our secret... our secret world. And I was very pretty. In camp when I was 15, I played my campmate Peter Sax's wife. It was an all boys camp. I played the girl's part. The nurse pulled out some kind of big costume from a barrel, a dress with big polka dots, and then she put lipstick on me. She looked at me, and I was really pretty at that age. And she said, "Oh my God, we can really do this." I'll never forget that. She got me all fixed up for this, you wouldn't believe it. I looked completely like a girl. I looked like a really pretty, with makeup and everything, 19- or 20-year-old—sexy, gorgeous.

I went out that night during the play and stunned the audience. The audience was from all the summer camps around us along with my group. At first they laughed and giggled. Then there was silence, then I got fucking applause like you can't imagine. It was my first big part, but I had played the Cuckoo Clock when I was ten years old, and I'd gotten a review that I thought meant I was the best thing in the play, and it decided I was going to go into show business.

Then the counselor who directed it said, "Everybody get on stage!" We're having, you know, soft drinks and cookies and all the audience comes up on stage and they all congratulate me, especially the girls who are guests from other camps. And they're going crazy for me. Two boys come up who had picked on me before. Then I became funny and they became like my bodyguards. I think they're going to punch me because of my history with them. They say the word "punch," and I realize what they're asking me, "Could they get me some punch?" They're treating me like a girl. They're, like, being deferential. And they were saying, "I asked first!" They're getting into an argument about who's going to get me the punch, these guys who used to scare me. They couldn't do enough for me, these guys.

I felt close to women. I got what the power of women was, and I also got the power of show business that same night. What I remember is, standing in this outfit feeling like a star, standing behind the flats, singing at the top of my whisper because I still was scared, singing, "There's no business like show business, like no business I know."

7.
"You're waving the white flag at me!"

In which we discuss the unanswered questions around his relationship with Orson Welles, the real root of his antipathy toward Steven Spielberg, an outrageous story involving Shelley Winters, and James Mason's love of bizarre prankster games.

DK: After you wrapped *A Safe Place*, did your close friendship with Orson just start right away, or did that take time?

HJ: Oh no, he went off to Europe after *A Safe Place*. I didn't see him for quite a while. Years later—after we'd spoken on the phone a few times—I started going to Ma Maison, and one day I ran into him. I say, "Hi hi hi, how are you?" And he said, "I lost my girlish enthusiasm." I said, "Oh my God!" I really got that. It hit me. I think he was going out and I was just coming in, so we were standing there. I said, "Why?" "You really want to know why? Let's meet at such-and-such a time, back here tomorrow." And he told me what he was going through to raise money for his films, whatever was happening at that time. Things had fallen through. That's when I determined I was going to get him money, or die trying. It was a bit romantic on my part. I didn't get him money and I didn't die trying, but I did try as hard as I could. No one wanted to give him money, but everyone wanted to have lunch with Orson Welles. There were a lot of promises. What was that one bastard's name? British guy, Andrew Braunsberg. I remember we opened a bottle of Cristal with him, he was totally on board, then I couldn't get him on the phone for months. He disappeared. And that was that. Never even apologized. That was just one of those disappointments. There were many of them, you know. Many of them.

They all wanted to have lunch with him, but not help him, including Spielberg, which is what got me very soured on Spielberg. He said, "I'm having lunch with Spielberg," and I said, "Oh, great," you know, "because all you need to do is get Spielberg's name. You don't need money from him. But if it says 'Steven Spielberg Presents a film by Orson Welles,' I can get you the deal." I would arrange with the studio—that's what they needed. It was low budget, but it was big budget by my standards. Low by studio standards. And if Spielberg's name were on it as the producer or the presenter or something like that, we were in. And Spielberg had just recently bought what he thought was the sled from *Citizen Kane* for a fortune, and it was hanging, he said, over his bed or something. Orson laughed privately at that and said, "Doesn't he remember the movie? The sled was burned! So how could that have been the sled from *Citizen Kane*?" But why would he object if he knows all he has to do is put his name on the thing, not even be involved?

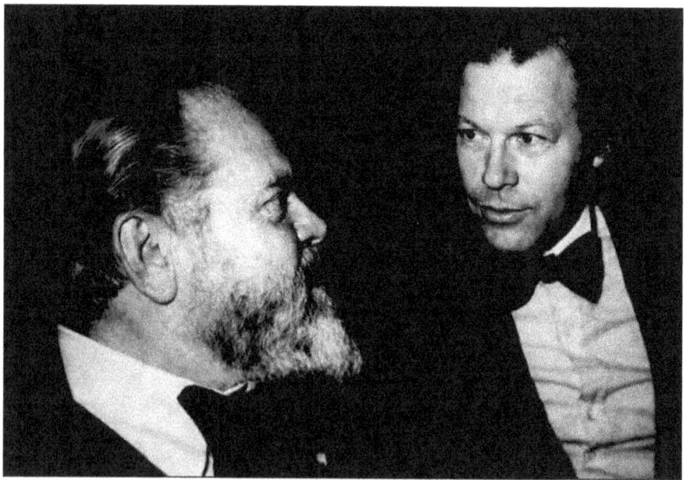

Henry and Orson: business partners and the best of friends
in Orson's final years.

So they had this lunch, and then he didn't call me afterwards. I couldn't get through to him. I spoke to the guys—his driver, whose name I have now forgotten; his faithful driver who was there when he died. He discovered him and then called me to apologize that he was dead. He was apologizing! What's his name, sweet man. I had said, "Do you want me to go with you?" "No, no, no, of course not. It's easier for me to do it alone, but just the two of us." Now I'm getting worried. Finally I called the driver again, and the driver went up to the room and got Orson on the phone, and he said, "I don't want to talk about this." I said, "Why? What happened?" He said, "First of all, he waited for me to ask for something, and I wouldn't ask." I said, "Why wouldn't you ask?" He said, "I'm not going to be put in that position, where I'm begging." I said, "So you never brought the subject up?" He said, "No, that was his job to bring it up! He knew why we were having lunch, and all he wanted to do was ask me about this shot in this movie and that shot in that movie, and talk about my old films. And then he left me with a check!" He said that was the final insult. He never even acknowledged.

I said, "Why the fuck didn't you say, 'Listen, while we're having lunch, the reason I'm here is I need you to do something for me. It's not a hard thing to do, and it's not going to cost you a penny. It'll just say 'Steven Spielberg presents a film by Orson Welles.'" He said, "I couldn't, I would have been humiliated because it was his job to. He knew why we were there." I said, "Well, what if I called to find out." "No! You don't dare call him or say this to anybody!" I said, "Orson, don't be proud now, this is silly." And, of course, Spielberg knew it. The people who scheduled it with him knew what it was about. They knew what I was looking for, and he knew it. "Everybody knows the trouble I've been having getting films made, and he knew that I would…"—you know. And he was stubborn, he refused to make the call to try the follow up, and he wouldn't let me do it. And that hurt him a lot. [*Author's note: Joseph McBride in his biography of Steven Spielberg notes that Amy Irving accompanied Spielberg to the lunch at Ma Maison, and acknowledges, "Rather than offering to help*

Welles with The Cradle Will Rock, *Spielberg spent most of their luncheon asking him questions about* Citizen Kane.*" In the footnotes, McBride also muses, "Spielberg may have been miffed over Welles's mischievous comment to the press that "the sled he bought was a fake."*]

HJ: Boy, that's... all those things I forget. You forget and then you remember. Yeah, so that's the Steven Spielberg story. That's the one that I wouldn't let Biskind put in the book. It's yours.

DK: Thank you. Were a lot of people intimidated by him?

HJ: Oh, absolutely! You see that in the *My Lunches With Orson* book. I never was that way with him. The type of things he would do that would intimidate people I found kind of amusing and charming. Sometimes he could be boorish, but I think he appreciated how I never acted like I was intimidated around him. He was my friend. I think he felt he could be himself. When we started shooting *A Safe Place*, he was difficult. He was trying to direct, he kept talking to the other actors and the crew. He was just impossible. I had to tell him, "This is not your movie, Orson. It's mine." I struck a deal with him. I let him repeat a line of dialogue in the middle of a take until he was satisfied with it, even though it was disruptive to the flow of the take. After a certain point, he didn't do that as much—the repeating lines thing—because he grew to trust me. And he did everything I asked him to do. And he even suggested things, like when it rained, he said, "Why don't I climb back out on the rocks and you can do another take with the rain coming down?" He was wonderful from then on. He also gave me one final shooting day free because of how he behaved on the first day.

DK: So, when did the lunches...

HJ: You know, my father said one day—I just felt like my father here, when I was taping him endlessly—he said, "There are a million stories in the naked city, like 1,001 Arabian nights." He loved telling all the stories, and he loved having me tape everything, but he didn't want to admit that ever. He'd say, "Why do you want to hear that story again. You've heard that story!"

DK: I think the *Train to Zakopané* story is incredible.

HJ: I am so excited about my book, which you're taking me away from. I hope you appreciate that. All these nights when I'm supposed to be working on my book. [*Author's note: Henry worked for years on a personalized Jewish history book, a literary magnum opus.*]

DK: Well, you're having a good time.

HJ: Yeah, a good time.

DK: And you're going to get more than one book out of it, so…

HJ: That's a good way to look at it, thank you.

DK: So when did the lunches become…

HJ: Become a thing? Habitual thing?

DK: Yeah.

HJ: God, I think around '81. 1980 or '81. The taping started 1983, I think. We went to Cannes together that year. Did I ever tell you that great story of the two of us at Cannes?

DK: I don't think so.

HJ: So, Orson and I are at Cannes. I was helping him raise money to get various projects made, but we were there mainly to dispel any doubts that he could direct again, because he was very large at that point, and not very ambulatory. We hid a wheelchair out of sight so that no one would see him in it, and were on a campaign to convince everyone he was ready to go, to make another movie. I put him in front of a table at this hotel, and we let it be known that he was there, and in no time, everyone starts swarming around. They came in from every direction. He's got his cigars, his Monte Cristos, and he's holding court. He's in this big white jacket, and he's got his scarf, and it's his larger-than-life self, and the press is loving it. I'm sitting next to him, and he's holding forth. He flicks his cigar and the ashes fall on his perfectly white jacket. He brushes off the ashes, embarrassed, and turns and whispers in my ear, "These ashes… Rita will kill me." He was talking about Rita Hayworth…

DK: Of course.

HJ: They'd split up decades ago by this point, and her career was long over. She'd contracted Alzheimer's and she was in ill health.

DK: Right, I know when they went public with the diagnosis, it was a shock.

HJ: Do you know when that was?

DK: I think early Eighties.

HJ: So she was going through it at that point, then. Later that night we were alone, and I said, "Orson, do you know what happened today?" He was blustery and said, "Yes, of course, you made me sit there like the fool in front of all those people!" I said, "No no no… do you remember, you dropped the ashes on your jacket and you said that Rita would kill you?" He was amazed, like he didn't remember. He said, "Did I really say that?" I said, "Yeah, you really said that." He just looked down, paused, like he was considering what I told him, and he said, very tenderly, "You know, once you love them, you always love them." This was right in the midst of my breakup and divorce from Patrice, so I was working with this very idea in conceiving the movie that would become *Always*.

DK: That's touching.

HJ: "Once you love them, you always love them." Isn't that something?

DK: Beautiful.

HJ: He was such a great friend to have during my divorce.

DK: So the taping started right when Biskind picked it up in the book. There weren't tapings before 1983, though there were lunches.

HJ: Yes, there were some untaped lunches that I wish I had taped. I only realized late how valuable recording them would be. And with Orson's permission… I'm remembering now something not on the tapes it was because this was before '83. I think I recall, Alan Arkin stopped by the table once to dish something to us about Shelley Winters and that turned into a really funny conversation. Did I ever tell you my Shelley Winters story?

DK: No. There's an item on IMDb that has her as having quit working with you on your movie *Always*.

HJ: What?! No, not true at all! No, this was when I was doing summer stock. I did summer stock in Westport, at the Westport County Playhouse.

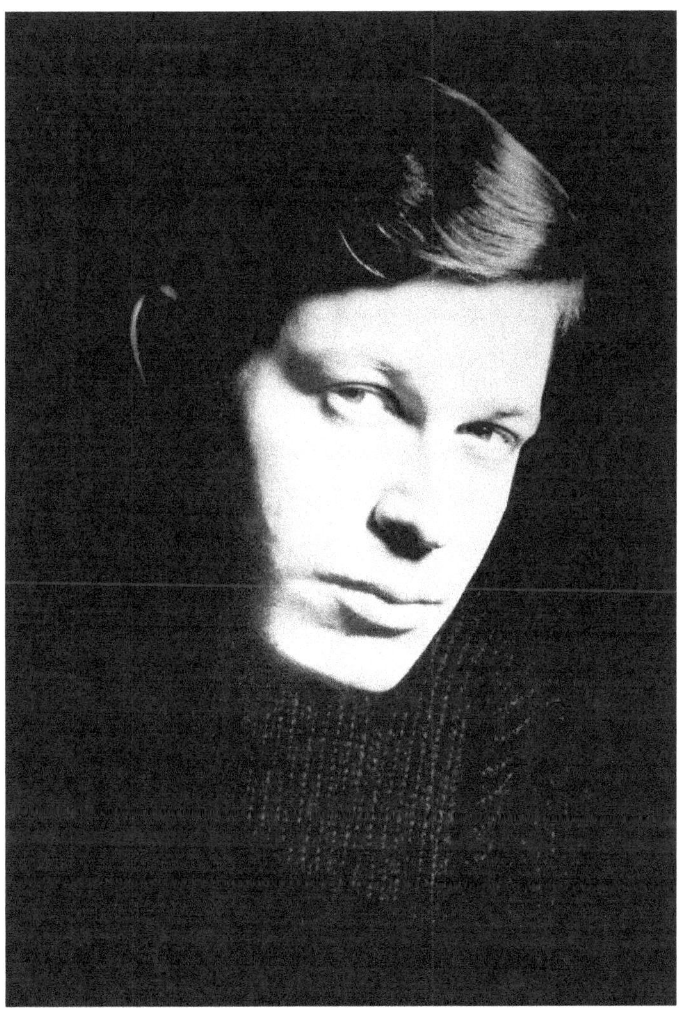

Henry's first actor's headshot, circa 1961.

DK: In Connecticut.

HJ: Yes. The woman who ran the props and everything, she was a point person at the theater, and she took me under her wing, kind of. Her name Marianne McKay. Tina Crawford was one of the apprentices along with me.

DK: *Mommie Dearest*!

HJ: She wrote *Mommie Dearest* much later. She told me all those stories about what Joan did. Oh, good God! We were very close friends, and… I'm talking about, I'm 19 years old. It's my first summer away from, you know, my college in Pennsylvania. I was studying journalism. They'd have a special performance there in the summertime, and you'd get a big star or, if you were lucky, two… they'd come up to do a performance of a play, whatever they were doing in New York, they'd bring it to Westport and the summer stock crew would work the theater for it. So, Shelley Winters is coming up with, I think, *Two for the Seesaw*. Marianne gives me the ventilation job, which involves handling these big blocks of ice, and the fans would blow the icy air into the audience. The whole evening, that was what I was supposed to do. Very primitive because this was an old building. This guy was telling me to put more ice into it, and I said, "No, that's more than enough."

I get so into learning my lines for the summer stock show, and get wrapped up studying that, that I forget to put the ice in place. That, and I was never keen on that type of labor. Keep in mind, this is the height of summer, in July, so it's sweltering. The audience starts fanning themselves with their programs. Little by little, you start to see the programs coming out, and people fanning themselves. Shelley is on stage looking out at this constant motion with the white paper programs is taking over, and it's distracting her. The place is getting so hot, you have no idea. I don't know what was going through my head — I was off mentally somewhere else, I guess.

In the middle of her lines, Shelley stops cold, pauses, then shouts out at the audience, "You're waving the white flag at me!" The audience continues to fan themselves. She calls out to them, "Ok, listen, he's in love with me, I say no, he leaves me, the end, curtain!" She explained the rest of the play in a sentence or two, then yelled out "Curtain!" and off she went. That was the end of that show, they couldn't get her back. Boy, did I get in trouble! And she got kicked out of Equity for, like, six months.

DK: She just stopped the show.

HJ: She stopped the show and ended it. She quickly told them what happened in the rest of the play, and then just left.

DK: That's wild. Mazursky had some wild stories of working with Shelley.

HJ: I later got to know Tony Franciosa, whom she married. I don't think they lasted long. She made him convert to Judaism.

DK: She would have been getting ready to do *Lolita* around that time.

HJ: I loved James Mason.

DK: "In later life"?

HJ: James Mason in all his days. You know, he owned 16mm prints of his films, some I'd never seen. He'd show them to guests. To see him fixing the projector and rolling it all up, that's a very nice memory. James Mason played those prints over and over again.

DK: This wasn't a *Sunset Boulevard* kind of thing?

HJ: No! He was the sanest man you ever met. He did like something that I couldn't get along with him about. He loved to play practical jokes and he loved these weird, elaborate role play games. I still have a letter from him somewhere. I'll see if I can find that. He'd say, "Look, this is the idea: I'm going with this friend to Spain. You write letters asking him to come to England, because you've got this big deal for such and such…" And then he'd say,"Porty is going to explain everything." And she'd say, "We've got a three-way plan and it looks so much fun, because we're introducing you as, you're a diamond dealer and financier from Rhodesia. So do it with the English kind of sound to your voice." It was to pull someone's leg, who was also there. And I said, "I'm not really good at this." I didn't want to do it because it was boring, a waste of time.

DK: Really? That sounds like a blast! I would have loved playing weird role play party games with James Mason and his company.

HJ: To each his own, I guess. But these elaborate games, he and his daughter—they had a great relationship. She died really young. I don't know why. She was such a sweet, sweet girl. When I was dating Sandra Smith, the three of us were inseparable for a long time. And I was at their New Year's Eve party—I remember being out in the rain. In a way, it was the first father-daughter relationship I'd ever seen, and it was a lovely one. The mother was a bit of a, you know… difficult. Pamela Mason. Someone I was with was just saying, "How could he have been married to someone like that?" She wasn't easy to like, and she wasn't entirely sure I was good company for her daughter. She didn't think Sandra Smith was good enough for her either. I don't know, she was a little snobbish, but they had great people over. All the British. Since I've learned to appreciate cinematographers, who was David Lean's cinematographer?

DK: Freddie… Freddie Young.

HJ: Very good, good for you. He was there. They were all there all the time at parties. And I met a lot of wonderful British actors, you know. The British colony here. And he liked getting away from… Oh! Interesting anecdote… It was the first time I had to shake hands with James Mason. It was a shock.

DK: Why?

HJ: It was like he was wearing a glove made out of string, a stringy glove. His hands were so brittle, wow. I don't know what the disease was. I learned later that he creamed his hands, and did stuff, and he avoided shaking hands. But I was, of course, like, "Oh hi," and so he took my hand. It felt strange, but I didn't react. Very strange because he was this gorgeous man, and I fight every time I see his old love scenes now, during his gorgeous period, I think about what the girl must go through because it felt like it was eerie.

8.
"You don't exist on the same planet"

In which Henry recounts his one and only encounter with Brando (a contentious one), we discuss Karen Black, whom we both knew (with Henry having known her much longer, of course), and his memories of the infamous premiere of A Safe Place *at the New York Film Festival.*

HJ: Brando saw *Tracks*. So I got very excited, I'll never forget this, of course, because it's Marlon fucking Brando. So I was at the house of what's-his-name? I don't remember his name. My friend, this older guy in the valley… Who's Brando's contemporary, his best friend?

DK: Not sure, you'd have to be a bit more specific.

HJ: Names again. First thing that goes. Brando calls this house and says, "I'd like to speak to Henry Jaglom." And I get on the phone and says, "What were you doing in that film?" I said, "What do you mean?" He said, "Well, it's all over the place." This is Brando! It's Brando's voice, but he's saying, "What was Dennis doing?" and he was putting down the film. He didn't like *Tracks*, which shocked whoever the mutual friend was. But I've got a big ego, you might remember, and I said, "Well, what are you talking about?" And suddenly I'm getting into an argument with Marlon Brando on the phone about Dennis's performance. I said, "I think it was brilliant, and I think *he* was brilliant." He said, "It was all over the place, and neurotic. That's just neurotic behavior." I said, "Yeah, well, he's the guy coming back from Vietnam." "Don't give me that!" It was weird because I was in a contretemps, you know, a feud suddenly with Brando on the phone, who I'd never met, who had just seen a movie of mine that this other guy loved and that I thought was pretty great.

What he was intent on doing was slamming Dennis's performance, which, as you know, since then has gotten praises as Dennis Hopper's best performance, ever in his lifetime. This thing is heralded now suddenly after forty years or whatever, but I want Brando to be alive so I can say, "Look at this." It was so complicated because I was so excited to be on the phone with him, but so depressed because he was putting down the film. He was so argumentative because I was defending Dennis's performance. He said, "The movie would have been great, would have been interesting. I was fascinated by the way you did this, this, and this. But with that performance, how could it go anywhere?"

It was really my only experience with him, beside Jack Nicholson. Nicholson said, "You know what happened last night?" I said, "No," and he said, "I had a weird experience." I have to give you the background. Brando kept eating, as you know; he had gotten bigger and bigger and bigger, and he finally put a chain around his refrigerator with a lock. He gave the key to a new housekeeper, and he said, "Whatever I say to you at night, do not give me this key." He repeated it in Spanish and English and everything. He said, "Hide it. Don't tell me where it is, and nothing that I say, never give it to me." So three nights went by, it was fine. The fourth night he came and they said, "Listen, where's that key?" She said, "Oh, Mr. Brando, you told me not to hand it over." And then he says, "No, that's okay, just tell me where it is." "No, Mr. Brando." He went over and in his garage, he takes an ax, smashes the lock and chain around the refrigerator, which also smashes the refrigerator. Jack was coming over to the house for some reason, late at night to see something they were going to discuss whatever.

DK: Maybe it was around the time they were doing *The Missouri Breaks* together.

HJ: I don't remember what it was, but he finds him on the floor in front of his smashed open refrigerator, eating bowls of whatever… on the floor!

DK: They were neighbors, right?

HJ: They were neighbors, yeah. Same compound.

DK: Up on Mulholland.

HJ: Jack told me that story first hand. That's the story.

DK: That's a full-on addiction.

HJ: Yeah, oh God, yeah. And he was smart enough to try to protect himself, and then just couldn't get through the night. It's touching, in a way.

DK: That was the only encounter, that phone call? I'm surprised, considering how looped in you both were at the studio.

HJ: Yeah, that was the only time.

DK: I love the way that Karen [Black] spoke of Brando. She must have done the cup thing with you?

HJ: Cup thing?

DK: She said the way that people in movies drank from glasses or cups was very normal, and then along comes Brando, who would hold the cup like this. [*demonstrates craning the arm over to pick up a cup from above, holding by the brim*] She said, "You'd never seen anyone do something like that before in movies," and how bewitching it was. This was a very specific behavior. I miss Karen.

HJ: Karen was a sweet, sweet, crazy girl. She always said we were more like brother and sister than anything, even when we were boyfriend and girlfriend. She'd make up these stories about us growing up together—she'd go off on some goofy rap about when we were little kids. Did I tell you about my mother's dress?

DK: I don't think so.

HJ: So one day Karen is invited to be on the Johnny Carson Show, or one of the big, big, big TV talk shows. I think it was Carson. I had three girlfriends that were in Carson, three in a row. Anyway, Karen was going on and she had nothing to wear, and she was kind of a funky flower child. She didn't have fancy clothes, so I took her up to my parents' place, and I said to my mother, "Maybe you can help find something among your stuff." My mother was a very elegant woman who dressed very beautifully. She took Karen, who was always the

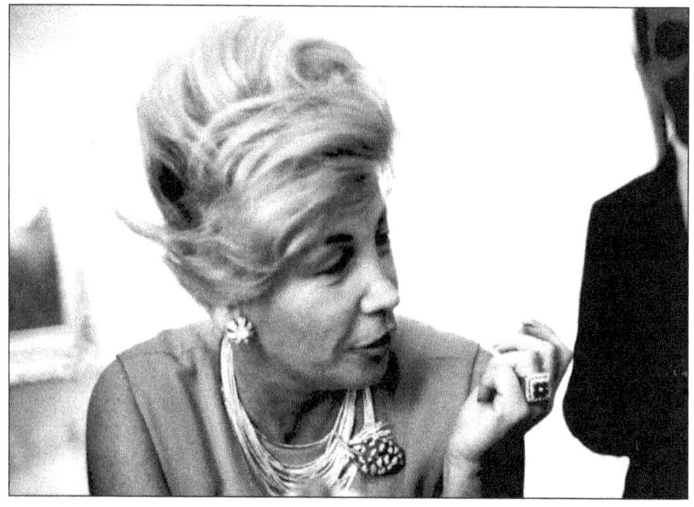

The elegant Marie Jaglom, Henry's mother, at a party in 1962.

sweetest, strangest little creature she'd ever met—she thought she was adorable—and she got her this gorgeous long, silk and satin skirt, with silver and this sheer chiffon blouse with long sleeves. It was just a gorgeous outfit. She looked spectacular. I was jealous, because women could wear such gorgeous things and men that get that lousy stuff, as far as I'm concerned. My mother also showed her a couple of things about doing her hair back.

She went on the show two nights later looking sensational. I hate to admit it, but we were at our height of our romantic period, a very nice romantic period, and we had an incredibly lovely romantic evening. I had to go back to my parents' house for some reason. I was going to sleep there tonight, not at Karen's. The next day, I was supposed to go there. She's running late—two in the afternoon, three in the afternoon, then she wasn't going to be there till five, but she wanted me to make sure that her cats were fed. She had a bunch of cats and she said, "Could you head over a little earlier to feed them?" I got the food and brought it over to where the cats were. She had big cushions for four kittens or five cats, I can't remember. And there in the middle of all this clutter was my mother's skirt. She had put it on this little pillow on which all her kittens pooped and peed. It just destroyed the skirt. Of course, I know it sounds very superficial and very not down-to-earth, but I couldn't handle it.

That was the end of our relationship. I could not possibly get past that—that difference in our sensibilities. She didn't mean anything badly. She thought the kittens would enjoy it because it would feel so nice to cuddle up on this beautiful fabric. We became very close friends. I brought her out to Hollywood, actually, and introduced her to Bob Rafelson and Jack Nicholson and all of those people.

She did *Five Easy Pieces*, the first thing she did was *Easy Rider*. There was nothing all that juicy for her on that; she just was added to that group down there. And she was with what's-her-name…

DK: Toni Basil.

HJ: That's right, in New Orleans. Scientology was always her thing. She got a lot of comfort from it, which is great. It worked for her. She never stopped trying to persuade me, to the end of her life, that it wasn't too late for me. She'd say, "There's still hope for you, Henry." It was loving though. It wasn't criticizing, it was more like, "I wish you knew what I knew." I told you the Karen Scientology story?

DK: You did, but let's get it on the record.

HJ: She was really committing herself to Scientology, and one day she called me up and told me she'd been very upset when we were going together that I wasn't interested in Scientology. I honestly wasn't putting it down, I just didn't know anything about it and I wasn't interested in it. So she had me meet some guy and she said she just wanted to spend the evening with him and me. I said, "Okay."

This guy comes, he sits down, he looks at me, no "Hello" or "How are you?" He just says, "What is something you don't remember from your childhood?" I said, "Sorry, I beg your pardon?" He said, "If you don't mind my asking you, is there something specific you *don't* remember from your childhood?" I said, "I'm sure there's a lot of things I *don't* remember." He said, "Well, tell me one specific thing." I said,

"Any kind of thing?" He said, "Anything at all. Something about your bedroom, your childhood bedroom." I said, "I don't remember that my childhood bedroom was painted black." He said, "Thank you. Now tell me one thing that you don't remember about your childhood." I said, "I just told you." He said, "Would you tell me another thing that you don't remember about your childhood?" So I said, "I don't remember that I could walk out of the window, crawl down eleven stories, and go across the street to Temple Shaareth Israel, where I was bar mitzvahed." And he said, "Thank you. Tell me one thing you don't remember…" I said, "You're just going to keep asking me the same question?" He said, "You don't want me to ask you that? Tell me why you don't want me to ask you that." I was losing my nerve and I said, "What is this?" And it was some process that they were using. I said, "I'm sorry, this is silly. I'm not going to play this game anymore." He said, "Thank you. Why don't you want to play this game anymore?" And I said, basically, "Fuck off." And Karen was suffering because I didn't behave well.

Keep in mind, we were going out to the movies together every Saturday night. We had a standing date, although we were no longer boyfriend and girlfriend. So on the next movie night, she didn't show up. So I call her, and a man answers, "Karen does not exist on the same planet that you do. You do not exist," and hung up the phone. I called again, because I was scared someone had kidnapped her. "She does not want to talk to you. You do not exist." The words "you do not exist" kept coming up. This was, of course, strange because, according to my perception, I was existing. I couldn't grasp what was going on until I realized this was part of her group that was protecting her against me, though I wasn't sure why. For two years, we didn't see each other. Even though we ran in the same crowd, we would avoid talking to each other. One day, she comes up to me and says, "Hi," in that irrepressible Karen manner, really warm and friendly. "Hi, pookie." I said, "Hi, are we talking?" She said, "Oh sure, I did my E-meter and I can say 'Henry Jaglom' and nothing happens. It's just steady. Before, I had to disconnect, because it was like with my father. The meter would go wild. I spent two years working toward this." I said, "Okay, let's go to a movie!" We never spoke of it again.

DK: You were a temporary suppressive person, it seems.

HJ: This was around 1975 or '76. You know, everyone finds their own path. She had found her path, and was the most charming, lovely, sweet, happy person possible.

DK: I think you know this… I think Karen or [her husband] Stephen told me this: Jack Nicholson used to call Karen "Blacky." Do you know who he called "Whitey"?

HJ: Oh yeah, what's her name?

DK: Carol Kane.

HJ: I used to see her all the time at Café Central in Manhattan.

DK: She has a funny little cameo in *Can She Bake a Cherry Pie?*

HJ: Oh, that's right!

DK: She's in it for just a moment, and she doesn't say anything. Blink and you'll miss her.

HJ: Yeah, we'd always hang out there. A whole bunch of us.

DK: How did you first meet Karen?

HJ: Philip Proctor was a friend of mine, an actor. I wanted him for a play, and we were discussing it one night at Jim Downey's Steak House. He left for the phone, came back over, and said, "My girlfriend is going to come over." I said, "You have a girlfriend?" "You'll love her. You'll just go crazy for her. She's the greatest girl in the world, and I'm going to marry her." I said, "Wow, Phil, that's fantastic!" We were both still very young. Then Karen shows up and we're sitting in these booths, and Karen and I start looking at each other. Long story short, she got something in her finger. I don't know what it was, whether it was a bit of a pencil, or splinter, or a piece of glass, or something scary. But she didn't shout, she didn't scream, but she did say, "I have to go to the hospital." So Phil and I accompanied her to the emergency room. This was like 2:30 in the morning. She didn't make a single noise as they were prying it out, she just concentrated on it. She just stared at it, they fixed it. It was ghastly to me and Philip. Up to that point, we were having a very good time. We got past all that, and it was time to go home. Karen says, "Phil, let Henry take me home." Philip was a little stunned, I have to say, but being the extraordinarily elegant gentleman he always was, he just said, "Oh good, that's great! You two get to know each other!" Nonetheless, unfortunately, that evening I kind of stole his girlfriend, a situation I replicated in the play of *A Safe Place*, which was originally called *The Snow Tree* in its first draft. I always felt a little bad about that, but not bad enough not to do it, I'm afraid, in those days. By the end of the week, she and I were boyfriend and girlfriend, and Phil was a very accepting friend in that situation. That was 1962.

[*Author's note: In Karen Black's* unpublished memoir, Conversations in a Burning Room, *she remembers the story slightly differently: "I had an infected cut on my finger that night and knew I needed to go to the emergency room to get it cut open, so it could heal properly. Henry decided to come along, and as he waited to leave at the very moment he saw the knife and the blood, he broke into little red hives all over his face. And that was the beginning of a lifelong friendship. I told them I had to watch the procedure, because it wouldn't hurt if I could see. Henry was very impressed with this idea about confronting things. He wanted to know more. He wanted to know and write and record what was in the room with him, as though it might overwhelm him if he couldn't capture it. We three then went to Henry's parents' apartment on Central Park West. We grabbed jams from England, and pots and tins of things, and then settled down to eat on the floor of that fragrant, pale room. All across the lovely walls were lovely vivid paintings. As I approached them closer and then closer, it stunned me to realize that I could actually see the pigment, the oils in relief in the living room light. They were originals: Renoirs, Chagalls and the like. Oh. Oh, yes. Henry was rich."*]

HJ: I wanted her to do the movie *A Safe Place*, and she turned me down unless I went to Scientology, and I wasn't interested. Some of the speeches in that play and the film came from her. It's word-for-word stuff I had written down from stuff Karen had said in her emotional explosions. My mother would always say, "She looks like a kitten who's been caught out in the rain." The studios initially had issues with her because she was only a little bit cross-eyed. That's Hollywood! That's what they say. Stupid.

DK: That reminds me of that scene in *A Star is Born*.

HJ: When Judy Garland goes to get that makeover.

DK: Exactly, and it's, "Oh no, her nose is terrible. We need to do something about her nose. And those teeth."

HJ: Yeah, that was Hollywood, no exaggeration. One of the wonderful things about that wonderful movie.

DK: I know she wished she had never done *Day of the Locust*. When I first met her, I complimented her on that performance, and she just erupted: "That film is an example of how not to treat people!"

HJ: I knew [the film's director John] Schlesinger. Perfectly nice man—not a difficult man. He told me she was making unreasonable demands. She could be difficult at that stage, with the types of demands she made, and it was driving him crazy. He really liked her at the beginning, then it went south. I had a long conversation with him about that.

DK: Did she ever do your colors?

HJ: All the time.

DK: She did mine. I remember I was first getting to know her, and I remember we were on an elevator. She told me the color I was wearing was all wrong for me.

HJ: Yeah, she loved that. You know, one of the things that surprised us was when she turned down Lee at the Actors Studio. He wanted her, he was ready to accept her, and she said, "No, I don't think so." Just astonishing! He'd seen her perform in my play and said, "Listen, we have a policy here where you audition to get into the Actors Studio. As you know, it's free and we can only take so many people. It's an absolute policy. Some people," and he pointed to Dusty Hoffman, "auditioned five or six times before they've gotten in. But you, miss, are admitted without an audition." Everyone gasped in amazement, they were just… stunned. Lee was very subdued, never really showed emotions, but he was very effusive and he was obvious about his enthusiasm for her. Without losing a beat, she said, "I don't think I want to do this. I don't want to learn acting in a class where it's restrictive." Lee panicked, "No, Miss Black, it's not like that at all!" She just said, "No, thank you very much, I know it's an honor, but... no." No one ever said that to Lee Strasberg, and in front of the *entire* class! Paul Newman was there, and I think a young Pacino. So many had fought to get in, and there she was. It was funny, and a unique experience. She went by no convention. Richie Pryor, I remember he said, "She's not gonna be given a second chance!" I said, "She doesn't want a second chance." He was like, "Wow, man! Wow! That's heavy!" It was shocking. That's Karen!

DK: You must have gotten to know her various husbands well. Like, [L.M.] Kit Carson.

HJ: Kit I never got to know very well, and I never liked him very much. I was on a panel with him and Otto Preminger and Jack at the New York Film Festival, after *A Safe Place* premiered. Did I ever tell you that story?

DK: You told me just a bit of that. Is there a bigger story?

HJ: Dennis was on the panel too. It's amazing when you think about it. Well, first of all, this immediately followed the premiere of *A Safe Place*. A large segment of the audience applauded, while the other segment actively hated it. And the critic, what's that guy's name?

DK: John Simon?

HJ: How the hell did you know that?

DK: Everyone knows John Simon was a notorious asshole.

HJ: Wow, again, good for you! He had already seen the film at a critic's screening and hated it so much that he brought his students out to boo the movie as it was playing! It was the John Simon Booing Section. I only found out afterward who it was. When others in the audience felt they were permitted to join in, they also started booing. The booing caused the applause group to applaud louder, and before you know it, everything devolved. Meanwhile, I'm like, "What's going on?" It was obscuring the sound, you understand. You couldn't hear what

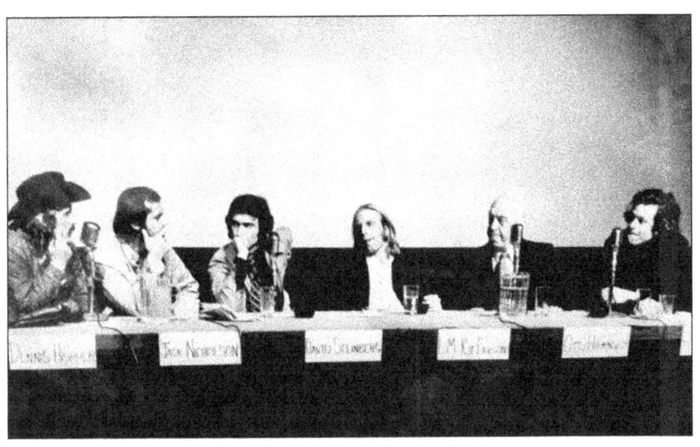

The New York Film Festival panel that followed the contentious premiere screening of Henry's debut film *A Safe Place* (1971).

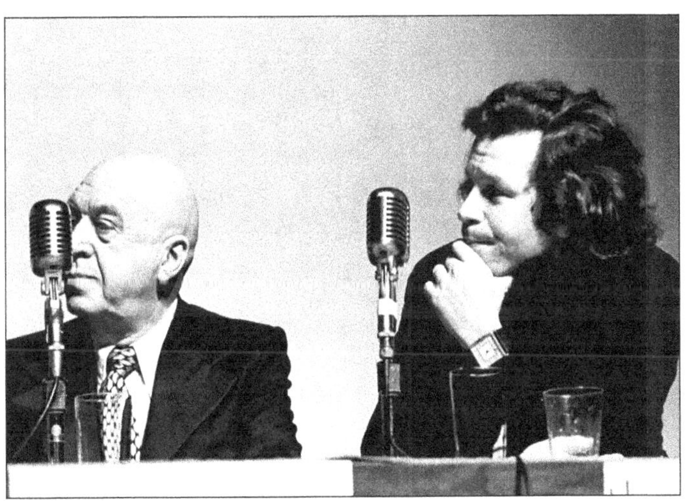

was going on in this poetic movie that you just have to get lost in. Imagine what that did to my parents! They're trying to pay attention to the movie, and the only thing they can hear is this booing and the war going on with the people applauding.

Then it's over. Then I'm on the panel with Otto Preminger sitting right next to me, which felt very strange. Of all people! You know? I don't remember exactly what he said. He was polite, I think, and said, "It's not my cup of tea," or something like that. I was trying to talk about the new changes in Hollywood and how film has to reflect all that was going on, in America and in Europe. As I'm talking, I'm getting applauded and booed. *A Safe Place* brought out a lot of antagonism in audiences. They didn't just dislike it, they somehow thought it was an insult to them, because they couldn't figure out what was going on. I never understood the big, titanic anger and hostility.

DK: Yeah, sounds like they were in need of a chill pill.

HJ: [*chuckling*] Very much in need of a chill pill!

DK: I guess Preminger would have been prepping his film *Such Good Friends* at this time.

HJ: I have no clue. I don't know that film.

DK: Kind of a sophisticated, jet-black New York comedy, written by Elaine May and starring Dyan Cannon.

HJ: Really? She's a good friend of mine, Dyan.

DK: I know, I met her at one of your parties a while ago.

HJ: Yeah, she used to come. I cast her daughter in one of my movies.

DK: Jennifer Grant.

HJ: Yeah. Which one was that?

DK: *Going Shopping.*

HJ: That's right.

DK: Looks like her mama. Back to Karen for a moment, what was *The Uncommon Denominator*?

HJ: Oh yeah, I had gone to Boston… David Shepherd was a legendary stage director, who had directed Mike Nichols and Elaine May and others, at the Compass Theater. It was second only to Second City, which became quite famous. David Shepherd auditioned a lot of people in New York. I was one of them

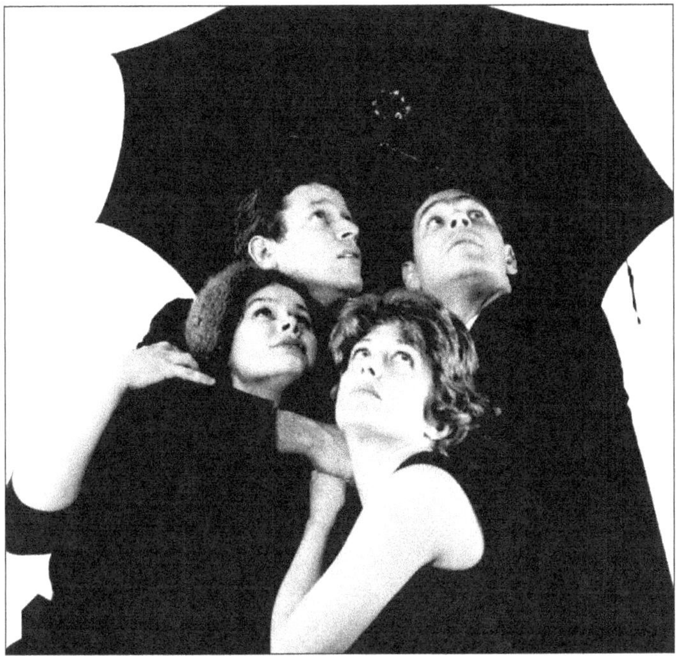

Henry and Karen Black's first collaboration, *The Uncommon Denominator*, an off-Broadway improv revue in 1963.

and I got the part. We went up to Boston to the Somerset Hotel where we performed, I think, for three or four months. We did improvisations on stage, asking audiences to participate and give suggestions. At the end of each session, we did the Kennedy-Khrushchev press conference. The guy who played Khrushchev, a good actor, had it easy because he just had to do a lot of gibberish in fake Russian. Then the guy who was playing his interpreter had time to think of a funny English translation. There were pictures of me all over Boston, calling me The Fourth Kennedy because I was playing JFK.

It all went great, Karen came up and said, "Why don't we do this in New York?" And I said, "Sure!" The next night, after Karen came up, that was the start of the Cuban Missile Crisis. I never worked harder and had a worse result than that night, trying to make that audience of people, and nobody feels like laughing. Nuclear war is upon us, and we didn't know if we'd all be alive in the immediate future. The cast was working harder to try to get them to laugh, and nobody was laughing. Then I get up as Kennedy, and I got boos and hisses, for making fun of Kennedy, as they saw it. It was a hairy night. But Karen was so impressed by that that we did it in New York, and it was a dud. We weren't spontaneously free the way we were up in Boston. We were trying to be more commercial. It was too middlebrow and now radical, and we closed in a few weeks. I directed it, and certain younger members of the audience laughed a lot. Older folks didn't get it. My folks said they didn't understand what any of it was about. Wasn't the last time.

[Author Note: In Karen Black's unfinished memoir, Conversations in a Burning Room, *she writes: "Henry Jaglom had gotten the agent Kevin Casselman to fly to New York, where I was starring in a Broadway play, to sign me. When I first got to Hollywood, I got a lot of guest-starring roles on TV, playing adolescent virgins. Henry took me to his favorite hangout: The Old World, and I watched him down cheeseburgers and write down everything everybody ever said in his diary. He introduced me to Jack Nicholson and, one fine day, Jack's friend Bert Schneider wanted me to meet an enthusiastic new director, one Dennis Hopper. Finding Dennis to be an absolutely brilliant impro-visational actor, I was thrilled to be cast in his film,* Easy Rider. *Once shooting in New Orleans, however, I was blown over by the disassembly, the drugs, the lack of any planning, and the absolutely unpredictable behavior. Embarrassed, I left the show off my resumé until a couple of years later it became the biggest hit in America. But Henry had a whole lot to do with where I lived and what I did with my life. If all that hadn't happened and he hadn't done what he did to help me, I would not have gotten an L.A. agent who drew up a quick contract for* Easy Rider. *I would still have been in New York, finding another Broadway show to do."* She acknowledges that Henry first set her on the path to movie stardom.]*

9.
"I would have strangled him
with my chiffon scarf"

In which Henry opines on Roger Corman, and he and I argue about Peter Bogdanovich's Targets *(a film in which he was nearly cast). We debate the idea of auteurism, with Henry looking back on one particular never-realized project. [Author's note: This conversation exemplifies the type of spirited debate that would crop up in the course of a lunch with Henry, at least in my case. He was always keenly invested in the stakes of the conversation, point-fucking-counterpoint, and I know how he treasured the stimulation of a studied conflicting view. I think our chats most sprang to life in moments like these—and these are some of the things I will miss the most about him.]*

DK: I know you were also originally cast in Peter's *Targets*.

HJ: Yeah, he hired me and then he fired me, and played it himself.

DK: You know, I think that's Peter's best film.

HJ: *Targets*?

DK: Yeah.

HJ: See, you're such an eccentric. That's so bizarre of you!

DK: It's such a great film!

HJ: Wonderfully bizarre of you, but… it's this silly movie with… what's his name?

DK: Boris Karloff. He's great in it!

HJ: Yeah, I was going to play the part of this movie director, which was what I wanted to be at that point. It was basically just a version of Peter himself. I went to his house, read for him a number of times, he was prepping me for it, then he decided to cast himself right before he started shooting. I was devastated.

DK: I'm not saying Peter drags it down, but I think you might have been better in the role. You can do cagey and agitated better than he can. I think Peter comes off as mopey and… kind of putting-on in it, but it doesn't detract from the film at all, which I think is a masterpiece.

HJ: *Targets* is a masterpiece?

DK: Yeah, I like *Targets* and *Saint Jack.* I think those two are Peter's best.

HJ: Oh, now you're really getting bizarre! He made some really wonderful things—*Last Picture Show*, *Paper Moon*, all that stuff—and *Targets* is like a little silly…

DK: Oh, it's not at all! Not at all!

HJ: Oh my God! What a strange creature you are! [*Author's note: Henry is the only person I've known who could use the word "creature" affectionately, as a kind of term of endearment.*]

DK: If we're talking about how powerful it is watching it today, with all the mass shootings and the gun culture in America, it's still a very important film. And the conceit of the sniper shooting at people through a big drive-in movie screen, that's such a rich kind of metaphor, one that I'm surprised *you* don't connect to more. It's about real horror vs. fake horror—

HJ: I know what it's about.

DK: It's just an exciting way to present that idea.

HJ: Why?

DK: Because it's this trashy horror film that's being shown, and the metaphor is there, if you want to see it. I think it's one of the most brilliant films of that time.

HJ: So you're more interested sociologically, not filmically?

DK: No, both, Henry!

HJ: No, those are two different things!

DK: A film can operate on both those levels! Who says they can't?

HJ: But what are you so turned-on by? The sociology or the filmic aspect?

DK: Both!

HJ: That's so bizarre of you.

DK: I mean, I'm not the only one, you've got to realize. It was, and *is*, extremely well reviewed. I think having the two stories coming together at the drive-in is just stunning. It's great storytelling. I like *Targets*, *Saint Jack*, and *They All Laughed.* Peter is all over that one.

HJ: That's interesting. So you're not liking just the film, you're responding to the fullness of the filmmaker's sort of… yeah, that's very much you and a lot of people who are on about auteurs being seen in their work, and all of that, right?

DK: I am an auteurist, yes. Devout. I respond to very personal, original work, where the personal aspect really emerges. I'll respond to those more than a superficially more "successful" work that is most popular with audiences. I want the feeling of the filmmaker with me, showing me things, showing me who they are, and what interests them. That's why I like *your* films. You benefit from that approach to film viewership, in my case.

HJ: Yes, but, that seems to sometimes not to be… it seems it should be distinct from the quality of the work.

DK: Quality in at least some cases is overrated. I find it very limiting sometimes. If I watched movies on a strictly pass or fail basis, I'd get pretty fucking bored. I mean, some films might be more popular than others, but I'll do you one more… I feel quality goes hand in hand with how personal a film is.

HJ: No, I think that you and people who think like you, like the fact that it is a certain kind of *thing*, a deviation from a tradition… I don't know, I don't know how to explain what I'm saying, really.

DK: I think the people, Henry, who appreciate your work the most recognize them as all yours. They're aware that no one else could make the films that you in particular make.

HJ: Well, that's true!

DK: Peter is more traditional. I know that, if I need to talk to someone about Classic Hollywood and the old directors, I go to Peter. For something a bit more… like, I think you're kind of a generational voice, and you're often doing something pretty sociological in your films. I don't know if Peter is capable of approaching that. I couldn't imagine a Bogdanovich

March 14, 1985

Mr. Frank Price
President, Universal Pictures

Mr. Martin Starger
President, Marstar Productions
100 Universal City Plaza
Universal City, CA 916008

Dear Messrs. Price and Starger:

We are writing to protest your censorship of Peter Bogdanovich's _Mask_, in clear violation of the director's artistic and expressive intentions — and probably his contractual rights as well.

In reversing the film's message behind the director's back, you have made it necessary to carry this controversy into the public arena. right, in the words of the nee or this fight, we support the director's right, in the words of Gilbert Cates, "to get his vision on the screen."

Sincerely,

Woody Allen
Hal Ashby
Budd Boetticher
Martin Brest
Mel Brooks
Frank Capra
John Cassavetes
Francis Coppola
Milos Forman
Samuel Fuller
John Huston

Henry Jaglom
Gene Kelly
John Landis
Jack Nicholson
Jerry Paris
Ivan Passer
Martin Scorsese
Don Siegel
Robert Towne
Billy Wilder
Fred Zinnemann

cc: Lew Wasserman
Sid Sheinberg
Marvin Antonowsky
Sean Daniel

Henry was one of a couple dozen director signatories for this full-page _Variety_ cri de coeur that came to Peter Bogdanovich's defense at a critical time.

documentary that wasn't completely reverential to its subject. But he's great as a classical picturemaker with a brilliant story-telling sense. No one is better for that than Peter. He's kind of the last of a dying breed.

HJ: He'd love to hear you talking like this.

DK: [*laughing*] I mean, movies increasingly suck. I don't like most of what comes out these days. I think the best thing about Peter is that he was hooked into the classical moviemakers he liked, from the American idiom.

HJ: This is all very interesting. Very interesting. I always say that my favorite movie is *An American in Paris*, but my favorite film is *8½*.

DK: To me, *American in Paris* is a film though. Minnelli is a filmmaker and a definite auteur.

HJ: No, but… you know what I mean, I think. *American in Paris* is my favorite for popular entertainment, and *8½* for the art of cinema. By the way, you say the word "auteur" incorrectly.

DK: I say it like everyone else I know. I think it's just been Americanized.

HJ: It's "auteur" [*pronouncing it more French-ly*] You say it like "haute couture."

DK: I know a little French, but I'll always be a gringo.

HJ: That's a great line. I want to write that down. [*he proceeds to do so*] "I know a little French, but I'll always be a gringo." [*pause as he finishes writing*] You know I got the BBS guys to see *Targets*. That's how Peter came to work for BBS.

DK: So *Last Picture Show* wouldn't exist if not for Henry Jaglom.

HJ: Highly doubtful it would, honestly.

DK: I've heard Peter admit to that too.

HJ: I've known Peter most of my life. We met in the late Fifties in New York.

[*Author's note: In a September 1992 piece in* Interview *titled "What's Up, Jag?," Peter Bogdanovich opens by stating, "Since Henry Jaglom is one of my oldest friends—we go back to the end of our teens, in*

Manhattan in 1959—I can never be all that objective about him or his work; sometimes I've been unduly critical, sometimes unduly admiring. We've each done the other some important favors. Henry got the partners in the BBS company to look at my first movie, which resulted in their producing my second; I arranged for Henry to meet Orson Welles, which resulted in Welles co-starring in Henry's first movie and eventually Henry directing Welles's last as an actor. We've managed to overcome some touchy show-biz moments."]

HJ: He would get so annoyed because he would run films on 16mm prints and invite people over. I hated the John Wayne and John Ford films, and he'd get really annoyed when I'd comment over them and make snide remarks. Once, he got so angry that he stopped the film and asked me to leave.

DK: You hit a nerve.

HJ: I just hated the macho wacho stuff, I really hated it, and you could never say a word against John Ford.

DK: That was crossing a line for him. Between us, I'm not a fan either.

HJ: Oh good! I'm so glad! I just… I couldn't stand those types of films, where the women were treated as second-class, and the men were manly men.

DK: We have the same issues there. Exactly the same! All this back and forth about auteurism, there's a story attributed to Orson that I'm thinking of right now, actually. He was directing and he told someone to place something random in frame, like a towel or something. This crew person did it and worked up the nerve to ask him why he wanted that particular item placed in the shot, because it just seemed irrevelant. He said, "Oh, no reason. It's utterly meaningless. It just gives the film snobs something to talk about." Something like that.

HJ: Yeah, he was always amused by the way certain people wrote about his films. He read the books about himself, and would always say, "This one's full of it, this one got this all wrong, this one is smart," and so on. He always had big opinions about the way he was depicted. I reviewed one of the Orson books for the L.A. Times. Or maybe two, actually. I introduced Orson to one of his biographers.

DK: Which one?

HJ: It was a woman. Barbara. Um... Barbara... Leaming! Barbara Leaming.

DK: Oh yes, I have that one.

HJ: And Simon Callow, who is the really great one, is coming here to interview me soon for his last volume of Orson books.

DK: What do you think is your... do you know the term "testament film"? It's from the French.

HJ: No, I don't think so.

DK: It means the one film of a director's career that best defines their style, their voice, their métier.

HJ: Where does that come from?

DK: I think it's maybe *Cahiers*, those guys. What do you think yours is?

HJ: I'd have to think about that. No, actually, probably *Venice/Venice*.

DK: Interesting, that would be a close second for me. My pick is *Someone to Love*.

HJ: I can see that.

DK: Friends of yours together in one single location, kind of hermetically sealed in that theater, in that single environment. That "singles" environment, maybe I should say. It has that great scrapbook quality that I like about your work, because you have your friends perform and show off certain talents on camera, and you're probing a big, big question about your generation, and the society that your generation was brought up in. Expectation versus reality, another big Jaglom staple. Orson's there, so that's also major. It's got a documentary essay... an essayistic feel, which you would develop more and more, the more you found your voice. I can point to that film and say, "That's Henry Jaglom!"

HJ: Yeah, I see your point.

DK: But *Venice/Venice* is close too. Movie dreams and how they impact the lives we lead. Reality vs. reel-ality.

HJ: Reel-ality. I like that! You know, there's one shot of that film that drives me insane.

DK: Which one?

HJ: It's the scene where I point to the camera and say, "What if this is all a movie I'm making?" This guy, like an asshole, he's holding up this lady's shoe in the shot.

DK: Who is?

HJ: I forget his name right now.

DK: Holding up a shoe?

HJ: Yeah, I want to climb through the screen and smack him. It's distracting! It's like the big, pivotal moment in that film, and there's this asshole holding up a woman's shoe.

DK: For whatever it's worth, I've never noticed that. Now I want to go back and watch that scene again.

HJ: Of course I didn't see it at the time because I was on camera acting. It's just always annoyed me. You know, I asked Orson if anything in any of his movies ever bugged him like that. I would have thought he said the cardboard crowd in *Citizen Kane*, which always bugged me because you can tell these are not real people. It's the only thing in the movie that looks fake. Do you remember what I'm talking about?

DK: When he's giving his stump speech?

HJ: Yeah. I made a big mistake… the only mistake I ever made in my relationship with Orson, I'd say. One day at lunch I said, "You know I rewatched *Citizen Kane* last night." And he said, "Oh God." I said, "Why are you saying 'Oh God.'" He said, "You've got a criticism, Henry. I know you've got a criticism." I said, "I don't have a criticism! But… I was surprised at one thing." He said, "*Oh God*!" I remember that so well. "So what's wrong?" I just said, "Oh nevermind." He said, "Is it something I should have done differently?" And I never told him. Then a couple nights ago I saw *Kane* again, and it stands out! Bogdanovich never noticed it either!

DK: Powell and Pressburger did that on my favorite movie of all time, *The Life and Death of Colonel Blimp*.

HJ: Not *The Red Shoes*?

DK: I love *The Red Shoes*. I love all of the Archers films, but *Colonel Blimp* is my favorite.

HJ: *The Red Shoes* is, to me, their best. That's interesting, because most artists would respond more to that one than they would *Blimp*.

DK: Well, what can I say? I love the sweep of *Blimp*, I love its romanticism, and it's…

HJ: Oh, I know. It's a sensational movie, but to me, *The Red Shoes* is the one. I love things about artists and the artistic process, like *8½* and *All That Jazz* and *Portrait of Jennie* and that great Alain Resnais film…

DK: *Providence*?

HJ: How did you know that?

DK: We've talked about it before.

HJ: Oh, I love that film! I just love it! I used to have a funny little tape copy of it, for years. I watched it a lot over the years. That one hits me at such a deep level. Just incredible!

DK: It's so underseen, at least in America.

HJ: And of course, *Sunday in the Park With George*.

DK: But I was going to say, in *Colonel Blimp*, they peopled a crowd with lots of mannequins. It's a scene in the middle, after World War I, when Clive is reunited with Theo and Theo gives him the cold shoulder.

HJ: That never called attention to itself like the ones in *Kane*. I asked Orson if anything bugged him in any of his movies. He always had a special love for *Chimes at Midnight*, and he just wished he had some extra money to do some of the bigger scenes in that better.

DK: That's my favorite Orson film.

HJ: That's a great pick. I still prefer *Ambersons* the most. I'm not griping, you understand. No one would argue *Kane* is a great film. You know, as a filmmaker, certain things bug you. You know, all this auteur stuff, you have me thinking about the guy—I knew him—he directed, um… *The Americaniza-tion of Emily*.

DK: Oh, Arthur Hiller.

HJ: Arthur Hiller. That movie gets me crazy.

DK: Yeah, great film. Paddy Chayevsky.

HJ: He drove me crazy, because he makes that one fucking fantastic movie, and the rest of his movies are junk! He makes that one great movie, and then was content to make a lot of shit. I asked him right up front, "You don't want to make another thing like *Americanization of Emily*?" He seemed to have no interest. It was almost a sin.

DK: I mean, I think he attempted a few times. I think, for instance, his gay film *Making Love* aspires to that type of thing, it's historically important, but it fell short artistically.

HJ: But he goes and makes *Love Story*, which I hated. The crew on *Love Story* wrapped that film and came to work on *A Safe Place*, including Dick Kratina, the cinematographer. All the same people—couldn't have been more different an experience for them, I would imagine. I had these white Capezio dance shoes, I had a ponytail, I was eating rice cakes which I was just throwing in my mouth all day. It was 1970, and the war was on. The second day of the shoot, they all showed up wearing American flag lapel pins, as a reaction to me. They were right-wing Republicans and I was a progressive leftist kid, and that's why they gave me grief.

DK: Spielberg reported having the same experience. It was 1969 and he shows up to direct Joan Crawford as a kid, early twenties, and the crew was all old, gruff types who didn't have much patience for this acne-faced kid coming in as their boss.

HJ: Yeah, that was the era, for sure. They gave me grief because I couldn't answer their questions. "Why do you want the shot?" I said, "I don't know, but could you shoot it through here?" "No we don't shoot through that, because we light it this way." And that's when I said to Orson, "I don't know what to do. Everything I ask them, they say they can't do it. 'It won't cut, it won't cut.'" And he told me, "Tell them it's a dream sequence."

DK: This is such a classic Jaglom story. I've heard you tell this many times. It's a great one.

HJ: Should I stop if you've heard it before?

DK: No, it's good to get it on the record anew, get it fresh.

HJ: Orson said it very compassionately, though. I don't know if that's been clearly said the other times I've told it. He very compassionately said, "You know, these people have hard lives.

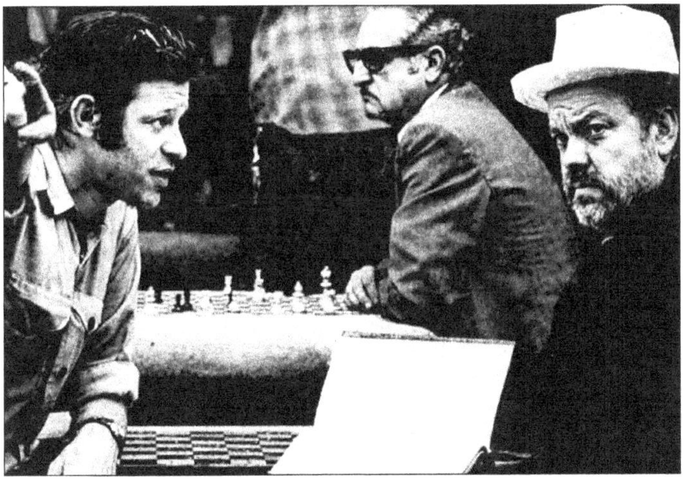

Henry directs Orson Welles in *A Safe Place* (1971)
during the summer of 1970 in New York.

They work, and they go home and rest. It's not full of easy diversions and a lot of luxury."

DK: Artistic fancy and all of that too, probably.

HJ: It wasn't about that. It wasn't about artistic diversion. Nothing to do with that. It's that they think of life as very structured.

DK: Right.

HJ: That's the key here. Because their lives are very structured, there's only one place in their life where structure is not important, and that's in their dreams. So if you tell them it's a dream sequence, they understand that all the rules can be thrown out. If you tell them it's poetic and you're just trying a different angle, they won't understand it. Or if you tell them it's artistic and you want to break the rules because it's a creative idea, they won't get it. But if you give them something about its relationship to dreams, they completely understand you. And that's what happened. And I must tell you that, to this day—I've made twenty movies—I think there's at least one time in each movie, somebody has said, "I can't do that" or "That won't work," and I use the dream sequence advice, and that person totally folds their resistance. It wasn't just that they gave up and didn't fight with me, but that they actually got it. That freed them. And the crew on *A Safe Place*, not only did they do what I asked, they started volunteering crazy ideas for "psychedelic shots," as Dick Kratina termed it.

It was a very interesting, very keen sociological observation on Orson's part, that people are coming from a certain socioeconomic class and it's all about work. They're lucky because they got good union jobs, and that's made them able to live pretty good lives—damn good lives in this country. But there are rules. They live within a world of rules. And you're asking them to break a rule about how they've learned to frame a shot. But we all have dreams that jump around all over the place. It's just amazing. Amazing. You wouldn't believe the people to whom I've said that, mostly non-actors, because actors get that. But for crew, over and over again—that is the best advice anybody's ever given a new director.

DK: I've related that story many times to others, and invoked you and Orson.

HJ: Oh really?

DK: There have been many occasions where it's been appropriate to tell.

HJ: That's good, but you gotta get the reason right. It's the rules, and in their dreams there can be no rules.

[Reference: Henry relates first meeting Orson Welles. "Peter Bogdanovich knew him, had written a monograph on him for the Museum of Modern Art. I told him I wanted him I wanted Orson in my first picture. He said, 'Orson won't do anyone's first movie.' I said, 'Why not? Citizen Kane was his first.' He said, 'I just know that he won't do it.' I asked him to tell me where he lives and to make an appointment with him on my behalf. He was in New York at the Plaza Hotel. I go there, knock on the door, the door opens, and this gigantic man in purple pajamas is standing there in front of me. He looked like an enormous grape. 'What is it?!' I said, 'I'm Henry Jaglom.' He

was in no mood. 'So what?' I told him I was here because Peter Bogdanovich made an appointment and I wanted to talk to him. 'About what?'—very stern. I said, 'Being in a movie.' 'Where's the script?' I said, 'Well, it's the kind of movie that, if you're not in it, it's not going to have a script for your part, because I'm going to create the part only if you're in it.' He says, 'I don't do that sort of thing!' I said, 'Well, I traveled 3,000 miles across the country to see you!' 'That's not my problem!' Then he learned this was to be my first film. We argued back and forth, and I told him to let me pitch him something. He said, 'Okay, I'll sit here, but I won't listen," and he crossed his arms and looked out the window. I started trying to sell him the movie, then I remembered that Orson in real life was an amateur magician. I started creating a character, of this lapsed wonder rabbi who's a magician and he's trying to make something disappear, but he can't do it. 'What is he trying to make disappear?' I said, 'Well, unless you play the part, you won't find out.' He looked at me very seriously and said, 'Can I wear a cape?' Then he asked if he could wear a hat. And I knew I'd gotten him. The ironic thing is, he didn't wear a cape in the final movie."]

DK: Back to Arthur Hiller. He would drop things here and there that intimated he could go deeper, but he just wasn't that interesting. I'm into Canadian directors, and he's Canadian, but he's the only one out of the early fraternity... he's just kind of bland. Outside of a handful of titles, I don't know what to say. There's not a whole lot there.

HJ: But *The Americanization of Emily*! I loved that film! I was very friendly with him as he was losing his eyesight. He was just a very conventional filmmaker. When I told him that Kratina went from shooting his *Love Story* to my *A Safe Place*, and how Kratina didn't like my crazy angles and all the style, he asked me, "Why did you want all those angles?" He really, honestly didn't get it—couldn't put it together. I liked him as a person, but it was amazing that he didn't understand, as a director or an artist, why anyone would go for something different. He was really set on doing things the conventional way, especially by the time I got to know him.

DK: Very set in his ways. Yeah, some directors are just content to play it safe, treat it like a job. He was good at comedy sometimes.

HJ: But *Americanization of Emily* was art though, you've gotta understand. It's just frustrating, because he seemed so capable based on just that one movie.

DK: Change of topic, but did you ever have much of a relationship with Roger Corman? I know many of your friends and contemporaries were close to him.

HJ: As little as possible. He seemed a nice man, but… you know, they were cheap. My movies were inexpensive, but I never wanted them to be cheap.

DK: Corman made and sponsored some important films. I mean, it's hard not to appreciate how *Targets* sprang out of Roger telling Peter, "I have two days with Karloff that he's already been paid for. Shoot with him, incorporate footage from *The Terror*, and you can make whatever you want."

HJ: Yeah, but that's Peter and *his* creativity. Roger always wanted something… not just cheap costing but cheap-looking. Jack loved him like family, you know.

DK: Well, A.I.P. is one story. Those days, he was at the mercy of Sam Arkoff, who was a schlockmeister.

HJ: So was Corman! He was schlockmeister too!

DK: I mean, Henry, Corman brought Fellini and Bergman films to America. *Cries and Whispers, Amarcord.*

HJ: He put his name on them.

DK: And exhibited them in cheaper theaters and drive-ins to audiences who otherwise would have never laid eyes on them. I know you had issues distributing *Tracks*. You never tried selling it to Roger?

HJ: No! Are you crazy?

DK: He put out a lot of high-quality arthouse type movies in that period. A lot of shit, but a lot of more ambitious stuff. *I Never Promised You a Rose Garden* leaps to mind. With Dennis Hopper in your cast, he might have yielded some results.

HJ: Monte [Hellman] worked with Roger at his own company… what was it?

DK: New World.

HJ: And his movie wound up retitled, recut, God knows what else. There's no way I was going to go to Corman with *Tracks*. Monte was heartbroken.

DK: In many ways, *Tracks* feels more like *Rose Garden* than Monte's *Cockfighter*. Far as I know, Roger didn't lay a glove on *Rose Garden*.

HJ: I don't know anything about *Rose Garden*, but I do know Monte was really hurt by all that. He would never speak ill of Roger because they had long history. I told you I met a lot of the people in my friend group when I was invited to see those Westerns with Jack that Monte directed.

DK: Yeah, *those* were Roger's!

HJ: Whatever. What can I say? I didn't trust him, partly just from association, and also partly because of Monte. Also, I read Jack [Nicholson]'s script for *The Trip*. I remember vividly him writing it and then showing it to me. It was far more interesting and better than what Corman did with it when he directed the movie. He made it into junk.

DK: Having met both you and Roger… I'm thinking this through—yeah, on second thought, I don't know if I can really imagine the two of you getting along.

HJ: Oh, I would have killed him if he touched *Tracks*!

DK: Not very girlish of you.

HJ: I would have strangled him with my chiffon scarf.

[*both laugh*]

DK: I know Roger didn't do overtly political very often, so that might have been another strike against it.

[*DK takes off his hat and scratches his head.*]

HJ: You don't wear a yarmulke underneath the hat?

DK: No.

HJ: I don't think I've ever asked this, but because you have that background… do Orthodox Jewish guys wear their yarmulke to bed?

DK: Many do. I never did, even when I was more observant.

HJ: Natalie [Wood] liked to talk to me about what it was like to be Jewish, which was very interesting to her, because she had starred in *Marjorie Morningstar*, in the lead role. She researched that role a great deal. She came from a Russian non-Jewish family. What year did she do that? Do you know?

DK: 1958.

HJ: Wow, that was at least five years before we met. She started investigating being Jewish. She asked me later on, "Was there relevance to doing that type of work for a role?" That was an international bestseller, and it was probably the first time they had been confronted with the question of Jews and Jewishness. She had grown up around plenty of Jews but she said it was a good early reminder about the bigger question of the Jews in America—the contribution of the Jews to America. In *Marjorie Morningstar*, that was the work to do, that was the center of the preparation. It's what she could do to ready herself. We had great conversations about all this, after the fact. It was never a superficial interest of hers.

DK: I've always found that film underrated. What do you think of it?

HJ: Oh, loved it. Loved it! It was the New York I knew, you know. It really captures something about that atmosphere. There was a script, a very New York script… it was the one I first came out to Hollywood to do. This was before *A Safe Place* and before I had a sense I was going to make a movie out of it. It was this thing called *All the Doors and Everything*.

DK: Interesting title, *All the Doors and Everything*.

HJ: Thank you. Very influenced by Salinger. And it was going to star a really young Richard Dreyfuss, and it was about a 17-year-old boy in this family. He's got a kid brother, but he doesn't go along with the family thing, with their traditions of the way their lives are supposed to be. I used certain things in my life about dating—taking a girl to a movie theater. As we come to Times Square, he pays the taxi driver, he gets out, and realizes the girl's still in the cab. He says, "What's wrong? Are you sick?" And she says, "All the young men who have ever taken me out have helped me out of cabs." He looks at her and he gives her a dollar—which is all it cost then to go all the way from 70th to Times Square—and he tells the driver to take her back home. This is his first date. That actually happened to me; I used it as part of this script.

DK: So she wanted all the doors and everything? Is that where the title came from?

HJ: No, not from her. No. The 17-year-old protagonist—I'm desperately looking for the script because I wanted my son to have it—is trying to find a reason to live, to justify his being alive. And all this stuff happens to him. Very Salingeresque. He always ends up talking to bears in the zoo. This was the Central Park Zoo as it was back then. There's a great scene where these two little girls walk up to him and ask what he's doing. He says, "I'm talking to the bears." "You can't talk to bears!" And they're leaving and the one says, "Ok, bye bye, crazy." The whole thing is him trying to figure out if he's going crazy. I had two friends who I was considering to play the part. Richard Dreyuss, or Rick Dreyfuss as we called him, and John Rubinstein, who was the son of the pianist Arthur Rubinstein, who Orson said was the greatest of all pianists. They both would have been perfect. I went to offices and agents, agents, agents, literary agents and talent agents. Couldn't get it done. I would go to places like MGM by taxi because I still couldn't drive yet at that point.

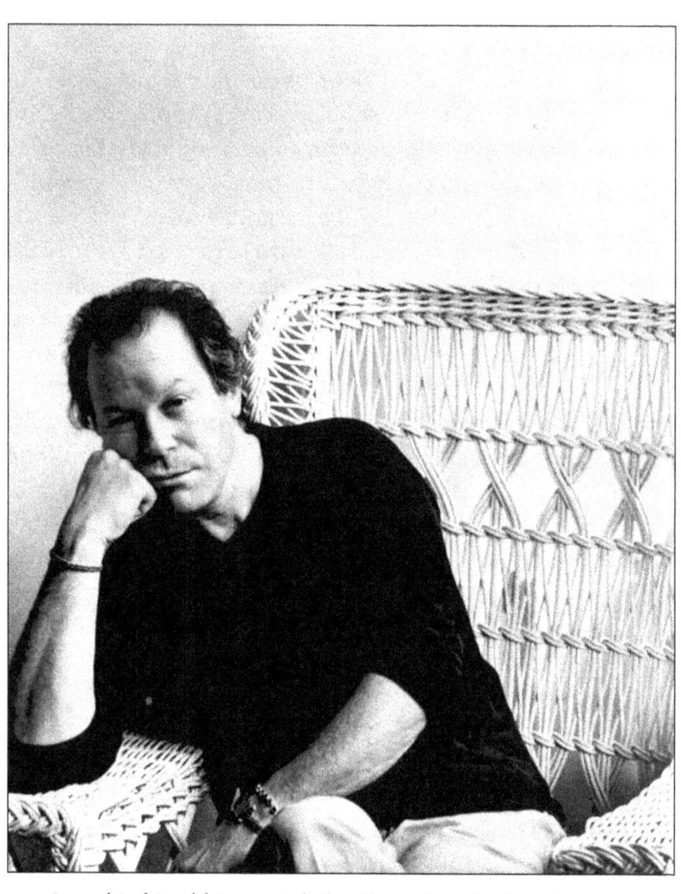

Seated in his old Sunset Blvd. office, where he lensed scenes from a number of his movies, notably *Venice/Venice*.

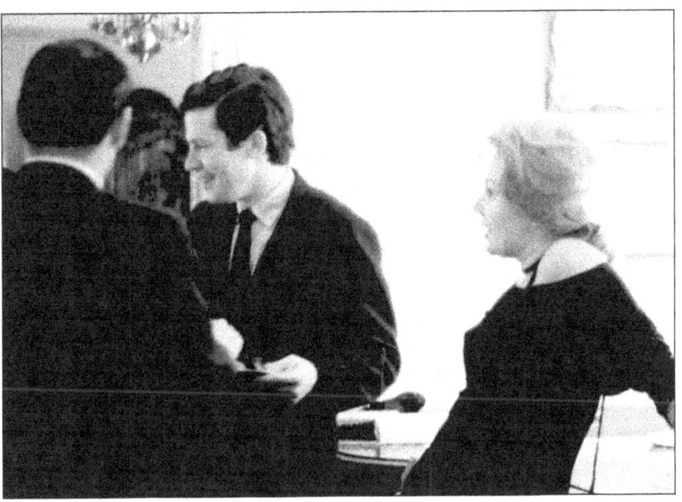

Henry was a "king of the Stardust Ballroom" from early on.
His parties were legendary, from the early Sixties onward.
One might have even called him a "prodigy of parties."

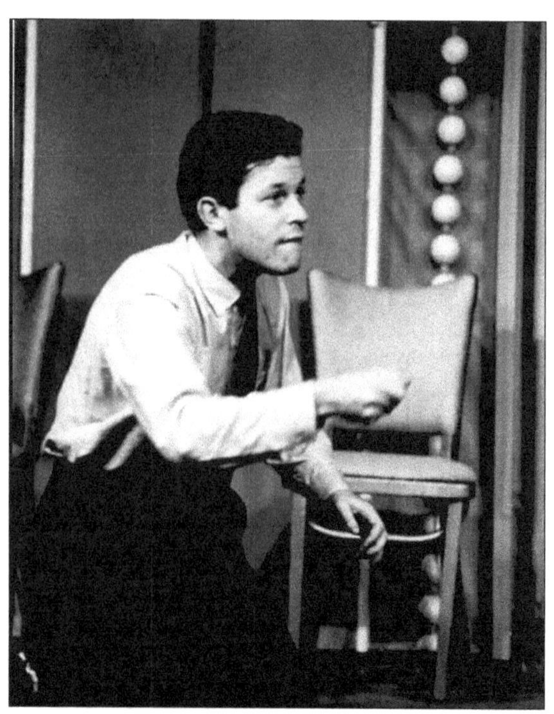

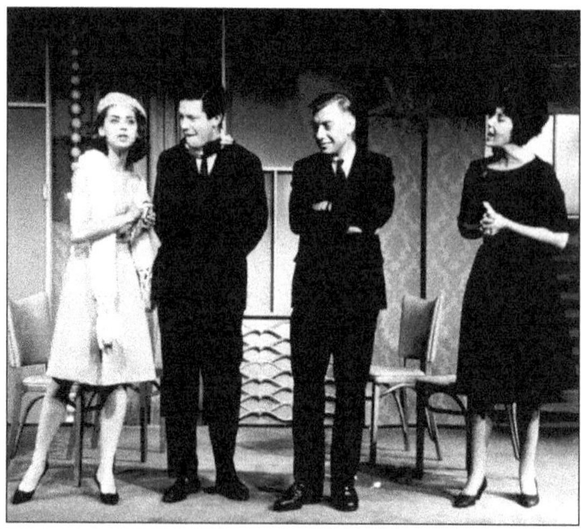

Henry as a member of the Compass Theater improv troupe in
Boston, with Peg Shirley, Freya Manston, Leslie J. Stark, and
Philip Baker Hall.

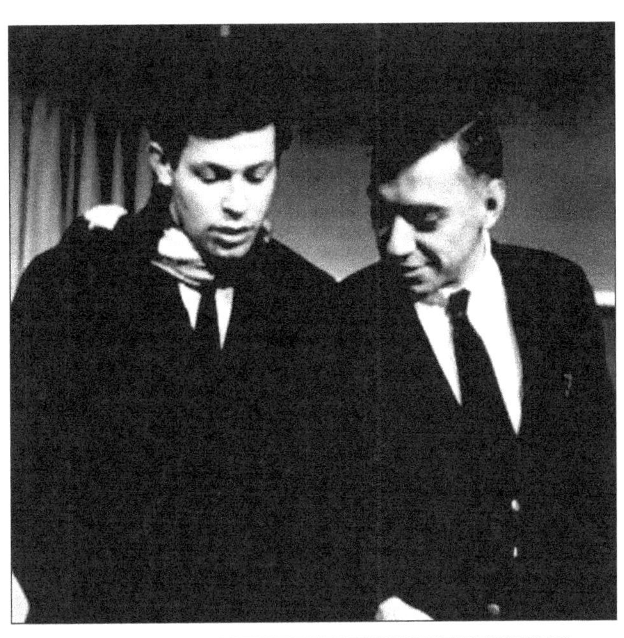

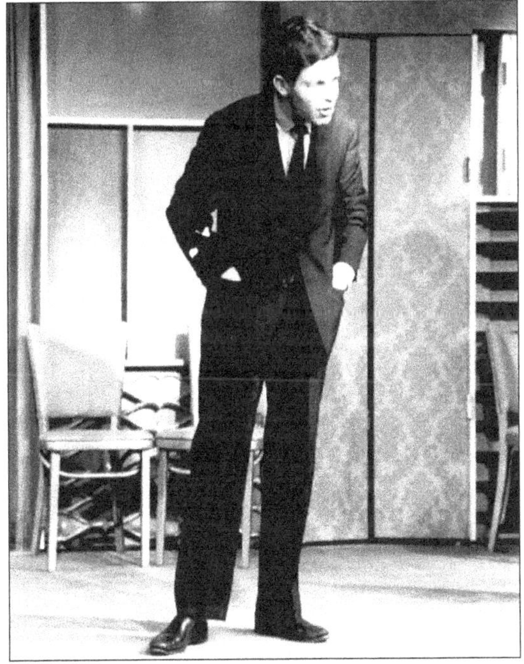

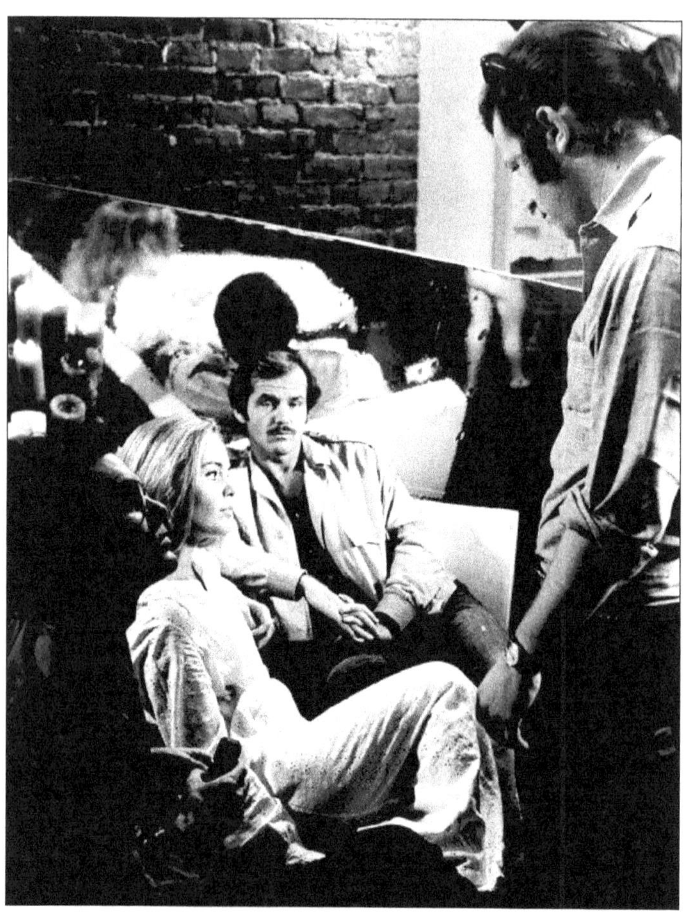

Directing Philip Proctor, Tuesday Weld, and Jack Nicholson
in his debut feature *A Safe Place* (1971).

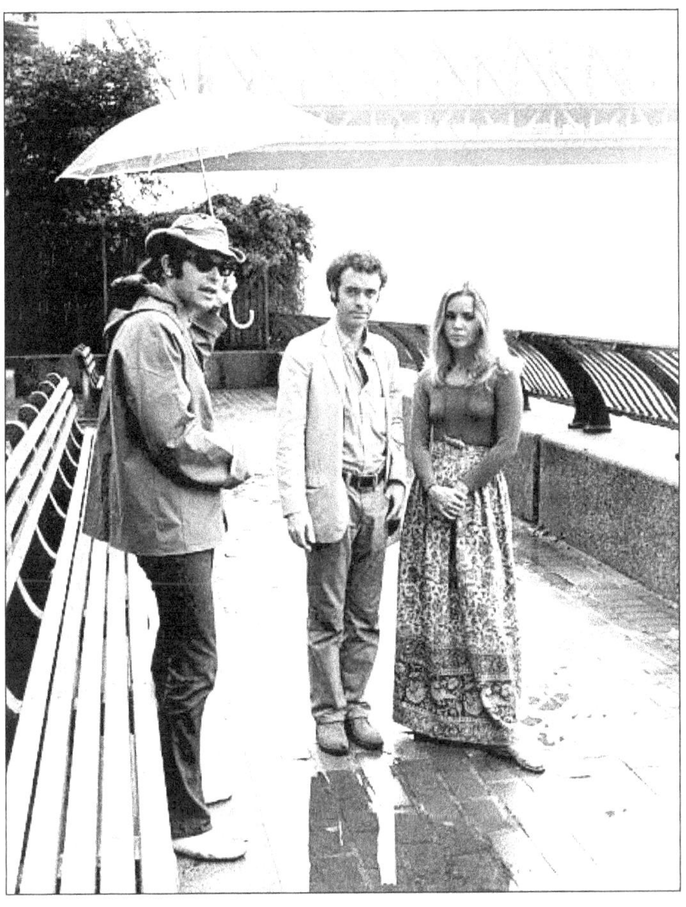

"I had a ponytail and wore these white Capezio dance shoes. The crew on *A Safe Place* obviously clearly didn't think much of me, based on my appearance," Henry remembered.
"They were conservative and wore American flag lapel pins every day after first meeting me."

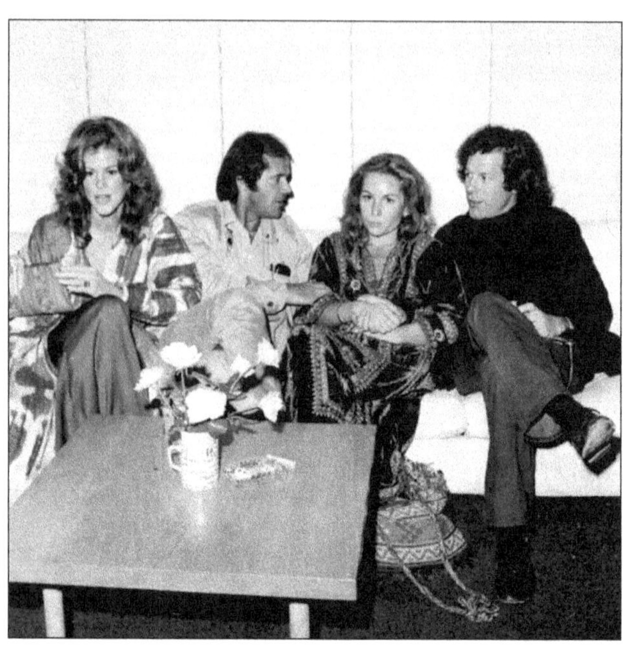

The after-party for *A Safe Place*, when it had premiered at the
New York Film Festival. Included in the photos are Barbara Flood,
Jack Nicholson, Tuesday Weld, Philip Proctor, and Henry.

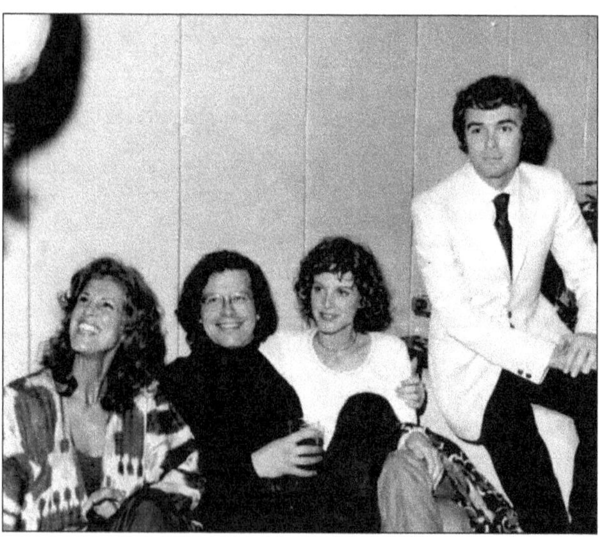

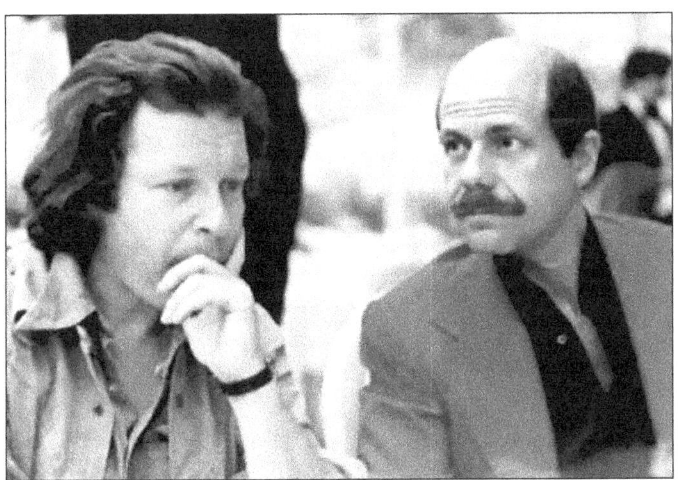

Henry met Zack Norman, a.k.a. Howard Zuker, shortly after
A Safe Place tanked critically and commercially. Without Zack,
it's unlikely Henry could have raised money for further films.
He became a Jaglom mainstay: producer, member of his
repertory company of actors, and friend.

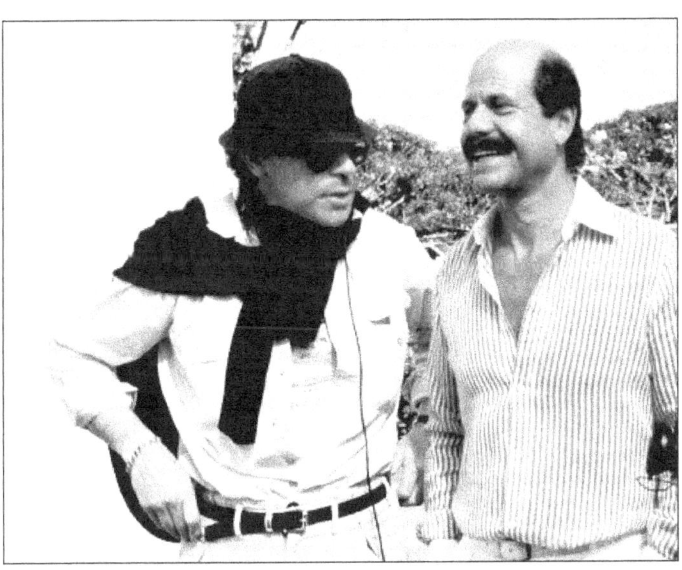

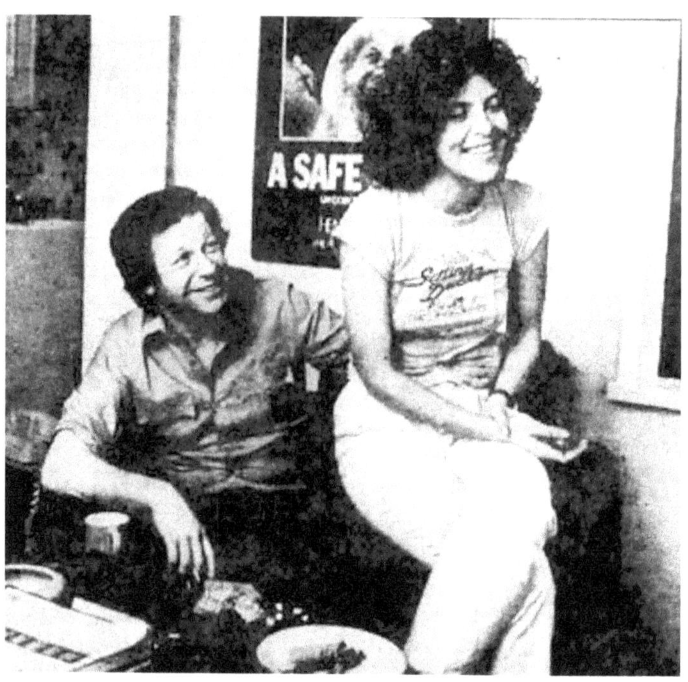

It didn't seem like a match made in heaven at first.
Henry's first wife Patrice Townsend stormed out of their first
meeting, only to discover during her furious exit that Henry had
directed one of her favorite films, *A Safe Place*. They collaborated
together on four films, as well as many unproduced scripts/projects.

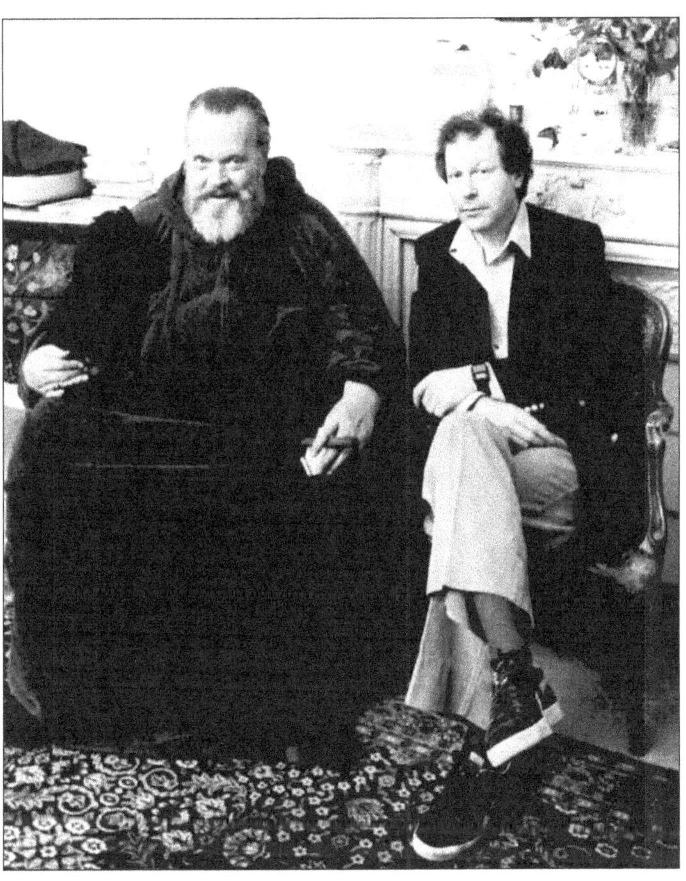

Henry's friendship with Orson Welles has been the subject of much conversation and debate—good and bad, informed and uninformed, speculative and grounded. It cannot be argued how committed the two men were to each other. In fact, they were inseparable during Orson's final years.

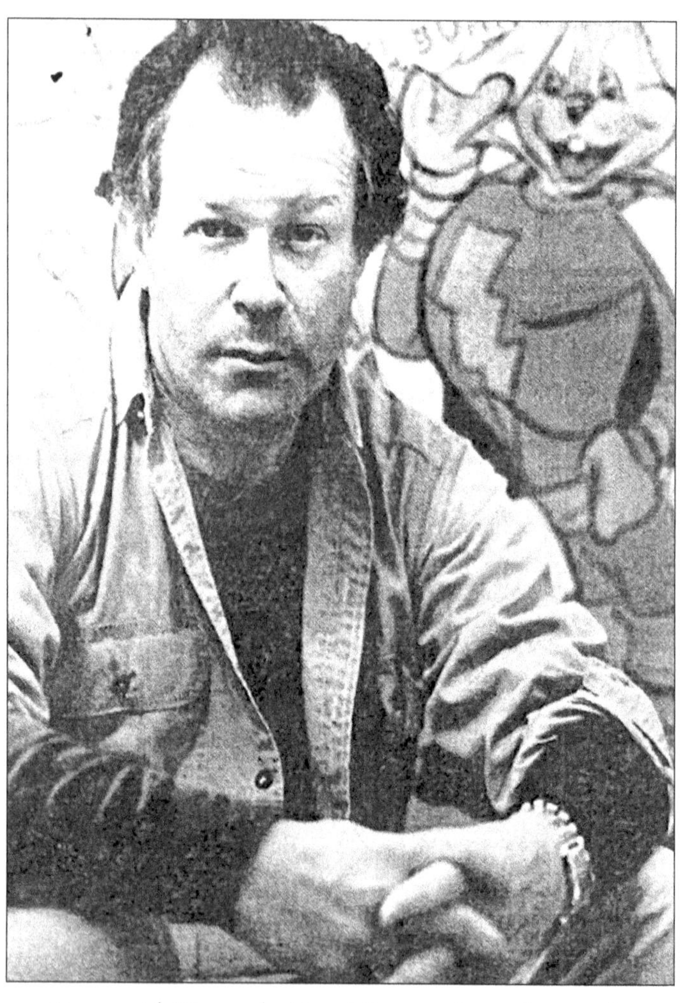

Henry with Hoppy the Marvel Bunny, who made a couple
of appearances in the dialogue of Henry's movies.
So many of Henry's films both reference and memorialize
a childhood he considered halcyon. Old home movies and
artifacts from his formative years are stitched into their fabric.

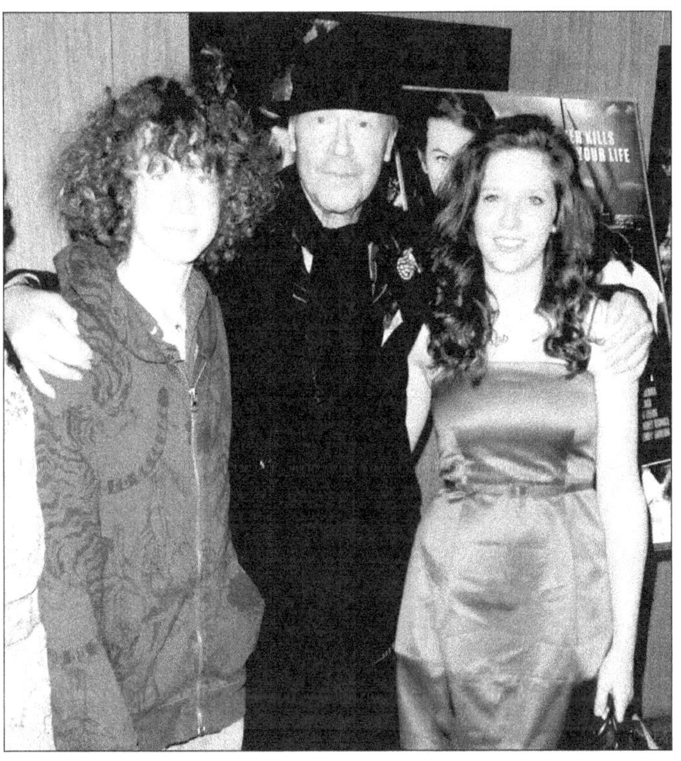

Henry was among the most committed of Hollywood fathers
—a rare family man in a town where that often proves
challenging. His daughter Sabrina and son Simon were the
apples of his eye.

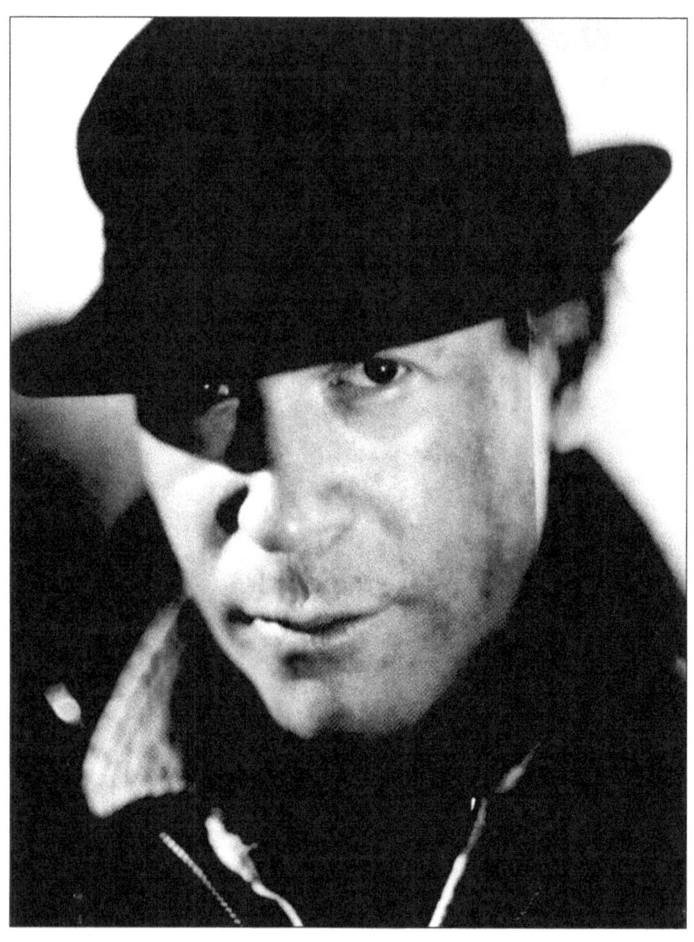

One of the classic Jaglomian head shots.

10.
"Did the magician make you disappear?"

In which Henry waxes nostalgic for his days as a stand-up comic, discusses the first star-studded party he ever threw in early Sixties New York, and ruminates on his biggest regret and his biggest weakness (which go hand-in-hand).

DK: I feel like I know about Henry the director, Henry the actor, Henry the writer, but very little about Henry the stand-up comic.

HJ: I saw Lenny Bruce perform once in Hollywood, and it blew my mind completely. I saw him in a period when a lot of hostile people were shouting back at him. It was a tentative time already, with the threat of police coming in to shut him down, and he was making comments related to that threat, daring anyone in the audience who was secretly there from the police to do something about it. He was taunting them and walking on the edge… or he made us think we were walking on the edge. I knew his wife…

DK: Honey?

HJ: Honey?

DK: Valerie Perrine plays her in Bob Fosse's movie. She was a stripper.

HJ: I maybe met her, but who was his wife when he died?

DK: I'm not sure.

HJ: Can you look it up? I can't remember right now. Names are the first to go. We used to hang with her at the Improvisation all the time. I was there from 12:30 at night onward. I was there with Dusty Hoffman and Richie Pryor. We'd get a chance to go up at like 2:30/3am, when it was largely empty…

DK: It's no wonder you have the body clock that you have today.

HJ: Right. I'd always get in early morning, and my father would be waking up. I remember him saying, "You've been up all night again? You better be careful. I'd ask where you go, but I don't think there's enough coffee for the answer." I was always on the verge of singing that song from *Guys and Dolls*: "My time of day is nighttime." But after a certain time at the Improvisation, it was just a couple of drunks and hookers and a couple of junkies. That's where we started. I started going up with each of them, with Dusty and Richie, and that was really exciting.

DK: Lenny's wife when he died was Lotus Weinstock.

HJ: Lotus! Of course! She'd be down in the Village, then she'd come uptown to us after hours.

DK: Did you ever know Lenny's mother?

HJ: I sure did, yes. Not well, but I did know her.

DK: You know, Paul Mazursky cast her in a little role in *Harry and Tonto*. She asks Art Carney if he's Jewish.

HJ: That's funny! I think, actually, Lotus was at my first party. Did I ever tell you about my first party, at my parents' apartment?

DK: No.

HJ: The guest list was incredible. John Gielgud was there. Peter Cook and Dudley Moore, and Brian Bedford…

DK: The actor?

HJ: Yeah, the actor!

DK: I know him mostly from John Frankenheimer's *Grand Prix*.

HJ: You don't know him from Orson?

DK: He made a movie with Orson?

HJ: The Falstaff! *Chimes at Midnight*.

DK: Brian Bedford? *Patrick* Bedford was in that.

HJ: Oh, Patrick Bedford. I think both were there!

DK: Patrick and Brian? Were they related?

HJ: I think so. I don't remember how.

DK: Seems like it set the pace for all the great parties you'd throw in the years after.

HJ: Brenda was there.

DK: Is there around the time you were dating?

HJ: Yeah, we were dating. This was 1962. Jessica Walter, Roscoe Lee Browne. It was a huge party. I've got tons of pictures from it. A lot of people I was getting to know from the Studio.

DK: Those were the days, huh?

HJ: They were, yeah. Stella Adler, whom I had originally met because she was a friend of my mother's. I first met Harold Clurman because he was married to Stella Adler. They used to come for our New Year's parties every year. That was before I knew anything about theater. I started reading about the Group Theatre when I was at the Studio. And then Clurman came in to take over the playwrights unit, which we had just created, basically, you know.

There's something about that party I only learned later, was kind of embarrassing. This is off-topic, but now that I'm thinking… it's funny how this free association works. Should I tell you the saddest thing for me? One of my saddest failures, one I never talk about? I'll be happy, for this occasion, to talk about it, because I don't want to do any bullshit with you.

DK: Well, with a build-up like that…

HJ: Anaïs Nin got cancer. She started losing weight, getting sick, on her way to dying. And I've always been very bad at hospitals when people are really sick, especially a terminal. It's not a gift of mine. But never has somebody as close to me gotten sick like that. I've been lucky myself, very lucky and spoiled, and I haven't had to face a real tough thing like death, which is as tough as it gets. But with Anaïs, this was the first person that that had happened with, and I just didn't know how to deal with it. I was still quite young and scared, I guess, of facing death and terminal illness. I don't know what happened exactly, but whatever it was—maybe I didn't answer her phone call, or I didn't show up—and I've got a postcard, which I've kept all these years. It's her writing. She wrote, "Henry. Did the magician make you disappear?" [*Author's note: A reference to Orson Welles's Magician character in* A Safe Place, *a film which Anaïs Nin championed.*] Devastating. She knew that I was scared.

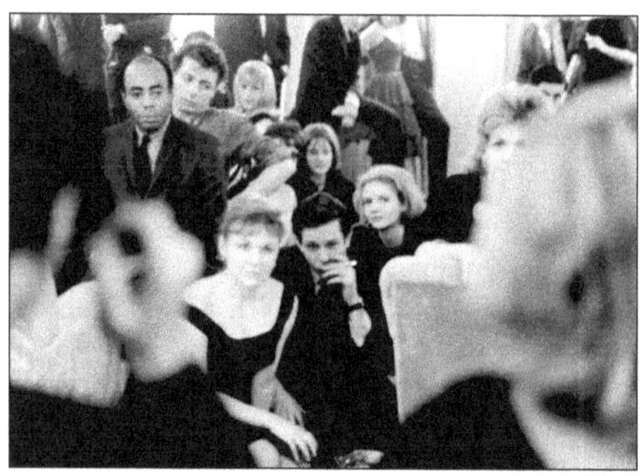

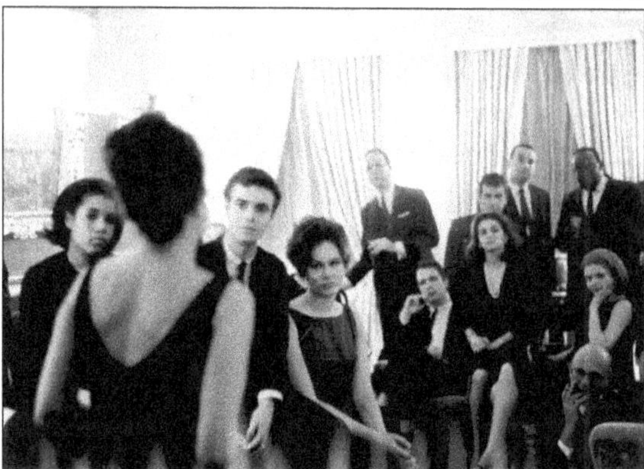

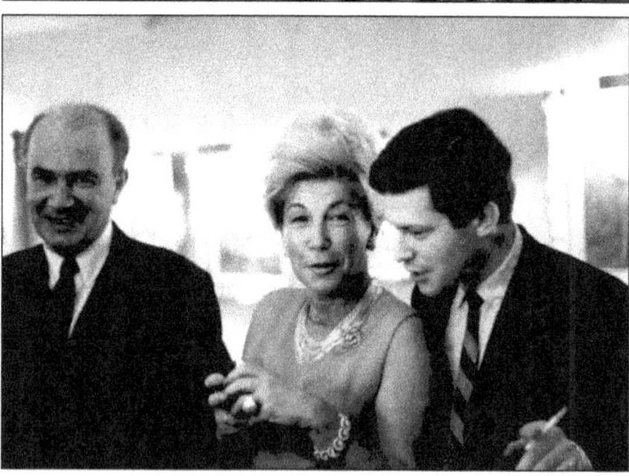

The impressive guest list Henry's first major party in 1962 included
Brenda Vaccaro, John Gielgud, Peter Cook, Dudley Moore,
Karen Black, Roscoe Lee Browne, and others.

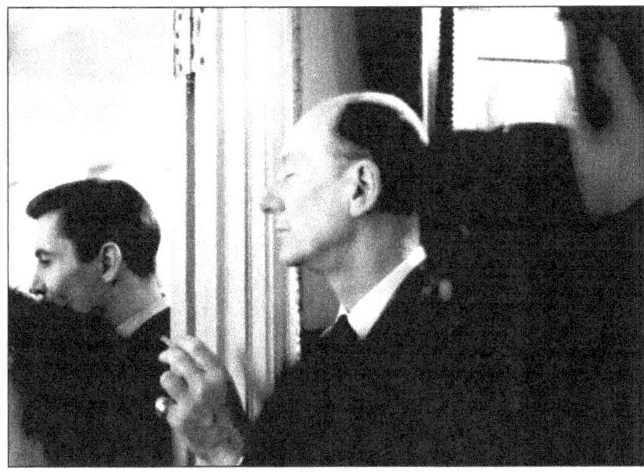

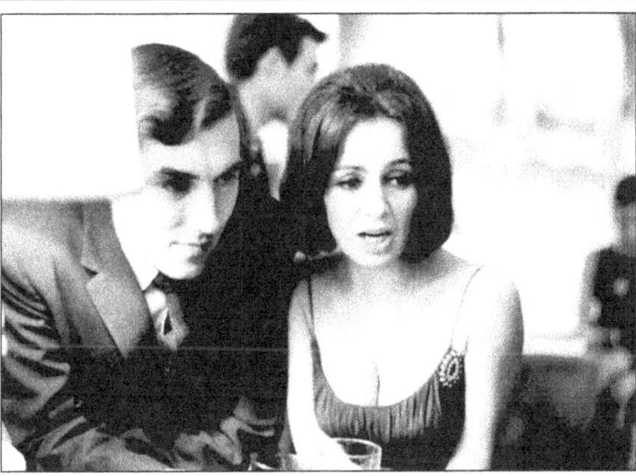

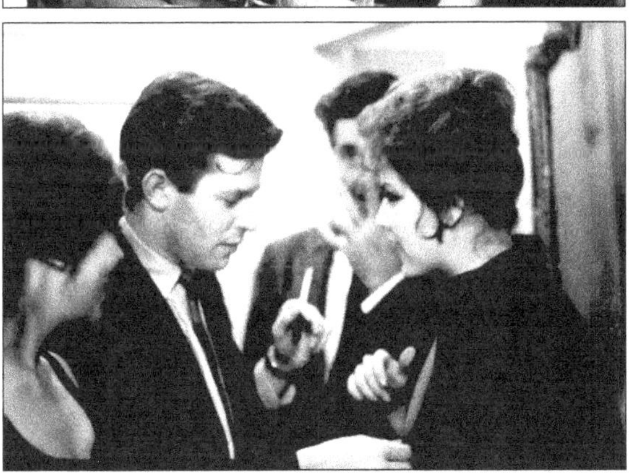

DK: That must have hit hard.

HJ: Oh my God! I still… I just couldn't face her with terminal cancer. I have that artifact among my souvenirs. That really hit me.

DK: It wasn't even directed at me, and I felt the impact.

HJ: Oh yeah, and it's true. I was full of shit. I was young and very happy to have all her support and everything, but I could not handle somebody dying. And then she actually died.

DK: That carried on fairly recently with Karen Black. Everyone noticed you didn't show up.

HJ: It's one of my biggest weaknesses and fears. I'm not proud of it. But I never saw Anaïs again, even after that postcard. I don't know, I sort of swallowed it. I didn't acknowledge to myself the full impact of that. That's my guilty secret that's sort of negative. I don't say a lot of negative things about myself because I'm very selfish, you know, a very arrogant type and I love myself a lot. But that really points to a real weakness of mine, always, and especially when I was younger. That happened to me more than once, with my friend Gwen Welles when she was dying. Bert Schneider was there every day dealing with it, taking care of her. With all his craziness and his drugs and self-destructiveness, he was there and I wasn't. So that's… that's my tragic flaw or Achilles heel. Then with Karen. That's especially amazing, considering how close we've been. Tanna went there and other people went, and she even wanted to be filmed.

DK: I was editing that material for a time. Stephen had me editing some of that material with Karen in the hospital.

HJ: Stephen was terrific. And I couldn't handle it. I don't go to funerals generally anyway.

DK: How were you with your parents?

HJ: That was as close as I got, and I had to be. My parents were the biggest influence on my life, especially my mother. My mother welcomed me into the world of women. She made me felt part of it, like it was the most natural thing in the world. My brother did not have my mother in the way I had my mother. And Michael became… not an artist. *I* became an artist. There's a logic to that, like with your mother.

DK: Funny thing is, my mom saw *Equus* on stage recently, with my aunt.

HJ: Oh my God! Really?

DK: Yes.

HJ: I can't even imagine my mother, who was very sophisticated, socialite and everything, going to see that play. She would have quickly gotten fed up.

DK: They have season tickets to the Pittsburgh Public Theater. She told me she was going and I said, "That's a real heady play, mom. I don't know if you'll like it so much." My aunt was totally perplexed by it, she told me, but she surprised me. She worked in the psychiatric field at one point, not as a doctor or nurse, but she worked directly with patients and got close to doctors. But it seems that that aspect of the play interested her.

HJ: That explains a lot. You have this wonderful, exploratory mother.

DK: She did say, "I have to say one thing though. The boy gets naked in front of everyone." She was shocked by the nudity on stage. I said, "Yeah, I know the play." And she said, "This actor…" And right away I'm thinking, "Is she going to say what I think she's going to say?" And she says, "He had such a small penis."

HJ: "My God, mommy!" [*laughing*]

DK: I was like, "I thought you were going there." She had some thoughts about the actor's micropenis. Because he wasn't well-endowed, she was amazed he would choose to expose himself that way.

HJ: That's funny. But that explains the making of an artist! It's the same with my mother. She was interested in watching all different kinds of human behavior. And my brother, like my father, was totally uninterested in that type of thing. They liked either scientific or historical stuff. My father went to James Bond movies. My mother was embarrassed by my father's taste. My father was probably the most brilliant man I've ever met in my life, and he loved James Bond and Westerns.

DK: I mean, I'm not saying I don't enjoy Bond and Westerns.

HJ: But you're eclectic. My father was a very, very, very, very big influence on my life. My mother and my father were so different and they were both gigantic influences. It's really amazing that they ended up spending sixty years together. Just amazing. Couldn't have been two more different kinds of people.

DK: I feel the same way about my folks.

HJ: But yours didn't have affairs and things…

DK: No, I'd be shocked if they ever did.

HJ: Mine had all these affairs. My mother arranged for me to find these letters when she died. She said, "If I go into the hospital and I don't come out, the key to the closet is there, and there's a thing in the back of the closet. She used to collect money there. 50s and 20s and even 100s because, though she had a joint account with my father and she could write checks for whatever she wanted, he would know because they had a joint account. When a girlfriend of hers needed an abortion for instance, or somebody was in trouble—like, once I got in trouble in Vegas and needed money—she could go into this secret stash and my father wouldn't know. And so when she died, before she died, when she went into the hospital, she said, "You know where the key is." So I thought I was going to find a lot of money. There was no money. There were love letters from five different lovers over a lifetime. And great, gorgeous—she was sharing with me this wonderful stuff, and she just wanted to make sure neither my father nor my brother came across this material.

I took it across the park where I was living at 68th and Madison, and I just had this incredible time reading this other part of my mother's life. These extraordinary romances. And it's very moving stuff.

DK: 68th and Madison—was that the apartment in [your film] *New Year's Day*?

HJ: Yeah.

DK: So, placing that, that would have been late Eighties.

HJ: She died in '90. And my father in '92, but she was gone basically after '86. Eventually she… I don't know if she withdrew inside herself. I'm not sure exactly. I could always entertain her with certain things. Otherwise, she was very quiet. She had nurses for the last four years. He took incredible care of her. He was really great, and she just withdrew. She was so used to being this beautiful woman, and flirting and having this attention based upon, you know, all that style and the looks and everything. And she just didn't want to grow old. She was the worst example of growing old. My father, who died right on his 96th birthday—at 94, he was walking a mile through the park to his office and, you know, he kept running his little empire, his world. Just, two examples, one the best example of aging, and the other the worst.

DK: Your dad also had affairs?

HJ: Yeah, I mean, I don't know much about them, but I heard from my mother, she said some sort of suggestive thing. Then I heard about this one woman, but his was reactive to hers, apparently. You never know for sure about other people. She never talked to me about hers. But she left those letters. She didn't want my father to see those. A lot of those wealthy Europeans, they had affairs and yet they wouldn't break up, you know. Once she showed me a picture of a guy, a G.I. in uniform, World War II. She said, "You know all kinds of strange people. You know people who do all kinds of strange occupations." I said, "What? Like what?" She said, "I don't know, say I want a private detective." So I said, "Yes, I know a few people who do that." She said, "Well, I mean, just say I wanted to find somebody I haven't seen in thirty years. What would I need?" "I'd say photo, name, any relatives you know about, last known address." So she brings out a photo of this really cute guy in his uniform and says, "You know, he was silly. He wanted to marry me. And I said, 'But I'm married!' But I'm just curious what happened to him." I told her I didn't think it was a good idea.

She was very flirtatious, but she was also very elegant. And she depended so much on her looks that when she got old, even though she read a book every night—German, English, French—that world so much depended on looks. That class, especially, with giving parties and having affairs.

One of those letters was one of her lovers saying, "Why are you telling me about Henry's grades in school and your new refrigerator? When will I next see you on the mountains above Geneva…" and so on. He's in the throes of passion and annoyed that she's writing him about her household affairs and her son's grades.

DK: Were your parents hands-off in some departments?

HJ: I wouldn't say that, no. They were very involved in their own lives, their social lives, but I felt cared for. Well, I will say… do I want to go into this? [*pause*] Toilet training was complicated for me, because this was during the war. I was in summer camp and I was much too young to be in summer camp—3, 4, 5. How old are you when you're toilet-trained? I can't remember with my kids.

DK: Like, 3 or 4, I think.

HJ: Whatever it was, it was my first year in camp. I was in a bunk with, I think, eight or nine other little boys, and there was a chart on the wall. I was born in 1938. So in 1943, that was probably my first year in camp. The chart was, "How many Japs have you killed?" or "How many Japs have you bombed today?" And each time you pooped, you got to mark one of the bombs. You got to check off that you bombed a Jap. Somehow, I guess you were supposed to imagine Japs at the bottom of the toilet. To think about it now is, of course, bizarre… but as a kid, right? You're impressionable and it impresses something on you. You make weird associations. And so the war effort and defecating were inextricably linked in my mind somehow. That I had this power! My mind was weird because it turned it into power. And I started winning stuff. The first thing I ever won in my life. I don't know, but I remember that great feeling of getting more bombs that day than other kids. Two, three when they got one or two at most.

DK: Flash forward to later when Jerry Lewis was filming you in the bathroom. That would tend to really complicate the picture of the bathroom for you.

HJ: I'm still convinced that film exists somewhere. Mortifying. But camp. Camp was incredibly important, and all of the teams were divided up there according to Army, Navy, Air Force, Marines. And we had Color Wars, as they're called in other places. I still get so moved by movies about World War II. You know, sometimes they're very corny, but they get me in a very visceral place because these were the first movies I ever saw. They'd show movies on these big sheets at night. I don't think we were allowed to see them till we were Cubs, Pioneers, or Juniors. I can't remember completely, but I do remember one of the first was *King Kong*.

DK: There are conflicting reports about the year of your birth. I've seen some say you were born in 1941. Others sources I've seen say 1939.

HJ: It was actually 1938. I'm glad there are still places that say 1941. I worked hard for that once upon a time. I cared about all that stuff. Now I don't give a shit, of course. At a certain age, you don't care anymore. I was born in London in '38, in January. In September of 1939, I'm a year and a half old, we go on the last ship out to America. They had bombed our sister ship and people were fearful on the boat that the Germans were going to bomb us. Our nurse or governess was apparently so nervous, really on edge, and my mother didn't understand, because my father and everyone had kept that information from her. A number of the other passengers were ignorant of it, I don't know. The governess knew because she apparently was having a little fling with one of the crew members, and he was telling her all about the precautions they were taking.

DK: So by the time America is in the thick of the war, you were 4, 5, 6…

HJ: Yeah, just old enough to remember the great war romances. Films like *A Guy Named Joe* and *A Matter of Life and Death* and…

DK: *White Cliffs of Dover*?

HJ: Oh, of course! That played a big role in [my movie] *Déjà Vu*, as you know.

DK: It's interesting the role that songs from that era play in your movies. You tend to prefer that World War II era music, as I also do. Karen [Black] did too.

HJ: Yeah, Karen loved to sing those songs, and all kinds of stuff. She was such a great singer.

DK: I remember driving somewhere with her, in a big van full of people, and she got so wrapped up in singing, I think it was "You're the Cream in My Coffee" and "Where or When" and then when the ocean was revealed to us on the drive, it just opened up before us and everyone was like, "Oh, so beautiful!" She just looked around completely lost and said, "Where?" I laughed, because she got so wrapped up in the music that she couldn't see what was right in front of her. She smiled and said, "He's always laughing, isn't he darling?"

HJ: She used to sing at the Improvisation way back in the Sixties. Dusty Hoffman and I wrote a song for her to sing, and she used to joke, "They're the worst lyrics you ever heard." It went, "The birds in heaven are lonely birds/They only fly by themselves./They always fly alone, always alone./Their feathers never feel./Their hearts will never heal." Dusty played the piano, wrote the tune, and I wrote the lyrics. God, I haven't thought about that in years! Completely inane lyrics. I wanted to be a lyricist at one point.

DK: There are songs that appear and reappear in your movies, like "La mer," which is almost like a trademark tune for you. But there tends to be a theme, or key anthem, for each movie. In *Déjà Vu*, it's "White Cliffs of Dover" and in *Someone to Love* is "Long Ago and Far Away" and in *Eating* it's "The Way You Look Tonight." I've always loved that about your films, because I love those songs so much, just like you.

HJ: That's interesting. You know, Frances Bergen, Candice's mother—do you know the story of how she came to sing that song in *Eating*?

DK: No.

HJ: She was so happy that, at this point in her life, I gave her the opportunity to sing. I remember when she first came into my office. I had this idea that I wanted to use her in this movie, in *Eating*. She immediately started crying. I said, "What's wrong? Why are you crying?" And she said, "This is where I met Edgar [Bergen]." I didn't know, but it had been Edgar Bergen's office, my office on Sunset.

DK: Really?

HJ: She said, "Is the blue bathtub in there?" I said, "Yes," and she went and looked at the blue bathtub, then she went into the kitchen. She said, "This is where he first gave me my first mink stole, and I ran down those steps so excited, I almost broke my leg." So I cast her and talked to her before I cast her, obviously. She said, "You know, I wanted to be a singer and, I was having a pretty good career. On my big opening night when my big career was just beginning, Edgar came into my dressing room and kissed me and brought me flowers and said, 'Good luck. You know, of course, that if you're successful tonight, the marriage is over.'" Candice was about 10, I think. She was taken aback and she said, "What?" He said, "Well, you know you can't have a career and be a mother." So she went out there to perform and she said she was terrible. She tried to sing her favorite song, but she was in such a painful situation, so she never had a career.

I said, "What was that song that you were trying to sing?" And she said it was "The Way You Look Tonight." I remember that when we came to shooting the movie, I didn't tell her she was going to sing that. I had all the other women sitting around on the floor. I told them, "Something's going to happen." Then I said to Frances, "I'd like you to sing a song." She know, "What? I didn't prepare anything. I don't sing anymore. That was decades ago." I said, "I'm sure you remember." She said, "I don't, I can't. I can't do nothing." I said, "However you remember it. I'm sure you remember." And she said, "Well, how can I sing? I don't have an accompaniment." I said, "We don't need any of that." She sang it a capella, and all these women started crying.

I had a moment with her that was so incredibly moving to me, because I had no idea it would mean that much to her. She wanted to be a singer so badly, and she had offers and a possible career ahead of her as a chanteuse, but… you know who Edgar Bergen was.

DK: Yeah, Charlie McCarthy.

HJ: Right. For whatever reason—old-fashioned ideals or whatever—he didn't want her to pursue a career.

DK: A dream deferred, it sounds like.

HJ: And she just did what he wanted her to. But then, on *Eating*, we were all in tears and everyone applauded and she was so touched, and she held my hands and thanked me. That was very important to her. And it was important to me.

DK: That's my favorite scene in *Eating*. Come to think of it, your movies are like *Field of Dreams* in many cases.

HJ: *Field of Dreams*?

DK: You don't know that movie?

HJ: A little through Tanna [Frederick], but I mean, it's baseball, right? *Field of Dreams*?! Really?

DK: Yeah, but you don't need to be some baseball fan to enjoy the film. Tanna would love this reference more than anyone. The idea in that movie is that people come to this baseball field in Iowa to realize dreams that got dashed in the course of their lives. They get one last chance. Whatever missed opportunities or regrets or whatever that they had, the field gives them a second and final chance. Frances Bergen got her chance to sing in *Eating*. I'm thinking of Vanessa Redgrave and her mom in *Déjà Vu*, because Kevin Costner [in *Field of Dreams*] is regretful to play catch with his father. Vanessa has that very touching scene…

HJ: With Rachel Kempson, yeah. Oh, that's so nice.

DK: A number of other examples.

HJ: That touches me, Dan. I don't know why, but it does. Thank you for making me think about the films like that.

DK: You did it for yourself in many cases—you could write yourself happy endings. *Cherry Pie* was born from a broken heart, and you gave your surrogate in that film Karen a strange but compatible partner who seems to be in it for the long haul. You give yourself and her a happy ending.

HJ: That's what you can do in art. You can create a world where things go your way.

DK: Precisely. And you could give yourself the crazy theatrical, creative families you always wanted in *Last Summer in the Hamptons* and *Just 45 Minutes from Broadway*. There's probably figurative things in *A Safe Place* too. You give yourself permission to fly away, like Tuesday at the end. *Festival in Cannes*, from the sound of things, you were settling the whole thing with Gene Kelly.

HJ: That's just fucking great, thank you. You gave me a new way of looking at the work. I appreciate that more than you know.

11.
"He's our homosexual"

In which Henry discusses his dominant feminine side, his complex-to-outsiders (but easily understood by friends) personal sexuality, his various run-ins, adventures, and misadventures with gay men and women early on in life, and the project of his that got away.

DK: Because you make all these movies about women and very female subjects and all that, I often have to explain to people that you're not gay. I try to define "male lesbian" to people, and I talk about how you've always been very enmeshed in the lives of women from the time you were a boy.

HJ: My entire world is female. Most of my closest friends are women. My mother would tell people, "Well, the men are going off skiing. Henry and I are going to go to Paris" or "go shopping," or wherever. I wasn't ever included with the men. I was included with my mother and her female coterie. I was fully part of that feminine world.

DK: Oh, you don't have to explain to me. But even with how much we've progressed as a society, people occasionally still have a hard time wrapping their minds around something like "male lesbian." I tell people that in no way are you attracted to men, sexually or otherwise. But then, someone will invariably say, "His company is called Rainbow, though," and the rainbow is an LGBTQ symbol.

HJ: No, that has nothing to do with LGBTQ. That's Orson pulling the rainbow out of the box.

DK: Oh, I'm well aware, but… people do talk.

HJ: I'm intrigued by sensitive men who are in touch with that feminine side and aren't ashamed of it, but it never meant sexual attraction. When I was 20 or 21, I was very friendly with these two women who lived together. I didn't know much about lesbians or gay people at that point. I was just out of college, and believe it or not, even at 21 — I can tell you a terrible story about myself and how naïve I was. I want to tell you that story, about my friend Gary, if you remind me. But I had worked in summer stock at 18 in Westport, at the Westport County Playhouse. I think I told you, I got to be very close with a woman named Marianne McKay, who took me under her wing.

A couple of years later in New York, I was still friendly with her and her girlfriend. They had a friend who came visiting and it was George Chakiris. George is now a friend of mine, but he wasn't then. He was just somebody. And he was the first man I'd ever met who was gay. But I didn't know anybody gay. I didn't know I knew anybody gay. I didn't know that the two girls were gay. I just though they lived together. I was so naïve. I did what we used to call second act-ing in New York. You know what that is?

DK: No.

HJ: You stood outside with all the people, because you couldn't afford to see the play. So, during intermission, you stood there and then you walked in with everybody. If you didn't find places, you had standing room always in the back. So I saw *West Side Story* twice legitimately, and then twenty times by second act-ing. You know… with Sondheim, *Sunday in the Park With George* is my favorite show of all.

DK: I'm well aware. But George Chakiris is interesting. He's one of a number of Supporting Actor Oscar winners or nominees who didn't have much of a movie career after his win. I was talking to F.X. Feeney recently…

HJ: Oh, you know F.X.?

DK: Oh yeah, we're movie-nerd buddies.

HJ: He's always at our parties.

DK: He and I were talking about Cathy Burns. Do you remember her?

HJ: Oh yeah, I knew her a bit. She was in…

DK: *Last Summer.*

HJ: What year was that?

DK: 1969. But she had no career after her nomination. No offense to Goldie Hawn, who won that year, but I would have given it to Cathy Burns. But she had completely vanished after *Last Summer*. Another one I loved is Mercedes Ruehl, but that was later. I always loved her.

HJ: She had some success on stage though.

DK: Right, but she should have had an incredible movie career, and it just didn't happen. Chakiris went to Europe and made some movies there, I think, but he was another one.

HJ: Who was the little guy in… that movie on the boat…

DK: Are you talking about *Ship of Fools*?

HJ: Yes.

DK: I forget his name.

HJ: He was nominated, I think. Tough business. I became a director because, though I love actors, I know how tough a life it is. *The Graduate* is what really killed me. I don't like talking about that. I really thought I had the part. But it's what Ron Rifkin says in *Last Summer in the Hamptons*.

DK: "If you can imagine doing anything else, for God's sake, don't be an actor."

HJ: You've really got to believe you can do nothing else with your life.

DK: So, you were going to say something about a guy named Gary.

HJ: Oh my God! He was my friend. I had no idea he was gay at all. That's the point of the story, how pathetic I was. I hate to admit that this has to be a year or two after college. So, around 23 years old. I'd been friends with this guy for five years. We're sitting on a table and I'm in this very romantic period, with Frank Sinatra music coming on and I'm mooning over some girl and at that point, and we were having a very complicated relationship. You know, she was in love with me, I was in love with her, but it was just a very complicated relationship.

So I'm with Gary, and Sinatra comes on the jukebox singing some song. "Oh my God, oh my God." I'm going on and on about how great this girl and how wonderful she is. He says, "Look, I can't continue this. I can't continue this." I said, "What do you mean?" He says, "I got to tell you something. I'm leading a fake relationship with you—a fake friendship." I said "No, what are you talking about? You're my closest friend." He said, "Can you stop listening to the music?" I said, "Well, can you wait till the song is over?" [*laughter*] "Oh God," and he waited.

I said, "I don't know if she's gonna call back because we're got into an argument." And he said, "I don't care! I don't care! Don't you get it?! I don't care!" I said, "Why don't you care? You're my friend!" He said, "Because you're making assumptions. You're making assumptions here." I said, "Assumptions? What are you talking about?" He said, "Look, I'm gay." I said, "I beg your pardon?" I beg your pardon! That's what I said. He said, "Don't beg my pardon." That's what I remember. He said, "I'm gay and you're aggressively heterosexual. I said, "Aggressively heterosexual? What does that mean?" He said, "I just feel like I'm living a fraud. I'm not telling you that I'm gay." I said, "Well, what do you mean you're gay?" He said, "I'm gay! You know, I like old men, boys, males. I'm homosexual." I said—and Dan, you have to forgive me for this because I was so green—I said, "Oh, don't be silly!" "What do you mean don't be silly?" I said, "You just probably think you are. You just haven't met the right girl yet."

DK: Oh boy!

HJ: That's how pathetic I was! I actually said what somebody's grandmother might have said. "You haven't met the right girl yet." And he looked at me like I was fucking crazy, and he knew me well enough to know that I was just so naïve. I was. I was not taking the mickey out of him. He just knew I was sheltered at that point. I said, "What about what's her name?" and I mentioned this girl who I knew he was very friendly with at the Actors Studio. He said, "She's gay too! She's a lesbian!" I said, "She's the daughter of a director." This was Robert Rossen's daughter. I said, "What do you mean she's lesbian." He said, "What do you mean what do I mean? I'm gay, she's gay, you know. Get with the program here!"

I just said, "You know, Gary"—and this is the most embarrassing thing I've ever done—I said, "Gary, you really probably just haven't met the right girl yet." I said, "I've got a girl…" He said, "Stop it, stop it! Do you know what I'm going to do when I get up from here? I'm going to go to Central Park South and pick up a sailor." I said, "You're going to go to do what?" I was trying to absorb. Pathetic! And I start saying, "What about what's her name?" I mentioned another girl. He said, "I give up, I give up." And he stormed out.

DK: Wow.

HJ: We eventually resumed our friendship. It shows you how times have changed and how different the world is.

DK: In that respect, thank God.

HJ: Yeah. My logic was, I knew him and therefore he couldn't be gay. I met him when my girlfriend was Barbara Flood; he was a friend of hers. Nobody said anything about anybody being gay. I didn't really have judgment about gay people. But my thinking was: Gary wasn't gay because he was Gary. Oh yeah—he also said, "I'm a chickenhawk." I said, "You're a what? What's that?" He said, "I like really young guys." I said, "Oh no, Gary, don't say that." But that was my that's how backward things were about being gay. No idea.

DK: So when did your epiphany come, if there was one?

HJ: Then! It stopped me from assuming, and I started paying attention. I still, probably for a year or more, had the idea that gay people just not hadn't met the right opposite-sex person. I mean, it was like something drummed into my logic from earliest life, because I didn't know anything about gay people. I went to high school in the Fifties and college at the end of the Fifties, you know. And here he was, a guy who I had known for a few years, so he couldn't have been gay because I would have known if he was gay. I felt like I was in the land of the Lilliputians, like, "There's a whole other thing going on here that I don't know anything about."

My favorite gay story, though, is my aunt—this you'll love because you're Jewish and you're gay. It's the best combination for this story.

DK: My ears are pricked!

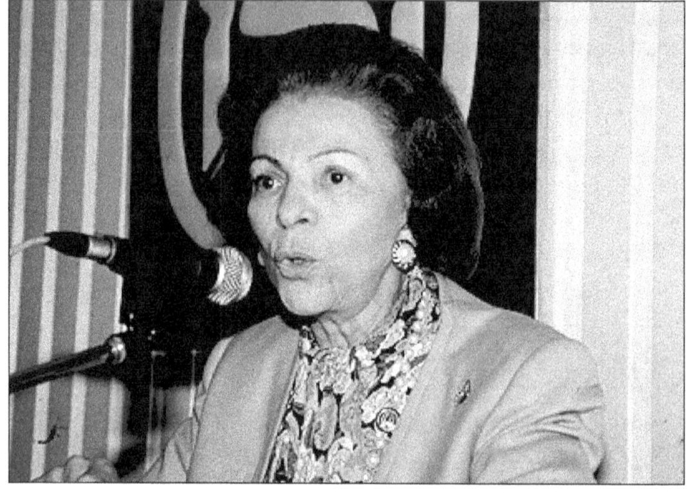

Henry's aunt, Raya Jaglom.

HJ: You don't know who my aunt is, right? In Israel, her name is…

DK: Raya?

HJ: That's right. She just died. There were things, big things, in the papers. She was 98. She ran the Women's International Zionist Organization. She was the president for thirty years. She traveled to sixty countries where she built orphanages, old age homes in Israel, and Jewish communities all over. She was very famous when I first went to Israel. The guy looked at my passport, and said, "Jaglom? Are you related to Raya Jaglom? Go through!" Everybody else, they were inspecting suitcases. Now, it's 1974 or '75. It was after the Yom Kippur War. It could even have been the end of '73.

I'm sitting at Kassit. Kassit was an artist's cafe on Dizengoff Street, right on what was then the main drag. And I'm with my aunt, I don't know how I happened to be sitting with my aunt Raya. There was another table near us, and she says, "Look, look." "That's…" she mentions the person's name, I forgot his name. She said, "He's the correspondent in Israel for *Variety*. He writes about movies and things. You know, he's our homosexual." I said, "What?" I had come a long way from Gary. I said, "What do you mean 'our homosexual'?" She said, "You know, he's Israeli." I said, "You don't think there's other homosexuals in Israel?"—making a joke, right? And this brilliant woman who runs her organization with great earnestness, when I asked, "If he's the only homosexual in Israel, what does he do for sex?" And I swear to God, she said, "He goes to Rome."

[*HJ and DK laugh together.*]

HJ: You know, it was insane. Look at the insanity of me, at the brilliant me, as I like to think of myself, at 23, saying "You just haven't met the right girl yet." It's just embarrassing, but it was just such a desert, culturally, intellectually, about homosexuality. It didn't occur to me in school that anybody was.

I wanted to do something, but several people told me not to, because I've been really interested. My graduating class was thirty-four people. Many are still alive. And I want to email, you know, "Are any of you gay?" just because I'm curious. We didn't know anything about that then, in the Fifties. And everybody persuaded me not to do that. Do you think there's something wrong?

DK: I personally wouldn't do it, but I wouldn't be offended by it. I'd answer… I have no compunction about that. There's no shame in it.

HJ: Maybe it's that age. People my age are still hardened or feel residual shame, but I'm fascinated, of course, because there was this complete false environment where everybody assumed that everyone had the same sexuality.

Tell me, did you get to know Miles Kreuger very well? [*Author's note: Miles Kreuger is the Grammy-nominated president and founder of the Institute of the American Musical, and was recognized as owning the largest private collection of vintage sheet music in the world. He was a longtime friend of Henry's, and I was introduced to Miles a number of times. On two occasions, I called to consult with on various old songs. He had the sheet music for even the most obscure title I ever broached with him, including obscure, never-recorded 1920s tunes.*]

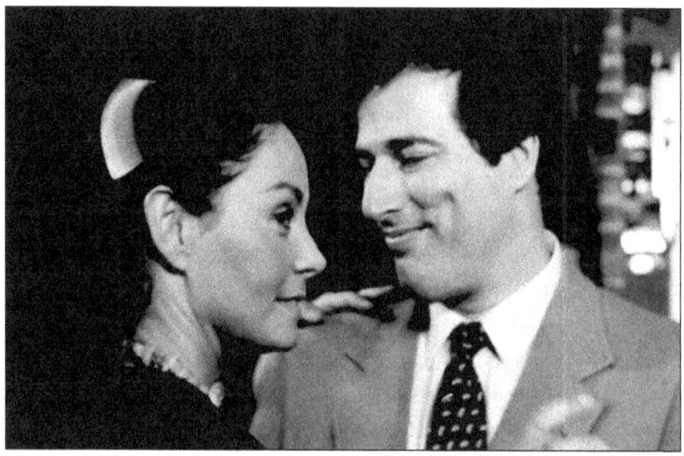

Miles Kreuger dances with Orson Welles' life partner Oja Kodar
in *Someone to Love* (1987).

DK: I don't know if I got to know him well, but I met him and
called him a number of times. I know he doesn't have email,
just a phone.

HJ: I've known Miles forever. We produced a play
off-Broadway when I graduated from college. It was mime
theater.

DK: Oh wait, I have something on this from Herrick [Margaret
Herrick Library, the Academy of Motion Pictures Arts and
Sciences]. This was on your Columbia Pictures press kit bio.
"*The Mime Theatre of Etienne Decroux*, which opened at
the Cricket Theatre in December 1959 and ran for 39 perfor-
mances."

HJ: That's it. Wow, that was in there?

DK: It's in your studio bio.

HJ: Wow. Yeah, what was his name again?

DK: Etienne Decroux.

HJ: I raised $3,600 from a bunch of my father's friends, and he
produced it and brought this great master of mime, the teacher
and mentor of Marcel Marceau. For $3,600, imagine putting it
on off-Broadway and it running for seven or eight weeks.

So I didn't understand that Miles was gay, because I didn't
know what that meant exactly. There was so much homophobia

then, and I remember somebody warned me, because I would go up to Miles's apartment and he'd play all these old songs for me, and he introduced me to all of that. He took me to 42nd Street and showed me the theater of the New Amsterdam, where all the great musicals were on the roof, and where the parties were after. "This is Fred Astaire and Ginger Rogers…" and Fred's sister. Astaire brother and sister were the stars of a bunch of musicals of Broadway—his sister was also a dancer. I loved this stuff! But someone had warned me about Miles, but I just had no idea what that meant. I mean, at that age! Can you imagine *today* someone that age not knowing anything?

I don't know how much of my attachment grew from my childhood and my mother, and how much from Miles re-introducing me. Judy Garland, for instance—he played me a tape of Judy Garland, about 14 or 15 years old, on a radio program, with what's-his-name—that funny, weird actor from *Dinner at Eight*. That gruff guy, what's his name?

DK: Wally Beery?

HJ: Jesus, you're good! Why he became a star, God only knows.

DK: His big movie was *The Champ*.

HJ: But what a weird fucking guy to become a star! But Miles played me this recording he made with Judy. And I didn't know about musicals, what the implications were about people who liked musicals. When people would warn me, I would say, "Miles is just theatrical. He's not like that." I remember thinking, "What a weird thing to warn me about, as if he was going to pounce on me." It's quite possible they thought I was gay. I dated girls, I expressed interest in them, they saw that, but they might have noticed I was into girly things.

I don't know if you know this. Judy Garland sang at the Palace, and I went and I stood there and suddenly realized I was the only heterosexual in the audience. There were no women. There were gay men everywhere. Just incredible. I didn't have a seat; I had to stand. You paid a much lesser price. I was in love with Judy Garland, and didn't know that was a gay thing. I told her this when I met her. I told you about when I met her. I remember telling her that and she laughed. She really laughed at that and I said, "I had no idea that you were so popular among"—I don't think we called it "gay" then. "I didn't know you were so popular with homosexuals."

DK: So, if she laughed, she must have picked up on that fact herself, at least by that point.

HJ: When did the word "gay" start? I don't even remember that.

DK: I don't have data on that, but I'd guess the Sixties somewhere.

HJ: "You don't have data"—that's a very interesting way to say you don't know. That's like an accountant or journalist. But it was the Fifties that I went to Judy Garland concerts. It was the first time I was conscious of, "Oh my God, there's no women here. And these are different kinds of men then what I'm used to."

DK: Would you have maybe said "effeminate"?

HJ: I mean, I was sympathetic to being girly, but I certainly didn't share their attraction with men. Roscoe Lee Browne was another gay friend at that time. I told you about his proposition to me?

DK: Yeah. Interesting approach.

HJ: "If you go to bed with me, it'll help you with women," is what he said.

DK: Gotta admire the effort… the hustle.

HJ: Roscoe introduced me to so much poetry, so much literature, so much stuff. He was very cultivated. He went around the country with what's-his-name, I forgot the guy. And they did poetry at all these things. Roscoe and him. He was amazing. But he was also a huge queen, and loved playing that up.

DK: That tracks. He always came off as extremely erudite and witty. I can easily imagine that.

HJ: But Downey's was an incredible place to grow up. You know, it was really coming of age with every show business person on Broadway, every actor and writer and director. It was so great.

DK: You had Roscoe and Roddy McDowall together in [your movie] *Last Summer in the Hamptons*. And Roddy was also gay.

HJ: Oh, of course! Robbie Baitz [playwright Jon Robin Baitz] was also gay, and he starred in *Last Summer in the Hamptons*. He and I used to tease Roddy terribly. Roddy was of that generation of gay people who never talked about being gay. And you couldn't even say it in front of them. Robbie and I used to tease him to try to get a rise out of him. So that's how weird it was with him, even then. That was in... what year did *Last Summer in the Hamptons* come out?

DK: 1995.

HJ: Yeah, even then, he was hung up.

DK: It's interesting digging down and parsing your gay history.

HJ: My gay history!

DK: You know what I mean. A history of your awareness and your evolution on the matter.

HJ: Did I ever tell you what my mother told me when I told her I liked Van Johnson?

DK: No.

HJ: The rumor was that he was gay, and I saw something in him that when I talked about why I liked him so much to my mother, she said, "Well, don't like him too much." And I said, "Why not?" She explained that he was a homosexual, and I said, "Well, what does that mean? I shouldn't like him too much?" And she said, "It's just a joke." I remember my being just conscious enough to say, "Are you worried about my liking him too much because..." I remember saying that. And she said, "Don't be silly! It was just a joke!" Was it widely known about Van Johnson, because she knew somehow?

DK: I wasn't aware of that myself.

HJ: I was surprised because she wasn't a person who studied Hollywood.

DK: Maybe you had to be around then. But with the type of gay history I'm talking about, my previous experience here is Sidney Furie, who is entirely 100% straight heterosexual man. Sidney is very hard-wired. But he would date girls in the Fifties in college, and because he was majoring in theater and active in the theater department at Carnegie Tech, many of the girls' fathers would warn them that Sid was probably gay. Just because he was in theater!

HJ: Some stereotypes were strong, even then.

DK: It makes me think of that Doris Day movie, when she says to this guy who is clearly coded gay, "Leonard, who has a lilac floor in their kitchen?!" And the guy is very indignant, and tells her, "*I* have a lilac floor in *my* kitchen!" She thinks fast on her feet and tells him, "Oh, well, Leonard, not everyone is as *artistic* as you are!"

HJ: It's funny, how the old movies did these things. I loved Doris Day. I told you that, right?

DK: That also might have tipped people off about you.

HJ: Tipped off? What do you mean?

DK: It might have made them suspect you were gay.

HJ: No!

DK: Ehh, I don't know.

HJ: Listen, whatever people thought, I was confident in who I was, but I was also painfully naïve, to the point now, talking about it is a bit embarrassing, but I don't keep many things a secret. I like talking about embarrassment.

DK: You're the only human being I know who does.

HJ: I remember this guy followed me home from a movie theater. I remember the movie—it was *Picnic*. Kim Novak does the dance with Bill Holden… she's at the top of the stairs wearing this gorgeous red dress. I was very turned on and I masturbated in the movie theater into a Marlboro pack. I went to the bathroom and this guy followed me, and I was uncomfortable. He started masturbating in one of the stalls—I heard him, and he's looking at me through the slit in the door. Before he'd gone in there, he handed me this magazine called *One* magazine, the first homosexual magazine. You ever heard about it?

DK: No, the earliest gay thing I know in this culture was the Mattachine Society.

HJ: This was put out by the Mattachine Society. Anyway, I left the theater and he kept following me. He kept pulling up his pants and kept shouting after me that he wanted to show me something. These swishy guys on the street kept on laughing and saying, "Oh, she's got a live one!" And I got stuck at this traffic light, and this guy caught up with me and said, "You don't understand, I love you!" And I said, "Well, love someone fucking else!" and I tear-assed off down the street. I couldn't believe it! I never said "fucking," but this guy just scared the shit out of me.

But it was all covert back then. I didn't totally understand, because I was so unsophisticated. I also remember Mr. John was a famous, high-priced hairdresser who lived in our building, with his boyfriend. I was 12 and I remember by mother saying, "They're sissies." And I'd say, "What do you mean?" and she was too embarrassed to explain to me. She'd say, "Well, you know." I was frequently in the elevator with Mr. John and his boyfriend. I kept on trying to figure out why they were sissies. Thank God I didn't actually ask anyone.

DK: *Picnic*, by the way, would have been 1955. So you would have been 16 or 17.

HJ: Yeah, that sounds right. I told Kim Novak later about this.

DK: You told her you jerked off to her image in a movie theater?

HJ: Yeah.

DK: Jesus, Henry! Really? How did she react?

HJ: Not well, I'm afraid. She was kind of horrified. I thought it was kind of charming.

DK: Oh, man. I could have never done that. Did you tell her you were preyed upon by…

HJ: No, it didn't get that far before she walked away somewhat horrified.

DK: I actually don't blame her. That wouldn't fly today.

HJ: I know. In a way, I don't know what possessed me, but I did tell her that, yeah. I thought she'd find it… I don't know what I thought. It was honest. But it was me as a kid, and it was mostly about the dress, for God's sake! I made that part very clear!

DK: It's hard to be delicate when you tell a story like that to someone you don't know.

HJ: I suppose, but… whatever, I didn't mean anything by it. I mean, at one point, I wanted to be a dress designer.

DK: You did? I never knew it went *that* far.

HJ: I wanted to be a dress designer, a civil rights attorney, a comedian, a painter. I remember, I was ten years old listening to the Lux Radio Theatre, which Cecil B. DeMille announced in this great booming voice [*inflecting his voice*], "The Lux Radio Theatre of the Air presents, from Hollywood" and then I'd rush to tell my mother that I was going to Hollywood to be an actor.

DK: I knew about comedian and painter and actor, but not dress designer and civil rights attorney. But I also know where both of those come from in you.

HJ: But anyway, with Kim Novak... I just saw that as innocent. She didn't.

DK: Fearlessly honest to a fault, aren't you? Would you have told her the rest of the story if she let you continue?

HJ: Probably not. The rest of it didn't apply to her.

DK: Yeah. Well... Novak aside, there's always been a market for twinks, and there always will be.

HJ: Twinks?

DK: Yeah, that's a gay category, or subgenus.

HJ: And what does it mean?

DK: Like, skinny, hairless pretty boy. Young.

HJ: Twinks! That's great! I never heard that.

DK: Twinks, bears, otters is another one.

HJ: What?! Wait a minute!

DK: You've never heard of any of this?

HJ: No! What are the other ones?

DK: Otters.

HJ: Otters are the ones who like the twinks?

DK: No, otters are skinny and mid-sized hairy gay guys. And they can be a bit older. Twinks are really young, like potential jailbait. And you've probably heard of bears.

HJ: No.

DK: Oh wow. A bear is a large, often fat or overweight, hairy guy. I can't believe you don't know this.

HJ: No, I've never heard any of this! I thought I knew things! There's got to be a joke: a twink, a bear, and an otter walk into a bar.

DK: It's not just a joke. It's every Saturday night for a lot of gay men.

HJ: I'm getting an education.

DK: But you were, to that guy, a twink.

HJ: Yeah, I was cute. Funny thing is that, yes, I found Kim Novak gorgeous, but it was her red dress in the movie that was turning me on. It was heterosexual, but at the same time, something else very girly. My connection is to that stuff and to women, there's no other way to say that. Speaking of which, did I tell you about the sequel to *Sitting Ducks* I was trying to do in the early Nineties?

DK: You told me about one you were planning on doing with Richie Pryor and Dustin Hoffman.

HJ: There were a couple. One was with Richie and Dusty. The other one was called *Lucky Ducks*, with Michael [Emil Jaglom] and Zack [Norman].

DK: That was listed on your IMDb for a while.

HJ: I decided it was so bad, and I was doing it for all the wrong reasons, mainly to make my brother happy and Zack happy, by following those same two characters. I actually started shooting. I was going to intersplice the story with interviews of various men. I was basically going to do all the stuff I was doing at the time. In the others, I was mostly interviewing women…

DK: Right, in *Eating*, *Venice/Venice*, *Babyfever*.

HJ: But I was going to try to get men talking about the kind of stuff that I thought would be important to them. They were just such assholes, giving me these one-syllable answers. And it was just a disaster. They were completely closed off emotionally and they didn't take anything seriously. I'd ask them, "What are you after in life?" or whatever, and they'd just laugh and say, "Tits," or "Pussy," or "A piece of ass," whatever. Disgusting stuff. It was an absolute disaster! Terrible mistake! I'm sorry for the actors, especially Michael and Zack. There was a lot of great stuff between *them*, but I never put it together. I just I gave it up. It was infuriating. When you ask women what they want, they tell you. And I could make movies about those subjects. Men cover up or deny what they feel.

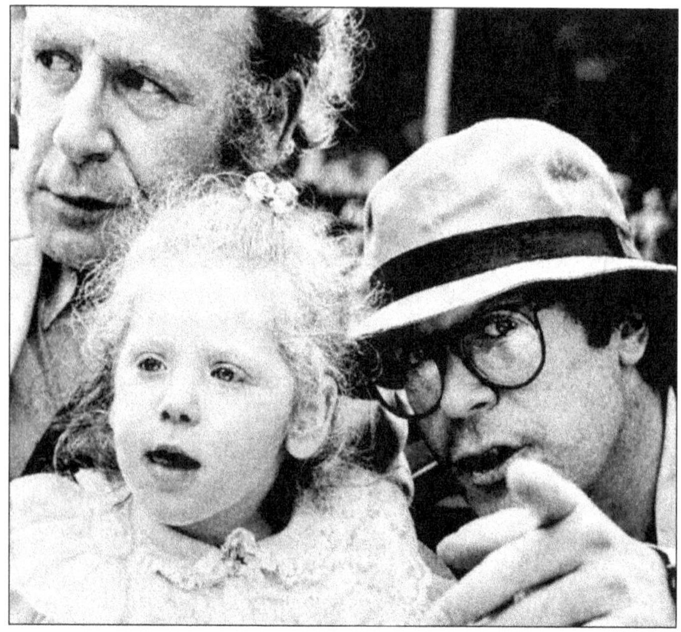

Henry directing his brother Michael Emil [Jaglom]
and his niece Ariella, Michael's real-life daughter, in
Can She Bake a Cherry Pie? (1983)

Those men were not prepared to really explore themselves at all. I got a great cast that's very interesting. I had a huge cast of men who individually had done some interesting work, like Roscoe Lee Browne. I had two women. One was Gwen Welles, the other was Daphna Kastner [wife of Harvey Keitel]. But it was impossible because the whole structure was based upon what men want. None of them told me anything. I just never tried to cut that together, which made my brother and Zack very unhappy for years. And they gave good performances, but they were not the key, the way they had been in *Sitting Ducks*. I should have left them the key and had them do the Abbott and Costello thing, but instead I tried to make something real, and to answer the question, "What the hell do men want?" and have them answer the way that the women did in my other movies. *Sitting Ducks* was, to me, nice but silly. The idea with the sequel was, at the same time, to make something silly, combine it with something real.

We went to this resort, I shot the whole narrative part of the film, and it was impossible to put together. It was just these same guys without the robbery. Like, imagine *Sitting Ducks* without the robbery. So it was the same funny stuff with Zack and Michael, but no story, no point. It was ridiculous. I didn't really want to do it because I wanted to make serious films by that point, but I was pressured. You can't make something real with nonsense. You can't do it.

DK: Where do you get those male interviewees from?

HJ: Friends, friends of friends.

DK: Where did the money come from on that?

HJ: Zack.

DK: Was there was there some fallout from that?

HJ: I mean, he could write it off. He got it from all these different people, different amounts. He talked to his lawyer, they made tax deductions so they didn't really lose anything. They still have the material somewhere. It's in a lab somewhere. You know, it was like forcing something you can't force.

DK: Did you begin to resent, the male sex more film from that experience?

HJ: I've never resented the male sex. I've just been aware of their limitations. I've kept company mostly with women. Men are terrified of themselves and their emotions, and they're angry at women for provoking them.

DK: That would have been interesting for you to somehow say in a movie, *with this footage you seem to hate so much*! There must be a way.

HJ: Twenty years afterwards, I tried to get Michael and Zack to sit down at a Kem, my Kem [film editing machine], and started asking them questions about it. I tried to turn it back into something and it just did not work. Zack kept on saying, "Come on, you got this material, you got that material. All we gotta do is shoot this and that." I thought about it, and it was just pointless. It was my biggest failure. That, and the National Lampoon thing, which wasn't even mine. [*See "The Cinema of*

Jaglom" chapter for more on National Lampoon Goes to the Movies.]

DK: You never thought about just using the bad stuff as a kind of indictment of men?

HJ: No, what point would there have been in that? You couldn't make a satire of any of it.

DK: It seems like you could have done *something* with that stuff.

HJ: I wasn't interested. I wanted to come back home, to continue working with women, because I knew I would get honest, emotionally truthful answers from women. The men just weren't serious. They were like teenagers. [*imitating*] *"What do you want out of life?"* "More, ha ha ha." *"No, what do you really want? What are you feeling?"* "I dunno. Hot. I feel hot. It's hot in here." *"No, what are you feeling emotionally?"* "Stupid." *"Why?"* "'Cause I'm doin' this." It pissed me off.

DK: I would have liked seeing the other sequel idea too. The one with Richie and Dusty.

HJ: There are any number of reasons why certain movies don't happen. That one came close to happening, though. I did get to call out male bullshit in another movie though, with I think some success. In *New Year's Day*, I play a scene with David Duchovny. He didn't see it coming at all, when I started in on him. He responded with all his real nervousness and defensiveness, but I called him out for his treatment—in real life—of my close friend Maggie Wheeler, who was then Maggie Jakobson, and of women in general. To his credit, he owned up to his behavior. I called it "the bullshit scene." I encouraged him to let all his complex male insecurity show, rather than cover it up.

My close director friend Dušan Makavejev loved that scene. Miloš Forman saw the scene, then came up to me at a New Year's party and asked to be in the movie because of it. I wrote a scene for him and the two women, using his real-life issues with women to imply an older version of Duchovny— an empty male future.

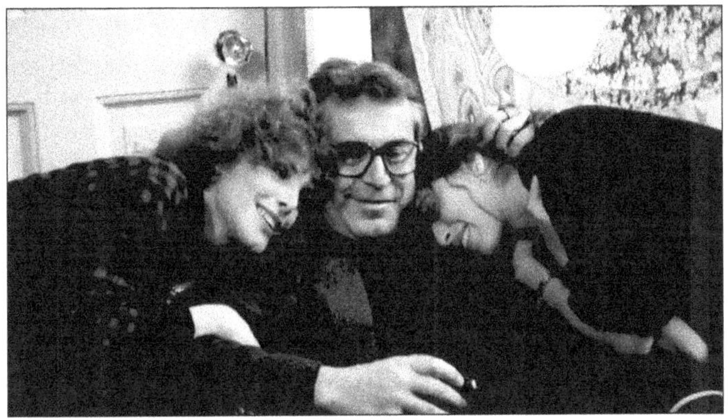

Miloš Forman appears in Henry's film *New Year's Day* (1989)
as a lovable landlord.

DK: I love Miloš in the film. It really makes me wish he'd acted more. You know, when I met him in New York about eight years ago, I mentioned that I knew Paul Sylbert, and it was kind of a blank reaction, even though they'd worked together on *Cuckoo's Nest*. Then I mentioned I knew you, his eyes lit up, and he went, "Chenry?!" with the Hebraic "ch" sound. It was so profound that I caught a big whiff of whatever he had for dinner, which was pungent, but just hearing your name, he was automatically in good spirits.

HJ: Oh, that's so nice! I don't think he's been well, healthwise. But David hadn't really acted before. He thought he was going to be a writer, not an actor, but that film changed his life. I always felt Maggie could have been a big star, but that didn't happen. Hollywood wasn't ready for her yet and only used her for comedy. She had that recurring role on *Friends*.

DK: In *New Year's Day*, you once again roast men with the character your brother plays.

HJ: Dr. Stadthagen, that my mother's maiden name.

DK: He called himself a psychosexologist.

HJ: Is that what he calls himself? That's priceless. Believe it or not, there were women who swore by him, and what he did for them. These women, I met them, saying how much he changed their sex lives and sexual experience for the better.

DK: I thought his character in that and some of your others was another great roast of the whole male thing, though.

HJ: That's always fun to do. One of my favorite review quotes was, "This film is a valentine to women and a letter bomb to men."

DK: You're such a girl.

HJ: [*laughing*] I do love that one song from… what's it called? The song is "I Enjoy Being a Girl." [*proceeds to sing*]

DK: Oh, *Flower Drum Song.*

HJ: Good for you!

DK: I can see how that would be your theme song.

12.
"Jaglom, your agony is hilarious"

In which Henry remembers Bob Fosse, which strangely bleeds into memories of his Zionist Jewish upbringing, which transitions into a discussion of the pet projects he never made, a prank played on Henry by a modern comedy legend, and an unpleasant encounter with Steven Spielberg over a movie title they shared.

HJ: I met Bob Fosse at Cannes, I think in the early Eighties.

DK: My guess, it would have been 1983. You would have been there with *Can She Bake a Cherry Pie?* and he might have been there with *Star 80.*

HJ: That sounds right, yeah. He had gone to great lengths to help me with *A Safe Place.*

DK: Fosse did?

HJ: Oh my God! He went to Columbia, he talked it up when no one was, he had some screenings privately arranged, and tried to get people to write things. Bob Fosse and Anaïs Nin, as well.

DK: That I didn't know. But you only met him at Cannes in 1983?

HJ: Was it '83? I don't remember. But he told me he couldn't relate to a film before that did what that one did, with editing. *A Safe Place* actually got to him.

DK: It's interesting, because his interview style, when he splices in kind of documentary interviews amidst the fictional or fictionalized narrative, in *Lenny* and *Star 80*, it reminds me of the type of thing you were doing starting in *Someone to Love.* Really, in a way, it started in *Always*, with you kind of interviewing Patrice in that style. It becomes this intimate conversation between the two of you, with you off-camera. But there was something cinematically Fosse-esque about your approach, once you start to get essayistic in your films.

HJ: That I didn't get so much from him. Rather than doing a documentary about why my generation was alone, I could frame it with a filmmaker character shooting a film with his friends. I wasn't thinking about Fosse so much at all. I wanted there to be opportunities to do scenes that I could set.

DK: Oh, there's no question that your style and your whole approach is original. But you can kind of see some connecting fibers there.

HJ: I did a drawing of Fosse, actually.

DK: Really?

HJ: Yeah, I drew him when we were together. Did you ever see my portrait of Francis [Coppola]?

DK: I have not.

HJ: How about the ones of Jack and Orson?

DK: Those two I've seen, but not the ones of Fosse or Coppola.

HJ: He understood—Fosse—he understood what I was trying to do with time.

DK: In terms of using film time emotionally?

HJ: Yes, because the way that people experience time is not linear. It's just not. And Fosse really understood that about *A Safe Place*. Time was presented emotionally. What's his name, who said "Time is"…"like a wagon"? No, not a wagon. "Always pulling up and going away…" What the fuck? I forgot his phrase. [*Author's note: Henry is likely thinking of the quote, "Time is a circus, always packing up and moving away."*] The guy was… I've always been fascinated by this Jew, he wrote with the other guy all this stuff, including *The Front Page*.

DK: Hecht?

HJ: Hecht. Not Harold Hecht…

DK: Ben Hecht.

HJ: Right. He wrote *A Flag is Born* about the state of Israel. Brando had a small part in that on Broadway. He, Hecht, was an American, very assimilated. And he became this passionate

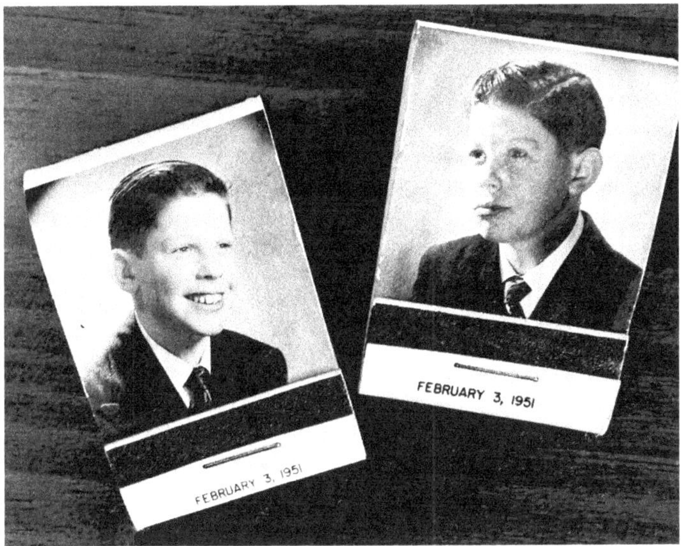

The matchbooks made for Henry's bar mitzvah
in February 1951.

Jew, very passionate Zionist. Brando was also a passionate
Zionist at one point, I was told. He studied with Stella Adler,
and he did this play *A Flag is Born*. Zionism was then the big
progressive cause.

DK: Well, Hecht also took that big ad out. [*Author's note: In
February 1943, Hecht famously purchased a full page in the
New York Times, with text that read, "For Sale to Humanity,
70,000 Jews, Guaranteed Human Beings at $50 a Piece,"
bringing the Holocaust to the public's attention.*]

HJ: Oh, you know about that. How do you know about that?

DK: I covered it in my first book.

HJ: It's mentioned in my book too. *[Henry's book on Jewish
history.]*

DK: That was when Sid Furie's first awareness of what was
going on in Europe with the Jews started. He was born in
1933, and he was becoming aware as a young boy…

HJ: Oh my God! That's so interesting. When I was about
twelve, my parents looked out the window at one of the
parades. This was on Central Park West, so we had the grand-

stand view. This would have been 1950, so two years after Israel. My mother—I never forgot this, it shows what happens with immigrants in America—she said, "Look, there goes our flag!" It was the Star of David and she was excited and proud. As you can imagine, coming from Europe and everything that happened, it meant a lot. But I was an American kid, and I said, "That's not our flag, that's our flag," and I pointed to the stars and stripes. And she said, as if she were shrugging, and said, "Okay, Henry," as if she were actually saying "Whatever."

We were very tied to Israel. My father, his whole life was about Israel. He was a very proud Jew. Being Jewish is central to me too, but I never had religion, I don't really what you'd call a Jewish culture. It's an idea for me, like being American. A lot of it has to do with trying to maintain an identity that others were always trying to eradicate. But at the time… it never meant anything to me except my thinking, 'Why is my mother thinking that's our flag?' When I went to Israel the first time, I went to Yad Vashem. I was 20 years old, and I suddenly got it. "I'm a Jew!" It was never of any interest.

My parents were always involved, and they were heads of, you know, she was in the women's organizations, he was in the men's Zionist organizations. He was president of the European division of UJA [United Jewish Appeal]. With the flag in the parade, I'm realizing now what it must have meant to them. I can't even imagine just two years after Israel when Israel was still new. Suddenly they were parading with the Star of David. This is just five or six years after the war and after so many Jews had been murdered.

She grew up in Germany, you know. So many things I didn't ask her that I would like now to ask her. I was so busy asking my father everything about his childhood. I'm so interested now in Weimar Germany. I keep thinking about my mother. She was born in 1908. She used to sneak away from her governess, go into the ladies room, put on a red armband, sneak out, march in the Communist parades and the socialist parades at sixteen. So in 1928, she was 20 or so, that's when all that shit was starting to happen. And then she married my father in 1930 and became a Romanian citizen, because he had a Romanian passport—God knows why—which is how they were able to get to America. Yeah, all those stories are amazing.

But I was so busy filming and taping my father with his stories, and now I'm really sorry, you know? Because she was easier to talk to than my father. And he liked telling the stories, but I never showed any interest in her stories. Strange. Now I'm fascinated by that whole period.

My mother used to get so excited in saying, "He's Jewish, she's Jewish," and I'd say, "Why do you care who's Jewish?" Now I'm doing the same thing she used to do.

DK: Did you parents have any brushes with anti-Semitism when they came to America? They were probably insulated by their wealth, no?

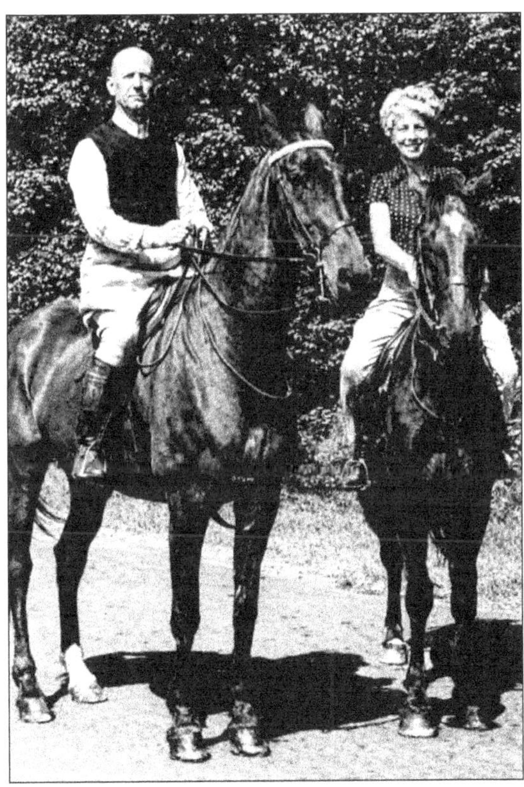

Henry's parents, Simon and Marie Jaglom.

HJ: It's funny you should ask that. I was just telling this one story to someone else. My parents—this was during World War II, and they'd recently come from Europe. They'd been in the country for a couple of years, and… I think you saw the photo of them on horseback. It's a very attractive picture of two very attractive people on horseback. So the manager of this hotel came to my mother and said, "We're putting out a big brochure about the hotel, and we'd love to use that photo on the brochure." My mother was flattered. She liked the picture, she liked the way she looked in it, and she said, "Sure, you can use it." They printed it and it came out a week later when they were still staying there. I think this was Upstate New York, but it might have been New England. This thing was spread around quite widely, pretty fast.

She was going to what had normally been her bridge game, with a few of her women friends who were also on vacation in that area. And they were very cold to her, very unpleasant. She wondered what was going on, why were they acting like this. Finally she asked one of them, "What's going on? I've got this very bad feeling," and they said, "Well, we really think you did something wrong." She said, "I did something wrong? What are you talking about?" One of them came out with it: "You put your photo on the cover of that hotel's brochure. You know that hotel is anti-Semitic. It doesn't take Jews." She said, "What?!" She was shocked. In Europe, with whatever else that had happened, they had never heard of a hotel that didn't take Jews. You know, that kind of "polite" discrimination didn't exist there, even though during the war, with all the horror… it was something that was unheard of by these Europeans in America.

So she went to the manager of the hotel and she demanded to see the person who was managing the hotel. He came to her and she said, "Is it true that your hotel doesn't take Jews?" And the manager said to my mother—and she she never forgot it, it was fifty years later when she told me—he said very politely, "Oh, we don't mean Jews like yourself and Mr. Jaglom. Of course not!" She was so offended that they were an anti-Semitic hotel. But they made exceptions for people who, in her case, were blonde

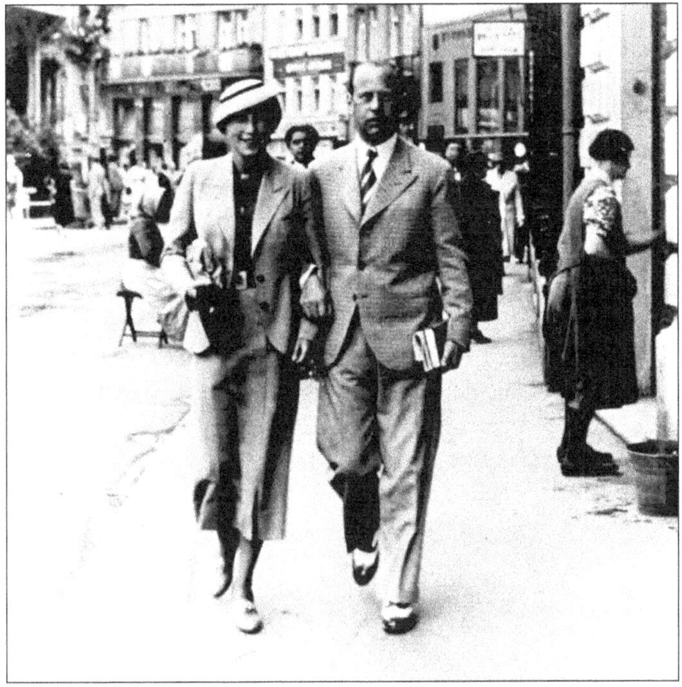

Henry's parents at the Carlsbad Spa in Karlovy Vary
in the mid 1930s.

and maybe Aryan-looking, or whatever, in America, with
America being at war against the Nazis. She immediately
demanded that they stop circulating this thing. They left the
hotel. I like that story because it was the first time my parents
had ever heard of the kind of gentle, "elegant" anti-Semitism that
existed in America. It just was like something unheard-of in first
class hotels in Europe, that they wouldn't take the Jews.

DK: "Elegant" anti-Semitism is a funny way of putting it.

HJ: You know what I mean.

DK: No, I get it. It didn't involve a hate crime or whatever.

HJ: It was polite and I guess you'd say mannerly.

DK: You were going to make a film in Israel at one point,
weren't you?

HJ: Before *Tracks*, I think it was, I had a deal with the producer
John Heyman. He was a British producer.

DK: I think he had worked a number of times with Joseph Losey.

HJ: That's right, I think he had. We had a deal with him going on distribution of other projects of ours too.

DK: I'm pretty sure.

HJ: This was a project I was very passionate about, *The Nili Affair*. I had recruited Israeli actors and an Israeli producer. It would have been my first time really integrating documentary with staged scenes. I filmed some interviews remembering the Jews who secretly helped the British defeat the occupying Turks. The lead character was a real figure named Sarah Aaronson, and I wanted either Candice [Bergen] or Liv Ullman for the part. Donald Sutherland was going to play her brother Aaron Aaronson, who was the leader of a Jewish spy network called NILI.

DK: This was a real spy network.

HJ: Yeah.

DK: So, World War I era. Wow, that sounds like it would have been quite an ambitious movie for you. It would have been your only period piece.

HJ: I had trouble with the screenwriter, and by the time I was making progress, I was shooting… yeah, I'm pretty sure it was *Tracks*. My brother was living in Israel at the time too.

DK: That must have been around the time you shot that little documentary about his sex life.

HJ: He was involved with one woman after another, making them feel good about themselves. At that stage of his life, he was trying to find women who were having trouble reaching orgasm, and he wanted them to know that it was the man's problem, that if they didn't have orgasms, it was the fault of the men in their life. And he would show them how they were perfectly capable of having orgasms.

DK: Just like he talks about in all the movies of yours that he's in.

HJ: And that was his mission. He was in Israel for three years doing that.

DK: What a riot!

HJ: Yeah, that's Michael.

DK: It seems that Candice was really your go-to at the time, because she was lined up for the Gene Kelly Cannes project as well.

HJ: She was a big star at the time too. I knew her for… well, I knew everybody in *The Group*, the movie *The Group*. I basically knew all the women in the cast.

DK: It's a shame she never did appear in any of your movies officially.

HJ: We were always very close. She's one of my best friends. Her book, did you ever read her book? *Knock Wood*?

DK: Not in its entirety, but I know it's dedicated to you.

HJ: Because I encouraged her to write it.

DK: When I went to the library [Margaret Herrick Library], I uncovered a number of other projects that were announced but never realized.

HJ: You mean scripts?

DK: No, like press announcements. There was another Jewish one, called *Ein Breira*, which I know means "There is no choice" [in Hebrew].

HJ: Oh, that's right. That was also Sutherland. That was earlier.

DK: This is right after *A Safe Place*. I have the Xeroxes with me.

HJ: You do? I'd love to see them.

DK: A lot of interesting stuff.

[**DK** *digs out his collection of Xeroxes.*]

DK: *Ein Breira*: Donald Sutherland will star as an alienated man whose parents were killed by Nazis, and Gwen Welles a drifting American girl who meets Sutherland in Israel.

HJ: When was that?

DK: December 1971.

HJ: Wow! Yeah, I was very invested in that project.

DK: There was also *Leon's List*…

HJ: Yes! That was my vehicle for my brother!

DK: …which was to star Michael as "an American who comes home from Israel and has to meet all his erstwhile girlfriends from 25 years before and make love to each of them."

HJ: Do you have a date on that?

DK: Summer of 1981. It seems like aspects of that were turned into *Cherry Pie*. I'm sure you would have had Michael going on and on about sex and his prowess in the bedroom.

HJ: This would have been all Michael, though. I would have used a lot of that footage of him that I shot in Israel—that film of him talking about his sex life.

DK: Might Karen have been one of the ladies?

HJ: Who knows? I never got to cast it.

DK: Oh wait, it's here. Lee Grant, Joan Hackett, Stella Stevens, Sally Kellerman, Brenda Vaccaro.

HJ: Really?

DK: Yeah, it was at the end of the paragraph. There was *Sunny Skies*, a comedy about "a group of health nuts and their concerns over dirty air, polluted water, and junk food. The ending involves the destruction of a chemical plant."

HJ: I tried to get that off the ground in Los Angeles and Paris. I had three versions of it at different times. My friend Dudley Moore was interested in doing it. You know I introduced him to Tuesday Weld, and they wound up getting married.

DK: Really? You introduced them?

HJ: Yeah, I was the matchmaker there.

[Author's note: I met Dudley Moore's biographer Barbra Paskin through Henry in 2016 or 2017, at one of Henry's parties. When I inquired about the Dudley-Tuesday matchmaking for this book, she responded: "I only know that, according to Dudley, when he was doing Beyond the Fringe in New York with Peter Cook, Tuesday called Dudley one night when she was feeling lonely. He went to see her and stayed. The two had already had a fling a few years earlier, when Dudley and Peter were doing another "Fringe" show in New York, but no mention of Henry. In fact, Tuesday first had an affair with Peter Cook before she and Dudley became a couple!" It is worth noting, however, that Henry had known both Pete and Dud since the early Sixties, both having been guests at his first big Upper West Side mega-party. Dudley and Tuesday were married from 1975 to 1980. Thus, things still line up.]

DK: There was a proposed cast named in the press: Dudley's in there with Joan Hackett, Brenda Vaccaro, Barbara Flood, Sandy Baron. Dory Previn was going to do the music.

HJ: Oh my God, Dory!

DK: I've pulled a lot of files at the Herrick and I have to say, you had two big envelopes and they were both really fat. You had a very friendly relationship with the press, it seems. They loved covering you, more than anyone else I've ever researched I daresay.

HJ: You know me, I'm a total attention whore! I loved it.

DK: I would have liked seeing the health nut thing. That sounds like that would have been a hoot. And hey, blowing up a chemical plant! A Jaglom action scene?

HJ: Don't get too excited. You know all my movies are low budget. It would have probably happened off screen. I think I was working with that producer on that… what's him name, who owns the world?

DK: "What's his name who owns the world." That's funny.

HJ: He had a cameo in *Cherry Pie*. Oh fuck, the names! The names are the first to go. He's an old friend, um… Israeli producer…

DK: Arnon Milchan?

HJ: Yeah, Arnon Milchan.

DK: He's in *Cherry Pie*?

HJ: He's in the background.

DK: That film is full of weird little cameos. You had Carol Kane in there real fast, and you had Larry David too, of course.

HJ: All at Café Central, because we used to all hang out there. This is a really good story I just thought of. My son and I were wearing hats and jeans, and we went to a party at this fancy club in Hollywood. My ex-wife Victoria, the mother of my son and my daughter, and two or three other people were waiting. We went in, jeans and hats, not looking as elegant, the way you were supposed to look in this particular club. The people out front said, "You can't come in here dressed like that." And I said, "My wife is inside and my daughter is inside, and this is my son." And they said, "I'm sorry, you can't come in." I said, "I want to talk to whoever's running this place." And they said,

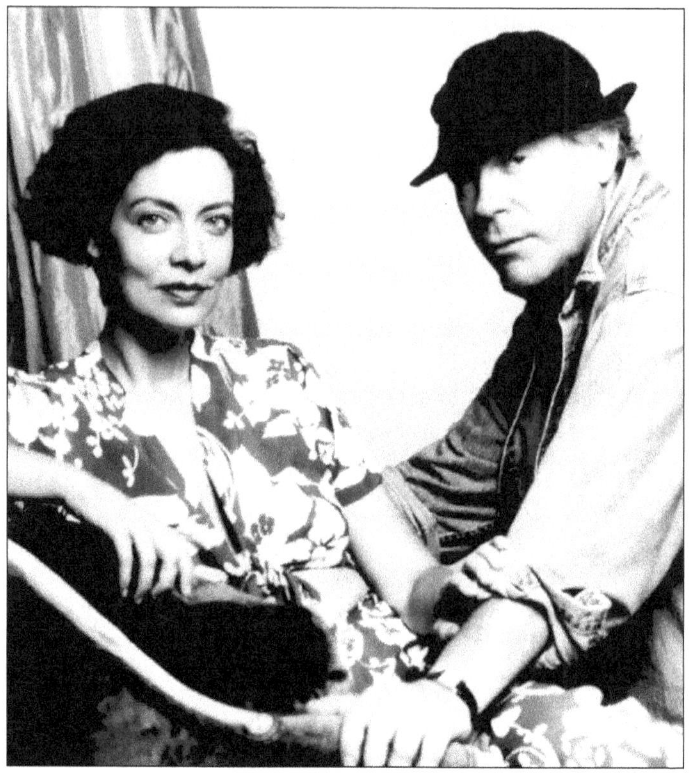

Henry with second wife Victoria Foyt.

"You can't talk to anyone. There's no one to talk to." I said, "Listen, this is an issue of religious freedom. I'm an Orthodox Jew, and that's why I've got the hat on. That's why my son has the hat on. We can't take our hats off."

They went and got somebody who came back. That person apologized to me and got us seated, with family members and a couple of friends, about eight of us at a big round table. A guy comes up from behind me and says, "Hey, you got to get out of here." And I try to turn around, and he's holding me back. I'm saying, "What? What do you mean?" He said, "You can't be here with hats on." I said, "Hey, this is a religious thing." He let me turn and I saw it was Larry David playing the part of the owner.

[**DK** laughs out loud.]

HJ: He had heard the commotion at the beginning when we walked in, but he held me for at least—I'm not exaggerating—four or five minutes, during which I was really getting angrier and angrier. He was really firmly holding me. Maybe it was only two to three, I don't know, but it felt like longer. When I saw him, I screamed with laughter. Larry David doing a number on me! Yeah, that was a great moment.

DK: That's hilarious.

HJ: What else do you have there? I really love this, going back over all these projects, films I never made.

DK: There was… *At Home*, based on a script you co-wrote with Patrice.

HJ: Oh yes, that's right!

DK: She was to play the lead. It's described as, "a kind of strange, anticipated love story, with the couple falling for each other before they ever meet." You were going to play a role. The prospective cast also lists Michael, Joanna Frank, Allan Rachins, Barbara Flood, and "Orson Welles in a mystery part." It sounds like the kind of thing you would do in *Déjà Vu* years later, like a blueprint.

HJ: Well, I always loved those magical realism love stories, like *Portrait of Jennie* and all those. It sometimes led me to humiliation and a lot of disappointment.

DK: What do you mean?

HJ: I remember I was having lunch at Mirabelle one day, back in the Seventies. I saw this woman, we locked eyes, and I was convinced we had some psychic or cosmic connection.

DK: Love at first sight?

HJ: It's like you see it and you know you're meant to be together, or at least that's what I thought. We keep exchanging glances, to the point where I'm just staring at her. The intense eye contact was so fantastic. I thought, "I really found her! This is my true love!" After I finished my meal, which I tried to do very casually, I went over and I asked her to accompany me to the bar. I told her, "I know what's going on. I know what's happening here. I know it's real and you know it's real." I just flat-out said all this… just came right out with it. I said, "This is incredible, let's talk about it. Let's get to the bottom of this. Tell me what you want out of life." And, I swear, in the worst voice, this horrifying voice with a hideous accent, very nasal, she said, "Ya got any coke?" I was like, "I'm sorry, what?" "Ya got any coke?" "Coke? No, I don't have any coke." She was suddenly chewing like a cow, this chewing gum—was she doing this the whole time and I just didn't notice?—and she just walked away. I felt like such a schmuck.

DK: That sounds like a comedy sketch.

HJ: It wasn't funny at the time. It was just humiliating.

DK: I can at least see it as a movie scene.

HJ: A bad movie scene.

DK: Well, I can see, like, Chevy Chase playing that.

HJ: It goes to show you what these romantic movies did to you. I loved them, and I still love them, but they fucked me up.

DK: By the way, that *At Home* project, that would have also been produced by John Goldstone for Gladiole Films.

HJ: It's thanks to him that I came to distribute the Monty Python films in America. We just got something with an old Terry Gilliam film.

DK: *Time Bandits*?

HJ: No, another one.

DK: *Jabberwocky*.

HJ: Yeah, that one.

DK: You know, I went to see *Monty Python and the Holy Grail* in the theater when I was in college. I went with a bunch of friends. And lo and behold, the movie opens with your Orson Rainbow Films logo.

HJ: It did? The logo was there?

DK: Yeah, definitely.

HJ: I'm happy to hear that!

DK: I was like, "Wow, I know the guy whose logo that is!" I felt really well connected, compared to my friends. I didn't make a thing of it, but it was cool at the time.

HJ: John Goldstone was involved when I was trying to get Orson money to make his projects. Arnon Milchan was too.

DK: Yeah, there are items I found at Herrick that talk about your efforts with *The Big Brass Ring* and *The Dreamers* and

King Lear. At various points, you were partnering with Arnon or Goldstone to make it happen for Orson.

HJ: So many close calls. We also held out hope. I told you what Warren Beatty said when we offered him the role in *Brass Ring*?

DK: No.

HJ: This was after his big movie *Reds*, and he was exhausted. He said, "Orson, it's as if I've been at a brothel all night and I've had all these beautiful women at the brothel, every single one of them. And then dawn breaks, and standing outside the brothel in the morning light is Marilyn Monroe, arms wide open, and she wants me, but I've got nothing left to give." He said, "I'm just worn out, I can't." And then he didn't want De Niro or Dusty Hoffman because he didn't think anyone in Kansas would ever vote for them. This was a story about a midwestern politician.

DK: Ironic, because Warren later made *Bulworth*, where he's a politician.

HJ: And there was Jack too, of course. All that's already in the Orson book. Jack was commanding this huge salary, and he didn't want to break that by working for Orson for less.

DK: Sounds lame to me, honestly.

HJ: I was sympathetic, but it just wasn't easy. So what else you got?

DK: There's *Night Club*, a project called *Night Club*, which you were going to do with Andrea Marcovicci.

HJ: Yeah, that was to showcase her as a singer. When was that?

DK: 1988. There's another project called *Evening Time*, that has this funny thing about Spielberg.

HJ: What do you mean "a funny thing with Spielberg"?

DK: It looks like this was around the time that his *Always* was released, and people were coming back asking how you feel about Spielberg stealing your title. You joked, "Maybe I'll just call *Evening Time E.T.*"

HJ: That's funny. You know my Spielberg story with *Always*?

DK: You had a confrontation?

HJ: Well, when I was releasing [my movie] *Always* in… what year would that have been?

DK: 1985.

HJ: These guys at MGM, they sent me a letter saying that Spielberg had registered the title with the MPAA, as well as other titles like *Forever*, *Eternally*, *Eternally Yours*, *Always and Forever*, *Forever and Always*. The language, "Steven Spielberg is making a *real* movie with that title." Something like that. It was contempt.

DK: That's awful.

HJ: I told Orson and he'd already had a negative impression of Spielberg based on his lunch with him. He said, "You must not change the title, because these arrogant idiots think 'real' and money are the same things." I said to Spielberg, "You can name your movie anything. You don't even have a script underway yet." His attitude was, "Why? Why would I do that? For you?" And I said, "I'm sorry?" It was rude. He had this big studio thing, I had a little independent film.

DK: I mean, for good or for ill, you can't copyright a title unless it's a trademark or something. You can't stake your claim on a common-use word though.

HJ: So yeah, I just started calling it *Always But Not Forever*. I benefited a bit from the confusion, I think. People would pick up my movie in the video store thinking it was his.

DK: It says in this one item, "Spielberg and his reps declined to comment."

HJ: I've always said, the budget of my movies is what Spielberg spends for lunches on his. I remember a studio head after *Sitting Ducks* or *Cherry Pie* told me, "I love your movies. Let me know if you ever want to make a real one." That's really how they think. Anything below a certain amount, it's not a "real" movie. I remember they offered me something with Bo Derek at one point. They were offering me a million-and-a-half salary on that, then the minute I tell them I want final cut, all the offers go right out the window.

DK: You called Spielberg the "Reagan filmmaker" here. He's "the ultimate Reagan expression of our age. He means to make films for the twelve-year-old boy that is alive and well in him and the vast majority of men in this country. He shouldn't try to be an adult. He's not." This is when he made *The Color Purple*, which was his first "adult" film.

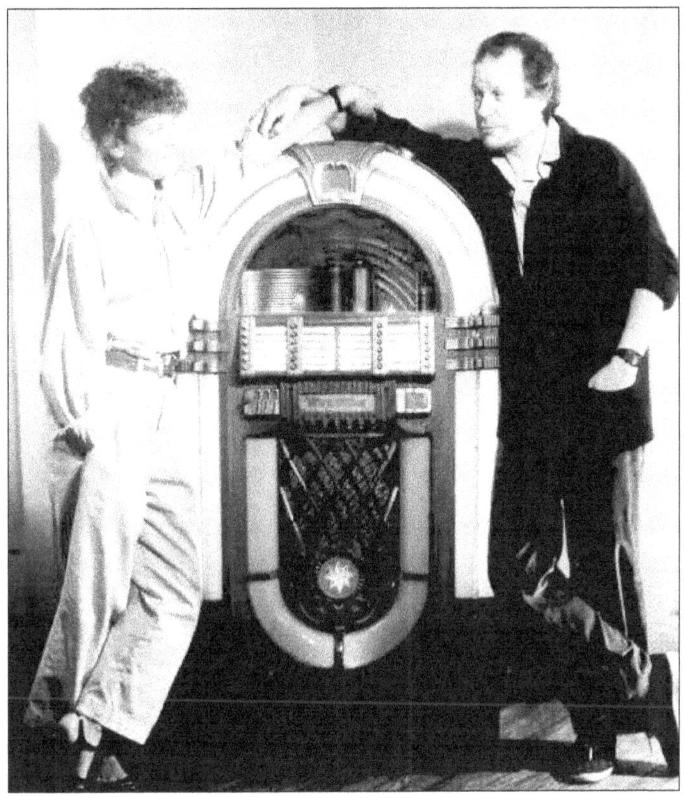

Henry with first wife Patrice Townsend, on the poster for
Always, a.k.a. *Always But Not Forever* (1985).

HJ: That still holds, as far as I'm concerned.
DK: You don't think he's done anything of value? You really
put down *Color Purple* in this piece here.
HJ: It's just Hollywood to me. I thought *Schindler's List* was
fine, but on another level it's glossy and Hollywood. It's about
the savior rather than the Jews he saved.
DK: Kubrick kind of had a similar complaint about it.
HJ: Did he? How do you know that?
DK: Frederic Raphael wrote a book about working with
Kubrick. He says that Kubrick said, "The Holocaust was
about six million Jews who were killed. *Schindler's List* is
about 1,100 who didn't."

HJ: Freddy Raphael I knew from many years ago.

DK: In London, I'd guess?

HJ: Parties, probably in England.

DK: Maybe around the time he'd written *Darling*?

HJ: Almost certainly. Maybe even before. Of course, he also wrote *Two for the Road*, which is just sensational.

DK: I remember when you and I met face-to-face that you compared me to Spielberg to someone who was with us. I knew you well enough from your commentaries and whatnot at that point that I knew, coming from you, that was not a compliment. It seems, especially now, that you were underhandedly putting me down in your way.

HJ: Well, I wasn't sure about you at first.

DK: I think my age and, for you, my sex were working against me.

HJ: Well, you were… you know you've grown.

DK: Okay, okay, I don't want this to turn into something about me.

HJ: That's right. Because it's about *me*.

[*DK and HJ laugh*]

DK: So, *Always* seems to have been first announced in the press as *Lovely Ride*.

HJ: That was from the James Taylor song. I wanted to use "I'll Be Loving You Always" but it was so expensive. It was crazy how much it cost. I paid James Taylor $10,000 for that song, way more than I'd ever paid on other music. But I wanted it to be called *Always*. Did I ever tell you what Steve Martin said to me when he was leaving a screening of *Always*?

DK: You sure didn't.

HJ: He said, "Jaglom, your agony is hilarious." I never forgot that.

DK: I guess it can be. *Someone to Love* was first announced in the press as *Is It You?*

HJ: Also from a song, the one that Andrea sings. We just used the title of that song.

DK: At first it was going to be set at a Halloween party. Then you were calling it *Valentine*. There was a project called *Other*

People, with Michael and Zack. This was…1977, right after *Tracks*.

HJ: It was called *Other People*?

DK: "Two guys, kind of middle-aged adolescents, are partners in an investigating firm who go to California looking for a runaway housewife."

HJ: Oh, that was a concept for a Zack and Michael movie before we came up with *Sitting Ducks*.

DK: It was going to "deal with male sexuality, and the attempt of men to use their sexuality to conquer women." A lot of the same people in that cast—Brenda Vaccaro, Joanna Frank, Topo Swope, Ronee Blakley. Ronee would have been just coming off her Oscar nomination for *Nashville*. There was another project with two titles, *The Spa* and *Undercurrents*, which was to take place at an all-female health spa.

HJ: Yeah, that would have been my first all-female movie, before I did *Eating*.

DK: That was 1977. It was to star Irene Forrest and Martine Bartlett and Martine Getty. There was an earlier project called *Déjà Vu*. "A musical about an extramarital affair between two people who are able to predict everything that happens to them."

HJ: You should know, you're a filmmaker. This is how long one project can gestate.

DK: You also alluded to walking away from a $20 million studio project in 1985.

HJ: That must have been that *Brenda Starr* thing, which was a disaster.

DK: Brenda Starr, like the superhero?

HJ: Yeah, I flirted with it for a bit.

DK: Jesus, a Jaglom superhero film?

HJ: The producer, I forget his name, was a really terrible person.

DK: That would have been hard to imagine.

HJ: You get offered all kinds of things, but at the end of the day, I needed to call the shots, I needed to edit my own movies and have final cut, and if I lose a big payday or whatever, it's not a big deal. I recognize that growing up in wealth and privilege, I never felt I had to bow to such offers. I think people who grow up poor or middle-class, I see how it becomes harder to turn down that type of thing.

DK: [*sings "I Gotta Be Me"*]

HJ: [*laughs*] That was unexpected! That scared me!

DK: I felt the Sammy Davis welling up in me.

HJ: Another thing is that Paramount would give me more money for videocassette rights on the finished movies than the movies actually cost to make.

DK: This one here I would have loved to see you do: a comedy about Old Hollywood, starring Bud Cort.

HJ: Bud's an old friend of mine.

DK: I met him at one of your parties.

HJ: You did? Which one? New Year's.

DK: No, it was back in like 2008. It was, I think Ron Vignone's birthday party at your house.

HJ: Good memory. He was there?

DK: He was leaving right when Karen [Black], Stephen, and I were arriving. He seemed quiet and maybe a little nervous. I complimented him on *Brewster McCloud*, because I was sure he got *Harold and Maude* all the time.

HJ: Yeah, I'm sure he does. I knew Hal Ashby, you know.

DK: Yeah, I know.

HJ: It's sad what they did to Hal. But he had problems. He was almost always high. I had the sense that he hardly knew where he was most of the time. But he truly… he was one of the sweetest men I've ever known.

[Author's note: In 2009, I emailed Henry to tell him that he was mentioned in the new Hal Ashby biography by Nick Dawson, Being Hal Ashby: Life of a Hollywood Rebel. *When I explained that the book recounted how he had recommended Tim Buckley to Ashby to play Woody Guthrie in* Bound for Glory *(1976), he replied, "I have no memory of this. Who the hell is Tim Buckley?"]*

DK: I have a director friend, Paul. He was involved in a fender-bender with Ashby outside the DGA once. He told me that it was like Hal didn't understand what had just happened, like he was up on a cloud.

HJ: Yeah, he was one of the people I knew who most abused drugs, where it became a real problem for him in his career. It's a shame, because he was so talented.

DK: Do you have a favorite Ashby film?

HJ: I love all his stuff. Probably the Peter Sellers one, *Being There*. And *Coming Home*. I wasn't nuts about the one that Jack did as a sailor.

DK: *The Last Detail*? You don't like that one?! That one and *Being There* are my favorites.

HJ: I haven't seen it since it came out, so who knows? It was too much a man's movie for me, I think was the issue.

DK: I think Ashby breaks all that down though. I think that's definitely one of his best. It feels like *Tracks* in some ways.

HJ: I'd be open to seeing it again. I just remember not being big on it at the time.

DK: But anyway, you were going to shoot with Bud Cort at your old house and it was going to be set in the 1920s.

HJ: Yeah, I remember that, but I don't think we pursued it for very long. It might have just been something I told the press.

DK: You had a project called *Happy Ending*, about a film-maker casting actresses to play his wife. Again, shades of *Venice/Venice* later on. Oh, I did find one announcement of the Gene Kelly Cannes project.

HJ: Oh, do you have it?

DK: Yeah, it's right here. It says Gene Kelly with Marisa Berenson. This was April 1976, probably when you were heading off to show *Tracks* for the first time. There were other news items that I found of note. You formed a production co-op called The Filmmakers Co-Op, with Jack, James Frawley, Carole Eastman, Barbara Loden, Penelope Gilliatt, Paul Williams, Dennis Hopper, and Martin Scorsese.

HJ: Yeah, that didn't last long.

DK: You were supposed to produce a film for Andrei Konchalovsky.

HJ: He never came up with a script.

DK: Then later in 1996 you were supposed to distribute a film of his, and also a film by Diane Kurys.

HJ: I only vaguely recall that.

DK: I think the most extraordinary thing I didn't know is that you launched a new division of Rainbow Films to support work by female directors.

HJ: That was very important to me.

DK: This was in 1987. You partnered with Women in Film, someone there named Marilyn LaSalandra.

HJ: I knew her all the way back from *Easy Rider*. She worked with Bob Rafelson for a long time. Marilyn, yeah…

DK: Especially considering all the initiatives today to give female directors their shot. They're still dogged by the system today. You were a pioneer and a visionary in that way.

HJ: I had big plans and high hopes for that. Dyan Cannon was going to direct her first movie. Another one of them was Jane Spencer.

DK: I know Jane. We're connected online.

HJ: Tanna is off now shooting with Jane on a new movie.

DK: I know Jane swears by you, and all you did for her. You helped her make her first feature, *Little Noises*. I always say, people either love or hate you and your films, but I don't think anyone would ever deny that you lived your word and your principles. Nothing was empty.

HJ: It was a desire to see more people make personal films that Hollywood wouldn't make, or put their muscle behind. And as I always said, love my films or hate my films, they're *my* films. Every frame of them is mine.

DK: Yeah, you've lived by your principles. No one could ever argue. And time has treated you well. You wouldn't happen to be "Henry Jaglom in later life."

HJ: I'm just Henry Jaglom.

A Colloquy's Conclusion

"This morning my phone rang; it was my office. There was a rumor he was dead; the press was calling. I called him on his private number. His man, Freddie, answered, said how sorry he was, yes it was true, he found him on the bedroom floor at ten this morning, and he couldn't rouse him. Freddie called the paramedics. He apologized to me (in lieu of Orson) for calling them, as if he had violated the trust for privacy that he still somehow felt he was expected to honor, even now. Orson was dead."

> Henry Jaglom, "Orson's Last
> Laugh" (October 11, 1985)

I read back the above paragraph in *My Lunches With Orson* upon finishing the full draft of this book. It renewed for me the kind of melancholia with which Henry was no doubt familiar when writing that.

I had gotten the news of Henry's death in a not too dissimilar way. It made re-reading the above passage all the more raw. The gravity then really set in that, even if I'd had questions for him, to help me clarify certain things he'd said in the course of our conversations, to relate certain stories he had hinted or started but never got around to telling me (or finish telling me), any desire I might have had for him to elaborate on this or that statement or musing… the time had passed. He was gone.

Someone close to Henry told me, "I would have liked getting him more on the record myself, but of course, I thought we had time." So did I. So did Henry when Orson died. We all think we have time. "Time" was one of Henry's major themes as an artist—he regularly acknowledged its most confounding and even mystical characteristics. As a film historian, I have what is referred to in Yiddish as "schpilkes"—I'm anxious to find people vital to cinema history in some way, get them on the record when possible, and let them know how appreciated they are in their own time. Many artists have died feeling alone, neglected, forgotten. That's one of my biggest overall heartbreaks in this life. There are a number of artists where I was born too late to have remedied such a need. Time is thus an adversary in my vocation, as we are steadily losing a whole vital generation of cinema history.

Do I have regrets about not following up on certain things with Henry? Without a doubt. I'm not a creature of regret really, but I live with it now—just a bit, anyway—pondering the things I might have potentially missed. It's neurotic in a way, sure. I have to remind myself that being comprehensive to the degree I desire is perhaps impossible, foolhardy at the very least.

I then have to consider the privilege I had, of having gotten to know Henry, of spending all this time with him, of being a friend he grew to actually count on in later years (I still have panicked voicemails relating to computer troubles he was having any given day), of being someone much younger who really felt he understood him in some way, or at least aspects of him. I think he felt that too, as Henry didn't suffer gladly those he thought were fools, or those wasteful of his time. During the times he and I were at odds, though, I'd think of the Neil Young song "Old Man" ("Old man, take a look at my life / I'm a lot like you. / I need someone to love me the whole day through. / Take one look at my eyes and you can tell that's true") and would feel this need to sneak up again and beseech him, "Give me a break, man." We were certainly not similar economically, but by virtue of what most interested us about life. By the time we enhanced our relationship and reached a

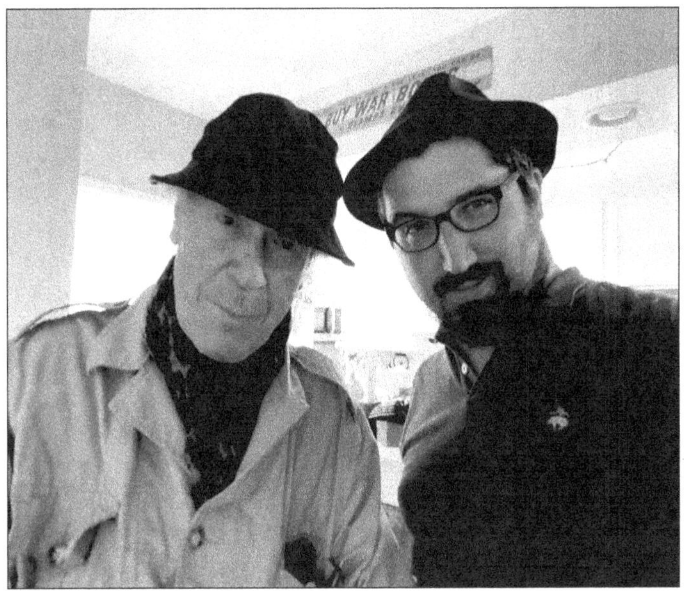

"Hats…people aren't wearing enough of them."
Henry with me, his biographer, just months before his death.

new understanding, a kind of friendship nirvana, I'd ironically grown to count on *him* in some ways.

He and my mother would talk on the phone during a certain stretch, after they had met each other over a wacky lunch. My mother is a gifted listener and a born empath, a kind of unlicensed therapist in some way. She later told me that a repeated line in their intimate conversations was him almost meekly asking her, "You really think so?" in search of "sisterly" affirmation (with Henry himself being a sister of sorts). It made me think of a speech he delivers in *Always But Not Forever*, about the importance and security of "being known," about "having to get up at the fanciest restaurant in the world, taking a shit on the table," then still being accepted and forgiven by those who know and understand you best, after everyone else has run away in horror. Beyond being known, it's about being "seen." That's what he consistently tried to do or to make happen: allowing himself and everyone to feel seen.

When I brought down my friend Tara for lunch, and when she befriended Henry, he said something to me later on, something to the effect of, "I respect you more knowing that you have all these amazing women in your life, and that they love and admire you as much as they do." That was a key to Henry's heart; if you were a man, it was the women in your life who were the truest reflection of you. He had no qualms showing me something girly he bought, a girly collection of something or other that he'd kept, and would ask my opinion as a gay man, albeit one that he felt desperately needed a shave. He also loved the World War II-era trappings of his childhood. Once at a party, surrounded by guests, I watched him rhapsodically hold forth on "cobalt blue," a very particular shade of blue embodied best in the Christmas bulbs from the winter resorts he would visit with his family.

I listened back to all these recordings with such tenderness. Henry was all too human, and he tried to capture on film the all-too-human aspects of those he placed in front of his lens. I do understand why, in my travails, the mention of Henry's name can provoke side-eye and sometimes outright distaste among certain people. I understand why his work divides. Cinematically, in some sense, Henry felt that to divide was to conquer. If people were talking about the work, positively or negatively, it was what he wanted. It was kind of a different take on the maxim "there's no such thing as bad press."

With all the stories he told, it's easy to see him as—as I once called him to his face in this book, to his quizical amusement—the "Forrest Gump of the counterculture" and of the film culture in his time. Did he embellish or play up some of these stories for my microphone? Truthfully, I doubt it. I found any number of sources that back up, or render likely or plausible, all he told me. Maybe, in certain places, he added a bold but stylish little brush-stroke, or an accent mark. Despite all his rubbing elbows with luminaries and affixing himself to history in the way that his *New York Times* obituary suggests he did, Henry to me was just Henry. He was the man who emailed friends and family in mass nightly messages—with photos, musings on recent experiences, and reviews both old and new—but never quite grasped the concept of a BCC, as actress Frances Fisher affectionately pointed out at his memorial, to quite a few laughs of instant recognition. Once, Francis Coppola got so peeved at the absence of a BCC that he fired back to the email group, in all caps, "WELL NOW THAT EVERYONE KNOWS MY PRIVATE EMAIL ADDRESS, I MUST PLEASE ASK YOU STOP DOING THIS. PLEASE!!!!!! STOP. FRANCIS." As I've said, he was so technologically hopeless that I couldn't help but just smile, sigh, and think to myself, "Oh Henry!"

Though it made sense to end the loose transcript section of the book with this encomium, the book ain't over yet. There are more Henry-related stories to come in the next chapter, which focuses specifically on the films of his that got made.

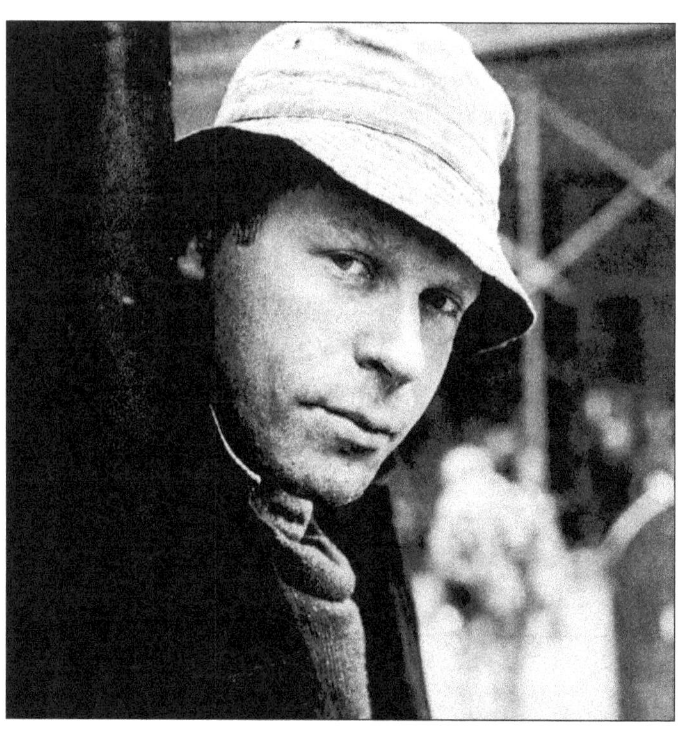

The Cinema of Jaglom

Henry Jaglom's films seems to incite a great deal of anger or passion. There's very little in-between—you either dig his cinema or you don't. Some swear by his work, others swear *at* his work. As the video box for the documentary about him inquires, "Genius? Fraud? Egomaniac? Maverick?" No one I've ever known in my life has been more invested in what makes people tick. He probed scenarios and people with unequaled vigor, inside his films and outside his films. The pursuit was "molto aggressivo."

In 1971, Peter Bogdanovich and Henry Jaglom appeared on film critic Molly Haskell's public access talk show in advance of their films' premieres at the New York Film Festival, namely *The Last Picture Show* and *A Safe Place*. In conversation, Bogdanovich accounted how he worked a day on Henry's film playing a juggler, but Henry cut him out of the final movie. "I think Henry just wanted that for his scrapbook," Bogdanovich quipped. There's something to that. Henry at his best makes what I call "scrapbook cinema." Some refer to his aesthetic as "home movie"-esque, but that's a glib and much too simplistic way of describing his métier. His Eighties films especially exemplify his sensibility.

The "Jaglomian Ethic" crystallized around this time. We see Henry's friends, family, lovers, and acquaintances captured in pressure-cooker environments wherein they bare their souls, wax philosophical (sometimes badly or awkwardly, sometimes profoundly), work out some animus or anxiety or complex, and reveal odd talents and hobbies (e.g. Michael Margotta's training of his pet pigeon in *Can She Bake a Cherry Pie?*, Maggie Wheeler's dolphin and chimp coaching in *New Year's*

Day, the science-educated Nelly Alard's cultivated physics metaphors in *Venice/Venice*, the various musical talents on display in *Someone to Love*, Henry's hilarious brother Michael Emil's sexually "enlightened" counsel on multiple pictures, etc). The films feel intimate not just because of what the people on screen reveal about themselves, but because so much feels like Henry keeping a scrapbook and bearing his own soul through others, by virtue of what he uses in the edit. It's the compulsive holding-on of moments, familiar to many filmmakers—a kind of custom auto-documentary. To many, "talky" films are inherently un-cinematic, by definition. Perhaps you'd say Henry's films are not "polished" in the classical sense, and sometimes they can be messy, but honestly, he wants it messy. His films are, so often, just a hairsbreadth away from chaos.

When Josh and Benny Safdie programmed a series at Brooklyn Academy of Music in 2010, they called it Emotionally Sloppy Manic Cinema. It's a great phrase and apropos here. Henry at his best is the messy voice of a generation—maybe not *his* generation or *the* generation, but *a* generation. I understand what he pursues, why he pursues it, and I think he has something to say, whether or not one is open to hearing it. For many of his films, you'd find a pithy, effective summary in the title of a Czech New Wave picture: Jan Němec's *A Report on the Party and the Guests* (1966). He creates his own class of essay film, of social document, of "actuality drama" (to co-opt Canadian filmmaker Allan King's term), of film form and content. The fact that the work divides only enhances its potency.

Few, if any, historians have probed Henry's films as sociological artifacts, tuned into their individual cultural and historical moments as vital pieces of cultural anthropology. *Daily News* film critic John Richardson wrote, "[Jaglom] wants nothing more, and nothing less, than to capture contemporary reality itself. Future scientists studying our times could find no films that tell more directly how we really thought and talked in the late twentieth century than those of Henry Jaglom." While Jonathan Rosenbaum obtusely reduces the work to

"New Age soul-searching" and formless psychobabble, as if to imply a kind of soft-headedness, works like *Tracks*, *Eating*, *Venice/Venice*, and especially *Someone to Love* are generational testaments. Bogdanovich called Henry's work "dramatized essays"—and few filmmakers trace (and rationalize) their own biographical imprint through an entire body of work the way that Henry Jaglom does. One can specifically follow a life, his own, on a clearly trodden path, an overall arc drawn by circumstance, in harmony or disharmony with life's more familiar drumbeats, along with the incumbent philosophical rationalization, film by film by film. In a way, one feels a strange intimacy with Jaglom merely by taking the journey in watching the films in chronological order. Each entry is a highly personalized "state of the union" address indicating Henry's current frame-of-mind as he works his way through new (and often comic) predicaments, and the vicissitudes of contemporary life. The films are windows into the filmmaker himself, a constantly evolving and revolving insight into what currently interests him about himself, his friends, his culture, and society at large. That's exceedingly rare in any filmmaker's oeuvre, at least in the outré way he does it.

For the better part of half a century, Angelenos—however familiar they were with Henry Jaglom—became acquainted with him through the same Sunset Boulevard billboard that advertised his films. The advertisements were inscribed with his squiggly signature in "Jagfont." He was a mainstay, a Los Angeles fixture in his way. Like Cassavetes (and then Jaglom's own improvisational indie filmmaking brethren Jon Jost and Rob Nilsson), he cultivated a go-to stock cast, a repertory company that audiences get to see grow up and grow old: Zack Norman, Michael Emil, Barbara Flood, Gwen Welles, Melissa Leo, many others. His camera zooms and hovers across a parade of familiar faces Jagfans come to hold dear through his run of twenty-one idiosyncratic features. Therefore, watching a Jaglom film becomes much like a visit with a group of eccentric old friends. It basically goes without saying that his films are actor's films.

Like documentarian Ross McElwee, I believe Jaglom to be a key contemporary cinematic essayist and experimenter who consistently and feverishly blurred the line between fiction and vérité/documentary in a way that few (or no) others dared. McElwee and Alan Berliner try to liberate formal documentary storytelling, in their own way, through not too dissimilar first-person testament. But Henry stages it in fiction, luxuriating in both the weave and the warp of the familiar, cheerfully tangling himself in its patterns, tensions, and all too human distortions. Others interpret that he is merely an insufferably narcissistic exhibitionist. The stratification and polarization of public opinion alone renders him worthy of serious study. How and why do his films elicit equally passionate praise and rancor? Shouldn't we applaud work that provokes such spirited (and often contentious) debate? Beyond all that, love or hate him, he's a singularly fascinating figure for having carved out a successful career helming stubbornly idiosyncratic pictures that make no excuses for what they are—and refreshingly so. They are confidently and emphatically his own. Pulitzer-winning satirist Jules Feiffer once wrote, "Henry Jaglom is one of the most exciting directors around. His movies are original, full of surprises, and full of life." No doubt, Feiffer saw in Jaglom a fellow satirist of sorts.

So, bearing in mind that the best way of making sense of Jaglom's life is by watching the films in chronological order, I here seek to chart the course, using his own words.

1. Finding His Voice

Henry's start in the industry was commercially faltering, to say the least. It took time for him to set himself up, at least commercially. During this time, he was the largely obscure "curiosity" among the successful class of BBS Productions alums (e.g. Bogdanovich, Nicholson, Rafelson, etc.)

A Safe Place (1971)

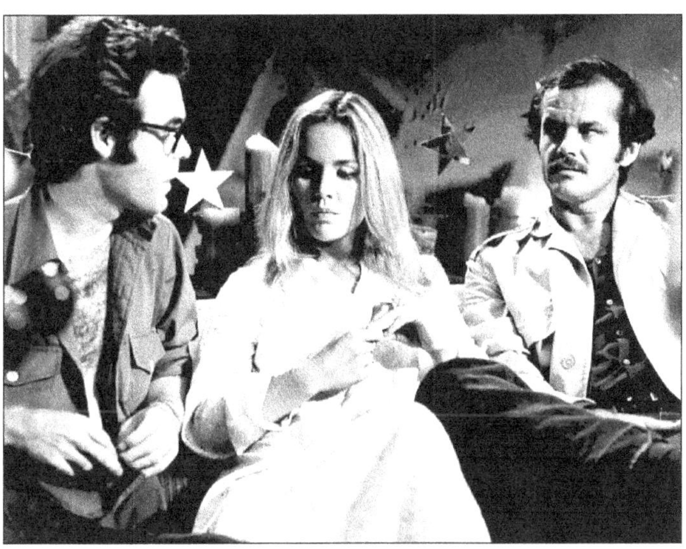

Henry: I personally had two different influences primarily. I had the influence of improvisational theater, which is what I started out in, and the influence of going to these European films—seeing Fellini, seeing Godard, seeing John Schlesinger, seeing Ingmar Bergman. It was a new kind of cinema. Plus, in America, Cassavetes had done *Shadows*, and was beginning his career. I think all of us were very influenced by that. When I adapted *A Safe Place* from the play I had written at the Actors Studio to the screen, I wrote a character who was one third Karen Black, one third Tuesday Weld, and one third me. There was this resistance to growing up, which was very endemic to that period. A lot of us did not want to grow up in the Sixties.

I still don't want to grow up. The Peter Pan thing is profound with me. There was a death attraction, a sort of romance of suicide—a lot of aspects of the popular culture, which I was part of. It's about the magic of our lives, the impotence of our life, the moments of excitement that dissolve—that we have to hold onto somehow but can't. It's about past and future and time and the elusiveness of time. It got the worst reviews possible, in the history of filmdom. Orson told me, "You're very lucky, Henry. You're starting at the bottom and have nowhere to go but up. I started at the top and had nowhere to go but down… and no matter what I did, everyone decided it was down."

Commentary: Orson Welles starring as a magician "wonder rabbi" in *A Safe Place* is an intriguing and rather marvelous prelude to his role as a kind of God-like father figure in Claude Chabrol's *Ten Days Wonder* (1972). His tenure as world cinema's favored supernatural, divine, or merely spiritual manifestation began in earnest around this time. The sense of Welles as mortal man is best manifested later in Jaglom's *Someone to Love* (1987), but here he is the presiding spirit over the Tuesday Weld character's web of arrested development, longing memory, romantic confusions, restless fantasies, and weltschmerz. It is therefore fitting that the word "remember" is the first ever spoken in a Henry Jaglom film.

At first glance and given its pedigree, one could have reasonably expected *A Safe Place* to command the stature, cultural footprint, and critical regard conferred on BBS landmarks like *Easy Rider* (1969), *Five Easy Pieces* (1970), and *The Last Picture Show* (1971). Or even *The King of Marvin Gardens* (1972). However, because its highly experimental cutting style is so radical—and thus confounding to the majority of viewers then and now—it quickly and tragically faded into obscurity, despite Anaïs Nin's passionate, unyielding support of it. Some of the more fragmented, fragmentary, stream-of-consciousness methods of montage in this, his debut film, echo the envelope-pushing editing in Dennis Hopper's *The Last Movie* (1971) and Jerry Schatzberg's *Puzzle of a Downfall Child*

(1970), both of which were also originally dismissed Stateside. There is also a kinship with Nicolas Roeg on the overall, and with what Frank Perry did in *Play It As It Lays* (1972), also starring Weld, the following year.

Hopper once told an interviewer that he wanted to use "film as film" in *The Last Movie*, in the same way that Jackson Pollock used paint as paint. Jaglom's approach is different, less about the materiality of film and more about its capacity for emotional subjectivity—using montage not to deconstruct narrative, but to replicate the movement of thought and feeling. It's less Pollock's splatter than Proust's reflection on the excavation of memory, and memory's traps.

Jorge Luis Borges writes in his essay "A New Refutation of Time" (printed in *Labyrinths, and Other Writings*), "Time is the substance from which I am made. Time is a river which carries me away, but I am the river; it is a tiger that devours me, but I am the tiger; it is a fire that consumes me, but I am the fire." No passage better distills the nature of Jaglom's methodology, his métier, for editing time in *A Safe Place*. They both impact—and are acted upon by—time itself. Fragments of dream and experience collide and externalize the tremors of emotion. In fact, Jaglom called its sense of construction "emotional time." In this pursuit, it constantly thumbs its nose at the typically American audience expectation, a demand, to feel in control (i.e. "make logical sense") of the viewing experience that is before them. Objections to its oneiric opaqueness aside, Jaglom stubbornly requires that we let the film wash over us as an experience. The more one fights that and defiantly chooses to intellectualize it, the more frustrated one becomes. When a picture demands control over its audience in this manner, many get either scared or, unfortunately, bored. *A Safe Place* is a film that one must completely hand oneself over to, without protest or resistance.

When promoting *Always But Not Forever* in 1985, Jaglom said, "When I made *A Safe Place*, I was so convinced that I was alone in this universe that I was almost defying people to 'get' it, so I reassembled pieces of time and logic into a new kind of structure." Describing *A Safe Place* in story terms or answering

"What's it about?" is futile. Writing in those terms about *A Safe Place* is akin to "dancing about architecture," to co-opt the old maxim about music criticism. This is stream-of-consciousness at its peak, uninhibited and stitched together purely for emotion's sake. Tuesday Weld's Susan/Noah, almost in the fashion of Kurt Vonnegut's hero Billy Pilgrim in *Slaughterhouse-Five*, has become "unstuck in time," but not because of any science-fiction machination. From first frame to last, the film dares to unflinchingly occupy a liminal space; a sleep logic ("perchance to dream" à la Shakespeare) tempers a cold, shambolic coherence that nevertheless insists upon itself in waking life—or what only vaguely passes for waking life. Even the opening lines speak to this: "Last night, in my sleep, I dreamed that I was sleeping. And dreaming in that sleep that I had awakened. I fell asleep." Jaglom lingers between, but clearly favors, dream states, with all their dominions destined to remain uncharted. That this understandably stymies the grand majority of viewers is almost part of its grand design.

The rational and logical is embodied by the Philip Proctor character, as he attempts to free himself, at least enough to find his own safe place ("I love you from Paris to Geneva," etc.). Susan/Noah has given him a kind of skeleton key that unlocks himself—especially the parts he works to shield from the world. In the most basic Jungian terms, the Proctor character can be interpreted as superego, while Nicholson's is id. (Henry once explained Nicholson's destabilizing role as someone who shows up to "fuck the girl, fuck the audience, and fuck the movie," essentially leaving it for all others to pick up the pieces.) But most of all, the film asks, what is true liberation? Is it "liberation" as we had come to define it in the Sixties parlance and paradigm, or is liberation being emotionally open enough to grapple with the pangs of our deepest loss and unrest, no matter how much it damages us (and Tuesday Weld's character)? There are portals that preternaturally guileless and liberated individuals can access, buried both in our personal past, (secondarily) our collective memory—overall, in the deepest and often most dangerous parts of ourselves. The film, like *Tracks* which followed, is an interior journey fraught with peril but also the lure of potential self-fulfillment, or self-destruction. Susan/Noah is finally released in a way that is wholly debatable. Death or flight, what is the safe place?

With a soundtrack that includes Thirties and Forties standards like Edith Piaf, Helen Forrest, Vera Lynn, and Charles Trenet ("La mer" is the film's wistful, wispy anthem—a song that would become a Jaglom trademark), the film is proudly, unapologetically sentimental. Henry thus defines himself as a sentimentalist right from the get-go. He once told a journalist, "All my movies, as I found out to my amazement when I saw a whole group of them together, are obsessed with the loss of childhood. I use old songs and use home movies of my parents or of my childhood. I have this strong attachment to, 'What did I first see with my new eyes? What did I first hear with my new ears? What did it do to me emotionally before I became conscious of putting it in this place or that?' So much of my films seem to be about love and the search for love in different kinds of ways. The example we have of love has a lot to do with the families we came from." Susan/Noah's insistence that as a child she flew, and that she could do it again if she could only remember how, epitomizes this overpowering need to recapture childhood for the sake of survival. The 8mm home movies projected onto Tuesday Weld's face in one sequence are Henry's own family home movies—and these same home movies reappear in later Jaglom pictures (most notably *Can She Bake a Cherry Pie?*).

This is a film about memory, the fragility and synchronicity of memory, and the sense of lost time. Hannah Arendt writes in *The Life of the Mind*, "It is in the insertion of man with his limited lifespan that transforms the continuously flowing stream of sheer change… into time as we know it." These ideas and elements all lie at the root of selfhood, especially when our always-in-motion world isn't ready to receive us, let alone accept us. Jaglom makes no mystery of the artists and the works he reveres and references in *A Safe Place*. He explicitly attempts to evoke a J.D. Salinger New York in a late Sixties Lower East Side context, one we can also define as a "hippie" context. The Central Park merry-go-round appears a number of times, and we can sense the specter of Holden Caulfield and sister Phoebe at the edges of these frames. Tuesday Weld's character Susan/Noah is shaded with subtle hints of Salinger's Franny in *Franny and Zooey*. Orson Welles underscores scenes as Weld's father surrogate with riddle-like rabbinical stories by Rabbi Nachman of Bratslov. The film's very construction evokes the French Nouvelle Vague. Henry has said, "You could have edited the film linearly—beginning, middle, end—and it might have been more of a success. Bert and Columbia might have made a bit more money with it and critics wouldn't have gotten as frustrated. The script was more linear, but I didn't want the film to be. It was to my career's great sorrow for many years that I went that way, but I have no regrets."

With the scene in which Weld chastises Philip Proctor for his lack of romance, as she manically waxes nostalgic over old telephone prefixes (e.g. Trafalgar, Algonquin, Butterfield), Jaglom chides and needles us to recognize that the inherent romance of a halcyon age is dying out, if it wasn't dead already by 1970. In making life ostensibly "easier" and more practical, the world strives to extinguish its traces of magic and wonder. As Weld's character declares, "Tomorrow is where the past is."

This isn't at all the "manic pixie dream girl flick" the most vapid detractors, cut-ups, and haters make it out to be. But alas, we all know it's easier to label than to dig. To the "old souls" in the audience, *A Safe Place*, *Someone to Love*, *Venice/Venice*, and *Déjà Vu* invoke the music, classic cinema, and literature that reminds us that, as long as these faded but no less potent remnants of a vanished past haunt the most unexpected pockets of life, the magic, wonder and hope that too many think we've lost forever can likewise exist. The vanished past is something Henry personally lived with and grappled with, day in and day out. It was acute, constantly guiding his conversation and where his mind wandered. *A Safe Place* is perhaps the most important picture in Jaglom's filmography. Basically everything—his preoccupations, his romanticization of the past, his obsession with memory and the safety of childhood, his Jewish sensibility, his love of old music, his femininity, his free-wheeling looseness, his regard for a certain mode of literature—can be traced forward from *A Safe Place*. It is the Jaglomian ur-text—a deeply misunderstood film, for people with an open mind about what cinema can be.

Cast: Tuesday Weld (Susan/Noah), Orson Welles (The Magician), Jack Nicholson (Mitch), Philip Proctor (Fred), Gwen Welles (Bari), Dov Lawrence (Larry), Barbara Flood (Noah's Friend), Sheila Oaks (Sister-in-Law), Julie Robinson (Noah's Friend)

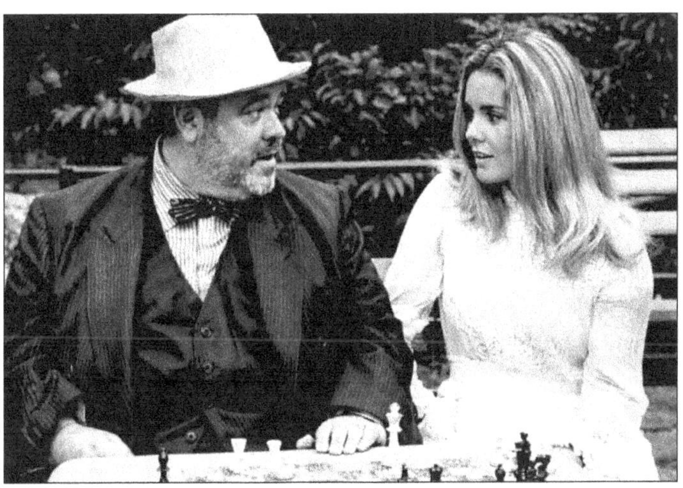

My Big Brother's Sex Life (1973) (unreleased, 45 minutes)

Henry: I filmed by brother in Israel talking about sex, because Michael was constantly bragging to everyone about his sexual stamina, including members of our family. So I just filmed him talking about all that. At one point, I wanted to incorporate the footage into a movie called *Leon's List*, starring him as a ladies man. But it's just kind of a little movie on its own. I call it my *2½*, because it's only about 45 minutes—half of a full movie. I mostly just wanted a document of Michael being himself. And he could never not be totally himself. This was

1972 or '73, so I had no idea I'd be casting him in all these movies later on. It took Jack Nicholson telling me that I had a comedy goldmine in Michael—and he said I absolutely had to cast him in something. In *Tracks*, he was with us on the train keeping track of the production money because he didn't trust Zack, so that was a test run. Then we did *Sitting Ducks* and the rest is history.

Commentary: In many ways, *My Big Brother's Sex Life* is an ideal primer to Henry's brother Michael and his appetite for discussing his colorful sexcapades, if you haven't seen him in his later starring vehicles and supporting roles. This lays a blueprint.

Cast: Michael Emil Jaglom (self), Henry Jaglom (voice)

Tracks (1976)

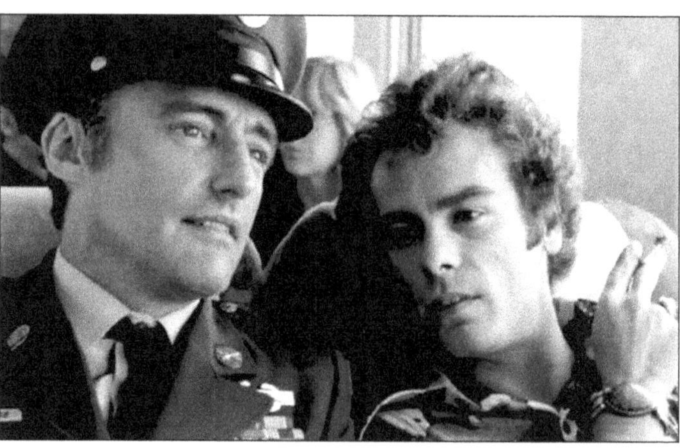

Henry: The soldier in *Tracks* grew up with all those heroic stories of World War II, but when he came of age and got ready to go to his war, everything was different. That's why I use all those great World War II era songs on the soundtrack. Langston Hughes wrote in a poem, "O let America be America again / the land that never was / yet still might be." It's another myth, America's dream of its own innocence, and it allowed us to do terrible things in its name. We believed the lie and we've been locked into these oppressive mythologies, personal as well as national, which we keep trying to break out of. Karen says in *Can She Bake a Cherry Pie?*, "Life isn't like what they told us it would be." That's also what *Tracks* is about, in a broader sense.

But in 1976, the only thing people wanted to see less than a film about Vietnam was a film starring Dennis Hopper. We had a very difficult time distributing *Tracks*, probably the most difficult an experience I've ever had with any film. The Vietnam War really defined my generation, and when I inherited the basic idea for the movie from Bob Rafelson, it presented an opportunity. We shot it as improvisationally as the actors performed it. The train in the film was real, not a set, and we never got permits. We would pay off the railway workers and get the use of a certain train car or compartment. We were also thrown off some trains as well. It's, in its way, a monument to guerrilla filmmaking. Beyond that, I think it says something important about where America found itself at the end of the war, which is why I started the film with Nixon's Peace With Honor speech. Dennis was not easy to work with, but I think his performance is just sensational.

Commentary: Independent filmmakers and cineastes chat about films and directors much like a bunch of jocks getting together to talk about sports and favorite athletes. Most of this ilk, even if they are not fans of Jaglom's overall body of work, usually admire—and many even outright love—*Tracks*, a sobering, barely post-Vietnam War remnant that follows Dennis Hopper as a battle-scarred veteran escorting the corpse of his fallen buddy cross-country on a passenger train. In attempting to woo young fellow passenger Taryn Power, a college girl heading home on holiday break, it becomes apparent that Hopper is psychologically "all sixes and sevens," to use the old British colloquialism. His mind gradually wilts to paranoia, fear, trembling, rage toward a society in a dazed rush to marginalize or discard veterans like himself (and his departed comrade). There is also yearning at play, specifically for a simpler time, when the good and bad binary was more recognizable and distinguishable. The lengthy trip is a faded red, white, and blue odyssey into America's heart of darkness. The soundtrack consists of the most sentimental World War II tunes and 1940s standards, juxtaposing the Vietnam quagmire with the previous "good war" of lion-hearted heroes who were welcomed home as such. By stark contrast, the disturbed Hopper is escorting a coffin home from an ignominious "bad war" and nobody seems to care all that much. Dean Stockwell co-stars as a man on the run who helps fuel Hopper's paranoid delusions.

The main reward here is watching the typically daredevil Hopper throw himself with typically reckless abandon down into the far depths of his character, a damaged "boy who did what he was told" who can no longer cope with a present-day reality that chastises old souls as freaks. In such a landscape, patriotism—even for an America that was lost—can only be freakish. "Do you ever think about your childhood," Hopper asks in the film's opening frames before the titles roll. "I think about mine, when the going gets rough." In a way, his character is not unlike that of Tuesday Weld's Susan/Noah in *A Safe Place*; that character likewise found it impossible to conform an idyllic past to a world now bereft of everyday magic. In Jaglomian fashion, Hopper and his director create a live-wire atmosphere that will electrify some and electrocute others. (This is indeed true even for his players. "The only filmmaker I ever had a problem with was Henry Jaglom," admitted Dean Stockwell in an interview with Patrick McGilligan.)

Just as Jaglom claimed that all of *A Safe Place* could have just played out in Weld's mind as she's listening to "La mer" on the jukebox, he also said that *Tracks* could have likewise taken place in Hopper's mind as he's sitting on the American-flag bench listening to his hand-held radio at the beginning of the film. Both pictures are, indeed, interior journeys—one might say journeys through "cities of the interior," à la Anaïs Nin—

that blur the line between external reality and psychic projection. They unfold as extensions of their protagonists' fractured minds, collapsing the natural course of events into purely psychological terrain. Both privilege subjective consciousness as governing logic, and as ontological anchor.

The Academy of Motion Picture Arts and Sciences' Margaret Herrick Library stores an early 197-page draft of the *Tracks* screenplay, inherited from a defunct talent agency's files. Dennis Hopper's Sgt. Jack Falen character is named "Johnny" in this draft, the Taryn Power college girl character, Stephanie, is a more worldly young woman named "Fran," and the Dean Stockwell character, Mark (named "Steven" here), is a nitrous oxide freak and uses the drug during sex (shades of both the later *Blue Velvet* and the Artie Ross story told earlier in this book). There are various other differences and departures from what wound up on screen, including Falen—or "Johnny"—being shaded as more explicitly right-wing. Highlights: There is a dramatic encounter with the coffin stored in the train's cargo, Johnny swaps war horror stories with a member of the train staff, and the film indexes more heavily on World War II musings and memories. At one point Johnny states, "World War II is the only war there is." A key exchange between Johnny and Fran has her recounting her father once telling her that no one got killed in World War II. Songs like "Someone's Gotta Slap a Dirty Little Jap" are written directly into the script, with one character calling its diegetic airing "sick, insane stuff."

This draft ends with Johnny delivering a big speech at the grave site, then proceeding to literally "bring Vietnam home" by turning the nearby town into a fiery, bloody, apocalyptic hellscape (very un-Jaglomian in nature). We can be grateful that Jaglom freeze-frames before we see any such massacre, which openly played into an unsavory trope: returning veterans as potentially dangerous ticking timebombs. What remains is Hopper's meltdown and his haunting "You wanna go to 'Nam?! I'll take you to Nam!" is more than enough—it has all the power and urgency Jaglom needed.

Tracks is like a male counterpart to Robert Altman's *Images* (1972), set in a time of national mourning over an unjust war. This and *Sitting Ducks* (1980) are Jaglom's most overtly "masculine" efforts, in a career he would later use to probe specifically feminine anxieties. But as the title of Anaïs Nin's essay "In Favor of the Sensitive Man" indicates, Jaglom never lacks any feminine fortitude, ensuring that a sensitivity is injected into even his most brawny and "manly" of stories. *Tracks* is one of the key "America looks at itself in the mirror" pictures of the Seventies. Considering that Jaglom co-produced the milestone Vietnam War documentary *Hearts and Minds* (1974), that film is directly tied in with *Tracks*, both thematically and financially (i.e. funds originally raised to shoot *Tracks* were used to buy back *Hearts and Minds* from a studio cornered into shelving it—Henry relates the full story earlier in the book).

The film had great difficulty finding distribution, playing the festival circuit for years until finally booking a theatrical run through the small company Trio Films in 1979. Though reviews were encouraging, the commercial strikes against it proved insurmountable. However, Anaïs Nin once again affirmed her role as vital ally, introducing filmmaker Alain Resnais to not only *Tracks* but also *A Safe Place*. Resnais wrote her in response, stating, "I agree with you, Anaïs. Henri (sic) Jaglom's *Un coin tranquille* [*A Safe Place*] was the first American film to make me dream in many years. Very beautiful. Now he has done it once more with *Tracks*, which I saw in rough form thanks to you. Here, though, it's more darkly, as in a nightmare, but strong and true. Now tell him for me, please, that he must cast Dennis Hopper and Tuesday Weld in a film together as brother and sister… or better, as lovers. Or both." Nin's fierce advocacy got Jaglom's early work in front of a number of other distinguished appreciators. Jaglom's cachet with European audiences grew apace; throughout his career, he remained far more respected in Europe than in his home country.

In later years, director Alex Cox joined in the praise for *Tracks*, even going to the extra mile to introduce the film on camera when it premiered on BBC TV's *Moviedrome*. Steadily, over the years, the film caught on with a cult audience, in a way that *A Safe Place* unfortunately still struggles to. Author Peter Biskind (*Easy Riders, Raging Bulls*), for one, heralded Hopper's performance as "the best and most powerful of his career."

Cast: Dennis Hopper (Sgt. Jack Falen), Dean Stockwell (Mark), Taryn Power (Stephanie), Topo Swope (Chloe), Alfred Ryder (The Man), Zack Norman (Gene), Michael Emil (Emile), Barbara Flood (The Lady), Cayle Chernin (Train Passenger), James Frawley (Train Passenger), Sally Kirkland (Train Passenger), Frank McRae (Coachman), Paul Williams (Tarot Reader)

Sitting Ducks (1980)

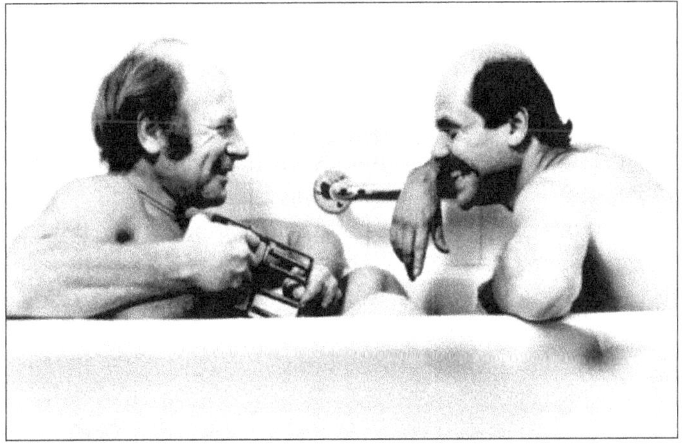

Henry: *Sitting Ducks* is a bit of a joke. *A Safe Place* and *Tracks* had been such financial disasters that I needed to make a more commercial movie if I was going to continue as a director. I came up with this story about two guys who steal money from the mob, but that wasn't really what it was about, to me. It was looking at these people who were obsessed with money, sex, and health, guys who were trying forever to satisfy some mythical American dream. It combines the influence of the Hope and Crosby movies of my youth, with the European films I grew into later on, which revealed to me how real things can be on screen. It was fun. It was the easiest film to make.

Commentary: There is an apt parallel to *Sitting Ducks*—or rather, a perfect analog within another "fellow traveler" filmmaker's career. John Cassavetes wrote the crime caper *Gloria* (1980), "to sell, strictly to sell," after his two previous pictures, *The Killing of a Chinese Bookie* (1976) and *Opening Night* (1977) resoundingly flopped both critically and commercially (though of course, both have gone on to become beloved classics in the Cassavetes oeuvre). Upon the successful sale of the *Gloria* script, his wife Gena Rowlands expressed interest in taking on the role and convinced her husband to direct her in it. He obliged, working within defined contours to deliver an unlikely buddy movie about a streetwise dame and a mouthy little Puerto Rican boy on the run from the mob. He thought of it as merely a "thoughtless" yarn. While not a raging financial success, it did bail him out of "director jail." Here with Henry Jaglom, we have *Sitting Ducks* to the rescue, after back-to-back commercial failures landed him a stiff "federal" sentence in that same director jail. And wouldn't you know—it's another story of unlikely buddies on the run from the mob. Both *Gloria* and *Sitting Ducks* were released the same year, to prove that a more audience-friendly pivot can spring you, or at least secure you a cushy parole. Both pictures had Cassavetes and Jaglom paying the piper, so to speak, but they both enjoyed some of the best reviews of their careers for these larks—to their eternal irritation. As one of the characters in Jaglom's later *Last Summer in the Hamptons* quips, "The dirty little secret of the avant-garde is that they are jealous of money." (This is not to suggest that Cassavetes and Jaglom were ever anything less than sincere in their artistic intentions, on the overall.)

This madcap road movie romp that many remember for its bawdy, sometimes raunchy, but—perhaps paradoxically—always tasteful, trenchant, observant human comedy. It was a lines-around-the-block success (rare for Jaglom) that drew the first critical raves of its director's career. This is an ostensibly more "straightforward" frolic about "sex, money, and vitamins" that put him on the map as a "bankable" director. Though, thankfully as mentioned, *A Safe Place* and *Tracks* were later lauded by critics and audiences in Europe (as Woody Allen quips in *Hollywood Ending*, "Thank God the French exist!"), Jaglom's dead-end, dire straits put any future directing career in serious jeopardy. What was the secret of its success? Looking back on the film in 1985, Henry told one journalist, "As my life got happier, the films got happier."

There's more to *Sitting Ducks* than the fun-loving, sunny-side-up spree that Jaglom himself often dismissed it as (and the public of its day loved it for being). Michael Emil—the director's incomparable, comic genius brother—and Zack Norman are a nebbish, randy Hope and Crosby for the burgeoning, sexually liberated Me Generation. A critic of the time also compared them to Abbott and Costello. Nervous, loquacious Simon (Emil) and manic, itchy-fingered, horny Sidney (Norman) are two small-time crooks who take off for Miami in a limousine, the wheels of which are stuffed with cash stolen from the mob. When they arrive there, they plan to fly off to Costa Rica on a permanent vacation. On the road, they pick up singer/chauffeur Moose (Richard Romanus) plus two women they meet in a Holiday Inn: Jenny (Patrice Townsend, the first Mrs. Jaglom), a duplicitous yoga maven with an aversion to kissing, and lonely waitress Leona (Irene Forrest), who abruptly quits her job after her supervisor berates her for socializing with customers.

Sitting Ducks plumbs the elasticity of male friendships. One of its most famous scenes is one that Jaglom staged like a trick or practical joke, in which Sidney intrudes on Simon's bathtub. His brother Michael had no idea that Zack Norman was about to storm in naked before it happened (he was told one of the women would be joining him), so his shocked, flustered reaction on film is nothing if not completely real. In addition to being hilarious as pure entertainment, this is a key moment in the film and also in Jaglom's overall career, registering as a reverse mirror image to a primary idea he would develop in later work. The principle or presupposition is that there is an intimacy and a kind of emotional maturity that heterosexual males mostly cannot achieve (at least collectively), that women, by and large, have no compunction sharing and exploring with each other, often with total emotional surrender.

When Jaglom tried to shoot the unreleased sequel *Lucky Ducks* ten years later, his position and perception vis a vis would be reaffirmed. Because men, as Jaglom sees them, are naturally guarded and stymied by both "virility" and sexual paranoia/panic, many cannot reciprocate or mutually surrender themselves to emotional vulnerability as women do with each other in later Jaglom titles. When that barrier is dismantled with men, even momentarily or in kamikaze fashion (à la the bathtub scene setup), a delicious comic set piece unfolds, in which the wounded male ego is royally roasted.

Whatever its director thinks of it (and make no mistake, he was not at all "ashamed" of it—he merely preferred that the other films get more attention), *Sitting Ducks* is not as déclassé as he often characterized it. This zippy, rambunctious farce opens itself to deeper consideration, inadvertently or otherwise, because as one critic opined, "It's a film made for laughs that has the immediacy associated with a personal film." It's also an attractively ragged artifact of a bygone era when neurotic read as sexy. Woody Allen was far from the only auteur answering to the demand.

A bit of trivia: Michael Douglas attended an early rough cut screening of *Sitting Ducks*. It was his idea to use the days of the week onscreen to help properly pace the movie, as to help the audience better get their bearings. Henry expressed his gratitude and adopted the idea. In the late Seventies and early Eighties, he attended a number of political fundraiser meetings at Douglas' house, with a guest list that often included the then controversial political gadfly Ed Asner.

Cast: Michael Emil (Simon), Zack Norman (Sidney), Patrice Townsend (Jenny), Irene Forrest (Cagen) (Leona), Richard Romanus (Moose), Henry Jaglom (The Bad Guy), Sheila Oaks (Other Woman), John Teranova (Mr. Carmichael)

National Lampoon Goes to the Movies (1982)
a.k.a. National Lampoon's Movie Madness

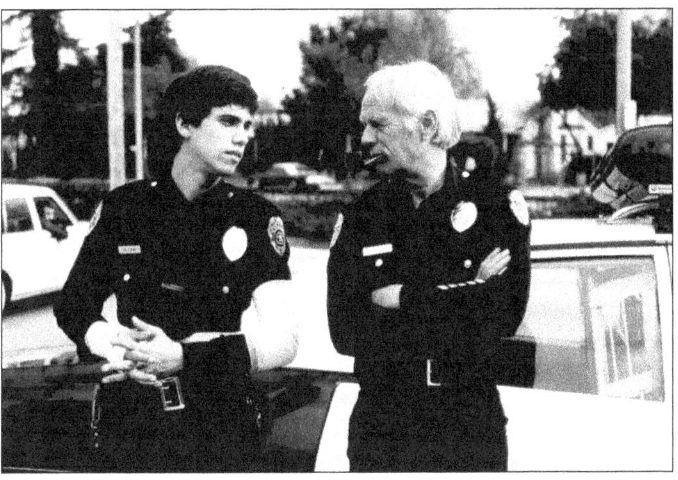

Henry: Orson Welles said I should try to find out whether I possibly could "work within their system" because, he said, my life would be so much easier if I could. So, after *Sitting Ducks* became my first commercially successful film, and Mel Brooks and everyone else thought I would become this big-time commercial comedy director after my first two dramatic "failures" [*A Safe Place* and *Tracks*], the National Lampoon people came to me. It was right after the huge success of *Animal House* (1978), and they offered me to direct two parts of their next film, a three-part "satire of the movies" thing. They were all dumb, full of breast jokes and sex jokes. Pathetic, but I thought I could maybe rewrite much of it. It seemed like I would have the freedom to do that. I told Orson it was going to take a month to shoot, and he said, "A month of your time, what is that? Do it. Find out if you can work within the system. It's worth your while, believe me."

I reluctantly took it. I had what was, for me, a big pay day, and actually had fun doing it because it harkened back to my days in stand-up comedy at The Improvisation with Richie Pryor and others. And also to my time in a Boston hotel with The Compass Theatre and doing improvisational off-Broadway comedy after college. They mostly left me alone, and I thought, "Huh, this is easy! Maybe I can do this." I took these garbage scripts and was working to turn them into something. Instead of my usual crew of fourteen, I had like 150. That made me uncomfortable and I said that I only wanted preferably twenty, but at most fifty. They told 130 of them to wander off to Sunset, take a paid day off. They were happy, I was happy. I was also trying to make political statements in my rewrites. I really thought for that time I *could* work in the system.

Then, after shooting it and planning it, as had already become my way with *A Safe Place* and *Tracks*, to really "create" it in the cutting room, especially important with comedy, they told me no. I walk into the cutting room and there's a guy sitting there. I said, "Excuse me, this is my editing room." He says, "No, no, this is my editing room." I said, "I'm the director." He said, "And I'm your editor. You can't touch the film. You're not in the editor's union." This is after I cut *Easy Rider*, keep in mind. I argued with him, but I had no choice. I could "supervise" an edit. So we're working and they decided, right in the middle, to cut out one of my two segments, a satire on the atom bomb. My brother, Zack Norman, and Patrice [Townsend] starred in the one that they cut out. I also cast Roscoe Lee Browne, Marcia Strassman, and Allen Garfield. I thought of it like a mini-*Strangelove*. Now, they were just going to have two halves, mine and this other guy's (he had directed commercials before that). [*Author's note: The other segment director was Bob Giraldi, known best for the Michael Jackson music video "Beat It."*]

My remaining half was a "satire" on police brutality and other stuff, but while I was supervising my cut, I found out that they had sneak-previewed the film at a screening at the Directors Guild. "How could they?" I asked, because I wasn't even near finishing it. But they did it and I saw it and it wasn't anything like my cut. It was just stupid and embarrassing and completely unfunny. Henny Youngman was now all over it. This footage turned up in my segment that I didn't shoot. All the sex jokes were put back in. It was completely unrecognizable. I never even got to finish my edit, because they just changed the whole thing, made it insanely stupid, put some insane music over it and I tried very hard with my then agent, a great guy who was then Scorsese and De Niro's agent as well, just to get my name taken off it. My name really didn't mean anything to them then, despite *Sitting Ducks*.

But this disgusting man who produced it, Matty Simmons by name, fought me and he insisted on keeping my name on it, God only knows why. I said, "My name is not worth anything to you. I've done two completely unsuccessful commercial movies. What could it possibly mean to you?" "Well, you read the contract and you signed it." I said, "Yeah, but I didn't do this movie. This wasn't my work." United Artists went with him, despite my protest, and my name remained on it, though it didn't in any way reflect my view at this time. Of course, the thing completely flopped, deservedly so, and was never even released theatrically. Now and then, it shows up on all these places as one of my films, which believe me it isn't. "A bigger, worse stupidity," as my father would say, you can't imagine than this film. The only good thing was that I did get to cast Richard Widmark in it, a hero of my youth in films (though comedy wasn't his thing). I also cast the guy who played the "gunsel" with Bogart in *The Maltese Falcon*, Elisha Cook, Jr. I never even saw the final movie. Anyway, that's the story. My agent, he was a serious guy, really worked hard and fought on my behalf, even though I'm sure he never made a dime on me the entire time I was his client. I felt protected.

There is one other "film" that pops up on my filmography, the would-be *sequel* to *Sitting Ducks*, called *Lucky Ducks*, shot in 1990 with my brother and Zack Norman and dozens of others, including Harry Nilsson, Roscoe Lee Browne, so many others. That one *was* mine. I *did* shoot it for a lot of complex reasons, but I could never cut it together. For the only time in my career, I just gave up on it after many months and never put it together.

Commentary: Otherwise known as *Henry Goes Hollywood…
Disastrously*. Though the *Variety* review of *National Lampoon
Goes to the Movies* erroneously states that the movie was never
released theatrically, it did have a (very) limited window in
April 1982 after being nearly shelved. A Rhode Island preview
audience so detested the film that the screening ended in what
might generously be called audience participation. That's the
most euphemistic or polite way of saying that the theater was
left in utter shambles. It was then inexplicably retitled *Movie
Madness* at some point in late 1981 or early 1982 (for plausible deniability reasons, perhaps?) before it premiered on
cable. The rocky production was nevertheless profiled in a
September 1983 *Rolling Stone* piece by Allison Silver, titled
"In the Can," about recently shelved studio product that never
saw the light of day.

When Henry heard at some point that *Movie Madness/…
Goes to the Movies* was not going to be released, he sent
everyone involved a memo describing a way to restructure the
picture with a wraparound to connect the individual segments.
This would have involved a few studio execs sitting around
discussing the "crap they could foist upon the public." The
real studio execs were outraged by the idea—no sense of
humor or reality, one assumes. Henry told *Rolling Stone* that
his experience on this picture "was a good lesson for me," that
"if people make deals with prostitutes, they have to expect
to get fucked." He also fumed to Allison Silver that "[Matty
Simmons] feels no obligation to an audience. His obligation is
to his own ego. He is an untalented, unfunny man." No love
lost, clearly.

One unnamed United Artists studio executive went on
the record stating, "The reason this movie wasn't releasable
was Henry Jaglom. His part was so messily conceived, so
badly shot, so atrociously directed that one segment had to
be abandoned." United Artists executive Steven Bach remembered the project as *The National Lampoon Picture Show* in
his now-classic tell-all book *Final Cut: Art, Money and Ego in
the Making of Heaven's Gate*. He called it "unreleasable," and
related one of the more unpleasant showdowns over its turbu-

lent post-production: "The director of the frankly terrible and distended segment [Jaglom] had his agent come to argue for it in the Thalberg Building, from which the agent was asked to leave after the abusiveness of his remarks about UA caused the meeting to degenerate into a worse—and more hysterical— shambles than the director's botch of the material." Contrary to Jaglom's account, he was given the opportunity to take his name of the final product, on the condition he kept quiet and refrained from badmouthing the studio or the people involved. He allegedly refused, wrongly believing that the permanent shelving of the project was inevitable.

It's quite possible, though, that such a hardcore Hollywood type would be ill-equipped to "read" Jaglom's improvisational footage the way he would something more traditionally executed with conventional coverage. Other improv cinema mavericks have shared war stories about "experts" explaining (read: condescending) to them that their raw footage was "uncuttable," only to be proven wrong when things came together in the edit. In some sense, only Jaglom can cut Jaglom footage. He was a born rule-breaker; Hollywood's rule-followers were rightly unnerved in this situation. To everyone else, the raw materials would likely be completely inscrutable. One can see why the disconnect between Henry and Hollywood proved untenable. There was no way forward, no potential for a modus vivendi.

Only stills from the ditched fourth episode, Henry's "The Bomb," still exist. The plot: Terrorists hide an atomic bomb in a ballet theater that has only one exit. Brenda Vaccaro was originally cast as a Russian ballerina, but she left to see to another obligation and was replaced by Patrice Townsend. The title of this lost segment would seem to be self-fulfilling prophecy. On the flipside, are there flashes of, well, anything in the surviving Jaglom segment, "The Municipalians"? Not really. All three segments are pretty dire (though I like Peter Riegert dragging his kids to see a Fassbinder flick in the film's opening segment, "Growing Yourself"). It's no wonder it was deemed wholly unreleasable in this form, because the best thing in it is the sultry, snazzy Dr. John main title tune.

It is interesting, however, to observe Henry directing his actors to play the comedy so broadly, like a television sketch. Robby Benson and Richard Widmark are in full-on caricature mode: good cop/bad cop. In that sense, and others, it's many miles away from something like *Sitting Ducks*, which is wild, woolly, and unpackaged in its pursuit of zany character truth. One assumes this was slated as a parody of the Joseph Wambaugh-style cop sagas of the time, à la *The New Centurions*, *The Choirboys* and *The Blue Knight*. In any event, a woefully bizarre detour in the Jaglom corpus. He never lost any sleep over it, though, as he never really considered it his work. It remains important to cover, however, as it still bears his name.

Cast: Robby Benson (Brent Falcone), Richard Widmark (Stan Nagurski), Christopher Lloyd (Samuel Starkman), Barry Diamond (Junkie), Elisha Cook, Jr. (Mousy), Julie Kavner (Mrs. Falcone), Henny Youngman (Lawyer), Bill Kirchenbauer (Crazed Husband) Irene Forrest (Cagen) (Crazed Wife), Martin Harvey Friedberg (Dispatcher), Rhea Perlman (Little Jewish Prostitute)

2. The Crisis-Comedy Era
(including The Quartet of Self)

Henry between marriages, dealing with the extended fallout from his first divorce (from Patrice Townsend), parlaying his personal pain into material for his films.

Can She Bake a Cherry Pie? (1983)

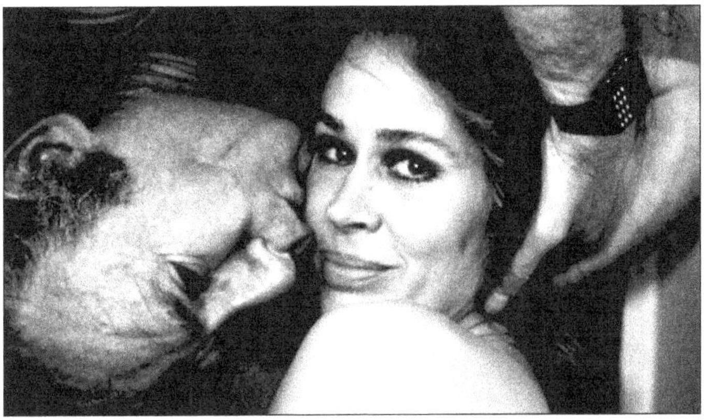

Henry: Here's a scene for you. I'm on the floor of my house with the TV on, watching the daytime soaps and crying. Total mess. Orson calls me up, because I hadn't been going to lunch with him, because I was so heartbroken. He asked me, "What are you doing?" I said, "I'm watching the soap operas. They're so truthful! There's such truth in them!" And I'm crying my eyes out on the phone there with him, a complete basket case. He bellowed, "Oh my God! Get out of there right now! Get out of there immediately, Henry! Put on sunglasses and put on a hat and get out of there! Come to lunch! I've got a story to tell you that will make you feel better." I get there and ask him, "So what's the story?" And he says, "What story?" He just wanted to get me out of the house—that's what kind of friend he was. But I was a total wreck, completely wiped out. Patrice had left me. Around that same time, I was walking all around New York muttering to myself, again crying my eyes out. I ran into Karen Black, I told her what I was going through, and

Can She Bake a Cherry Pie? was born. I paired her with my brother Michael and set them loose. The film was an attempt to give myself a happy ending. I wanted children desperately and I was losing hope that I'd have them, so the film ends with Karen announcing her pregnancy. I'm also proud that the film documents life at Café Central in Manhattan in that era. There was always so much going on around Café Central. [See Appendix titled "Karen Black on working with Henry" for her version of the project's conception.]

Commentary: *Can She Bake a Cherry Pie?* is one of the best American independent comedies of its era, along with Joan Micklin Silver's *Between the Lines* (1977), Paul Bartel's *Eating Raoul* (1982), Jarmusch's *Stranger Than Paradise* (1984), and Jaglom's own *Sitting Ducks* (1980). It would make a great double bill with Robert Altman's studio-released *A Perfect Couple* (1979), in which Paul Dooley courts computer date Marta Heflin. The best comparison, however, is to John Cassavetes's spiritually adjacent *Minnie and Moskowitz* (1971), another shaggy romance of two oddballs whose union is unlikely but somehow inevitable. Both relationships are built on the combustible coalescing of envelope-pushing eccentricity. Cassavetes lays a foundation for tearing down romantic convention while Jaglom cross-examines such conventions.

The connection between the two films runs deeper, though, with Jaglom consciously or unconsciously building upon a scene in the Cassavetes film. Peter Bogdanovich, in conversation with Jaglom in 1992 astutely points out that his then-new release *Venice/Venice* seems to have been built upon a Gena Rowlands speech from *Minnie and Moskowitz*: "Movies are a conspiracy, because they set you up. They set you up from the time you were a little kid. They set you up to believe in everything. They set you up to believe in ideals and strength and good and romance and, of course, love. So you believe it. You go out. You start looking. Doesn't happen, and you keep looking. There's no Charles Boyer in my life. I never met Clark Gable. I never met Humphrey Bogart. I never met any of them. They don't exist! That's the truth! But the movies set you up. And no matter how bright you are, you believe it!" Jaglom, for his part, starts building upon this notion long before *Venice/Venice* comes into the picture. In *Can She Bake a Cherry Pie?*, Zee tells Eli, "Life's just not what anybody had in mind. It's just not the way they told us it was going to be." This re-emerges in *Someone to Love*, when Jaglom's character Danny says, "None of us has settled into what we thought grown-up life was about when we were children." Only later on, in *Venice/Venice*, are movies and their seductive power factored into the equation.

Both *Minnie and Moskowitz* and *Cherry Pie* are romantic comedies for people with a deep and abiding distrust for the genre. *Time Out* critic Chris Peachment praised *Cherry Pie* for "a personal style that is pure innocent delight," remarking that "it ought to fall apart in its own cheerful indulgence, leaving all concerned with egg on their faces; but somehow it's all done with such a loopy benevolence that it emerges as the damn nicest film since Astaire stopped dancing." It's a loose, improvisatory, comic pas de deux—a curious romance between two New York neurotics, shot as the filmmaker was coping with a traumatic breakup that would end in the divorce covered in his next film *Always But Not Forever* (1985). Karen Black revels in her comic gifts as Zee, a sweet but paranoid blues-singing kook who picks up the equally eccentric Michael Emil at Manhattan's Café Central. Along with the now equally now-defunct Elaine's, it was a choice hangout for folks in the arts and intelligentsia.

Be it noted that Henry always had "his restaurant" (some made their way into his movies) with circumstances dictating each migration—from Old World to Café Central to Dan Tana's to Ma Maison to Mirabelle to Spago, all the way to his final hangouts of choice on Montana in Santa Monica, where I would regularly meet him. He and his dietary idiosyncrasies (one being a default mountain of lemons, delivered worldlessly immediately upon his arrival) was known by every wait staff at every establishment. Such restaurants would work themselves into the films—even in the *National Lampoon* debacle, a major scene is staged at Mirabelle. His final havenly haunts and hangouts were the now defunct Art's Table and the still-standing R+D.

Emil's usual screen persona, the loquacious, bald, but sexually confident oddball with virtually every manner of peccadillo, gets ample airing here. The film is also a robust document of the New York of that era. Its streets are vivid, and just as much a character in the film as the actors themselves. One can tell that many shots and scenes were done guerrilla-style, with random passersby occasionally gazing at the lens (or at the leads) quizzically. Some look starstruck, clearly recognizing Karen Black (a repeat occurrence, just as Seberg and Belmondo are clocked by local Parisians Godard's *Breathless*). But this contributes to an atmosphere of anything-can-happen. The streets of New York supply a sense of endless possibility, heightening each dramatic situation or comic set piece—and Jaglom is there to take full advantage. *Can She Bake a Cherry Pie?* is the ne plus ultra of Jaglom's infatuation with neurotics on screen. It's as scrappy and infectious as the Lost Wandering Blues Band, which performs the opening title tune. It may be the best of his broad comedies because it is gently tinged with pain.

Cast: Karen Black (Zee), Michael Emil (Eli), Michael Margotta (Larry), Martin Harvey Friedberg (Mort), Frances Fisher (Louise), Anna Raviv (Young Woman at Café), Robert Hallak (Young Man at Café), Paul Williams (Zee's Husband), Madeline Silver (Eli's Ex-Wife), Larry David (Mort's Friend), Arnon Milchan (Café Customer), Carol Kane (Café Customer), Meir Tepper (Café Customer), Geraldine Baron (Café Customer)

Always, But Not Forever (1985) *a.k.a. Always*

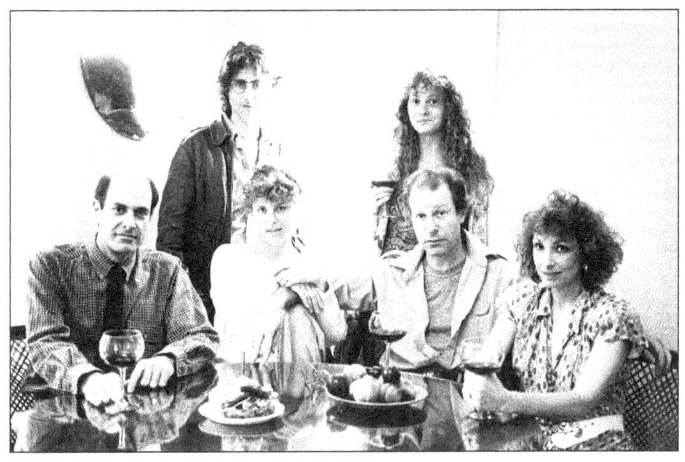

Henry: I was still dealing with the emotional fallout of my divorce. It was the type of cataclysm I had no frame of reference to deal with. Orson encouraged me at lunch to make a film about my pain. I approached Patrice, who was willing. I put together the production, all the time still very much in love with her. The happy ending for Patrice was that the film was enough of a hit that it helped her buy a new house for herself. All in all, for me, it was one of the most painful artistic experiences I've ever had. My father told me I was crazy for putting myself through it, and asked me who I thought would care. At various points, I asked myself that, but I was encouraged when people connected to it very strongly. At early screenings, they laughed in the right places, out of recognition more than anything, and I remember many people holding back tears during discussions after the movie.

Commentary: One critic dubbed *Always But Not Forever* (1985) "the greatest home movie ever made." It inaugurated the cycle of four films in which Jaglom played a version, or versions, of himself, using cinema to publicly examine his private life. The resulting "Quartet of Self" seems to divide audiences the most among his output. In this case, he cast his real ex-wife Patrice Townsend as his soon-to-be-ex-wife, shot the whole film in the house where they had lived as a couple, and explored their own divorce. In spite of her unexplained abandonment, chalked up to a vague existential dilemma, he still loved her. He cast their real friends as their friends, his own brother as his brother, etc. Director Bob Rafelson (*Five Easy Pieces* and *The King of Marvin Gardens*) shows up as a surly neighbor, and the incomparable André Gregory appears (typecast?) as a Party Philosopher.

As almost by procedure at this point, critical detractors found it a tacky piece of exhibitionism, but most critics responded quite positively. A critic from the *Boston Globe* famously/infamously proclaimed, "*Always* is the film Woody Allen would have made if he had the guts." No comment. In our recordings, Jaglom said something that fascinated me: "I grew up on movies, but my influence comes from both movies and films." Of course, "movies" meaning classical Hollywood entertainment and "films" meaning art cinema. Through the prism of that self-analysis, consider how he could have framed *Always* as a 16mm *David Holzman's Diary* or *Coming Apart*-style picture in which he bared his soul with rugged, unpolished, boldly avant-garde street-cinema techniques native to homespun confessional cinema. But the shot-in-35mm *Always* is purposefully told in somewhat more classical style, with periodic detours into what might be deemed more avant-garde devices. As his other films prove, Jaglom renders his own branded romanticism with a "movie logic" and a filmic approach. This would become kind of a métier the more he pressed on in his filmmaking.

As a stylist, he poses three questions: (1) To what extent can a filmmaker effectively hybridize documentary and fiction filmmaking? (2) Practically, how does one blur the line between the two? (3) How malleable are both forms when in concert with each other? Jaglom would address these questions even more in his follow-up film, *Someone to Love*, which certainly defies any simple categorization.

This is all a very heady, "intellectual" way of discussing a very emotionally charged film. Jaglom even later admitted that *Always* was an elaborate attempt to win his wife back. This did not happen; sadly, this was the radiant Townsend's final film appearance, as she married a fellow yoga instructor not long afterward and moved on with her life. The emotions themselves are messy, and much of the technique along with it.

The framing story works on the level of entertainment, and is compelling on those terms. On the night they are supposed to officially sign their divorce papers, David (Jaglom) and Judy (Townsend) shock and bewilder the visiting notary with their various antics of undying affection. Comedically, the notary protests and refuses to let them proceed with the signing of the papers because he is convinced they still love each other. After ostensibly getting poisoned by a dinner that David cooked especially for the occasion, Judy stays the night. The next day, David and Judy's best friends, long-married couple Eddie (Alan Rachins) and Lucy (Joanna Frank), arrive as houseguests to celebrate the Fourth of July weekend. ("Independence" Day, get it?) Soon after, Judy's sister Peggy (Melissa Leo in her debut film performance) arrives with her nebbishy boyfriend Maxwell (director Jonathan Kaufer). Together, the six of them (one married, one just recently dating, and the third about-to-be-divorced) comfort and afflict each other, resulting in a kind of extended ad-hoc group therapy session.

Always does what I call an "artful meander," a description or tendency (proclivity?) that might apply to Jaglom's work in general. There's a fair amount of hugging, rapping about feelings, and pop-psychology. No one can deny that the characterizations are genuine and that their pain and struggle to find happiness and fulfillment emerges as very real and often very touching.

Again, its use of vintage music of the Thirties and Forties is sublime in that it yields an unexpected kind of emotional reward. Some might say that, by this point in the filmography, the soundtracks are evocative of Woody Allen, but Jaglom's purpose is not one of novelty, humor, or mere fancy. It's the filmmaker's acute longing for the past—his own past, a shared collective past, and the past as an idea or general concept. The films' vintage music is a means of wistfully lamenting time having slipped away, despite his best efforts to stop it and live forever in a golden moment. Not an average nostalgia, this.

Andrea Marcovicci observes in the documentary *Who is Henry Jaglom?*, "If the blossoms are falling in a particular way when Henry takes a walk, it might actively hurt him to experience that beauty and not be able to stop or preserve it." Jaglom refers to his "Trigorin complex" in *Somone to Love*: the need for the artist to compulsively observe and record (Trigorin in *The Seagull* was often referred to as Anton Chekhov's avatar, alter ego, and spirit animal). After sonically front-loading the picture with Fred Astaire, Charles Trenet, and Benny Goodman, Jaglom ends the film on a more contemporary song, James Taylor's "Secret O'Life" which contains the lyrics, "Now the thing about time is that time isn't really real / It's just your point of view / How does it feel for you?" (shades of *A Safe Place*, again). Henry once wrote a poem that was printed in the *New York Times*, with the line "Everything becomes the past too fast." He would often quote this line in conversation.

As suggested in the recent bestselling book *My Lunches With Orson*, Welles helped Jaglom concoct the film's set-up scenario. It remained a difficult film for its director to watch. For those obsessed with blurring the often thin line between fiction and documentary, this is absolutely essential viewing. See also: Canadian documentarian Allan King's "actuality drama" *A Married Couple* (1969) as a kind of prototype. Jaglom's take on divorce is certainly novel in terms of its tender, soul-searching approach, but Claude Chabrol's *Une partie de plaisir (Pleasure Party)* (1975) provides an abrasive and much uglier cinematized portrait of a real divorce, specifically the one between Chabrol's associate Paul Gégauff and his wife Daniele. Both of them plus their daughter play slightly fictionalized versions of themselves, much like Jaglom and Townsend here. The major difference: a question of tenor.

Cast: Henry Jaglom (David), Patrice Townsend (Judy), Joanna Frank (Lucy), Alan Rachins (Eddie), Melissa Leo (Peggy), Jonathan Kaufer (Maxwell), Amnon Meskin (The Notary), Bud Townsend (Judy's Father), Bob Rafelson (Sam), Michael Emil (Mickey), André Gregory (Party Philosopher), Peter Rafelson (Sid), Sheila Oaks (Party Guest)

Someone to Love (1987)

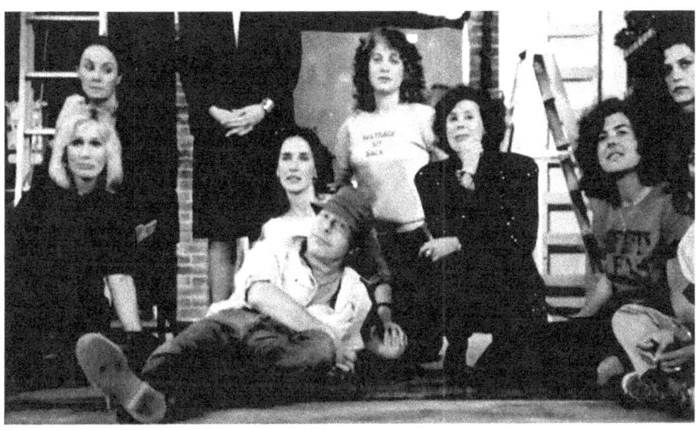

Henry: I was hung up with something about my generation. More and more people seemed resigned to a life of being alone. The life that we were told to expect, that we were set up for, is not the life many of us got. It felt like everyone was saying they were "okay" but they were hiding something about themselves. To me, it was something unique about my generation. I also wanted to showcase Orson as he actually was — the Orson that I knew so well. When he died, I toyed with the idea of titling the film *Orson Welles Says Goodbye* because I was so touched by his footage. I was filming him and he was beginning to get uncomfortable. So much of the real him was getting revealed — his sweetness and vulnerability, as opposed to all the stuff that he used to protect himself. You see it, he said, "Okay, that's enough. It's gotten too sweet," and he turned to the cameraman and said, "Cut" really forcefully. My cameraman, Hanania Baer, this tough Israeli guy, got intimidated because it was Orson Welles telling him to cut. I ran over to him and I was hysterical. "Are you crazy? You can't cut! I'm the director!" He said, "But it's Orson Welles!" I flipped it back on, but Orson didn't know it was on, so he reached behind him for his cigar that he'd hidden and he started laughing uproariously. That wonderful, all-embracing laugh. If he'd lived to see the final movie, he would never have allowed me to use the laugh because he had this stupid thing about how "a fat man," as he called himself, "shouldn't laugh" because "it's unattractive." He was embarrassed. But really, it was nothing of the sort. It was him getting the last laugh on all his problems, on sixty years of making films. It was a wonderful thing to share with audiences.

I'll tell you another story about Orson and *Someone to Love*: I'm working on the film after Orson died, editing it. I get a visit from John Huston! Orson, of course, had directed Huston in *The Other Side of the Wind*, and they'd been very close friends. He says, "You have footage of Orson that I haven't seen." I said, "Yeah, come in and I'll run it for you." He's watching the big Orson laugh and he turns to me, amazed, and says, "He let you do that?! Oh, that's wonderful! I always wanted a record of Orson laughing. I'm so glad you captured it." And he really started crying, right in front of me. Really crying. He said, "Thank you," and walked out.

But yes, never in a million years would he have let me use it in the final movie, if he'd lived. *Someone to Love* is also the movie on which he said I was like the old Eskimo in *Nanook of the North* who was carving a piece of walrus tusk. When he was asked what he was making, why he was doing this, he said, "I'll find out what's inside." He said, "You're like that old Eskimo, Henry. You're carving away at me, at your friends, at your generation, trying to find out what's inside all of us."

Commentary: The presence of Orson Welles alone, who eloquently ruminates in real time about life, love, art, the sexual revolution, and his predictions for society's future, could easily be the basis for a doctoral dissertation. *Someone to Love* (1987) is, to me, the quintessential "Jagfilm." While *Venice/Venice* might be his "testament film," *Someone to Love* has the heft to speak to the filmmaker's quintessence. Beyond being a personal reckoning, the film's sociological bearing is of remarkable import. This is truly the closest Jaglom comes to a generational statement, a pronouncement about all the things that addled his generation's pursuit of happiness.

Someone to Love is a meta-film that, picking up narratively and stylistically where *Always But Not Forever* left off, permanently distorts any line between fiction and documentary. The party in this "report on the party and the guests" is a gathering of familiar faces all by their lonesome, who congregate in a majestic art-deco theater (the Mayfair in Santa Monica) on Valentine's Day, at the invitation of filmmaker Danny Sapir (Jaglom). The surname "Sapir" is used throughout the Jaglom filmography, by various characters. The name was inaugurated in *A Safe Place* by Philip Proctor as "Fred Sapir" (who, in a kind of wordplay, becomes enmeshed in Tuesday Weld's liminal state between "appear" and "di-Sapir," à la Welles' magician).

Thanks to his businessman brother (again played by the brilliantly comic Michael Emil), Danny has become part-owner of this theater, which is soon to be demolished and turned into a shopping center. In an effort to memorialize it as a temple of art and drama, the frustrated, lovelorn Danny hires a film crew (led by his real longtime cinematographer Hanania Baer, who appears onscreen) and asks those assembled why they are alone. The presence of a lens—and Danny's lack of a sense of boundaries with that lens—has ramifications on how this rather peculiar lonely hearts-by-default party proceeds, and how these guests choose to rationalize their culturally-encouraged isolation.

Who shows up? Sally Kellerman, Oja Kodar (Orson's real-life companion), Monte Hellman, Stephen Bishop, Kathryn Harrold, Ronee Blakley, songwriter David Frishberg, Jeremy Kagan (director of *The Big Fix*, *The Chosen*, and *The Journey of Natty Gann*), his wife Elaine Kagan, and the always lovely

Andrea Marcovicci, who plays Danny's girlfriend (she was Jaglom's own at the time).

This film's sense of itself as "scrapbook cinema" (per the earlier observation) is more potent here than in any other Jagfilm. A piece here, a piece there, a musical interlude over here, some choice interview soundbites over there, a proper dramatic scene, a bit of poeticism or lyricism, another musical interlude, etc. But beyond a normal scrapbook, which consists of photographs and mementos that, more often than not, lack proper context, Jaglom attempts to dose the "hodge-podge" with the overarching thrust of thematic logic, emotional urgency, intellectual rigor, an oddball sense of structural integrity, and a method of montage that builds and then establishes. More simply put, it invents its own syntax. Comparisons? It's hard to think of any.

By the time Orson shows up to explicate the woebegone partygoers' angst, and button Jaglom's essay as a whole, what we have on top of everything else is perhaps the best living document of the real Orson Welles. (I'd also point to Dick Cavett's 1970 interview with Welles, taped while he was in New York shooting *A Safe Place*.) As Oscar and Pulitzer Prize-winner Jules Feiffer is quoted as saying on the film's poster, it's "the most apt eulogy to Orson Welles's life." Indeed, it is "a movie not frightened of its own intelligence," especially when Welles, with all his gravitas, is given such a poignant send-off. He died suddenly (in October 1985), not long after filming wrapped that July.

As Jaglom said, "I wanted to give Orson the last laugh. He never would have let me use that joyous roar of his if he'd been alive to see the film put together, but that's who he was to those who knew him and loved him." The rich discussion that Henry and Orson share towards the film's end constitutes a rare time when Welles let his guard down on screen, allowing people to see him as warm, familiar, and familial, rather than the imposing presence his monumental reputation suggested. One can immediately sense how close he and Jaglom were as friends (or "girlfriends" as Welles once jokingly put it). The way that Jaglom lets us in on that rapport is a gift for the ages.

There has been much grumbling vis-à-vis the nature of their relationship in the intervening years, but the filmmaker's deep and abiding affection for his departed friend feels very real and very immediate, and nearly impossible to cynically doubt, in *Someone to Love*'s final stretch.

Jaglom, as exemplified by work like *Someone to Love*, is the cinema itself in a way. It's a work that could exist in no other medium. Whether one loves it, likes it, is apathetic, or hates it, there is simply no other film like it.

Cast: Henry Jaglom (Danny Sapir), Andrea Marcovicci (Helen), Orson Welles (Danny's Friend), Michael Emil (Mickey Sapir), Sally Kellerman (Edith Helm), Oja Kodar (Yelena), Stephen Bishop (Blue), David Frishberg (Harry), Geraldine Barron (Attendee), Ronee Blakley (Attendee), Robert Hallak (Attendee), Kathryn Harrold (Marilyn), Monte Hellman (Richard), Miles Kreuger (Theater Manager), Maggie Wheeler (Jakobson) (Attendee), Marcia Jacobs (Attendee), Elaine Kagan (Attendee), Jeremy Paul Kagan (Attendee), Amnon Meskin (Attendee), Peter Rafelson (Attendee)

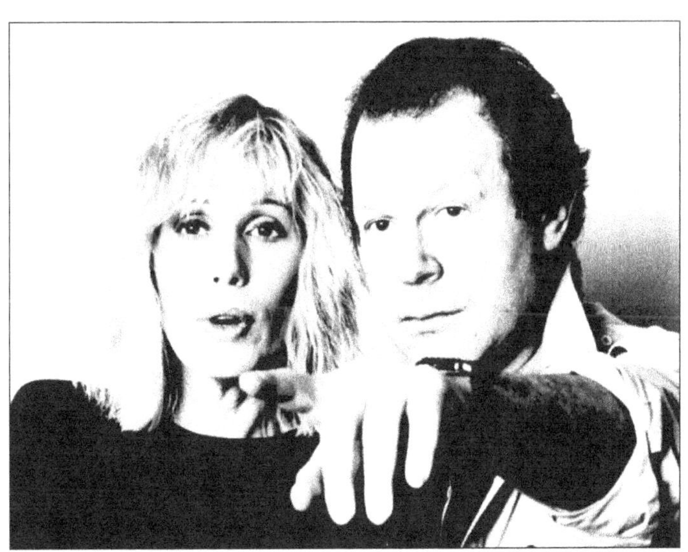

New Year's Day (1989)

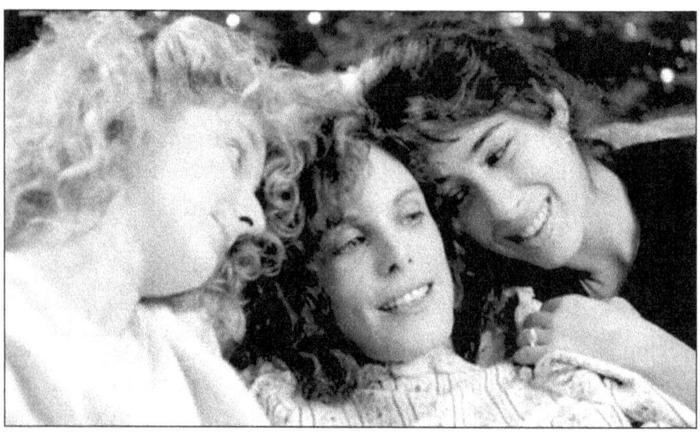

Henry: New Year's Day was a way to wrap up what I perceived was a trilogy. "Time to move on" was the idea. I had met Maggie Jakobson, or Maggie Wheeler, a few years before and thought she had an extraordinary presence. I put her in a bit of *Someone to Love*—she was one of the people in the theater interviewed. I was living during that time at my place in New York, at 11 E. 68th Street, near Madison. I thought that would be a good location, so we shot it in around New Year's in January 1987. My films, around this time, were therapy, but I've always thought that if I can make people feel less alone in whatever they're going through, the movies will have succeeded. I'm also happy I got to cast Miloš Forman, who asked me at a New Year's party if he could act in one of my movies one day, and I just told him to show up to the *New Year's Day* set and I'd give him a role. And he did, and he was magical.

Commentary: *New Year's Day* was selected as the official American entry at the Venice Film Festival. It's the final picture in Jaglom's Divorce/Coping/Moving On trilogy. It's the third in his "Quartet of Self" if you include *Venice/Venice* (1992), which incidentally was shot at the Venice fest when *New Year's Day* was in competition.

Opening on a summation of his character(s) from the trilogy's previous installments ("Okay, so I was miserable"), *New Year's Day* sees Jaglom return to his hometown New York after the period of intense emotional pain that followed the dissolution of his first marriage. His character, Drew (his third of four alter-ego D names), is looking to start over in a new city. Upon arriving at his Madison Avenue apartment, he discovers the three previous tenants still residing there due to a misunderstanding; they claim they maintain the lease through January 1st, whereas Drew believes the place is his on the 1st. Lucy (Maggie Wheeler, née Maggie Jakobson) is a cartoon voice artist whose life is in disarray as she prepares to set off for Los Angeles to start her own life over after a recent breakup; Annie (Gwen Welles) is a photographer and Lucy's best friend, who is uncertain about what she wants to do with her life; Winona (Melanie Winter) is a baby-crazy magazine editor who hears her biological clock ticking. With nowhere to go until they move out the next day, Drew gets to know the women.

An assortment of others soon arrive at the apartment for a New Years (and farewell) party. Chief among these guests is Lucy's lothario ex-boyfriend (David Duchovny, Wheeler's real-life ex-boyfriend, in his first major role), whose maddening mixed signals only confuse her more. Drew, the gathering's most objective presence, draws amusement, irritation, bewilderment, and ultimately inspiration from the various conversations and strange encounters that ensue. In helping Lucy move on with her life, he gradually finds himself readier to move on with his own. Forman plays a "dirty old man" landlord who shares a special (maybe too special) relationship with Lucy, Annie, and Winona. The incomparable Michael Emil also turns up as a party guest, the "psychosexologist" Dr. Stadthagen (Jaglom's mother's maiden name), who insists on having intercourse with female patients before deciding on whether to treat them with psychoanalysis.

Jaglom is a seasonal filmmaker, a holiday auteur. Many of his pictures revolve around parties thrown for holidays and special occasions, and a number of them are shot on a single set. *Always But Not Forever* (1985) is an extended weekend Fourth of July in Jaglom's real house, *Someone to Love* (1987) is Valentine's Day in an old theater, *New Year's Day* is self-explanatory, *Eating* (1990) is a triple-birthday bash in a large mansion, *Babyfever* (1994) is a baby shower in a similar type house, *Going Shopping* (2003) is Mother's Day in a dress shop and its adjacent café, and *Just 45 Minutes from Broadway* (2012) is Passover at a sprawling country estate. *Irene in Time* (2009) has one reference to Father's Day.

Elia Kazan was very impressed with *New Year's Day*'s finale scene between Maggie (Jakobson) Wheeler and Gwen Welles. "It's chilling because it's fired by a desperate want," Kazan wrote to Henry. Jakobson-Wheeler is bewitching in the lead female part; she went on to act predominantly in television. Gwen Welles is likewise stunning; she starred in one last film, Jaglom's *Eating* (1990), before leaving us way before her time in 1993. Filmmaker Donna Deitch (*Desert Hearts*) documented Welles's brave struggle with breast cancer in the harrowing documentary *Angel on My Shoulder* (1998).

Cast: Henry Jaglom (Drew), Maggie Wheeler (Jakobson) (Lucy), Gwen Welles (Annie), Melanie Winter (Winona), David Duchovny (Billy), Miloš Forman (Laszlo), Michael Emil (Dr. Stadthagen), Harvey Miller (Lucy's Father), Irene Moore (Lucy's Mother), James dePriest (Lucy's Shrink), Robert Hallak (Delivery Man), Katherine Wallach (Delivery Man's Friend), James Hurt (Winona's Brother)

Eating (1990)

Henry: Food is and was an issue of primary importance in the lives of all women that I've ever known, almost universally. To me, food was always just there. I could eat it and forget about it. I realized after spending enough time with enough women, food had a lot to do with their identity, with their sense of themselves—it could be obsessive and frightening. It's tied into how they deal with the world. When Jane Fonda first came out and told the world that she was bulimic and had been

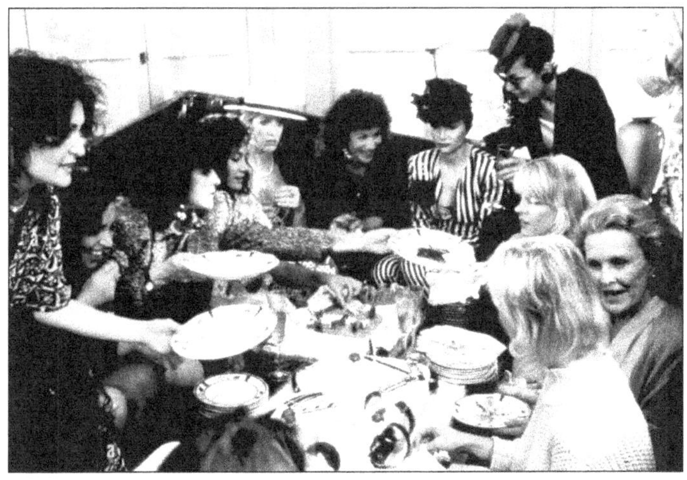

for twenty-five years, people were stunned. They looked at her saw this perfect body, and they realized that this is not an issue that is just related to overweight women or women who are, according to conventional society, twenty or thirty pounds more than what they should be. This problem is in the mind, it's what society does to women. And it's nothing really to do with an objective reality about how they look. Men didn't understand it and they certainly didn't make movies about it.

Men aren't given the message daily that their success in finding love and fulfillment revolves around the number of inches they can take off their waist or hips. No man is told by society that his essential worth is non-existent because he doesn't look "right" in a bathing suit. Quite simply, men don't have it hammered into them from their earliest childhood that happiness and all the good things in life can only be bought by starving themselves. So I thought it was very important to try to make a movie that was dealing with it from the point-of-view of the women experiencing it. It's the first of its kind, I'm quite sure. That's what the papers used to say, anyway. Men were very angry with me. They would storm out of the theater when their wives and girlfriends had brought them. The women would defiantly stay and the men would leave. Then the same women would come back to see it again with their girlfriends or mothers. I was proud of that. People suggested all kinds of things to do to make it more appealing to men. I wasn't the least bit interested. That wasn't my job.

Commentary: Like George Cukor's *The Women* (1939) and Joseph Losey's swan song *Steaming* (1985), Jaglom's *Eating* (1990) features a 100% all-female cast. There are two centerpieces in this film, which became one of Henry's biggest commercial successes, arguably the film with which he is most identified, and the first in his quintet of films specifically about women, and their unique set of dilemmas, problems, obsessions, and challenges.

One centerpiece involves the distribution of pieces of birthday cake prepared for three women respectively turning 30, 40, and 50. A plate is passed around the all-female gathering… and it just continues being passed round and round. In an exquisitely simple visual for a knowingly dialogue-heavy picture, Jaglom succinctly communicates the many pertinent talking points that orbit this crucial, symptomatic collective gesture.

In its other centerpiece, Frances Bergen (Candice's mom) sings an a cappella rendition of "The Way You Look Tonight," a tune that appears in many other Jaglom films, including *Tracks* and *Can She Bake a Cherry Pie?* With motherly affection and abiding concern for this group of women, she delivers a potent musical message after learning or directly witnessing their complexes around body image, food, or eating. According to Henry and an eyewitness I know in San Francisco who saw it in 1990 during its initial theatrical run, some audiences were so moved by this musical performance that they applauded in the theater.

When the women refuse to eat the birthday cake (at least in public, as "sneak eating" is also examined), puzzled French documentary filmmaker Martine (Nelly Alard) decides to interview the guests. As often happens in this era of Jaglom's output, a film that begins as narrative transforms into something much more essayistic and documentary-adjacent. The "story" is interspliced with the women's direct-to-camera confessions, probing their secrecy, shame, self-loathing, and powerlessness. What is it about food that… "consumes" them? If *Eating* was not the first major work to address women, food, and eating disorders such as anorexia and bulimia, it was pivotal in legitimizing these disorders as manifestations of a broader cultural, psychological, and systemic condition that demanded attention rather than customary dismissal. Thankfully, the issue is taken much more seriously today. It earned a fair amount of publicity, including the talk show treatment on a downright bizarre episode of Phil Donahue, in which the cast members are assembled behind a long table of culinary delights, as if to ridicule their disorders.

As Roger Ebert writes in his original review of *Eating*, "We eat for all sorts of reasons having little to do with hunger and nutrition. We eat for security, for reassurance, for companionship, for social reasons, for something to do." The film's most famous line, "I think I'm still looking for a man who can satisfy me as much as a baked potato," exemplifies the role food can assume in daily life beyond its utilitarian value.

As a male author, I am not totally secure addressing pictures like *Eating*, *Babyfever* (1994, about women and their biological clocks), *Going Shopping* (2003), *Irene in Time* (2009, about women and the complex relationships they share with their fathers), and *The M Word* (2015, about menopause). I can remark on a purely cinematic level—and as a male outsider—about these pictures. Henry said it best: "If men enjoy *Eating*, great, but it's aimed at women."

Post-Script: The 1990 *Movieline* Jaglom profile piece "The King of Spago" by James Kaplan, published just in the wake of *Eating*'s success, opens on a funny scene: various Spago denizens in search of Debra Winger's missing Armani purse. In the middle of the dragnet, Winger quips, "I feel like I'm in a Henry Jaglom movie! You know, one minute it's serious, and the next minute it's completely bizarre," only to be promptly told by a waitress that Jaglom was seated down at the other end of the restaurant. Somehow and in some way, Winger had been in "Jaglom country" before this Spago misadventure.

This amusing salvo evoked, for me, a scene in *Terms of Endearment* (1983), when Winger's character, a plainspoken Nebraska-by-way-of-Iowa housewife visits her dearest friend Patsy in New York City. Following an upscale luncheon with Patsy's well-heeled, career-driven, urban-sophisticate lady friends, Winger marvels, half-appalled, "In less than two hours, two of them told me that they'd had abortions. Three of them told me they were divorced. One of them hasn't talked to her mother in four years. Another one told me she has a yeast disease and vaginal herpes, and another had to put her daughter in a boarding school because she has to travel for a job. If that's fit conversation for lunch, what's so god-awful about my little tumor?!" Ironically, it would seem as if Winger's character suddenly, if only for a moment, wandered into and out of a Henry Jaglom movie, especially the track of female-centered pictures that *Eating*, *Babyfever*, and *Going Shopping* established. It took Jaglom to come along and make whole movies about those types of gatherings. The very part that *Terms* director James L. Brooks elliptically cuts away from (and only sums up later) forms the lifeblood of Jaglomia. And it was *Eating* which set the pace.

Cast: Frances Bergen (Whitney), Lisa Blake Richards (Helene), Nelly Alard (Martine), Mary Crosby (Kate), Gwen Welles (Sophie), Elizabeth Kemp (Nancy), Marina Gregory (Lydia), Daphna Kastner (Jennifer), Beth Grant (Carla), Taryn Power (Anita), Hildy Brooks (Mary), Savannah Smith Boucher (Eloise), Sherry Boucher (Maria), Toni Basil (Jackie), Jackie O'Brien (Janet), Catherine Genender (Lily), Aloma Ichinose (Joanna), Rachelle Carson-Begley (Catherine)

Venice/Venice (1992)

Henry: *Venice/Venice* is a movie about how the movies affected our dreams of life and romance, and how the movies made it impossible to have a sane love life. But it's also a film about what it's like to be this weird thing called a filmmaker, especially making the types of films that I do. But I was also in the kind of push and pull between illusion and reality. I met Nelly Alard when I went to Paris in 1983, and I found her very exciting. She was a student at that point. I told her then, "I don't know how, but I want to put you in a movie." When I was doing *Venice/Venice*, she seemed the perfect person to cast. She could have been a star, I think, but she became a very successful novelist. When *New Year's Day* was invited as the American entry in competition at the Venice Film Festival, I used that as the backdrop. The idea is to use everything, use whatever you've got. Suddenly I had a thousand extras, the fans, the journalists, the paparazzi with all their cameras, at these great hotels. Nobody interfered and no one looked into our lens because we were just another film crew.

I had always wanted to make a movie at a film festival, because each festival seems to create its own universe. And they are all about movies. But the people who make movies themselves get caught up in their own fantasies at these events, and I wanted to capture that. To me, there's a very romantic thing about a film festival. Anything can happen, you might meet somebody, it could change your life. They are intense periods of shared time, rather like sea voyages. I made an arrangement with the press when I was there. I told them, "You can interview me, I'll do anything you want. All I ask in return is that you let my crew film you filming me."

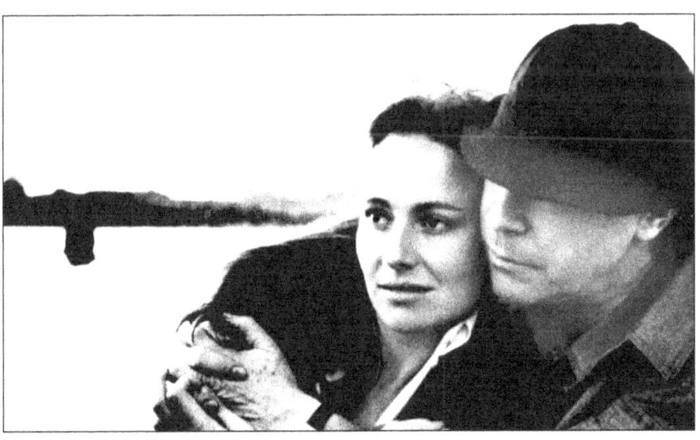

Daphna Kastner just showed up in Venice and said, "Here I am! Use me!" I only brought a few people from the U.S. because I was keeping the budget tight. I told her that she could play my assistant, but that that I would treat her very roughly, to get even with you. But the way I work, she probably knew deep down that I would adapt. And I did.

Commentary: About midway through Thom Andersen's three-hour essay documentary *Los Angeles Plays Itself* (2003), an essential piece of urban and cinematic anthropology, the sardonic narrator snipes, "If New York has Woody Allen to live down, we [Angelenos] can't feel superior. We have Henry Jaglom, who's even more narcissistic and even more solipsistic." These snarky remarks introduce and bleed over into a clip from Jaglom's *Venice/Venice* (1992), which one critic called "the egomaniacal Jaglom's commercial for himself." Jaglom himself prefers the headline of a Colorado newspaper's review of the film: "Jaglom on Jaglom again - Who cares?"

Despite the filmmaker's amusement at these cheeky denunciations, *Venice/Venice* is the picture he claims most expresses his personal philosophy and outlook on life. I admire it especially for its structural audacity. As the title suggests, the film's first half is set in Venice, Italy, while the second half is set in Venice, California. Of course this alone is not novel, but this structural bifurcation reveals itself in a Möbius strip final twist as an eloquent expression (and manifestation) of the film's key thematic preoccupations. Is there a kinship between reality and illusion, and how is this reflected in movies? How has this magician's medium embedded dreams of romance into our collective psyches? What impact have movies had on our lives, our expectations, our standards for living? How does the slippery nature of time and our often tenuous perception of past/present define how we interpret the dance between reality and illusion? Do movies infuse or instill in us any ability to make sense of it all? The ending is a master stroke at stirring debate around these pregnant questions.

In other ways, *Venice/Venice* is Jaglom's own take on Fellini's *8½*. His filmmaker character Dean grapples with many quandaries and crises similar to Marcello Mastroianni's character Guido's. Like Mastroianni, Jaglom must answer to all who have grown to depend on him (for either emotional support or for work on his films), while juggling that responsibility with attempts to rectify his own existential and creative predicaments. About *8½*, Jaglom once wrote, "The film changed my identity. I realized that what I wanted to do was make films. Not only that, but I realized what I wanted to make films about: my own life, to some extent." And between its skewering of show business and the interspliced interviews with various women discussing all these ideas in their own words and from their own experience, we know we're firmly in Jaglom country. Building off Gena Rowlands's speech in Cassavetes's *Minnie and Moskowitz*, in which she bemoans men not measuring up to their cinematic models and laments how movies build us up just to let us down, one of Jaglom's interview subjects rues, "Men were Cary Grant, men were Gregory Peck. But in reality, men were not Gregory Peck. Men were assholes."

Venice/Venice is precisely the type of culminating achievement one might—and should—expect from a filmmaker who spent many years, great effort, and emotional rigor creating full-length, intensely personal autobiographical portraits that strive to comment on contemporary reality itself. Incidentally, we also get to hear Jaglom distinguish between "good narcissism" and "bad narcissism" rather early in the film. This is a philosophy that he held near and dear for most of his life. "The way we experience the world is initially through ourselves. If we're not willing to admit that, we're not really looking at each other. Bad narcissism is when you stop at only looking at yourself. Good narcissism is when you use your healthy initial self-love to then turn it to somebody else, and try to get a sense of who they are. And you're open to who they are because you know something about what you are, otherwise I don't think you can love anybody else, if you don't love yourself first." In later years, Henry would refer to this as "empathetic narcissism."

The beguiling Nelly Alard, who transitioned into writing novels, commands the screen in her co-starring role. She's sensational as Jeanne, the journalist and fan who arrives at the Venice

Film Festival with the intent of interviewing Dean, just as Alard herself had once interviewed Henry at length for her own documentary *On the Tracks of a Filmmaker: Henry Jaglom* (1988). In her memoir cum novel *The Life You Had Imagined*, Alard writes of her director and short-term lover/fling, "We were opposites in every way. The list of our differences was so long that what was most astonishing was the mysterious alignment of stars that had attracted us to each other in the first place." (Incidentally, she vividly recounts being introduced to Orson Welles at Ma Maison, so this helps place their affair on the biographical timeline.) She does consider *Venice/Venice* "a movie about [their own] aborted love story," but one that also ruminated on "the romantic illusion conveyed by popular cinema, and the subsequent disillusion that inevitably results." The film's specific reflection of their personal history and shared reality was, to her, Henry's standard operating procedure. "Nothing was ever created out of nothing with [Henry]," she states, "and nothing was ever lost, either: everything was transformed into film, theater, or books." She compares the process of acting and improvising in Jaglom films to "a litter of kittens being thrown into freezing water, thrashing about to keep from sinking straight to the bottom in front of the camera's merciless eye." From this objective perch, she succeeds admirably and, vis a vis "feline aquatics," even Olympically. Unfortunately, Nelly's acting career ended prematurely after *Venice/Venice* (at least outside her native France), but she remained friends with Henry to the end.

David Duchovny co-stars as a shallow boytoy star-to-be who fences and feuds with Dean in preparation for a role in his new picture. Melissa Leo is affecting as an emotionally scarred lady friend whose role in Dean's life is gradually usurped. Shostakovich's Concerto No. 2 for Piano and Orchestra hauntingly underscores this cobweb of cross-purposes.

Venice/Venice is a kind of capstone. The narrative, emotional, and stylistic arc from *Always* to *New Year's Day* is fairly clear. Across three films, we witness Henry's transition from a broken, desperate man, to one who "forces his misery onto others" (as Orson Welles tells him in *Someone to Love*), and finally to the scarred, quiet interloper at a party at which he finally sees himself reflected back unfiltered. Jaglom bookends these pictures with direct-to-camera addresses, in which he speaks with sincerity as himself on behalf of thinly disguised alter egos. Within the context of the quartet rather than the trilogy, Jaglom reigns victorious in *Venice/Venice*, as the "orchestra conductor" (read: film director) known for "making movies about himself," who finally is able to juggle then arrange the elements of filmic time to definitively illustrate and interpret reality and illusion, at least for himself, all after spending years making autobiographical pictures that blur those lines. I cannot name another similar progression in another cinematic series.

Cast: Henry Jaglom (Dean), Nelly Alard (Jeanne), Melissa Leo (Peggy), Suzanne Bertish (Carlotta), Daphna Kastner (Eve), David Duchovny (Dylan), Vernon Dobtcheff (Alexander), John Landis (Himself), Zack Norman (Dennis), Diane Salinger (Stephanie), Victoria Foyt (Interviewee), Marshall Barer (Mark the Singer-Songwriter)

Lucky Ducks (circa 1993)

Henry: [see his comments in Chapter 11]

Commentary: I remain convinced, even in light of Henry's complete dismissal in our conversation, that enough of it exists to create a satisfactory final product. I do believe Henry's disenchantment with men, and the male nature and thought process, prevented him from seeing clearly in this case. Even in their monosyllabic slob disposition, Henry could have provided fresh insight into the limits of men, in equal measure to a high-quality, high-temperature roast—customized to his sensibility. But he wanted to go home, where his heart was... with women. And that's what he did.

Cast: Michael Emil (Simon), Zack Norman (Sidney), Roscoe Lee Browne, Gwen Welles, Daphna Kastner

3. The "Victorian" Era

Henry meets second wife Victoria Foyt around the time of editing Eating. *They marry in 1991, he casts her in the lead of* Babyfever, *and from there, his films start to get less essayistic and more story-oriented. They have two children together, Sabrina (b. 1991) and Simon (b. 1994)—he begins featuring them in his films, in both small parts and flash appearances.*

Babyfever (1994)

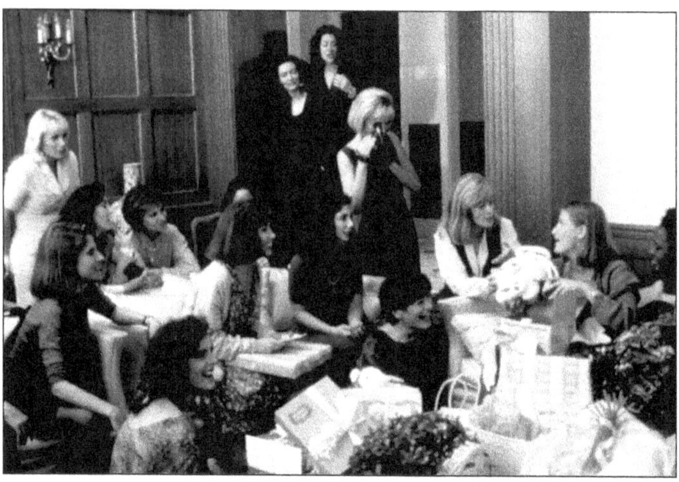

Henry: Having babies was such a topic of conversation among every woman I knew at that time. For many men too— I obsessed over it, for decades. I really wanted to be a father before it was too late. Women and their biological clocks seemed the perfect way to continue what would become my series of women's films. Victoria gave me the idea, I think when she was pregnant herself and I was promoting *Eating*, and I thought it was brilliant. So I told her to start writing it— I think it was the first film of mine on which I'd shared a writing credit. The amazing thing is that so many of the women in the film went on to have babies directly after the movie, including women who'd had trouble conceiving for years. It seemed that everyone got pregnant after *Babyfever*, including

Frances Fisher. Tracy Avildsen asked me if I put something in the coffee, I remember.

Commentary: Michael Musto joked in the *Village Voice* that *Babyfever* copied the *Eating* formula so closely that it should have been titled *Ovulating*. I would never say that *Babyfever* is the Jagfilm that most interests me, but as I've grown older, the prospect of parenting has put *Babyfever* in front of me anew, in a different light. In 2024, when I recorded the Blu-ray commentary track with Henry for the film, it seemed to be the biggest film for which he developed "scissorhand syndrome" upon rewatch. He told me, and the listeners, that he would have cut Zack Norman and his entire subplot completely out of the movie if he were editing the film today. Be that as it may, he remained happy with the extant work, as he was with mainly all his films.

Cast: Victoria Foyt (Gena), Matt Salinger (James), Frances Fisher (Rosie), Eric Roberts (Anthony), Elaine Kagan (Milly), Zack Norman (Mark), Eliza Roberts (Dr. Hilda Glass), Charlayne Woodard (Eartha), Irene Cagen (Forrest) (Sylvia), Tracy Brooks Swope (Avildsen) (Maggie), Robin Curtis (Carol)

Last Summer in the Hamptons (1995)

Henry: *Last Summer in the Hamptons* is really my love poem to actors. Even though I have been a director for a long time, first and foremost I am an actor. When I am directing, I am acting at the same time. I'm part of it. Even though I am behind the camera, I'm still one of the characters in the film. I took Chekhov's *The Sea Gull* and *The Cherry Orchard* as a kind of model structure, and I created the type of crazy theatrical family I would have wanted to be part of, in contrast to my very upper-crust, business and society-oriented family. I'm certainly not complaining, because I had an amazing childhood and I love my family. But I was also this crazy creative in a family that didn't totally understand that. When I met Viveca

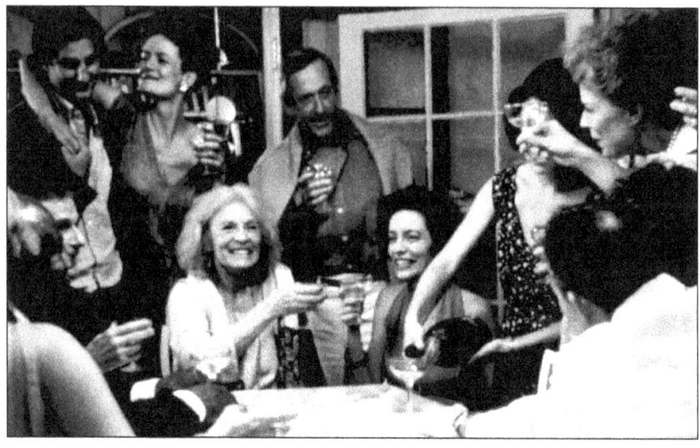

Lindfors, she became a muse for the matriarch figure in this theatrical dynasty. It sometimes wasn't the easiest film to make, because we had that boisterous ensemble, but as my valentine to actors and to the theater, I think it's one of my better films.

Commentary: A boisterous theatrical family lights up the first section of Ingmar Bergman's *Fanny and Alexander* (1982). Its next section gives way to a rigid, hushed, punitive asceticism. Exorcised of Bergman's most sobering tribulations and somber trappings, *Last Summer in the Hamptons* is a Jaglomian pageant of another boisterous theatrical family: show people in a spasmodic spiral of neverending performance. As the playwright character Jake barks at one point, "This family is just a barrel full of theatrical eels poisoning and electrocuting one another over and over again." Or as one character says much more simply in Henry's favorite musical *Sunday in the Park With George*, "Artists are bizarre." Imagine spending a weekend with a large theatrical family of crazed, high-strung thespians and artistes, many of whom are flaming drama queens, played by the likes of Viveca Lindfors, André Gregory, Melissa Leo, Martha Plimpton, Ron Rifkin, Jon Robin Baitz, Roddy McDowall, Roscoe Lee Browne, Holland Taylor, Kristoffer Tabori, Diane Salinger, and Brooke Smith. This is the irresistible proposition hoisted onto Tartuffe-ian protagonist Victoria Foyt in *Last Summer in the Hamptons*, a delicious ensemble comedy that is certainly the closest Henry ever came to directing an all-star cast.

Critic Scott Foundas, a longtime supporter and admirer of Henry's, praised *Last Summer in the Hamptons* as the peak of his career. I see it as his *Midsummer Night's Dream*, with Lindfors as a matriarchal Puck abroad in Chekhov Country, who bears witness to the furtive comings and goings, secrets, lies, seductions, and all the resulting complications during one last stay at the generations-old family retreat, which economic hardships have required them to sell (again, "Anyone for Chekhov?"). Appropriately, the estate is abuzz, preparing for a special family workshop production of Chekhov's *The Seagull*, to be staged on the grounds for invited guests. This is similar to André Gregory's late invite-only theatrical productions, which were always years in the making.

There's the young genius gay playwright (real playwright Jon Robin Baitz, fresh from his Broadway smash *The Substance of Fire*) at the center of the family's attentions. Much revolves around him. There's his eccentric, horndog director father who has shunned him (André Gregory), the opportunist apprentice who flirts aggressively with him (Nick Gregory, André's son), his possibly incestuous sister who is hung up on her Chekhov lines (Melissa Leo), his beleaguered, desperate-for-a-hit actor cousin shamelessly vying for the lead role in his hot new play (Ron Rifkin), Rifkin's tomboyish daughter ravenous for constant attention (Martha Plimpton), and the "normal, well-adjusted" Lindfors son who strikes up *un petit affaire* with Foyt's visiting Hollywood movie star interloper (Kristoffer Tabori, real-life son of Lindfors and George Tabori). Like any multi-character mosaic worth its salt, there are other characters too, but these are the principals.

There is a "loaded" reference (if you will) to what Jaglom himself refers to as the gun "McGuffin" in Renoir's *Rules of the Game*, which is ironically a very literal "Chekhov gun." There are the actorly games the characters play with each other as both a stealthy communication of hidden agendas and as a self-absorbed evasion tactic. Jaglom himself appears in a single scene as a hilariously overbearing Hollywood producer-director disingenuously extolling the "bold feminist statement" in Foyt's box-office smash superhero character Mary Marvel. He plays the anti-Jaglom, and it's a hoot. Many Hollywood producers approached Jaglom after the film premiered, asking if he was specifically roasting them in that role. Unfortunately, though, this marked the last time he ever appeared onscreen in one of his own movies.

There is also a tenderness and sincerity to the film as a valentine to actors and creative artists when, at the bittersweet finale, the spellbinding Lindfors recites O'Shaughnessy's "Ode" ("We are the music makers, / And we are the dreamers of dreams") knowing full well this last summer performance marks the end of an era for herself and her marvelously dysfunctional family. Jaglom would create another similarly mercurial theatrical brood in his later play/film *Just 45 Minutes from Broadway* (2012). I can imagine a member of the Mora/Axelrod family (*Hamptons*) marrying a member of the Isaacs/Cooper clan (*Broadway*) and foresee a grand opera of emotional nuclear-fallout level at such a gathering.

The film was shot in the East Hamptons at the actual Jaglom family summer house, named "Proskurov," after Henry's father's childhood home in Russia. The entryway sign over the driveway is visible in a few shots. Like in the film, the house was on the market during shooting. Documentarians Henry Alex Rubin and Jeremy Workman can be spotted in the background of a couple scenes shooting their profile doc *Who is Henry Jaglom?* (1995).

Cast: Victoria Foyt (Oona Hart), Viveca Lindfors (Helena Mora), Jon Robin Baitz (Jake Axelrod), André Gregory (Ivan Axelrod), Melissa Leo (Trish Axelrod), Martha Plimpton (Chloe Garfield), Ron Rifkin (Eli Garfield), Nick Gregory (George), Savannah Smith Boucher (Suzanne), Roscoe Lee Browne (Freddy), Roddy McDowall (Thomas), Diane Salinger (Marian Mora Garfield), Brooke Smith (Lois Garfield), Kristoffer Tabori (Nick Mora), Holland Taylor (David Mora Axelrod), Henry Jaglom (Max Berger), Barbara Flood (Wealthy Lady)

Déjà Vu (1997)

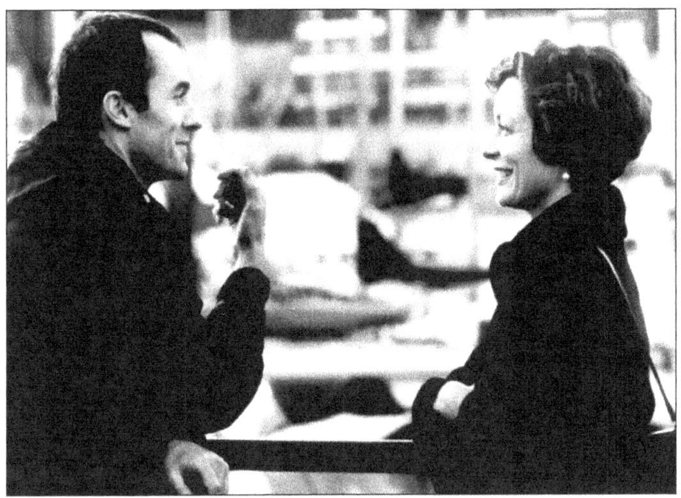

Henry: I wrote *Déjà Vu* as a short story in 1974. It was very different then — different characters, a much different storyline, but one thing remained constant between that initial piece and the finished film nearly twenty-five years later: the story of two people, each of whom is settled in life, each of whom is committed to a reasonably happy and satisfactory relationship, who suddenly meet one another and feel that they belong together, feel as if they somehow have been together already, although they have never actually met before. I've always been haunted by that concept, best expressed in Lorenz Hart's great lyric, "It seems we've stood and talked like this before. / We looked at each other in the same way then, / But I can't remember where or when."

I wrote it out in different forms and Patrice [Townsend] even had a go at writing a script with me at one point. Something I couldn't define was always missing, so I kept putting it away to work on other films. In 1990, my very first meeting with Victoria Foyt was so redolent of the *Déjà Vu* story that I knew it was only a matter of time before we would be working on it together. We realized, as the lead characters began developing, that the film should be shot in timeless foreign locales. When we found ourselves in Israel for the Jerusalem Film Festival, we decided to shoot the opening scenes there. The rest of the script, however, required extensive location shooting in London, Dover, and Paris, something I had never done before. It was going to require a higher budget.

[Producer] John Goldstone and I had been close friends for years and he has been successfully producing films in the U.K. for a long time, including all the Monty Python movies. I sent him a copy of the script, he liked it, and we decided to make it together, with him producing. I was most excited by getting Vanessa Redgrave to play the crucial role of the emotional catalyst. The unique quality of this piece required that I stick pretty much to the script, more than I ever had, following a strong narrative with all its twists and turns. And after all these many years of resisting it, I discovered much to my surprise that I really love telling a story!

Commentary: *Déjà Vu* is a globetrotting piece of romantic cinema with a level of originality one would likely not anticipate from such an enterprise. It is nevertheless a film of many antecedents. One can easily appreciate it on its own, but I guarantee a richer experience when you consider it within the larger context of Jaglom's career.

As for these antecedents, first and foremost is William Dieterle's *Portrait of Jennie* (1948)—produced by David O. Selznick, starring Jennifer Jones and Joseph Cotten—a movie that haunted Jaglom almost his whole life. Looking at the arc of his collective work, you start to understand why. Its themes of memory, time, timelessness, the elusiveness of time, and the emotional ramifications of time also impacted the way Jaglom approached *A Safe Place* (1971), *Tracks* (1976), *Venice/Venice* (1992), and the appropriately titled *Irene in Time* (2009).

In *Portrait of Jennie*, Jones plays the eponymous romantic vision, who exists outside of a rational understanding of time. She emerges in frustrated painter Cotten's life, inexplicably wearing antique clothes, to inspire him during a dry spell. She grows conspicuously older each time he re-encounters her.

Cotten's ultimate tragedy is his inability to sustain neither a moment in time nor his inspiration at its source. In *A Safe Place*, Jaglom spoke incessantly that his edit of the film "used time emotionally," but in *Déjà Vu*, the two principals experience time as emotion. Time arranges them, whereas previous Jaglom heroes grappled with rearranging time in their own favor.

Victoria Foyt stars as Dana, a soon-to-be-married American woman visiting Jerusalem. At a café, she has a chance encounter with a mysterious woman who approaches her and tells her personal story of lost love that revolves around the antique ruby pin she's wearing (shades of Max Ophuls's *The Earrings of Madame de…*). When the woman leaves abruptly, suddenly Dana realizes that things are not as they seem. Present time seems to have at least momentarily slipped away—she's re-emerged from a time warp. In her quest to find the woman (who might very well have been some kind of ghost), she chances to meet British painter Sean (Stephen Dillane) at the white cliffs of Dover. Or have they met already? Whatever their case may be, they feel irrepressibly drawn to each other, but their first rendezvous is spoiled by Dana's guilt over her fiancé, Alex (Michael Brandon). Fate or chance, or what-have-you, dictates that they haven't seen the last of each other, however. As Dana heads off to London to meet Alex at a house owned by family friends of his (Noel Harrison and Anna Massey), who else should cosmically pop up there but Sean and his ten-years-married wife (Glynis Barber). Vanessa Redgrave stars as Skelly, an aging free-spirit who passionately prescribes living a rollercoaster existence that lunges at any opportunity for romance, no matter the consequences. She shares a supremely touching scene with her real mother, Rachel Kempson, appearing here in her final film role at age 87. She died five years later.

As *New York Times* critic Stephen Holden observes, "*Déjà Vu* goes on tangents of a sort you won't find in the work of any other filmmaker. The most delightful is a throwaway bedroom scene between an older married couple. The husband, who has an insatiable appetite for candy bars, tempts his wife with sweets.

After bickering, the two fall into a voluptuous reminiscence of their childhood tastes in candy. It's an utterly real moment in a movie whose insights into tenacious grown-up longing are a lot more penetrating than many of us would like to admit." The candy confab is perhaps my own favorite scene in the picture. It whimsically captures the simultaneous urgency and delight in the act of remembering, and how it binds couples, and grounds us in a stability of permanence.

Déjà Vu is one of Jaglom's most critically and commercially successful pictures, for good reason. The film tunes into the romantic yearnings we all have at some level, seizes upon them with wit and improvisational magic rather than cheap sentiment and hackneyed knock-off Hollywood scripting. Both would be easy default approaches to this material. The story is one that Jaglom groomed over a period of decades (including as a musical at one point), culminating in his collaboration with second wife, lead actress Foyt (also the co-writer). This is the director at his most ambitious, his most epic, his most (dare I say) timeless. And though, as a hardened atheist, he rejected this claim, it is Jaglom at his most theistic (the film believes in some sort of human puppeteer orchestrating our paths, à la the way that Alan Rudolph broached this same idea in his *Made in Heaven*). This is the pinnacle of "spiritual Jaglom," and the film of his that is most embracing of life. By the finale, as their final moment onscreen is crystallized in an artistic expression—a painting rendered by the director himself—Dana and Sean begin living moment-by-moment together, now knowing that tomorrow is where the past is, as Tuesday Weld declares in *A Safe Place*. Most simply expressed, *Déjà Vu* is one of its director's crowning achievements and one of his very best pictures. It's also his most successful "story film."

Cast: Victoria Foyt (Dana Howard), Stephen Dillane (Sean), Vanessa Redgrave (Skelly), Glynis Barber (Claire), Michael Brandon (Alex), Vernon Dobtcheff (Konstantine), Graydon Gould (Dana's Father), Noel Harrison (John Stoner), Aviva Marks (Woman in Café), Anna Massey (Fern Stoner), Rachel Kempson (Skelly's Mother)

Festival in Cannes (1999)

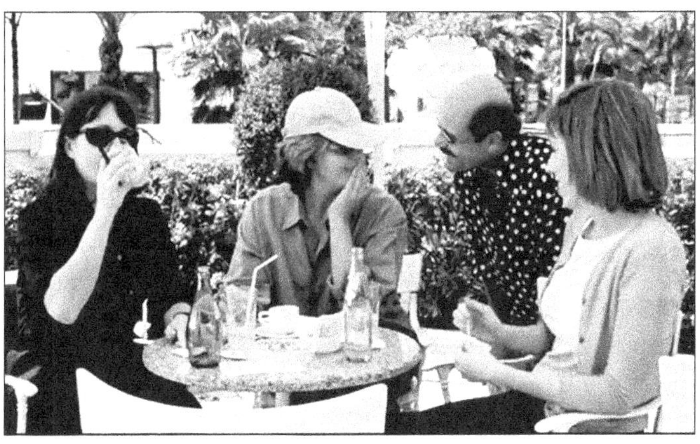

Henry: I met Anouk Aimée and got the idea to resurrect the Cannes project I was going to originally do with Gene Kelly all those years ago. That's how *Festival in Cannes* happened. We went in 1999 and we shot around the actual festival. It's the second of my film festival movies, next to *Venice/Venice*.

Commentary: In the spirit of Michael Ritchie's unjustly forgotten Cannes caper *An Almost Perfect Affair* (1979), *Festival in Cannes* is the final result of a project Jaglom devised in the Seventies for Gene Kelly, under Daniel Melnick's reign at MGM. Kelly was to play an aging, nearly forgotten movie star who is re-invigorated when he ventures to the festival and unexpectedly finds romance. Slated to be shot while MGM promoted *That's Entertainment!* (1974) at the festival, the film would have likely featured Fred Astaire, Cary Grant, Cyd Charisse and other noted legends in walk-ons and cameo roles. A couple of weeks before shooting was to commence, Kelly got cold feet and backed out, citing insecurity on a few fronts, especially the idea of playing an older, faded star (after all, he had danced and romanced Catherine Deneuve in *Les demoiselles de Rochefort* just seven years before, doing so as if he hadn't aged a day). Melnick implored Jaglom to get Kelly back on board, but that version of the project was ultimately abandoned.

Over twenty years later, when Jaglom met Anouk Aimée at the Academy of Motion Picture Arts and Sciences 50 Years of Cannes gala, he resurrected the idea. Because he loved Lelouch's *A Man and a Woman* (1966), Jaglom knew he just had to work with Aimée. "I wanted to address how women are treated when they get older—both generally in our culture and especially in the film world. Women are discarded and 'dealt with' at a certain age." Jaglom had already proven himself a man who lived by his words and his beliefs to the contrary of the mainstream, having cast the beautiful, radiant, 74-year-old powerhouse Viveca Lindfors to lead *Last Summer in the Hamptons* (1995) just five years prior. Anouk Aimée (then 68) is the epitome of intelligence, loveliness, grace, and strength in *Festival in Cannes*. That these incredible women would ever be deemed obsolete, anywhere or in any context, is an unforgivable sin.

Established actress Alice Palmer (Greta Scacchi) has come to Cannes to write, develop, and raise funds for a feature-length feminist character study she intends to direct, hoping to cast someone like Gena Rowlands as her principal. Along comes a blarney-gifted grifter Kaz Naiman (Zack Norman), who overpromises but seemingly wheels-and-deals a $3 million deal if she agrees to cast Millie Marquand (Aimée), a screen legend attending the festival for a tribute. Millie in turn must decide whether to take a handsomely paying but thankless supporting part in a Tom Hanks blockbuster produced by Rick Yorkin (Ron Silver), or the meaty lead role in Alice's independent film, which she would personally prefer. At a career crossroads himself, Rick manipulates veteran director Victor Kovner (Maximilian Schell), Millie's philandering director ex-husband, to get her to accept the offer in the Hanks film. Meanwhile, naïve ingenue Blue (Jenny Gabrielle) becomes the toast of the festival with her debut performance in a low-budget smash that takes Cannes by storm. Faye Dunaway, William Shatner, Peter Bogdanovich, and Louise Stratten appear in amusing cameos.

I honestly can't name another picture that captures the frenetic energy of a major film festival as adeptly as this one, with all the dreaming, scheming, finagling, and sleight of hand one would expect from such a conflagration of talent, tradesfolk, and tricksters. To me, the only picture that comes closest is the aforementioned *An Almost Perfect Affair*, but Keith Carradine and Monica Vitti's amour fou (though compelling) doesn't quite hold a candle to Schell and Aimée's tender, even poignant rekindling of a failed romance amidst the hullabaloo of a shark convention on the French Riviera. The denouement, during which both of them address the camera directly and confess that which is in their hearts about each other, is supremely poignant. *Festival in Cannes* is yet another picture that proves Jaglom, despite whatever pronouncements were made against him, was first and foremost a filmmaker of the heart, unabashedly.

Paramount Classics picked the film up for distribution, thus constituting one of the only two Jaglom pictures released by a major studio (though Paramount had released many of Jaglom's earlier titles on home video). Zack Norman plays a character based on the version of himself he seemed to become when Jaglom ventured to Cannes with him for the Oscar-winning documentary *Hearts and Minds* (1974), which they produced together.

Cast: Anouk Aimée (Millie Marquand), Maximilian Schell (Viktor Kovner), Greta Scacchi (Alice Palmer), Ron Silver (Rick Yorkin), Zack Norman (Kaz Naiman), Peter Bogdanovich (Milo), Jenny Gabrielle (Blue), Alex Craig Mann (Barry), Rachel Bailit (Nikki), Vernon Dobtcheff (Millie's Escort), Louise Stratten (Milo's Girlfriend), William Shatner (Himself), Faye Dunaway (Herself)

Going Shopping (2005)

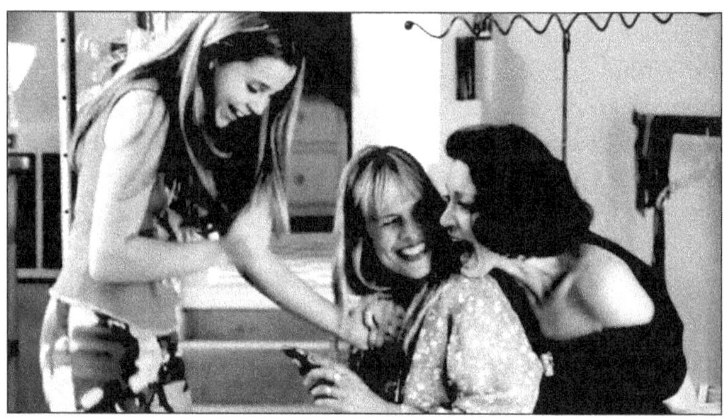

Henry: I had a lot of fun on *Going Shopping* because, of course, I love clothes and women's things, and I got to talk to women about dresses and colors and jewelry and all of that. I could really be a girl on *Going Shopping*. I got more men in the film. I'm not sure that I was as honest as I was in *Eating*. It's maybe more entertaining because I made it more male-friendly. I was a little concerned about having done that, even though I don't think I did anything dishonest.

Commentary: As Arthur Miller put it in his play *The Price*, "The main thing today is shopping. Years ago a person, he was unhappy, didn't know what to do with himself. He'd go to church, start a revolution, something. Today, you're unhappy? Can't figure it out? What is the salvation? Go shopping!" Jaglom, of course, couches these notions of American consumerism into another essay on, and outing for, women—women in the wider world, and the women he had known personally throughout his life. *Going Shopping* is, from where I personally sit, the most outright entertaining in Jaglom's series of "women's films." It is more approachable for male audiences because the subject matter is not sexually exclusive. Though he does not lose or in any way soften the essayistic, documentary-like interludes—considering that a parade of women are once again asked to profess the nature of their obsession with shopping direct to camera—this time he has fastened it to more of a narrative, that being the struggle to save a Montana Avenue boutique from financial ruin and closure. Lee Grant, as always, is a joy to behold.

Cast: Victoria Foyt (Holly Gilmore), Rob Morrow (Miles), Lee Grant (Winnie), Mae Whitman (Coco), Bruce Davison (Adam), Jennifer Grant (Quinn), Juliet Landau (Isabella), Robert Romanus (Jimmy), Joseph Feury (Richie), Angela Garcia Combs (Mother), Jenny Gabrielle (Waitress), Kim Kolarich (Waitress), Robyn Peterson (Nicole), Pamela Bellwood (Landlady), Cynthia Sikes Yorkin (Lisa), Martha Gehman (Melanie)

4. The "Tannic" Era

Henry meets Tanna Frederick around 1999-2000. When she gets his play A Safe Place *produced in Los Angeles in September 2003, and stars in the lead role as Noonie ("Noah" in the film), she becomes his muse. By this point, the films are altogether almost entirely story-oriented. He returns to the stage, writing plays, staging them, then adapting them for the screen. Note: It becomes tricky to be objective in any way about these pictures, because I got to know everyone involved with them very well.*

Hollywood Dreams (2006)

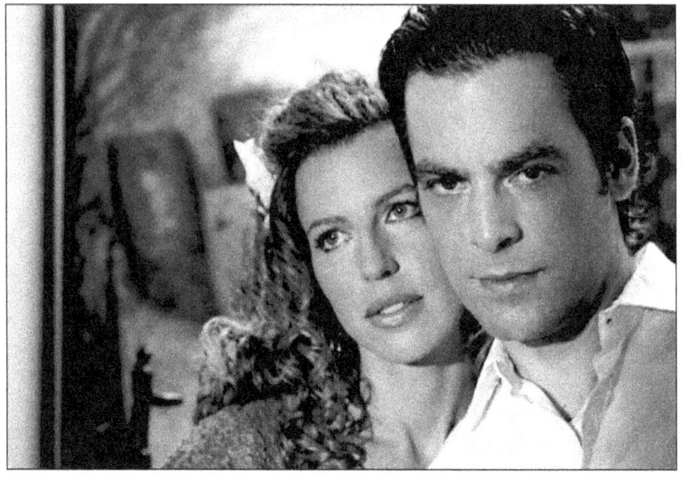

Henry: Tanna is an astonishing talent. She is the most spontaneous and the most in-the-moment actor that I've ever worked with. She has the fullness of life, the fullness of expression. You can throw anything in her direction, which is perfect for my way of working. She has the range to go into comedy—profound, hysterical, almost broad Lucille Ball-type comedy—and then the next moment, she can go into tragic, touching, serious pathos. And she never "acts" it. She feels it, she behaves it. I knew I wanted to make a movie, so we started coming up with *Hollywood Dreams*. I did a screen test, a so-called "audition," where she reads some bits from the play *A Safe Place* and burst into tears in the middle of it, in character. We turned into a brain trust. I talked to Cassavetes about this, with Gena Rowlands. He felt the same way about Tanna, of course. I revolved the entire movie around her, taking little biographical details, like the fact that her character was from Iowa and had come to Hollywood to make it as an actress.

Commentary: For as much as Jaglom hated being compared with Woody Allen in his lifetime, particular case-by-case comparisons are apropos and certainly there to be drawn. *Sitting Ducks* is a sort of a shaggier *Small Time Crooks* or *Take the Money and Run*; *Can She Bake a Cherry Pie?* is like a rugged, earthier *Annie Hall*; *New Year's Day* centers three women just as mixed up as *Hannah and Her Sisters*; *Venice/ Venice* is just as contentious a filmmaker disquisition as *Stardust Memories*, and so on.

I thought for years that *Hollywood Dreams* was a featherweight affair, until I realized how thematically akin it is to Allen's unfairly dismissed *Celebrity* (1998). Beyond being a mere opening salvo for Tanna Frederick's career as a movie actress, it's saying something more penetrating about a very particular sickness. Those who crave celebrity status and show business success, so often driven by deeper needs—and sometimes psychosis—are constantly performing. They are just as propelled by the art of skillful manipulation as they are by the socially acceptable art forms we celebrate. When does performance stop, the true self begin, and the wounds that the constant performance conceals open?

Henry loved being the subject of a "good con," even when there was something on the line. He liked being manipulated by a skilled performer, and got annoyed when he was the subject of a "bad con," as he deemed it. He misread something about me personally, many years ago, and gave me this whole speech about how "shitty" "bad cons" and "bad hustles" are. He considered that the most insulting. In the profile piece "The King of Spago" by James Kaplan, he admitted how delighted he was when Gwen Welles pulled the wool over his eyes about something during the making of *Eating* ("*You* manipulated *me*! I can't believe you got away with it—it's so great!"). Tanna Frederick also conned him at the outset, beguiling him with a lengthy letter about how much she had loved *Déjà Vu* despite never having seen it. When she copped to the hustle, he was thrilled rather than offended. What is the root of that? Henry loved a good performance and loathed bad or emotionally dishonest performances, even if a con was at the root of it.

Why is all this relevant? The manic Margie Chizek character in *Hollywood Dreams* is the consummate hustler, a skilled manipulator, so much so that she is almost an anti-hero from time to time. Many critics and audiences were unsettled by her tearful excesses, the revealed nature of her Machiavellian perfidy, and her delirious, generally performative schtick—the performance of a performance, one might say. She's the most "movie crazy" of all Jaglom's often movie-crazy characters, re-enacting scenes from classic movies to beguile, confuse, or charm her targets, or her "prey" if you will. It is in the scene Frederick shares with Melissa Leo that the stakes of her conniving are revealed as trauma-related psychosis. On top of this, there's the deception and day-to-day "performance" of the Justin Kirk character, an actor sold to the press as gay and typecast as such (all the more ironic because Kirk is a heterosexual who had then recently played one of the leads in Mike Nichols's *Angels in America* film adaptation). As he cavorts around as the red-blooded heterosexual he actually is, he must avoid detection and operate under the radar, before "coming out as straight." *Hollywood Dreams* is a film of precarious pretenders flirting with disaster. Jaglom sees an industry of people hungry for fame, and in a constant state of performance in its pursuit. It's the director at his most cynical in a way, but as established, he relishes a "good hustle" and a "good con." Everyone in Hollywood, in the biz, operates on a wavelength that we're often not privy to. Karen Black's big moment near the climactic scene likewise speaks to this thesis.

To my chagrin, I find that the later Margie Chizek/Maggie Chase movies eschew these constructs, in a way. There is something about *Hollywood Dreams* that is knowing, informed by experience, and seasoned by hard-bitten industry savvy. There is fresh insight into the machinery of fame, and how ambition erodes sincerity and true human connection. I was amazed on my last viewing at things I noticed that I hadn't previously pondered to any conspicuous degree. It's an ideal entry in Jaglom's line of show biz chronicles, in many ways a darker vision, but made oddly charming by the fact that the director truly is in Margie's corner and clearly forgives her everything. In the scene of her masturbating to the image of herself in the newspaper, he underscores the more bitter comic implications of runaway narcissism.

In the final scene, the character sits alone patting herself on the back for the manipulative real-life "performance" she's just given in her break-up with a heartbroken Kirk. That pang of recognition that falls over her face when she realizes she is likely consigned to a life isolated from meaningful human connection, in favor of the fame she craves, is perhaps the most tragic of all Jagfilm conclusions. No character in the Jaglom-verse is more damned to a life of torment than Margie Chizek at the end of *Hollywood Dreams*. And this from the man who loved his happy endings! This is not to detract from the film's comedic humanism, especially present in scenes shared between Zack Norman and David Proval, deliciously working outside their comfort zones as an aging gay couple. Seymour Cassel's one-scene character is named Rupert, in honor of his and Henry's mutual friend Rupert Crosse.

Cast: Tanna Frederick (Margie Chizek), Justin Kirk (Robin Mack), David Proval (Caesar DiNatale), Zack Norman (Kaz Naiman), Melissa Leo (Aunt Bee), Karen Black (Luna), Keaton Simons (Jimmy DiNatale), Kim Kolarich (Kiki), Jon Robin Baitz (Jonathan Harrington), Eric Roberts (Thomas Kurt), Seymour Cassel (Rupert), Sally Kirkland (Minister), F.X. Feeney (Journalist), Sabrina Jaglom (Zoe the Child Director), Simon O. Jaglom (Johnny, Boy on Swing), Richard Schinnow (Leon), Philip Proctor (Theater Director).

Irene in Time (2009)

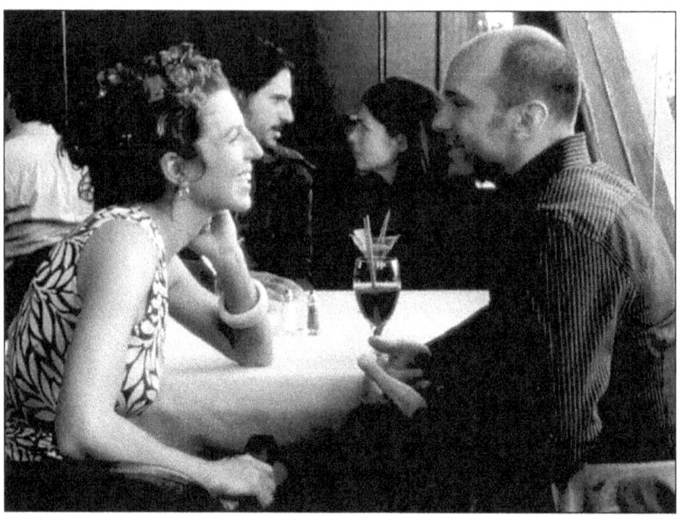

Henry: Long before becoming a father in 1991, I had been fascinated by the complex relationship between fathers and daughters—ones that I would see or hear about, the often profound effect that fathers seem to have on their daughters' lives, often even long after the fathers themselves were gone. In literature, works such as Dickens' *Little Dorrit*, Sylvia Plath's *Daddy*, or *King Lear* have held a singular fascination for me, one that has been compounded by the tales told to me by the women I have come to know in my life. The many different father-daughter dynamics seemed uniquely compelling, long lasting and fraught—sometimes in wonderful, loving ways, sometimes with devastating results. So many women have told me "I never got over my father" or "I married my father" or, as Barbara Walters repeatedly wrote in her biography, "I could never be with him, he reminded me too much of my father."

Orson Welles stunned me one day as he sadly confessed out of the blue, "I never knew how to be a father to girls. I could have been a good father, I think, to boys, but I never knew how to do it with my three daughters." So that is one theme that has been of lifelong interest to me. Also, ever since early childhood, I have been fascinated and even obsessed with movies in which, one way or another, love beats time: *Portrait of Jenny*, *A Guy Named Joe*, *Here Comes Mr. Jordan*, *Stairway to Heaven* [*A Matter of Life and Death*], *The Life and Death of Colonel Blimp*. When I finally got to work on *Irene in Time*, I had a teenage daughter of my own and had come to understand the complex father/daughter thing that I mentioned earlier, in a way that only the father of a daughter (or the daughter of a father) can fully get.

Commentary: Critic Jonathan Rosenbaum once wrote that Jaglom "reduces" the women in the interview sections of *Venice/Venice* to an "obsessive theme." He huffs that "one doubts that these real-life women are as unoriginal as Jaglom makes them sound." I think that's an unfair critique, selectively applied in the case of *Venice/Venice*. The fourth entry in Jaglom's series of "women's films" is, however, rather an odd mixture. I find it frankly just a bit odd that characters wander through the film incessantly discussing their fathers, often in awkward, incongruous, or downright peculiar situations. It's a question of format, really. Considering the extent to which viewers are smothered with the father-daughter theme, I told Henry once that I think he should have set the film at a Father's Day party (or at least had the film culminate at one), keeping in line with the holiday-party format of *Eating*, *Babyfever*, and *Going Shopping*. That would have given all the daddy-talk some motivation and grounding in basic logic. I wouldn't say he was fully receptive as he never apologized for his work, but he did understand my point on some level. His defense was that he took some artistic license. I understand the intention, but I don't think the magical realism "plot" aspect of the story works as well as the essayistic aspects, or the "bad date" scenes. It feels as if our filmmaker is trying to merge the mysticism, romance, and story-consciousness of *Déjà Vu* with the documentary essayism of *Eating* or *Babyfever*, and the unlikely blend of chemicals just doesn't ignite. An intriguing experiment, nonetheless. Note, once again, the idea/theme of "time," present even in the title.

It is, however, wonderful seeing Andrea Marcovicci return to the Jag-verse, playing once again (appropriately) a chanteuse. A tip of the hat to Grammy-nominee Harriet Schock for some of the catchy songs she contributes to the soundtrack here. Some critics complained, but I think it was a means for them to hide the fact that they likely left the theater singing "Learning at Starbucks" to themselves. I would never begrudge any woman who connects with this material the joy or relief they feel in watching *Irene in Time*, however—and the same thing goes for any of Jaglom's "women's films." I enjoy them from a certain (maybe not so terribly distant) perch, but I admit I'm not the target audience, and I could never be by virtue of my sex, despite whatever gayest part of myself feels stimulated. That is simply as it should be.

Critic Scott Foundas labeled Henry "the mumblecore forefather" in his review, writing, "Moments of genuine insight alternate freely with those of banal psychologizing, but even then, there can be no denying that the filmmaker has an ear for a certain brand of self-absorbed discourse often overheard in restaurants and bars in the shadow of the Hollywood sign. And, given the choice, I'll take Jaglom's home movies over Jonathan Demme's any day of the week." He likewise found *Hollywood Dreams* superior. There's something to that—and be it noted that Foundas was mainly referring to Demme in his final career chapter rather than on the whole. (Incidentally, I think Jaglom and Demme in their respective primes are both to be treasured.)

Cast: Tanna Frederick (Irene Jensen), Andrea Marcovicci (Helen Dean), Victoria Tennant (Eleanor Jensen), Karen Black (Sheila), Lanre Idewu (Jacob), Kelly De Sarla (Jo Jo), Jack Maxwell (Mikey Cagney), David Proval (Norm Forentino), Reni Santoni (Sam), Harriet Schock (Sandie Fuse), Sabrina Jaglom (Gigi), Simon O. Jaglom (Ollie), Louise Stratten (Hostess), Barbara Flood (Phyllis), Joe Manganiello (Charlie)

Queen of the Lot (2010)

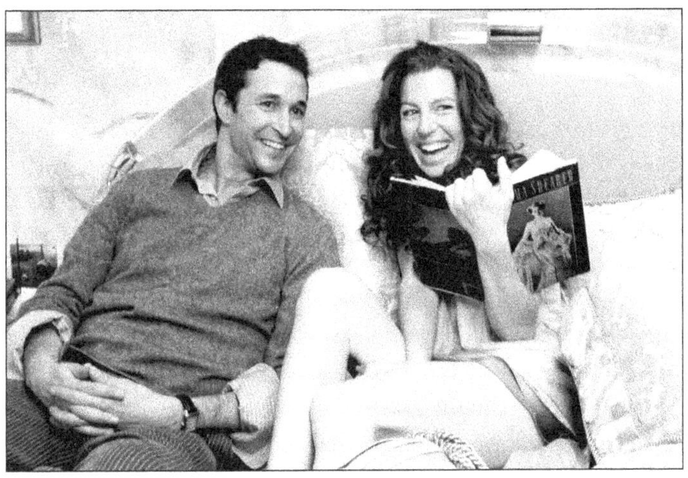

Henry: We wanted to continue the story of Margie, or Maggie, saga from *Hollywood Dreams*. It was my bid at a series… or franchise, if you think about it like that. In the headlines at the time was all the stuff about Lindsay Lohan, with the substance abuse and DUIs and all that. So that seemed to be the way to take her story.

Commentary: *Queen of the Lot* certainly lacks the teeth that *Hollywood Dreams* has. Gone is the sentimental cynicism and the heroine's mile-wide Sammy Glick streak, and out in full force is this sequel's sense of itself as an airy spree. That said, Noah Wyle and Jack Heller are both excellent, an ideal romantic foil to Tanna Frederick, who is as fearless as ever. My favorite Tanna Frederick Jagformances, however, remain her heartbreaking turns in *Hollywood Dreams* and especially *Train to Zakopané*.

Chris Rydell (son of actor-director Mark) makes a contribution that is made all the more fascinating when one takes into account how the character was partly inspired by Christopher Jones [Henry's always fragile relationship with Jones covered earlier in this text]. It is also of interest to see Henry answer to pop culture developments like reality TV.

Most amusing of all, perhaps, is a major plot point that revolves around whether a temperamental veteran director character played by Peter Bogdanovich will dare helm a major motion picture remake of Ernst Lubitsch's *Trouble in Paradise* (1932), or refuse to on "religious" grounds. Of course, the "religion" in the Bogdanovichian sense is The Cinema, though one could all too easily imagine the real Bogdanovich committing to such a project, as he made a name early on his career by skillfully parroting the likes of Ford, Hawks, Capra, et al. and fitting their sensibilities around his emerging own. Why not add Lubitsch to the repertoire? It could be argued he already had, with his box-office disaster musical *At Long Last Love*, but a proposed formal Lubitsch remake becomes a serious bone of contention in the *Queen of the Lot* story.

It still feels like Henry is playing a lot for farce here, and I miss the bite (there go those teeth, again!) in the commentary of its predecessor. That's not to say that it lacks for entertainment value, but mileage will vary. One could of course say that about any Jagfilm, depending on one's constitution.

Lastly, I recall Henry telling me how the gambling scenes in the film were based in part on gambling adventures with Elliott Gould and other esteemed company, but I did not get that on the official record. I phoned Elliott himself to possibly clarify this detail (I first met Elliott at Jaglom parties, then got to know him better later on). He remembered, "Henry might have accompanied me to some poker games at some point, but I don't remember specifically. It's certainly possible. I first met Henry because Jack Nicholson told me that he knew, or had met, another eccentric Jew. He told me that we had to meet. And he was determined to introduce us." It would seem to me that these *Queen of the Lot* poker scenes are also vague manifestations of the nightly private poker games he played at Robert Walker, Jr.'s house, with Maureen Stapleton and Marilyn Monroe's masseur.

Cast: Tanna Frederick (Maggie Chase/Margie Chizek), Noah Wyle (Aaron Lambert), Christopher Rydell (Dov Lambert), David Proval (Caesar), Zack Norman (Kaz Naiman), Paul Sand (Ernesto), Peter Bogdanovich (Pedja Sapir), Dennis Christopher (Odin Johannessen), Jack Heller (Louis Lambert), Kathryn Grant (Elizabeth Lambert), Mary Crosby (Frances Lambert Sapir), Sabrina Jaglom (Zoe Lambert), Diane Salinger (Hildi), Ron Vignone (Gio), Kelly De Sarla (Crowley), Simon O. Jaglom (Michael Lambert), Eliza Roberts (Erika), Wendel Meldrum (Kylie), Michael Emil (Saul Greilsheimer), Robert Hallak (Client), F.X. Feeney (Journalist), Charles Matthau (Poker Player), Philip Proctor (Journalist).

Just 45 Minutes from Broadway (2012)

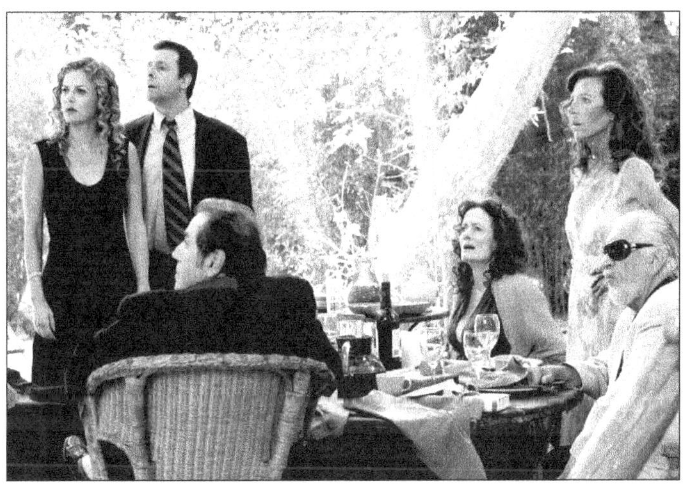

Henry: Our family Passover seders were rather notorious, even on a national level. In my cousin Ralph Gardner's Wall Street Journal piece, he accounts how I had brought my then-girlfriend actress Sandra Smith to a seder one year. She was not Jewish so it was all new to her. She went onto the Johnny Carson Show soon after and proceeded to explain how all the kids would scurry under the table to steal the afikomen, then attempt to haggle and negotiate for a good going rate. Cash envelopes were handed out. Carson got all these protest calls the next day, including from a handful of rabbis, and he was forced to go on the air the following night to explain that the Jaglom family seder wasn't really representative of what happens at a normal seder. But that was our family. The next year, when I was thinking of coming home with another actress girlfriend, I was told, "Our family doesn't need any more publicity." When I was writing *Just 45 Minutes from Broadway*, it was important to me to write a boisterous seder scene, just like the ones I used to know, to invoke Irving Berlin, another Jew. Beyond that, the play and film of *Just 45 Minutes from Broadway* is another valentine to actors, just like *Last Summer in the Hamptons* was.

Commentary: The play and film of *Just 45 Minutes from Broadway* are closely blood-related to *Last Summer in the Hamptons*. Every character is the star of their own show: needy narcissists hurling emotional napalm. Or per Jon Robin Baitz's early *Last Summer in the Hamptons* metaphor, another barrel of theatrical eels. As in *A Safe Place*, Jaglom's previous stage-to-screen adaptation (or quasi-adaptation), he uses the original play as a scaffold to construct a cinematic sandbox where the actors improvise around the foundational story, situations, and essential structure. *Just 45 Minutes from Broadway* is a far more linear and conventional film product than *A Safe Place*, however, to say the least. It is not without a few noteworthy formalist twists, though.

The film opens like a dress rehearsal for the "theater-film" approach that is expanded and enhanced in Jaglom's swan song *Train to Zakopané*, his other late, personal stage-to-screen adaptation. Our players are introduced on an obvious set in what is obviously an otherwise empty theater. A complementary bookend scene on the same set towards the end fully reveals a 35mm camera dollying back in a heretofore unseen wide master-shot. It's a rug-pull not dissimilar to the one in *Venice/ Venice*. In between, the play is opened up, transplanted from that stage to a real location, a family hacienda in the country.

A theatrical layer or membrane does still remain, especially in a climactic scene played out on this country house's veranda, as if that veranda were a proscenium. One could dismiss the flat, distanced staging here as staid or cinematically pedestrian, or (more generously) reminiscent of live television, but when Jaglom then cuts back to the theater proper, with his reveal of the Panavision camera to break the illusion and thus tie everything up, we instantly glean that there's a bit more up his sleeve. His extrapolation of this artifice in the superior *Zakopané* takes flight, thanks to the prototype in *Just 45 Minutes from Broadway*.

Paul Mazursky featured a Chassid in each of his movies, sometimes in the background and other times in bit parts, as a kind of trademark. In commentary tracks, Mazursky would proudly proclaim "There's my Chassid" at the sight of each. Henry's Jewishness has lurked at the edges of his movies, occasionally poaking its head up and making itself further known. Orson Welles's Rabbi Nachman stories in *A Safe Place*, the TV program starring two Reform rabbis in a motel room in *Sitting Ducks*, Michael Emil's Talmudic references in *Can She Bake a Cherry Pie?*, and the centrality of Israel in *Déjà Vu* are just a few examples. In his later period, with *Just 45 Minutes from Broadway* and especially *Train to Zakopané*, Jaglomian Jewishness became more than a general mien. It lived large. Around the time these projects were being conceived (the latter in particular), I was consulted on various Jewish "points of order," as it were. The big seder sequence in *Just 45 Minutes from Broadway* is a consummate Jaglomian gathering. By this point, we had seen an Independence Day cookout, a Mother's Day mega-sale, two film festivals, a baby shower, a triple birthday blowout, and parties for both Valentine's Day and New Year's. All have given the filmmaker grounds for quirky ensembles to gather, ruminate, kibbitz, philosophize, self-dramatize, and overanalyze. A boisterous seder brings so much in the Jaglomverse full circle.

I do tend to prefer this particular work in its original form as a stage play, but a number of scenes and lines added for the film lend that loose, patently Jaglomian comic verve.

Cast: Tanna Frederick (Pandora Isaacs), Judd Nelson (Jimmy d'Angelo), Jack Heller (George Isaacs), Diane Salinger (Vivien Isaacs Cooper), David Proval (Larry Cooper), Julie Davis (Betsy Isaacs), Harriet Schock (Sally Brooks), Mary Crosby (Sharon Cooper), Michael Emil (Misha Isaacs), Simon O. Jaglom (Willy Lewis), Sabrina Jaglom (Judy Cooper), Jack Quaid (Danny), Eliza Roberts (Aunt Kit).

The M Word (2014)

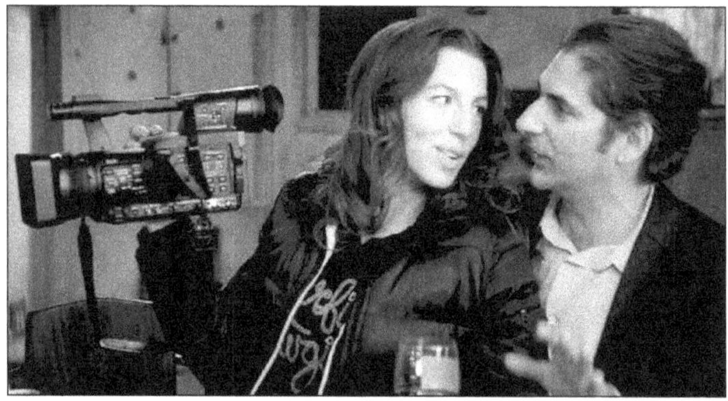

Henry: Menopause affects women, and it affects the way you perceive a woman, and how it is affecting her work and life, and any compassion and empathy you feel for that woman. It should not be a secret. Women told me while making the film that their own mothers didn't talk to them about menopause and didn't prepare them for it. There are no women who if they live long enough, don't get menopause. I never found a woman yet who didn't want to discuss it. But women my mother's age would be shocked by this. My mother was shocked by *Eating*. I think it's important that we talk about it. Tanna had a huge sensation playing Sylvia the dog in the A.R. Gurney play. I filmed a bit of that, and I wanted to get the funny animal things she did into *The M Word*. So we said, let's have Moxie play a dog on the children's program, even though she's interested in making a documentary on women's lives.

Commentary: *The M Word* is the final entry in Jaglom's run of "women's films," this time about menopause and the "change of life." Henry first mentioned this as a future film subject back in 1994 when he was promoting *Babyfever* ("Menopause is a topic I want to do"). The chemistry between Tanna Frederick and Michael Imperioli is the film's best element; a romantic montage shot guerrilla style and set to Sarah Vaughn's "Speak Low" is supreme and effective, and in point of fact, one of the better romantic sequences in this final movement of Jaglom's career. Filmed at the height of the "Occupy" movement, this marks the first time a Jagfilm broaches labor and class struggle. Jaglom had been confronted multiple times throughout his career vis-à-vis his resignation to covering the "cushier" problems of the privileged. He at least acknowledges, in some stride, how the other half (or, cough, the 99%) live in this film.

Cast: Tanna Frederick (Moxie Landon), Michael Imperioli (Charlie Moon), Corey Feldman (Benny Becker), Frances Fisher (Carson Riley), Gregory Harrison (Mack Riley), Mary Crosby (Aunt Rita Stephenson), Eliza Roberts (Aunt Louise Steiner), Stephen Howard (Doug Dengrove), Robert Hallak (Harry Rubinek), Cathy Arden (Sherry Baum), Zack Norman (Louie Hess), Ron Vignone (Rich Rizzoli), Michael Emil (Sam Sapir), Simon Jaglom (Johnnie Sapir), Lisa Pescia (D.D.), Gary Imhoff (Lloyd Duff), Harriet Schock (Sheila).

Ovation (2015)

Henry: *Ovation* was shot entirely in this theater where Tanna did the play *The Rainmaker*. I decided that what's interesting is not onstage but backstage. You never see the play in the film. That gave me inspiration. I have to create a story that takes place entirely in the theater. There's another reality, which is economics. I can't have vast sets. I need things that take place in a limited area.

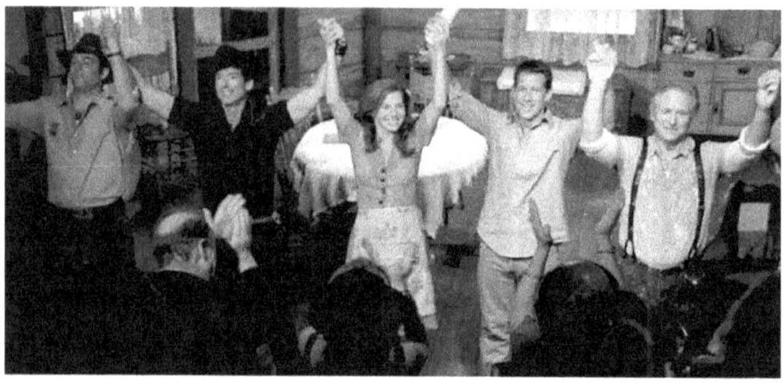

Commentary: Otherwise known as *The Henry Whodunit*. Also, simultaneously, the third in the "Maggie Chase Trilogy" inaugurated with *Hollywood Dreams*, so this is a "sandwich" or "salad" movie in its way. James Denton proves a welcome addition to the Jaglom retinue. I admire the concept of a multi-pronged, many-moving-parts backstage drama, and I admire that the central play is the seldom staged *The Rainmaker* by N. Richard Nash, rather than something more expected or perfunctory. Not everything quite coalesces, however. The most effective of the thematic threads stitched into the movie is the art vs. commerce question. Maggie has grown a helluva big conscience since her first time out in *Hollywood Dreams*—when her character is offered a stable gig in a plum TV show, one gets the sense that the fresh, green Margie Chizek of the earlier film would have leapt from the footlights into the arms of the hunky star dangling the opportunity. Evolution? She dithers because she knows it would hamstring the strapped *Rainmaker* company, who are dealing with financial hardship and possible closure. What emerges is Jaglom's perennial love of the stage, of actors (once again, forever, and always). But also, elements such as the Tarot subplot were sharper in something like *Tracks*. The abusive relationship subplot does not move the needle much at all.

Cast: Tanna Frederick (Maggie Chase/Margie Chizek), James Denton (Stewart Henry), Stephanie Fredericks (Sybil Edwards), Cathy Arden (Rosalind Goodman), Simon Jaglom

(Michael "Mouse" Lambert), Zack Norman (Kaz Naiman), David Proval (Caesar), Diana Salinger (Hildi), Ron Vignone (Gio Vitale), Sabrina Jaglom (Zoe Lambert), Stephen Howard (Harry Falen), David Lee Garver (Earl Bigbee), Benjamin Chamberlain (Gideon Garrett), Robert Standley (Bill Breck-nell), Kim Kolarich (Kiki)

Train to Zakopané (2017)

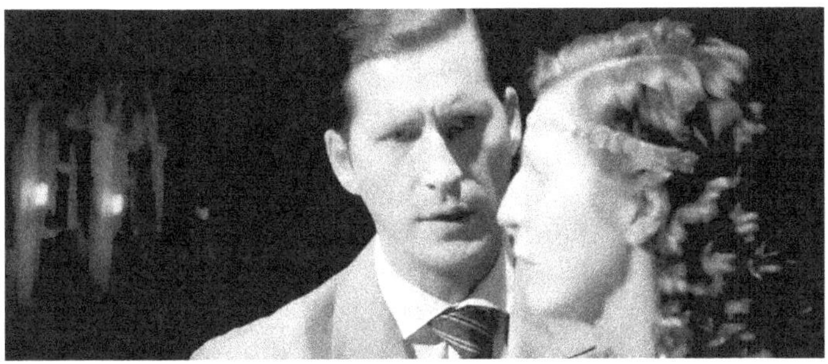

Henry: I followed my father around with a tape recorder for more than thirty years. I was determined to capture as many of his extraordinary stories as I could—stories which started with his astonishing privileged childhood and youth in the last decades of Czarist Russia, his subsequent experiences during the Bolshevik Revolution when he was imprisoned as a "capitalist," his escape to the newly created post-World War I State of Poland, and his subsequent business activities in Central Europe between the wars. In the late 1920s, my father was indeed on a business trip by train to Warsaw, like the one that takes place in this play and the movie. On that crowded train trip he did meet an attractive Polish Army nurse, along with several others, who invited him to join them in their cabin. That meeting, and its consequences, are what this play, *Train to Zakopané*, is about. The nurse did say those terrible anti-Semitic things, and my father did react to it the way he does in the play/movie. And he made the decision to act as he did. The incident that takes place on the train and its aftermath in the ski resort of Zakopané are all true. Only the dialogue and secondary characters are invented.

The events in this play occurred a few years before my father met my mother. The night he told me the story of what happened to him a half century before, we were sitting in the library of my parent's Manhattan apartment in the mid 1970s. They had been married over forty years at this point. It was past midnight and although we had thought my mother had gone to bed, she suddenly appeared in the doorway in her nightgown, asking us why we were talking so late, telling me to let my father go to bed. "In just a minute," my father answered. When my mother left, he told me the rest of the story in a whisper. Only in writing *Train to Zakopané* has it become clear to me how profound this encounter had been in my father's life. I wondered, for the first time, if he ever wound up telling my mother. They were married for sixty years when she died in 1990. He died two years later, at 96.

When we put the play on, it did very well. At first I didn't know how I would make it as a film, because we couldn't actually go to Poland to shoot it. My brilliant editor Ron Vignone did a lot of hocus-pocus, and it took me back to my days first working on editing *Easy Rider*. The magic of editing, and the magic of movies!

Commentary: *Train to Zakopané* is one of Jaglom's finest achievements and an ideal, even perfect film for him to go out on. It was Peter Bogdanovich's favorite among all Henry's films, as well. After its premiere at the Aero Theatre, Peter wrote to Henry, CCing a number of mutual friends, including myself: "Congratulations! What a touching and beautifully wrought movie. And probably your best film, certainly your most personal. I'm really sorry I couldn't stay afterwards. I have a very early call in the morning (8:30—ugh) for color timing on the OW [Orson Welles] picture. Just wanted to give you wholehearted and warmest good wishes: A very troubling, moving, superb work. All the best with it. Let's get together soon! Much love to you, and love to Tanna too. She's really great in it. As ever, Peter."

Beyond any ties to subject matter and theme, this much is certain: Only a veteran filmmaker could have written such a play and directed such a film. It is a mature (and matured) valedictory statement, about love, time, memory, blinding emotion, and regret. *Train to Zakopané* is Jaglom's first period piece and his least improvised work. It surges with the age-conferred virtuosity and circumspection displayed by filmmakers like John Huston with *The Dead* (1987), Max Ophüls with *Le plaisir* (1952), or Luchino Visconti with *L'Innocente* (1976). Even if Jaglom ain't your thing, this one is by no means your usual Jaglom film.

To quote Henry at the film's Aero premiere Q&A, "I felt like Billy Wilder on this picture." It's easy to see the parallel. *Train to Zakopané* is a quasi "studio lot" picture in the sense that it is shot in a single space that doubles for a variety of locations, à la the pictures of classic Hollywood. The comparison doesn't end there. The glossy, shimmering lighting palate recalls the Warner melodramas of the Forties—Tanna Frederick is at her most luminous under this soft, retrofied glow. One knows from having spoken with Henry about those classic movies that he never stopped loving them, and, deep down, had always wanted to recreate their feel, somehow, somewhere. This aesthetic is reflected and replicated in the film's poster design as well. Editor Ron Vignone's visual effects, which expand the stage space in which the film was shot, suggest a studied artifice. It's just unreal enough to evoke the past as dream or glistening memory. Thus, it becomes much more than merely the filmed record of a stage production. It's the closest we can get to a Bette Davis romance of conscience in these modern times.

While some critics faulted the film's artificiality, the look, feel, and artifice recalls the on-stage aesthetic of Luis Valdez's *Zoot Suit* (1981) and Éric Rohmer's *Perceval le Gallois* (1978). The writing is literate and the cinematography recalls everything from classic Hollywood melodramas like *Now, Voyager* (1942) and *Waterloo Bridge* (1940) to Lars von Trier's *Zentropa* (1991, a.k.a. *Europa*). This is a very different kind of film for Jaglom, and this is not in any way to denigrate the work that came before. His most personal films are enshrined in a glow of palpable nostalgia for lost times and lost chances. What connects his work "auteuristically" is deep yearning for the promises of the past when it comes into conflict with hard-bitten present reality. In *Always But Not Forever*, Jaglom laments that his "happy future" is in his past. More succinctly stated, Jaglom's last is the apotheosis of all the most vivid, compelling elements that reverberate through his curious, unique canon.

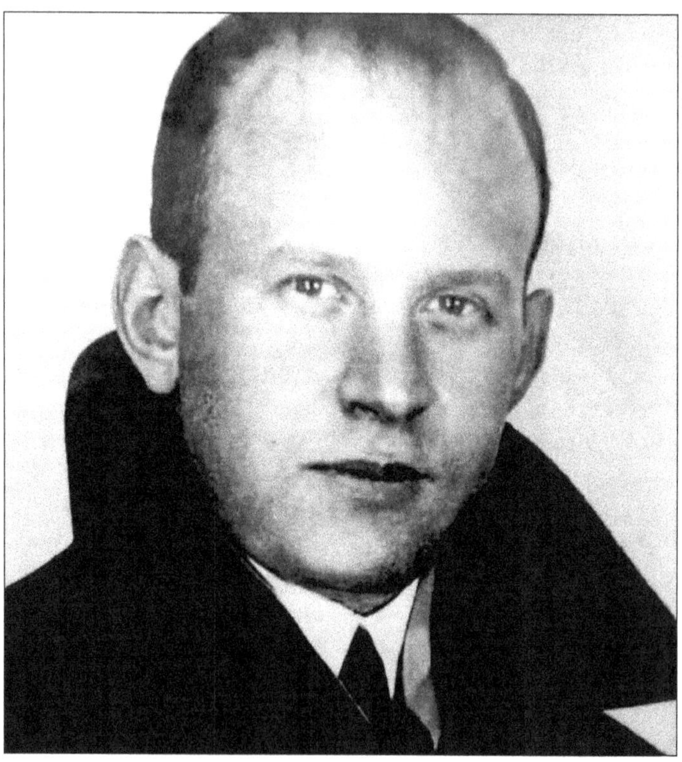

Henry's father, Simon Jaglom, at the time
Train to Zakopané takes place, in the 1920s.

The tune "Pour moi toute seule" ("For Me Alone") (as performed in two versions by Jacqueline François and Bernard Hilda's orchestra) is much like Trenet's "La mer" as used in many a previous Jagfilm. It provides a haunting anthem to the two star-crossed lovers hobbled by an interpersonal prejudice later to be seen writ large as it engulfed Europe under Hitler and the Nazis. *Train to Zakopané* tells the story of Jaglom's father Simon as he crossed Poland via train in 1928. Anti-Semitism was, at that time, rampant in much of Europe, especially in Poland. In the film, Simon "Sioma" (Mike Falkow), a successful young Russian businessman, meets Katia (Tanna Frederick), a nurse in the Polish army on a train-trip to Warsaw. He is faced with a life-changing dilemma when they fall madly and mutually in love: he discovers that she is fiercely anti-Semitic. Will he reveal to her that he is Jewish? Will he move toward love, or will he move toward revenge? Will he kiss and tell? Their weekend stopover in the resort town of Zakopané haunted Jaglom's father for a lifetime.

Jaglom integrates analog video clips he shot with his late father before his death in 1992. He reticently discusses his memories of this whirlwind affair, and its aftermath. These grace notes are all accented by dynamic performances by the entire cast, especially Tanna Frederick, who gives her best performance in a very difficult role. *Zakopané* and *Hollywood Dreams* are her crown jewels. Here, she must be wretchedly hateful, yet still alluring to Sioma and to the audience—a very difficult balance to strike. The ending, in keeping with the Old Hollywood and theater-film aesthetic, is shattering, especially when the film cuts back to Jaglom's real father finishing his own account of the story.

Cast: Tanna Frederick (Katia Wampusyk), Mike Falkow (Semyon "Sioma" Sapir), Cathy Arden (Madame Nadia Selmeczy), Stephen Howard (Father Alexandrov), Kelly De Sarla (Marusia Petronko), Jeff Elam (Dr. Nachum Gruenbaum), Simon Jaglom (Himself)

Henry's Last Word: Nearly all my movies have been made for around $1 million, sometimes even less. If my movies make $5-10 million, they are a massive success. If a Hollywood film makes that same amount, they're in the toilet! And I have found that, quite naturally, women and I had much more in common than I felt was the case between me and most men. I still suffered certain male problems, whether inherent or conditioned: aggression, impatience, arrogance, insensitivity and other male stupidities never were—and I'm afraid never really are—completely unknown or unavailable to me. But I tried, and I continue to try, to sit on the worst parts of my gender, to openly and insistently pursue an honest and unafraid look at my interior and share it in my life—and my work—with those, mostly women, who care to join me. The point is, we're all "bozos on this bus," if you know that expression. To some extent, we're all going through the type of things I cover in my movies, and to share in that means we're going to feel less alone, less in trouble. (*From the Filmmaker's Statement in the published screenplay of* Eating.)

Credits

AS ACTOR

Stage
The Uncommon Denominator (May 1963) Off-Broadway
    Dir: Henry Jaglom

Television
"East Side/West Side" (1964, "Here Today" Season 1,
    Episode 26)/Reporter
"Gidget" (1964, "All the Best Diseases Are Taken" Season 1,
    Episode 10)/Billy Ray Soames
"The Flying Nun" (1967, "The Dig-In" Season 1, Episode 15)/
    Bill Watkins

Film
Psych-Out (1968)/Warren/Dir: Richard Rush
The Thousand-Plane Raid (1969)/Worchek/Dir: Boris Sagal
Drive, He Said (1971)/Conrad/Dir: Jack Nicholson
The Last Movie (1971)/Minister's Man/Dir: Dennis Hopper
Lily, aime-moi (1975)/Guest at Flo's Party/Dir: Maurice Dugowson
Sitting Ducks (1980)/The Bad Guy/Dir: Henry Jaglom
Always, But Not Forever (1985)/David/Dir: Henry Jaglom
Someone to Love (1987)/Danny/Dir: Henry Jaglom
New Year's Day (1989)/Drew/Dir: Henry Jaglom
Venice/Venice (1992)/Dean/Dir: Henry Jaglom
Last Summer at the Hamptons (1995)/Max Berger/
    Dir: Henry Jaglom
Hollywood Dreams (2006)/Casting Director/
    Dir: Henry Jaglom
The Other Side of the Wind (2018)/Henry/Dir: Orson Welles

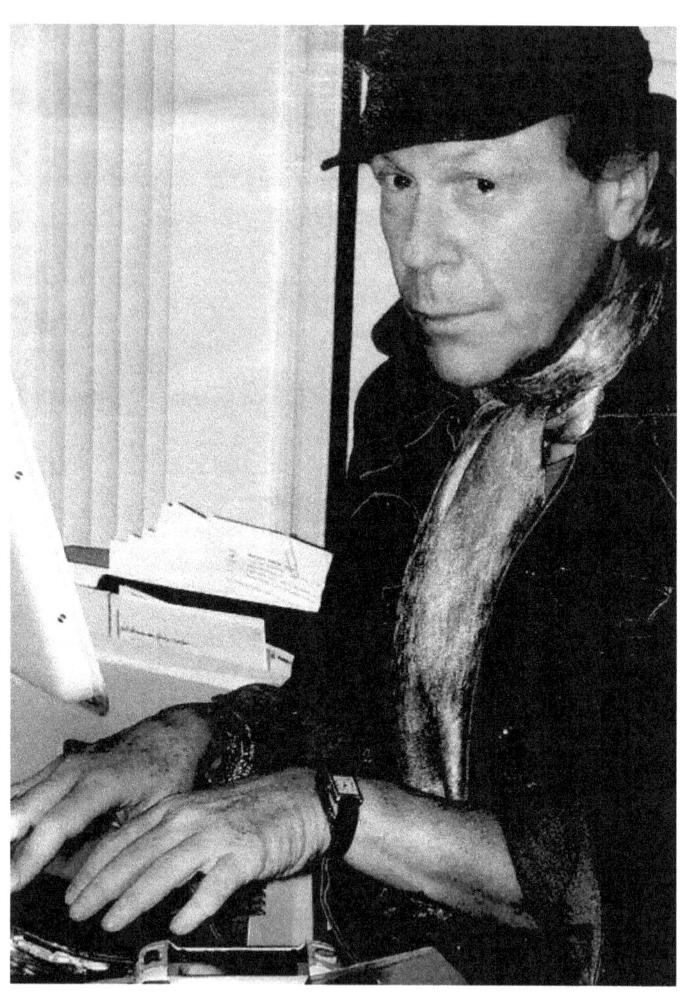

AS PRODUCER

Stage
The Mime Theatre of Etienne Decroux (December 1959)
   Cricket Theatre, New York

Film
Hearts and Minds (1974) (uncredited, also Presenter, via
   Rainbow Pictures) (Henry's name is engraved on the
   statuette)
Little Noises (1991) (uncredited)/Dir: Jane Spencer
Runaways (never completed)/Dir: Elizabeth Swados
Phyllis and Harold (2008) (as presenter)/Dir: Cindy Kleine

AS HIMSELF

Notes on the New York Film Festival (1971) with
   Molly Haskell and Peter Bogdanovich
Out of the Blue and Into the Black (1987)/Dir: Paul Joyce
On the Tracks of a Filmmaker: Henry Jaglom (1988)/
   Dir: Nelly Alard
L'homme qui a vu l'homme qui a vu l'ours (1990)/
   Dir: André Labarthe
Who is Henry Jaglom? (1995)/Dir: Henry Alex Rubin and
   Jeremy Workman
"The Phil Donahue Show" (1990)
CBS-TV "West 57th" (1990)
"The Roseanne Show" (1997)
"E! Mysteries and Scandals" ("Orson Welles") (1999)
Wheatfield with Crows (2002)/Dir: Brent Roske
Easy Riders, Raging Bulls (2003)/Dir: Kenneth Bowser
The Mystery of Natalie Wood (2004)/Dir: Peter Bogdanovich
Z Channel: A Magnificent Obsession (2004)/
   Dir: Xan Cassavetes
Edge of Outside (2006)/Dir: Shannon Davis
Searching for Orson (2006)/Dir: Dominik and Jakov Sedlar

*To My Great Chagrin: The Unbelievable Story of Brother
    Theodore* (2007)/Dir: Jeff Sumerel
BBStory (2010)/Dir: Greg Carson
Scene Missing (2012)/Dir: Alex Cox
Magician: The Astonishing Life and Work of Orson Welles
    (2014)/Dir: Chuck Workman
This Is Orson Welles (2015)/Dir: Clara and Julia Kuperberg
Orson Welles: Shadows and Light (2015)/
    Dir: Elisabeth Kapnist
They'll Love Me When I'm Dead (2018)/Dir: Morgan Neville
I Am Richard Pryor (2019)/Dir: Jesse James Miller
King of Cool (2021)/Dir: Tom Donahue
Now, Irving Rapper (2026)/Dir: Daniel Kremer

AS CHARACTER

Played by Rupert Reid in *The Mysteries of Natalie Wood*
    (2004)/Dir: Peter Bogdanovich (in addition to
    documentary-style footage of Jaglom himself)

BOOKS AND PUBLISHED PLAYS/SCREENPLAYS

Eating: A Very Serious Comedy About Women and Food (1991,
    Samuel French Trade)
Babyfever: For Those Who Hear Their Clock Ticking (1994,
    Samuel French Trade)
Last Summer in the Hamptons (1996, Samuel French Trade)
Déjà Vu (1998, Samuel French Trade)
Festival in Cannes (2001, Samuel French Trade)
Hollywood Dreams (2007, Samuel French Trade)
Just 45 Minutes from Broadway (2012, Samuel French Trade)
*My Lunches With Orson: Conversations Between Henry
    Jaglom and Orson Welles* (2013, Picador) (with Peter Biskind)
Train to Zakopané: A True Story of Love and Hate (2015,
    Samuel French Trade)

Appendix 1
The Kazan Letters

Henry saved virtually everything from his past. He was the greatest of sentimental pack-rats. So here for posterity is the full Jaglom-Kazan correspondence, as referenced in Chapter 2.

INTERNATIONAL RAINBOW PICTURES

12 July '89
Los Angeles

To Kazan:

I hate you.

But I believe you.

And I'now understand you, which makes me
not hate you.

You are despicable in what you allow yourself.

Yet honest. So profoundly, astonishingly honest
that you make me empathize with you, even as you
rationalize your terrible, flawed being and behaviour.

What an extraordinary book. Sad and disturbing.

What a great piece of work. Insightful and fascinating.

What compelling, manipulative, brilliant story-telling.

I can't put it down.

I never want it to end, so I keep putting it down.

I've learned more about directing (and that is my job
and I think myself very, very good at it) than I thought
there was to learn.

I am being forced to understand what I have absolutely
despised as an article of faith for more than 30 years; even
as I always recognized your creative work as truer and deeper
than any other American's of the period of my adolescence and
young, impressionable adulthood, my social and moral and
political conscience was simultaneously disgusted and horrified.

You have now taken my human outrage and my artistic
respect in your two hands and somehow re-fashioned the whole,
re-defined the totality into something much different, something
far more deeply felt and comprehended:

A Person.

A Life.

HENRY JAGLOM

KAZAN ANSWERED MY letter. Here it is:

ELIA KAZAN

July 24th, 1989

Mr. Henry Jaglom
International Rainbow Pictures
9165 Sunset Boulevard
The Penthouse
Los Angeles, CA. 90069

Dear Mr. Jaglom:

Thank you for your letter.

I've had a great many responses to my book
but yours was the most intriguing. What might
be even more interesting would be if, in the
spirit of my book perhaps, you would write and
tell me what impressions or convictions you had
that were altered or modified by what you read.
In that sense your excellent letter was incom-
plete.

Yours,

Elia Kazan

New York to L.A. via TWA
July 30, 1989

Dear Elia Kazan,

This is harder to write than my earlier note to which you responded in such a perfect, director-fashion: Be more specific.

I will try to be more specific about what you were to me and what has changed as a result of reading your book.

Your book is the single most impactful and powerful thing I've read in many years. I bore all my friends about it, buy them copies to read, force them to get into it. I am excited when others tell me, on their own, that they read it and how strong their reaction to it was. You should be aware of how *often* this happens, how many, frequently unlikely people are knocked over by it. And many, like myself, are as *surprised* as they are overwhelmed.

Now if I understand what your question to me *really* is, it's: Why the surprise? What had I, or others, thought of you *before* that makes our reaction not only so powerful, but so unexpected in ourselves. Why are we so amazed that *you,* of all people, have made us react this way? I will try to explain, at least for myself – and I think it's true for many others.

You represent a lot of things to a lot of us. You, your image, your work and your mythology have created – until now – a disturbing, contradictory portrait, vivid as hell.

Take me.

I grew up in the 1950s, went to school then and had three dreams: Romantic, Artistic and Political.

You were irrelevant to my romantic hopes, but in the remaining two arenas that excited my early emotions, you played significant roles in opposite directions, *each extremely powerful* and lasting, and ever at war.

Artistically, you offered great hope to an aspiring actor/writer/director/filmmaker. In a time when Hollywood churned out unreal, overblown, meaningless and artless fantasies, your films looked real, felt true, contained uniquely powerful and honest performances and were *about* something. Your work in the theatre seemed to give us the few important experiences to be found there. You etched a deep, creative consciousness in my young brain. And I was lucky: *I* learned the vital lessons you talk about at the end of your book – of self-esteem, a sense of self-worth, not needing exterior approval to define yourself – very early in my life. It has enabled me to make eight movies to date entirely my way, with no compromises – good or bad, each film is totally *mine*, frame for frame, I don't know if you know my work, but it's completely free and unique, as honest as I know how to be, and so *from myself* that quite a few critics have a field day with charges of self-indulgence and narcissism. I've starred in the last three as well, and ask from myself and my actors *not* the realization of a predetermined character, but full exposure of themselves, which I later, taking a year or two in the cutting room, fashion into my "story."

I tell you all this so you will understand who wrote you that intense note, and as a way to try to answer your letter and its question.

Orson Welles, in the last decade of his life, was my closest male friend, despite the generation between us. I remember running "America, America" for him and explaining why you had been such a significant creative influence on me. He had an easier time with "Waterfront" and with "Streetcar" and we had a long, fascinating evening about you. He said many things which I'll be happy to pass on to you should you wish. But I kept asking him: "How can an artist with that much vision, honesty and power have been such a *shit?*"

Which brings me to my political dream.

I was a young leftist, non-doctrinaire but passionate about injustice and oppression. Paul Robeson was my early hero and Pete Seeger concerts fed me dreams of a decent world. I grew up very comfortably in the 50s, so I never experienced any of the real world's suffering or displacement, except in my feelings. I called myself "progressive," and you know the rest. I cared and tried to do what I could. I still care and still try.

McCarthyism was the first evil I knew, however indirectly. And my heroes were those blacklisted actors and writers who were named and lost what they lost and didn't give in.

They are still my heroes.

That doesn't mean I am simplistic or naïve. I know the difference between doctrinaire party-liners and sweet, humane, decent people who hoped for a better world with less pain and injustice.

And you named them. You cooperated.

You committed the inexplicable sin, one I could only believe you did for comfort and self-protection and security. You were selfish and weak.

And you took The Ad. *That* made it seem so much worse. You justified it, rationalized it, and tried to make it seem right, moral, necessary even. You and Shulberg even made a film to justify yourself. And it was a *great* film. And you *are* a great filmmaker, no matter how much you minimize the importance of your work. It stands and it *is* truly important, significant, first-class art. And I always recognized that, just as I always despised you for your betrayals.

And I never knew how to reconcile the two things.

And then I read your book.

And now I do.

I studied with Lee for ten years. Harold gave me my first encouragement, when he took over Molly's writing-and-directing unit at The Studio, and I presented my first play there, and he told me I'd created "a whole new sound, a language of today," and so on. I was 23 or 24 and that strengthened my ability to withstand temptations and seductions and I turned that play into my first film six years later for a very befuddled Columbia Pictures, and have happily gone my own way ever since. If I had no other way of knowing the truth of your book, the astonishingly complex accuracy with which you describe so many people I know or knew would make it completely clear to me that you have somehow managed to do that hardest of all things: *Not to lie*. The fact that you do it so wonderfully well, so artfully, makes the book important *beyond* its honesty; but without that honesty I really wouldn't give a shit. I know your talents from the work you've done on films and plays that live within me for life. But this book, being *your* truth, being such a difficult, angry, sad, loving, frightening and finally *all-embracing* truth, being the fullest expression of one person's life that I have *ever* read (and biographies, and most especially autobiographies, are *all* I really am interested in reading anymore) – this book truly *is* some kind of great work of art! I have been telling people "great as the great novels" but I do that to make sure they get it; I *really* mean great in a way *no* work of fiction can ever quite be – great as a *life*.

I hope you can receive this praise. I am as arrogant as anyone you have ever known, so I have absolutely no doubt that I am right about what an important work you have created: you have taken the pain and loss and confusion and need and resultant turbulence of your years, and turned it all into a spectacular gift for all of us living (and many yet-to-be-born) to be able to finally find an honest mirror to look into about what it means to be alive.

Henry Jaglom

ELIA KAZAN

August 15, 1989

Dear Jaglom:

What a wonderful letter! I'd guess it all
but it was great to have it from you and in your
own ardent, troubled, impassioned words. I'd
guessed it all because several others have had
the experience - and conveyed it to me - of
having trouble liking the book but liking it
nevertheless.

Now you have a job, kid, that you stop just
short of: you have to put the two conflicting
images together. Orson, for whom I worked once,
had the same problem and he never put them together. It's easy to say, "Shit!" But how can
a "shit" write a book that you respect so much
and praise so highly? That's the question, not
for me but for you.

I feel affectionately toward you and send you
those regards.

Elia

Mr. Henry Jaglom
International Rainbow Pictures
9165 Sunset Boulevard
The Penthouse
Los Angeles, CA. 90069

Henry Jaglom

August 19, 1989

Elia Kazan
174 E. 94th St.
New York, NY

Dear Kazan,

I'm a bit disappointed by your response to my letter – *my* response was *acknowledging* that I *had* reconciled, at long last, the very human complex capacity to both act like a "shit," yet produce a brilliant and important piece of work – *thanks to that very work* – i.e. your extraordinary book! *That* is *precisely* what made the book so remarkable; that it *did* allow me to see the complete being and comprehend *all* the contradictions that had been so hard to incorporate prior to it.

So I must have failed to make that clear, to elicit a response so seemingly defensive – re: my use of the word "shit," and that my "job" now is "to put the two conflicting images together."

And what do you mean by the throw-a-way line: "Orson had the same problem and he never put them together." ???

Please, please explain that! And please do understand that *now*, thanks to *your* phenomenal achievement, I finally understand the fullness of what Walt Whitman meant when he said: "Do I contradict myself? Very well then, I contradict myself. I am large; I contain multitudes."

You certainly are and you certainly do and I *get* it now, I really do and I hope, you get that I do.

Best–
Henry J.

ELIA KAZAN

                                    September 7, 1989

Dear Jaglom:

I was away from this office so I am answering
your letter late.

Sometime we should meet. Letters don't do it.
Expression is a total thing.

When can I see your film NEW YEAR'S DAY?

I'm going to Europe October 1st for a year
at least, more likely a year and a half.
Making another film. Time to move on.
                                    E.K.

Mr. Henry Jaglom
International Rainbow
Pictures/Jagfilms
9165 Sunset Boulevard/
The Penthouse
Los Angeles, CA. 90069

September 12, 1989

Elia Kazan
174 East 95th Street
New York, N.Y. 10128

Dear Kazan,

    I heard about you going to Europe, in Venice, just this week.
I would love to meet you before. I'm in Toronto at a film festival,
then going to Boston on the 16th. Can be in New York the 18th,
but must go to L.A. to shoot a film. Is it possible to meet on
the 18th some time in the afternoon or evening? Any way you'd
like. Can you contact my office, preferably my associate, Judith
Wolinsky, (213)271-0202, with an answer?

    I would hate to wait a year.

    Best,

Henry Jaglom

P.S. If possible, to facilitate a meeting, could you pass on a phon
number to my office? Hope to meet you soon. H.J.

9165 SUNSET BOULEVARD/THE PENTHOUSE LOS ANGELES, CALIFORNIA 90069 (213) 271-0202 FAX: (213) 271-2753

Journal Entry
2:30pm New York City
September 1989

A bit unreal, my having just spent a couple of hours with *Elia Kazan* in his East 94ᵗʰ St. townhouse. Another part of the dream.

On a street of wide-open, surprisingly unprotected buildings, I came upon #174 and recognized it as having to be his, immediately. Heavy black iron gating, must be opened trickily, from the inside, if you are coming in you must reach *over* and unlatch it from under the other side. Once you do, you're confronted with a tight gray stone building, the ground floor of which is enwrapped in more black iron, jail-like encasing.

I ring the door. A dog barks wildly, keeps barking threateningly as a woman of probable Latin American origin opens warily and says nothing. She looks at me, the dog continues to bark, I try to reassure the dog that I am not a danger to those within, I enquire of the Latina if this is Mr. Kazan's house. She nods, doesn't move, says nothing. 'He's expecting me,' I say, inbetween reassuring words and looks at the dog! Still saying nothing, she walks in and I follow her. She points toward a flight of stairs. I now suspect that she is deaf. I say, simply and clearly, 'He's up there?' and she more or less nods and disappears.

I walk up.

At the top of the stairs, an elegant, early-middle-aged, casually pulled-together blond woman says, "I'm Mrs. Kazan. He's up those stairs. I'll show you." She walks up the 2ⁿᵈ flight and I follow her. She walks up a 3ʳᵈ flight and I keep following. "Just wait right here."

I wait on the landing, near the top of the stairs, surrounded by posters. There they all are: Streetcar, Death of a Salesman, they are all there and here am I. It's nice to still get excited by things, I think. It's nice to still have people to meet for whom I am able to get a little bit worked up. Earlier I had almost felt nervous with the anticipation, and tried to dive into that young, unsure feeling, but it went away.

"Henry? Come in ..." A familiar voice behind a door. Kazan and me. "Come on in."

Me and Kazan. He jumps up, bantam cock tough handshake. So complicated and so simple. I start to talk. "You always talk so fast?" he asks me. I talk more. "I really like you," he decides.

A lot inbetween, but it's the 'liking' part that worries me. This man has been, by all my definitions, a bad man. Selfish and very harmful and the cause of much pain to many people.

And yet I like him too. After reading the book, I thought I would, but I almost hoped I wouldn't. But I did. A lot. And that does mean, just as I realized in reading the book, that life is even more complicated than even *I* had understood it to be.

A slight shyness and eye-averting at compliments, but other than that easy and fine and trying to find out about me.

"You live alone? That's tough."

And about him.

"There were always some people who didn't like each of my wives," the strangest comment.

I talk about the book, characterize it as "neither an apology nor a defense."

His eyes avert, at first it looks like shyness at the compliment, then I sense the subsequent distraction and realize what it is – he likes the *phrase,* is holding it in his brain and wants to write it down. I let him know I know and understand and he gets up and writes it down, checking with me first: "Neither an apology nor a defense." I nod. "That's good," he says, writing it.

On leaving he insists on walking me down all the flights of stairs, taking me to the door. He pumps my hand again, the same bantam cock stance and handshake at an angle, feet planted too solidly on the ground. Only then does he seem like the little kid determined to make his way at all costs to him or anyone else in the big, tough world where no one gets any favors from anyone for anything.

He will make it.

                        ELIA KAZAN

                                        September 27, 1989

Dear Henry:

I'm writing you despite the fact that I am not sure it's
wise. I've lost friends telling them what I believe.
But here is how I see what I saw in your films; I   ran
two of them NEW YEAR'S DAY and SOMEONE TO LOVE. I enjoyed them but not as much as I wanted to. You have
sensitivity, energy, money, some daring, curiosity about
your fellow humans, the memory of pain, a history of some
trouble, and perhaps above all the beginning of a confrontation with yourself, and the readiness to use your
own experience. I thought your films interesting but
that is not a word I'm fond of in our field. I felt the
films should have been better. I believe you will do
better.   There is something irresolute about both films.
The characters seem to be in some way protected, never in
genuine danger. Protected by what? By intelligence, by
custom, sophistication, an adequate income, a seamless
philosophy. But mostly by the author who sits over them
with a gentle and understanding smile, one that does not
sufficiently challenge his people. Or himself. They all,
characters and author, seem to be finally safe. There are
no genuine penalties, no genuine risks, no genuine rewards.
The people mooch along, talking bout themselves, but the
author-director has not thrust them into situations where
they have to strike out for themselves, that is, raise
holy hell in their own behalf. They are all protected by
that understanding smile on the face of the author-director.
He won't let them get hurt. They are not, for the most
part, troubled enough or desperate enough to make drama.
They don't hate, they don't truly love, or if they do,
they are not ready to do something about it. You tell me
what the characters think, but what do they want and what
are they prepared to do about it. There is one great
scene, the one at the end of NEW YEAR'S DAY with the
woman in the bathtub. It's chilling because it is fired by
a desperate want.

Somebody or other said that there is a similarity between
drama and a prize fight. The combatants climb into the
"ring" and there is no easy way out, only bloody triumph
or bloody disaster. Perhaps NO WAY OUT is the essence of
dramatic structure. I speak for myself; you see life differently or so it appears. Your characters can talk themselves out of any situation. When the leading man wants a

                                        - continued

woman (sort of), he gives her the key to a house he owns
(lucky man). He doesn't have to fight for her. She
smiles. He smiles. Then what? What did happen? As I
watched your films I often had a wish for you, that you
would someday be in trouble so deep that there appeared
to be no way out of it. The certainty of safety can be
a curse.

I hope you don't think the above patronizing. I hope
you don't get mad at me because I do like you. And, of
course, I have my own problems.

                              Elia

P.S. Then I received and ran ALWAYS. The best of them.
It has a unified theme and a central story. I thought the
end brilliant and I congratulate you on it. But what was
really eating JUDY? The explanation of wanting "perfection,"
etc., is insufficient for this viewer.

I haven't time to write more as I'm just about to leave
for Europe.   Good luck always.
                              E.K.

Mr. Henry Jaglom
International Rainbow Pictures
9165 Sunset Boulevard
The Penthouse
Los Angeles, CA. 90069

JAGFILMS, INC.

16 October 1989

Dear Elia -

I just came home (to the house in "Always") after a good
long day's shooting, and found your letter. I very much hope
that this reaches you before you leave; or in Europe.

I greatly appreciate the honesty of your response to my
three films. I in no way find you patronizing, nor am I mad
at you, nor like you any less in any way. On the contrary,
my respect which you so completely earned by your book, is
simply <u>confirmed</u> by the fact that you would do no less than be
completely honest with me.

And I find your response to my work fascinating. Not
because I think you are right, in any way, nor because I feel
you have "a point" from which I can learn something. I believe
I would be very open to that, but I respond to your responses
differently. I have heard them before, they consistently come
back to me from a significant percentage of my audience (and
critics), in much the same way. But <u>your</u> means of expressing
your response has something else in it, something you show
(and openly reveal) in your book: Your anger at people who
haven't had to struggle for physical comfort, your dismissal
of work not about BIG dramatic, life-threatening, risk-taking
events.

Now maybe its because of the fact that I've always had
enough money, that my life (and the lives of 90% of the people
I know) hasn't been confronted yet with what you call "trouble
so deep that there appears to be no way out of it." Thanks
for wishing it for me, I <u>mean</u> that; I know what you're saying,
I really do and you're <u>right</u>, of course. As you say: "The
certainty of safety can be a curse."

Yes. But what about those of us who <u>have</u> been and are,
essentially "safe." Do you feel <u>our</u> internal concerns, <u>our</u>
struggles for love, for happiness, for meaning, for connection
with one another, is meaningless? Should not be taken seriously?
Is less true or felt or significant than the struggle of
millions for food or physical safety? I think you <u>do</u> feel this
way, and so do many others, especially <u>men</u>, who tend to define
the important issues of life as external, societal or political.
In this you share a response with a large group of the people
whom you once identified with politically, who gave you a
feeling of home and shared meaning. I understand all that, and
how angry it must still make you some place inside the young,
hurt you, to see work about nothing more important than feelings,
nothing really less trivial than the search for love among the
small percentage of people on the planet who have enough to eat,
to house themselves, to clothe themselves, whose skin color
doesn't make them the object of oppression, whose fortunate
circumstance of time and place doesn't make them the victim of
war or some other societal madness brutally expressed.

JAGFILMS, INC.

Page Two

What sort of betrayed you, I feel, were the several
references to my "money." The fact that each of these films
cost less than the lunch budget for any studio film,isn't seen
as relevant; but the fact that I have "energy, money, some
daring," is. Think about that. My films you find irresolute.
But I'm dealing with people in situations, in <u>life</u> for many
of us, that <u>have</u> no resolutions. Only questions exist, not
answers, only trying to figure it all out. But, you say,
I and my characters are "protected." By what? Your answer
includes: "custom, sophistication, an adequate income." Hmmm.
Does that mean they don't feel pain? Loneliness? Loss? Are
their feelings <u>less</u> because they have more material security?
How strange that you would hold on to this"workers philosophy"
today. Poor people are in need because they are <u>poor</u>, not
because they <u>feel</u> more.

The one scene you like, the bathtub scene with the two
women in NEW YEAR'S DAY, you like because "it is fired by a
desperate <u>want</u>." It <u>is</u> more dramatic than most of my stuff,
she has taken pills, has hidden a love, etc. But why does that
make her situation more worthy of being looked at? What an odd
statement: "The similarity between drama and a prize fight."
Isn't that only one <u>kind</u> of drama: conventional, focused,
intensified, explosive circumstances or situations? What about
the drama of two people who love each other, one leaves, the
other is devastated? Are my responses to the end of my
marriage, the end of my dreams, less meaningful "drama" than
fists beating faces bloody? Than wars blowing bodies apart?

How can you not see what I am saying? I expect this from
many others, but I admit I was disappointed in hearing them from
you. It is the <u>same</u> you who doesn't value sufficiently the great
work <u>you</u> have done, because you were "interpreting" Miller or
Williams. You say "no way out" is the essence of dramatic
structure, and here I agree with you. There <u>is</u> no way out of
the dilemma of life, love, relationships, searching, finding,
losing, searching again. Is that only the stuff of soap operas?

You resent "the leading man" because he "owns a house,
and can give a key away"? By now <u>you</u> own quite a few things.
Are your feelings and longings less worthy now than when you
were poor? Can you truly believe that?

Finally you ask, about my ex-wife, "what was really eating
'Judy'?" You don't buy the explanation of wanting perfection.
You say it was "insufficient." Many men have had the same
response. Do you know, do you care, that millions of women
feel the same way as 'Judy', know it sounds "insufficient",
but <u>feel</u> that? I have just finished a film with 38 women
obsessed in one way or another with food and the "imperfection"
of their bodies.

Page Three

They suffer <u>real</u> pain and cry <u>real</u> desperate cries and many
of them have tried suicide and some have succeeded. How can I
care about this in a world full of hungry people? I don't know.
I <u>do</u> care. I care about the hungry people <u>and</u> I care about
the white, middle-class trapped people for <u>whom</u> food and much
else has become a complex means of self-destruction.

     Don't you? Maybe deep in all this is the reason you've
allowed yourself some of the crueler behaviour you've levelled
against others as you so honestly document in your book: The
women in your life, your co-workers, your former co-dreamers
of a better world. Forgive me, but is it possible that not
valueing sufficiently the small human needs and feelings of
others, the <u>importance</u> of those needs and feelings, is what
gave you permission to hurt them so?

     Now it is <u>I</u> who must ask <u>you</u> not to get mad at me. I like
you a great deal, genuinely and strongly, but I must tell you the
truth as I see it. And <u>your</u> honesty gives me the freedom to
do so.

     As you said, I'm not sure how wise it is to write you this,
but I must. I think you should, if possible, re-think your
notion of what is and isn't art, what is and isn't drama, what is
and isn't important and what is and isn't risk-taking. I believe
I am able to look at some very difficult, very uncomfortable,
very painful truths about myself and about others. While I don't
share some people's perception of this as being particularly
brave or daring, it certainly <u>isn't</u> avoiding risk-taking and
even my strongest critics don't accuse me of that. On the
contrary, it is some of the <u>deepest</u> risk-taking for myself and
my actors to open one's insides up, in all their pathetic,
unsure, flawed, and needful ways, to public inspection and
exposure. Precisely as <u>you</u> yourself do with such amazing and
powerful honesty in <u>your</u> greatest work of art - your brilliant book.

     Can you continue this process with me and not be too put
off by my direct and perhaps excessively personal zeal? I truly
hope so. And I <u>fervently</u> hope I hear from you soon.

All My Best,

HENRY JAGLOM

P.S. You didn't mention "TRACKS," which I also gave you. I
would think this may be a more "life-and-death" oriented work,
and more male-centered, and as such maybe more up your alley.
Can you let me know?

ELIA KAZAN

November 9, 1989

Dear Henry:

That was a fine letter you sent me and I liked it a lot and will read it again, taking it to Europe with me. But I can't answer it properly now because I'm all bogged down in this production and in differences with my producer and etc., etc.

I send you my affection and my admiration in the meantime.

Elia

Mr. Henry Jaglom
International Rainbow Pictures
9165 Sunset Boulevard
The Penthouse
Los Angeles, CA. 90069

November 16, 1989

Dear Henry:

As I wrote to you, I can't answer your excellent letter
as it deserves because my mind has been on a family problem.

It is, your letter, the best you've written me and
focuses on an abiding fault of mine, a kind of perverse
snobbery which I developed in the CP. I used to write
myself notes in the early 30's - "Don't trust anyone
except working class people," and so on, all shit. Of
course the concerns and struggles of those "who are
economically safe," for love, happiness, etc. are meaningful.(The
list is in the bottom paragraph of your first page, I
don't have the energy to transcribe it since I'm still
struggling with my family problem.) But you're right
and I still think like I used to and get impatient unless there is a BANG at the climax where it "should"
be to tell the proper theme. Of course they "feel
pain," and poor people do not feel more. Agree. Give
me hell! Yes, the pain they suffer is REAL, of course.
Why don't I respect it as much?

I still like the bathtub scene best. You figure out why.
I can't today. As for getting mad at you, I never will
because it's rare that people can have the kind of discussion we've been having. I appreciate, do not duck,
the paragraph urging me to RE-THINK my notion of what
is and what is not art. O.K.?

But Henry. That's advice for a critic. It does seem
to me that an artist cannot have it all right. An
artist is narrow, maybe deep but narrow! He can only
say what he feels and in most cases, yes, it is twisted
and "wrong," and so on but it is what he feels. What
matters is how intensely he feels it and how well he
tells it.

Shit! Another interruption. I can't go on now. Thanks
for your letter. It was first class.

                                  E.K.

P.S. TRACKS I didn't see yet. In time, old coot.

PPS. Maybe I'll see you in Paris.

                                    e.k.

                    1 December 1989

Elia Kazan
174 East 95th Street
New York, NY 10128

Dear Elia:

Many thanks for your open, willing-to-hear, non-defensive
response. Terribly impressive. Knocked me out! Your
honesty continues to overwhelm. Your ability to listen
to difficult and unpleasant things. Wow!

BUT:

What a dangerous description of an "artist":   "... yes it
is twisted and 'wrong' and so on but it is what he (the
artist) feels. What matters is how intensely he feels it
and how well he tells it."

Bullshit! I'm sorry, but bullshit! What an excuse for
one not having to behave humanely, what permission - by
placing one's self in a rarefied category, even if apt -
to not be responsible for one's personal behaviour.
"Wrong" should not be in quotes. There _is_ such a thing as
wrong and being special doesn't make it any less wrong.

I think I understand now. Scarey, though. Justifies the
artists who survived and functioned under repressive
regimes, during Stalinist - even Hitlerian - times.
"Mephisto" - did you read or see it? Orson told me a story
that has never left my brain: Emil Jannings, on the front
doorstep of his house in Germany at the end of World
War II, holding his Oscar (for "The Blue Angel") above
his head to show the occupying American GI's that he was
all right, even if he _had_ stayed and worked and prospered
in Nazi Cinema after the Jews were purged and after Lang
and Dietrich and the rest left. Did that Oscar give him
a clean bill of moral health? Some very dangerous thinking
goes on when one puts one's self beyond the criteria that
others must adhere to. You know?

Sorry to hear of your family difficulties. Hope you're
okay.

Best,

HENRY JAGLOM

ELIA KAZAN

March 11, 1991

Dear Henry:

Belatedly, thank you for sending the book on your latest subject, "Eating - A Very Serious Comedy About Women and Food." Not only do I admire you and your work - but I wish I could be as open as you are.

Always good luck.

Elia

Mr. Henry Jaglom
International Rainbow Pictures
9165 Sunset Boulevard
The Penthouse
Los Angeles, CA.   90069

INTERNATIONAL RAINBOW PICTURES

22 March '91

Dear Elia –

Thanks for your note on the book of "Eating" – I meant to send you the cassette of the film, not the book, so here it is. I'd love to know your as-always candid responses to it – whatever they are. Please.

Since we met, my life has changed profoundly. I remember telling you that for the last 10 years I'd been living alone + your reaction went deep – you looked at me sharply + said – "that's very tough" – and I felt it. It stayed.

Happy to report that's all changed, thanks to a wonderful twist from out of the blue – (it's marked in the enclosed piece – I thought that would be easier than trying to go into it here).

Point being – in additional to my being happier than I've ever been – we just went to Paris for the opening of "Eating" there, and the sub-text for our entire first trip together was + continues to be, her reading of your magnificent book and her daily – even hourly – intensely felt, excited responses to it which exactly duplicated mine. So you've given us – and me – a really memorable gift.
And when she finishes, next week or so, I'm going to start reading it all over again. Hard to explain exactly what I mean, but I hope you get it. Somehow you shared with us a dimension of experience in addition to the one you gave each of us – and so many, many others – in our individual reading of what you have put down so extraordinarily. A unifying experience that I really think only great art can give –

Which I was reminded is what your book truly is.

Hope all is well + hope to hear from you soon –

Best – and thanks from Victoria –

Henry

9165 SUNSET BOULEVARD/THE PENTHOUSE LOS ANGELES, CALIFORNIA 90069 (213)271-0202 FAX: 213/271-2753

August 17, 1992

Dear Henry:

Everything is as well as things can be.
You and your bride look happy which is the
point.

I haven't played your video as yet, but I
will pretty soon. I'm about to work with my
editor preparing my book for - for whoever will
be reading it.

             E.K.

Mr. Henry Jaglom
JAGFILMS, INC.
9165 Sunset Boulevard
The Penthouse
Los Angeles, CA. 90069

ELIA KAZAN

October 26, 1992

Dear Henry:

Sorry I'm late responding to
the film you sent me. The fact is - sorry! -
I preferred you in your other mode, less conventional and with less of an effort to organize your experience into a meaningful order. I see the film is
being shown to people here in New York City and you
know I wish you all success. In your marriage most
of all.

Best,

Mr. Henry Jaglom
International Rainbow Pictures
9165 Sunset Boulevard
The Penthouse
Los Angeles, CA. 90069

ELIA KAZAN

November 16, 1992

Henry:

I would not, absolutely would not, pay too much
attention, put too much weight moral or aesthetic
on my opinion of your films. Generally I like them.

The one I liked best was EATING. I got something
lasting out of that one. You were telling me a
truth that possibly I knew but didn't realize that I
knew. I valued the film.

Somehow this one missed me or blew right by me.
I'm glad you're receiving some general public attention.

Someday I'll play this one again and maybe I'll
say (to myself, that is) how the hell did I not appreciate that goddamn picture the first time? But right
now I'm editing my book which started at 1100 pages
and although I want it shorter, I don't like everything I sweated over lost. You can understand that.
So even on my benign days I'm ornery and see the
world darkly.

Know that I always wish you luck.

Elia

Mr. Henry Jaglom
The Rainbow Film Company/Jagfilms
9165 Sunset Boulevard/ The Penhouse
Los Angeles, CA. 90069

ELIA KAZAN

December 27, 1993

Dear Henry:

      I have your card and the picture of your beautiful wife and that lovely child whom you are kissing, as you damn well should.

      Will you do me a favor, Henry, throw that hat away, get a new hat , have yourself photographed in the new hat and send it to me immediately so I will stop worrying about your hat. It's a miserable garment and not worthy of your talent and your energy. Do you need money? If so, I'll send you some. Buy a hat!

                           E.K.

Mr. Henry Jaglom
9165 Sunset Boulevard
Los Angeles, CA.90069

Appendix 2
The Welles-Nicholson-Michan Deal

Henry was helping Orson Welles put together a film project called The Big Brass Ring *in the early Eighties. For a certain period, it appeared that Jack Nicholson would play the lead role, of a midwestern American politician. Henry worked hard putting together a deal with Israeli producer Arnon Milchan. In typical fashion, Henry preserved much of the deal's paper trail, and the memos are presented here for posterity.*

MEMO

Date: 20 May 1982

To: Jack Nicholson   From: Henry Jaglom

Jack:

I spoke to Orson at length. As we discussed, I tried to do it without getting him too excited, explaining to him all your involvements, etc.

He wanted me to tell you that he is 100% ready, he has done 6 months of pre-production work and is totally prepared. He has every location selected and could shoot in July in Spain.

The budget is completed and thoroughly detailed, as is the shooting schedule. He knows day by day, hour by hour, each technical move he has to make. His whole crew is together, with back-ups for those who are not available. Same with his cast - he says that he has cast it in triplicate - all he has to do is find out which actors on his first list are not available when he knows the day, and then he goes to his second choice, and then his third. He has picked many wonderful actors, but he emphasizes that this is a movie about two men, and everything else is very much secondary.

About the story: He describes it as being about a man who fate has determined has to be the next President of the United States. He, and everyone else, knows that that is his fate, that that is inevitable. But there is some devil in him that wants to destroy that destiny, and that is what the film is about.

Orson: "He is a great man - like all great men he is never satisfied that he has chosen the right path in life. Even being President, he feels, may somehow not be right. He is a man who has within him the devil of self-destruction that lives in every genius. You know that you're absolutely great, there is no question of that, but have you chosen the right road? Should I be a monk? Should I jerk off in the park? Should I just fuck every body and forget about everything else? Should I be President? It is not self-doubt, it is cosmic doubt! What am I going to do - I am the best, I know that, now what do I do with it? Hannibal crossed the Alps with the second greatest army in classical history. He

20 May 1982
Jack Nicholson
Page two

arrived at the outer gates of Rome and Rome was in his hands,
ready to be taken. At the outer gates, he stopped and went
back. What made him stop? That same devil - this thing that
always stops conquerors at the moment of victory. That is what
'The Big Brass Ring' is about. Also: There is this foolish,
romantic side of us all, that puts us into these absurd, even
ridiculous situations and positions in life. That is what the
circumstances of the film are about - the theft of the necklace,
the situation with the monkey, etc. All these idiotic events·
that one's romantic nature leads one into."

Jack, I've put all this into writing because I didn't trust
myself to accurately convey it verbally. As Orson told it
to me, it seemed to address so clearly the questions you had
about his intent, and so wonderfully, that I thought I should
pass it on to you this way.

I'm dictating this to my office in Los Angeles and having it
sent out to you tomorrow. I'll call in a few days.

Best,

Henry Jgw

HJ/jrw

INTERNATIONAL RAINBOW PICTURES, Inc.

24 May 1982

Jack Nicholson
12850 Mulholland Drive
Beverly Hills, CA 90210

Jack:

A follow-up to the memo I sent you May 20. I've just gotten off
the phone with Orson. Much as I tried to keep him from getting
too excited at the prospect of you playing Blake Pellarin, I am
afraid that inevitably I failed. He does understand all the
possible reasons why you may end up not being able to do it. But
the possibility that you may do it was too much for him - and in
a very positive way, I feel. He sat up the last three days and
nights, rewriting the script. It's rewriting focused on deepening
and clarifying the relationship between Pellarin and the old man.
He read it to me on the phone just now, and I think it's really
superb. One of the most significant changes is actually not a
change at all: Originally, with you in mind, he had Senator Pellarin commit the murder of a beggar. By doing so, Pellarin's character and the whole sense of the Presidency, past and future, reso-
nates with an undertone, a darkness, that deepens the character
profoundly. He goes from this incidental and meaningless murder
on to becoming President. The power of the Presidency, its use in
recent years to affect the lives and deaths of countless people,
all comes into play at a very important sub-textual level. When
it seemed that you were not available, Orson discussed with me the
fact that none of the other actors we were considering could make
that act credible. The possibility that you might, after all,
play Pellarin, was enough to send him back into an intense
re-examination and rewriting of the script. He is sending you
a copy of the new script and asks you not to look again at the
old script. And, as I say, is very excited and hopeful, since
you were his very first choice and he feels the character of
Pellarin would be most fully realized by you.

Also: He has completed the shooting schedule in such a way as
to require the actor who plays Pellarin to be available for
exactly eight weeks. This is all, he insists, not a day more.
He has structured the schedule so that everything else will be
shot after that. And he repeated that he could begin easily in
July. I cautioned him once more that you had all of these potential projects that might get in the way. He said he understood,
but could not help being extremely hopeful and excited.

Best,

Henry/jw
HJ/jrw

SUITE 202 933 NORTH LA BREA AVENUE HOLLYWOOD, CALIFORNIA 90038 (213) 851-4811

INTERNATIONAL RAINBOW PICTURES, INC.

MEMO

Date: 27 May 1982

To: Arnon Milchan   From: Henry Jaglom

Arnon:

I went over the budget in some detail with Sandro Tosca,
Orson's Production Manager. As I told you, Orson's fees as
writer, director and actor are all included in the 8 million
dollar budget. The good news is it includes ALL Above The Line,
including a large portion of Jack's salary, whatever that should
turn out to be. In fact, if you manage to put through either
of the deals with Jack as we discussed, the total budget still
stays at 8 million or very close. It seems to me that if it
is necessary to pay Jack more than the 1 million plus 50/50
or the 2 million against 10% of the gross, this new look at
the budget makes that more possible. Do you agree?

What I'm talking about is the following budget breakdown:

$3,500,000:	All costs Below The Line.
1,500,000:	Orson salaries for script, directing and co-starring.
500,000:	Seven other supporting actors' salaries.
500,000:	Fee for completion guarantee.*
300,000:	Finders fee/Exec. Producer salary - Henry Jaglom.
200,000:	Production Manager salary - Sandro Tosca

$1,500,000: Toward Jack Nicholson's salary.

The above does not include any fee you may want to take for
yourself. It does include a half million dollars for the
completion guarantee*, that you may want to do without, or
to arrange yourself.

The above includes absolutely all other costs. There are no
hidden expenses that I can determine. Even at that, both Orson
and Sandro assure me that they have allowed themselves a comfortable cushion.

By the time you receive this, I may have gone over all of these
points with you, but I wanted to get them down on paper in any
case.

Best,

Henry

HJ/jry

SUITE 202   933 NORTH LA BREA AVENUE   HOLLYWOOD, CALIFORNIA 90038   (213) 851-4811

28 May 1982
Arnon Milchan
Page two

One last thing: There is a very important directorial factor
that is a vital concern to Orson. He considers it to be his
only prime visual concept, and one that is irreplaceable to
him. It requires at least one full week of shooting before
sunrise. Madrid was selected not only for its significance
to the story, but for the fact that in Madrid for one and a
half hours each summer morning before sunrise, there is a
special, haunting, intensely surreal light and totally empty
and deserted streets. There is a profound menace to the idea
that the sun is going to come up, and it is in that context
that Orson has created what he considers to be the single most
significant scene in the film. In order to accomplish this,
he must shoot no later than the first week in August. His pre-
ference is, of course, July. September would be impossible,
as the days have grown short by then and the streets are full
of people, street lights are on and the magical hour vanishes.
Therefore, I want to emphasize that it is in no way merely a
whim of his that he shoot before the first week in August is
over. It is, rather, central to his entire creative concept
of the dramatic vision of the film.

Appendix 3
Anaïs Nin's letter to Henry

Henry's note: *This is a 1976 note from Anaïs Nin, who wrote in her seventh and last diary a lot about me. She sent me this after we met these Paramount Studio guys about* Spy in the House of Love, *fascinated, she said, about how I handled (and controlled) the businessmen like only a lady would.*

Dear Henri—

I was fascinated about how you gained control over those unpleasant businessmen by completely "throwing them," by doing all those little feminine things that I have never seen you do, like insisting that they please put their cigars out, then asking them for a light for your cigarette, and how you accepted it when they lit it for you, putting them in this position to help you, somehow.

Later reaching into your shoulder bag and extracting your silk scarf and tying it around your neck while he was talking, looking for another cigarette and having it in a very jeweled cigarette case you pulled out of your quilted shoulder bag (and needing a light again till that tall thin one reached over to give you one, he seemed completely enchanted and confused by you (Prada isn't the bag?) and black and with that pretty gold chain—all very feminine. I had never seen it before, did you pick it on purpose for this meeting?

Another time you're putting perfume on your wrists from your bag again (can I say from your "purse" because that is how you handled it, didn't you?) just while he was making that aggressive business point. All of that sort of thing, you know? All very feminine tactics which somehow took away their sense of control and power and which I saw distracted them from the points they were trying to focus on, that they were trying to make to control the situation.

Were you doing that on purpose, you minx? You confused them, you totally undercut them by all these feminine moves. I was so fascinated by the entirely casual and natural way you did them, while smiling nicely at the men as if you were interested in what they were saying, but just a little bit distracted. The way you were going in and out of that little black bag in your lap, it was brilliant and <u>so</u> female. How did you learn to do that? You threw them off-guard constantly with all that, then chimed in and said what you and I wanted to accomplish. In your words, they "just caved," didn't they?—which I felt you laid the groundwork for by all your feminine distractions.

When I asked you how you knew to do all that, all you said was that you watched the way your mother and her friends would take the power from the men in their conversations by using the one thing the men didn't have: their femininity. But to see a young *man* do that—a straight man at that—was truly amazing! You are the only man I have ever seen take control of a room full of men-men that way. (I had to control my laugh so hard when all three put out their cigars out of deference to you, *not* to me.)

And you let them think they won those two stupid points we didn't care about and we won all three major business points that way. So amazing, my dear Henri! I want to thank you again & really congratulate you. I do remember that the bag was a black Prada with a chain link shoulder strap. Where did that come from? I can't remember the scarf, but it was a big flowery silk one which I never saw before. Did you set all that up on purpose? I am just fascinated. And, of course, very grateful that now they won't be able to mess up our film, if they really do it. I'm afraid I still suspect they will back out of it. But I wanted you to know how impressed I was by your wonderful feminine wiles. Please tell your mother about it, and tell her *merci* from me.

(Do you say "wiles" in English?)

Much Love,

Anais

Appendix 4
Karen Black on working with Henry

I remember everything about filming Henry's *Can She Bake a Cherry Pie?* because it was one of the most difficult but exciting roles I ever did. There is something called improvisation, and then there's something called writing/performing, where part of your consciousness is actually writing the movie while you're acting it, and writing the character as you are in it. What Henry has invented in all his films is some amazing combination of the two. I can't quite explain it. I never ever encountered it from Bob Rafelson to Alfred Hitchcock.

Henry and I first worked "professionally" when Henry wrote and directed the play *A Safe Place* (it was called something else then), which we did for Lee Strasberg and Harold Clurman in both the Acting Class and the Directing Class at The Actors Studio. But when he shot it as a film six or seven years later, he wasn't satisfied with shooting the written script, so he created it improvisationally along with the actors as he filmed it (I've described it as Tuesday Weld playing Henry playing me), even though it was his first film. Then he re-re-created it in the editing. Then he did that again with *Tracks* and Dennis Hopper and it's brilliant. When he met Patrice Townsend and married her, he was truly happy for quite a few years. It was wonderful to see him that way, and just for fun he made *Sitting Ducks* with her and Michael and Zack, the silliest, happiest romp you can imagine. Strangely, he had his first, great commercial success with that, after what I would call his two neglected masterpieces.

When I ran into Henry on Columbus after not seeing him for a year or more, he looked so miserable. He said he felt that his life was over. He looked terrible and was clearly devastated. He was holed up in a hotel nearby, around the corner from his parents' apartment where he grew up on Central Park West. They were the most elegant European couple you have ever seen. She was so beautiful, he was so handsome, both in that old-world way. I hadn't seen Henry in over a year, I think, and he told me that Patrice had left him for good. He was crying his eyes out in that terrible hotel room with a window facing a wall. He described how incredibly hard it was for him to get off the floor there—he meant that *literally* and he explained it to me. He said that he was now walking the lonely Manhattan streets and all his old childhood paths in Central Park talking to himself and crying his eyes out and eating endless qualities of ice cream and chocolate, nothing else. He told me that he wanted to make a movie about it all somehow, and now—upon seeing me—he suddenly pulled himself together and decided on the spot that "*he wanted me to play him*" and he suddenly shouted out, "*You're going to play me so I can find out what my happy ending could possibly now be.*" He wanted me to play him walking the streets and around Central Park, crying my eyes out, eating ice cream and chocolates, and talking to myself. We would take it from there." "To where?" I said. "I don't know, we'll find out," he said.

Orson Welles had said to him when Patrice left, "If you were a poet, you'd write poems about where you are now, if you were a singer you'd write songs, you're a filmmaker so you must make a film about it." That became *Can She Bake a Cherry Pie?* and then *Always*, which starred Patrice. It's one of the most brilliant and honest films of all. Henry now said that he doubted whether he could even have a happy ending anymore and thought that the only way for him to survive now was to make this movie so he could maybe somehow feel safe again, so he could hope again. In seeing me, he said, he realized that he couldn't have a man play him, because it wouldn't seem real. (He's never felt very connected to men, as a whole.) We had been boyfriend/girlfriend for a year or two and had done so much of that work when he created *A Safe Place* with me at The Actors' Studio. I really knew him so very well. I had typed up that whole play while he was writing it (because Henry couldn't type).

Now, we were out to "find his happy ending" as he kept repeating, "like the Doris Day movies of my childhood" which made him feel romantic and safe and upbeat about life. He started writing the outline right there with me, but wouldn't write the dialogue. He would get it out of me. "How terrifying," I said. We started to cry together, both of us sitting there, eating our eclairs. "Careful," I said to him between tears, "you'll ruin your mascara!" Henry was always such a girl and loves being teased about it. He's this amazing heterosexual male girl—I can't really explain it. But we couldn't stop laughing and crying.

Making the movie was amazing, Henry came up with a distinct through-line, like a guided improvisation. You have strict guidelines to where you have to go next, and often what you have to include in the scene before he will say "Cut." There is a sense of what you have to "accomplish," as he would call it. But along the way, anything else at all was what Henry called "fair game." I always knew how Michael [Emil] would respond in our scenes, because I knew him so well too. (He's Henry's big brother, you know? And he's so wonderfully odd and predictable.) I could simply gear up and create the scene off of my motivation and commit myself fully to the storyline that Henry wanted.

In one scene, I open that closet door and find Michael hanging there inside upside down. That was Michael's idea. I jumped about a mile, and that was completely real. I was so very tired when we finished that movie. I don't think I've ever been that tired. It was incredibly draining, using all of myself that way, with Henry always wanting more. He worked so fast because of the small budget. We jumped in cars to change outfits and then hopped out to do a scene, then jumped in again to change again, in Central Park or at the Museum of Natural History.

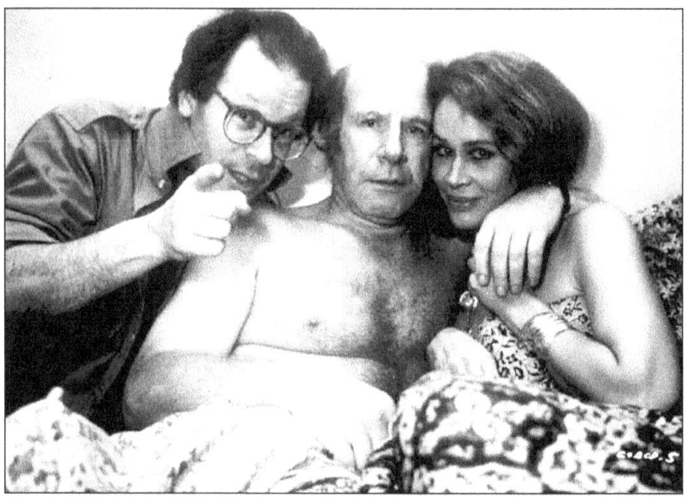

Henry led me to thinking that the character's pregnancy at the end was my idea, but of course it was his from the beginning. He had so wanted a baby and feared now that he would never have one. The scene telling him I'm pregnant I wrote on a napkin. Henry would always say excitedly, "Wow, that didn't turn out the way I thought it would! It's better! You're better at playing me than I could play me!" I was also always very much keeping Henry himself in mind: his sadness, his sweetness, his irritability, his sharp edges.

Henry knows women better than any male director I ever worked with. I mean he really knows them, from the inside somehow. He knows how to direct them so they don't feel directed, so they feel as if they are making the whole thing up every moment on. But that takes a lot of preparation and hard work, believe me.

Appendix 5
Henry's poem about making *A Safe Place*

This piece was written by Henry for the January-February 1972 edition of Action. *I've included it because it's a peek into Henry's mind as a young director. Many of the insights and modes of thought glimpsed here would develop as throughlines in his life and career.*

It's really weird.
I made this movie: *A Safe Place.*

> "The Lux Radio Theatre of The Air
> Presents Live From Hollywood…"
> Hollywood?
> What am I doing here?

Hollywood is an idea, not a place. I'm living in an idea. I'm lying in the dark, 10 years old, New Year's Eve, listening to the radio, the shiny ball is about to fall off the top of the N.Y. Times Building, the crowds below in Times Square are cheering as the plastic icicles on my Christmas tree shine in the dark and now Lux presents Hollywood.

I'm here. But I'm there, in bed, 10 years old, watching myself here, in Hollywood, 20 years later, putting together my movie, remembering my future.

My movie: *A Safe Place.*

> I wrote it.
> Re-wrote it.

Broke it up.
>Put it together again.
Cut it.
>Directed it.
The piece of my mind.

You can't do it that way, they said. Too personal. Too subjective. No one else will understand it. Movies are made by committees, by consensus. Find common denominators, things everyone will identify with. Things everyone will understand. A kid named Billy Batson. But he had a magic word. *Shazam!* Lightning struck and he *became* all-mighty, Captain Marvel.

That's it. If only I could find my magic word I would be able to fly. Even Hoppy, a regular kid rabbit, could do it. *He* said Shazam, too, and he became Marvel Bunny. Mighty Mouse, Dumbo, Peter Pan, they all had their special tricks that made them able to fly.

I had to find mine.
>I tried,
I said "Shazam" a lot, whispered it, shouted it, pronounced it every possible way.

Nothing happened,

I started looking for *my* magic word. *My own magic word.* I put all kinds of syllables together. Made all kinds of sounds and noises.

No good.
>I couldn't fly.
Or could I?

It seemed at times as if I *was* flying, soaring up to buildings, floating from tree to tree, gliding up there, nice and easy, cape trailing behind me in the wind…

Were those moments dreams? Or were they happening? Aren't dreams happening? When I remember them now, are they happening now, or are they happening then? How can now and then, dreams and non-dreams, be separated

I am sitting in a classroom,
10 years old, looking out of a window,
remembering the future.

I am sitting on a park bench,
50 years old, anticipating the past.
No such thing as a straight line, said Einstein.

I came to New York, where I'm from, went to the Central Park of my mind, found Orson Welles, seals, Jack Nicholson, squirrels, Tuesday Weld, chess players, Philip Proctor, cracker jack, Gwen Welles, rowboats, Dov Lawrence, merry-go-rounds.

Friends. Myths. Images.

I put them all together, juxtaposed the realities, sank the fantasies, tried to break through the myths, creating anti-myth, feelings, thoughts, vibrations.
Painted my movie, changing colors and shapes as I went along, exploring childhood, loss, pain, loneliness, isolation.
Worked it out. Re-traced childhood paths, re-found magic, renewed memories, re-visited my mind.

Songs, movies, tastes,
radio, smells, comic books…
Comic books.

It all started with comic books, reading with a flashlight under covers after lights out. Identifying myself. Superman wasn't me, he was *always* Superman, even beneath the Clark Kent number. Nothing could happen to him. *He could fly*. He acted vulnerable, but he wasn't, really.

I was.
     Lonely. Scared.
Powerless in a world of adults,
          rules, classrooms, groups.

Alone. Where is everybody? I'm a kid, not Superman. *I can't fly.*

But, wait a minute.
     Maybe…

Captain Marvel, you see. *He* wasn't always together, always all-powerful, always in charge. He was a kid, like me.

Emotions, I said. They'll identify with emotions. If I put them together straight, my way, as they come and go, appear and disappear, change and contradict. My emotions must be universal. How can I feel differently from how everyone else feels? I can only translate it differently, personally, as it happens. Feelings are for everyone.

They looked at me.

I went to Hollywood. Felt. Thought. Wrote. Acted. Tried to get my movie done.

Write me a story, someone said
          Direct *this* story, someone else said

No. You don't understand. It all has to be coming from me. One person translating himself up there, on the screen. How can I translate someone else? How can someone else translate me?

They said Thank You Very Much.

I hung out, listened, talked, met people, found company, others trying to do the same thing.
I worked things over at the Actors Studio.

I spent eight weeks with Dennis Hopper, cutting *Easy Rider* with him.

I went to Oregon to be in Jack Nicholson's movie, went to Peru to be in Dennis's. Other places, other people putting it together, their way.

Finally got my shot. Total freedom-make it, do it, anyway you want, your way. No intrusions. Support all the way. BBS productions let me loose.

Bert Schneider released me.

Time must curve like everything else, must bend, ultimately join itself, make a circle.

It is always Now.

They lied to us, out of their fear.
Parents, Teachers, Movies, Newspapers, Songs—our entire culture based upon myths—all lies.

"Oh, give me something to remember you by…"
But Bogart didn't lie. Batman didn't lie.
Bugs Bunny didn't lie.
Did they?

"You must remember this. A kiss is just a kiss. A sigh is just a sigh. The fundamental things apply, as time goes by…"

Where is everybody?

Why am I alone on my bicycle, hot out, sun, wind, walking on boardwalks, playing on rock-mountains, looking for the future, the past, the always.

When I grow up—
What?

* I'll Always Buy Chesterfield and work at
Paramount Pictures,
like Bob Hope and Bing Crosby.

*I'll meet Doris Day and settle down,
after one wild fling with Lauren Bacall.

*I'll have a job, a career, a house, a family,
ambition, guts, a war to fight, a future to win.

"Someone to watch over me…"
Put it all together.

Break up the movie myth. Make an anti-movie. Nostalgia kills. Use nostalgia to kill it before it kills all of us.

"I'm old-fashioned. I love the moonlight.
I love the old-fashioned things…"
Feel it.
No lies. No numbers.
Just the way it feels.
Felt.
Will feel…

A jigsaw puzzle of my mind. My friends. Our needs. Our fantasies. Our emotions. A tapestry woven with our feelings.

An internal movie instead of an external one. Why can't it be done?

Proust said it: "The past is hidden somewhere beyond the reach of the intellect."

Don't think it. Reach back and feel it. Ben Hecht said it: "Time is a circus, always packing up and moving away."

Follow that circus, your circus, follow time, go with it, into it, enter it and let it enter you. Connect events emotionally, not logically. Logic is false, the ultimate lie, the lie of a structured, frightened, oppressive society, trying to impose rules, "shoulds," upon the chaos of life.

Accept the chaos and echo it. Dive into the chaos and only come up for air. Don't be afraid like they are, like they tried to make you be. Don't try to understand why or where or how. *They don't exist*! Illusions created to cover the fear of being.

> Just be.
> > And it'll be all right.
> Pedal faster on that bicycle.
> > Downhill now.
> Slide—Get behind it.
> > Feel the freedom of that cool air.
> Lose fear.
> > Lose what-if and if-only.
> Puff up your chest like Mighty Mouse.
> Hoppy Rabbit is becoming Marvel Bunny.
> > Happy New Year.

The shiny ball is about to fall off the top of the New York Times Building.
> Fall with it.
> > Share it.
> > Put it all together.
> Make a movie: *A Safe Place*.
> > * *Shazam!*

And for 93 minutes, in the dark, you'll be able, at last, to fly…

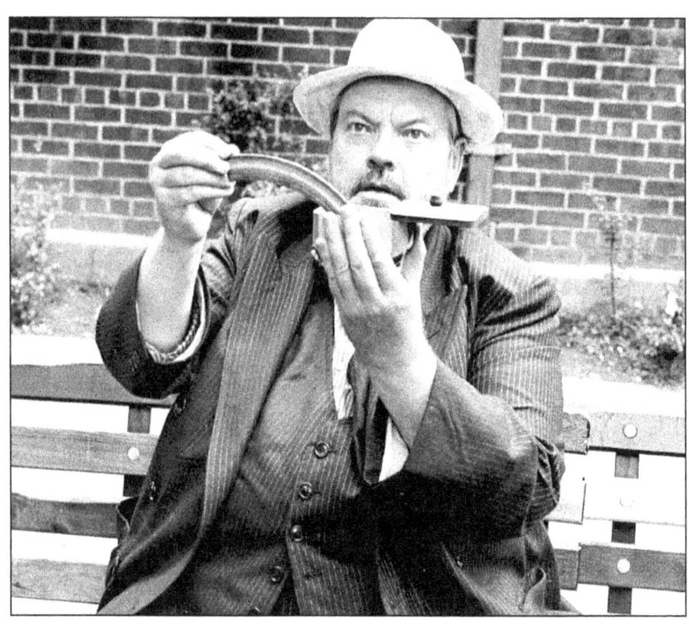

Shazam! Welles the Rabbinical Magician in *A Safe Place*.

Afterword by Noah Wyle

I worked with Henry Jaglom on his film *Queen of the Lot* in 2009, but we had established a rapport well before I ever walked onto his set. Like Daniel, I was a lunch companion of his, and he was the best lunch date you could ever ask for. I couldn't be more pleased that someone has written a book on him, especially one that so captures his voice, as does *My Lunches With Henry Jaglom* (a fitting title considering his indispensable book of conversations with Orson Welles). Actually, the only person who would have been more pleased with this book and its publication is Henry himself, and it's a shame he didn't get to see it happen in his lifetime.

As his daughter observed at his memorial, Henry was an open book, a man without secrets. He forever wanted to make himself known. I knew him, I loved him, and I miss him. He was a singular artist in that he made other people his art. You might say he was an artist of others. He was deeply invested in people and was obsessed with getting to the bottom of what made people tick. On a personal level, he could be either tremendously flattering or witheringly condemning, but he was always honest. He was never less than honest. He couldn't help himself but be totally himself. The point is, you knew right where you stood with Henry. And the closer you stood, the more special you felt. I kept in touch with him well after we wrapped shooting on *Queen of the Lot* and always counted him as a friend.

A few of us, Daniel included, were granted front row seats to Henry's "show" and gifted a chance to be warmed by Henry's exuberance and incandescence. I'm eternally grateful for my time with him, and grateful to Daniel for sharing his

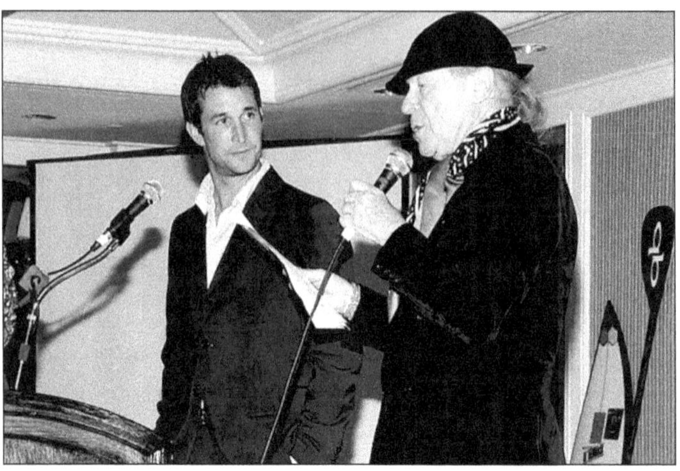

recollections and his recorded conversations. I heard Henry's voice in my head as I was reading them, almost as if he were in the room with me again. Henry had a singular way of relating to people, and he was of course a great, colorful raconteur. The stories in this book are incredible—some of them I'd heard him tell before, others I was experiencing for the very first time. All of them are vivid and made all the more believable by Henry's eye for detail, his impeccable memory, and his wit.

I remember once calling Henry "an L.A. institution" and an "indie film institution" during an interview years ago. He worked like no other director worked, in that he created a sandbox where actors loved to play. He created a dynamic environment at work just as much as when you sat down to share a meal with him. I'll miss those lunches greatly, and I'll miss calling him up to chat, but I can always return to this book to summon his unique, unmistakable presence again.

Noah Wyle is the winner of two Emmy Awards for his work on the medical drama The Pitt *decades after having risen to fame on NBC's* E.R., *for which he was nominated for five Emmys, three Golden Globes, and won four Screen Actors Guild Award.*

Acknowledgements

Thanks above all go to my husband, Evan, whom I love more than words could ever express. Two book projects in one year was a big ask, and he was a champ throughout it all. I must also, once again, thank the Academy of Motion Picture Arts and Sciences and their Margaret Herrick Library, a vital institution and wellspring of film research which is mentioned a number of times in this book's dialogue.

I must forever thank Candice Bergen and Noah Wyle, who didn't even hesitate for a moment to contribute a foreword and afterword to this book.

My friend Joel Roth read some early chapters and encouraged me to keep going, so I must thank him for giving me a dose of confidence. Also, a nod to my longtime best friend, Aaron Hollander, who listened to my Henry stories for the better part of twenty years. Joe Dante and Larry Karaszewski, men of great cinematic achievements, were two of this manuscript's early readers, and their enthusiasm for the material (despite whatever respective misgivings they had about Henry's films) was also just the tonic I needed to see this project through to its completion.

So much gratitude must go to Paul Cronin and Sticking Place Books, who didn't even think twice about agreeing to publish. Additional gratitude to Dudley Moore biographer Barbra Paskin (who drove me home from one of Henry's New Year's Eve parties many years back), for her insight into one key historical question. Filmmaker Paul Williams gave me an afternoon to discuss his own history with Henry, for which I'm most grateful. My friend of nearly eighteen years,

Stephen Eckelberry, who is mentioned in the text as having taken such great care of his departed wife Karen Black, when she was terminally ill, was also a great help and support. He graciously granted me permission to use excerpts from Karen's still unpublished memoir *Conversations in a Burning Room*.

All praise goes to the technicians at Adobe for their Premiere Pro transcription service. I don't know if this book would have ever gotten done (and in record time!) without their speedy, user-friendly software having transcribed so much of my audio.

Index

Films directed by Jaglom are denoted by their date of release, in brackets, e.g. (1985 film). Bold denotes a photo representation.

Sticking Place Books (stickingplacebooks.com) is a New York-based publisher specializing in cinema, offering interview books, memoirs, critical and historical studies, screenplays, and essay collections. Our titles include:

Lessons with Kiarostami, edited by Paul Cronin

In the Shadow of Trees: The Collected Poetry of Abbas Kiarostami

Still Film Crazy (After All These Years) by Patrick McGilligan

It's Only a Movie by Bruce Joel Rubin

Three Visionary Screenplays by Bruce Joel Rubin

Playing Among the Stars: Conversations with Damien Chazelle by Nathan Réra

The Magic Eye: The Cinema of Stanley Kubrick by Neil Hornick

A Shared Cinema: Conversations with Michael Ciment by N. T. Bihn

The Naughty Bits: What the Censors Wouldn't Let You See in Hollywood's Most Famous Movies by Nat Segaloff

Mexico: The Aztec Account of the Conquest by Werner Herzog

Werner Herzog/Rogue Filmmaker by David LaRocca

De Palma on De Palma: Conversations with Samuel Blumenfeld and Laurent Vachaud

Publication as Autobiography: Occasional and Forsaken Texts— and Endangered Cinema Species by Scott MacDonald

Filmmakers Thinking by Adrian Martin

Secret Cinema: The Rise and Fall of the Blue Movie by John Baxter

Casualties of War: An Investigation by Nathan Réra

Hollywood on the Tiber by Hank Kaufman and Gene Lerner

What Made Cinema? Essays on Visual Culture and Early Film by Ian Christie

Travels in the Cities of Cinema: Conversations with Jonathan Rosenbaum by Ehsan Khoshbakht

Camera Movements that Confound Us by Jonathan Rosenbaum

Upon Open Sky by Guillermo Arriaga

Ambrose Chapel by Brian De Palma

Russian Poland by David Mamet

The Archival Impermanence Project by Ross Lipman

These Fragments I Have Shored Against My Ruin by Caveh Zahedi

Cinema Now and Then: Conversations with James Naremore by Craig S. Simpson

* 9 7 9 8 8 9 9 7 6 0 5 0 1 *